MOLEHUNT

OTHER BOOKS BY DAVID WISE

Nonfiction

The U-2 Affair *(with Thomas B. Ross)*
The Invisible Government *(with Thomas B. Ross)*
The Espionage Establishment *(with Thomas B. Ross)*
The Politics of Lying
The American Police State
The Spy Who Got Away

Fiction

Spectrum
The Children's Game
The Samarkand Dimension

MOLEHUNT

The Secret Search for Traitors That Shattered the CIA

■

DAVID WISE

Random House New York

Library of Congress Cataloging-in-Publication Data
Wise, David.
Molehunt: the secret search for traitors that shattered the CIA/by David
Wise.—1st ed.
p.   cm.
Includes bibliographical references and index.
ISBN 0-394-58514-3
1. United States. Central Intelligence Agency. 2. Intelligence service—United
States. 3. Intelligence service—Soviet Union.
I. Title.
JK468.I6W54   1992   327.1′2′06073—dc20   91-53114

Manufactured in the United States of America
24689753

Book design by Lilly Langotsky

Book text set in Times Roman

TO MY BROTHER, BILL

Contents

MOLEHUNT

Chapter 1

Escape from Helsinki

It was early evening, ten days before Christmas of 1961, and the snow, crisp and white, had covered Helsinki. Frank F. Friberg, the chief of station of the Central Intelligence Agency, was shaving, getting ready for a holiday cocktail party, when the doorbell rang at his home in Westend, a suburb four miles west of the Finnish capital.

Since few people knew where the CIA station chief lived, it was with some puzzlement, mixed with caution, that he went to the door and opened it. A short, thickset man stood there in the snow with a red-haired woman and a little girl, who clutched a doll. A Russian fur hat covered most of the man's dark hair.

"Do you know who I am?" he asked.

Friberg said he did not.

"I am Anatoly Klimov."

The CIA man opened the door wider and quickly motioned the family in. He knew the name Klimov well; a KGB officer working under diplomatic cover in the Soviet embassy in Helsinki. Friberg had even studied Klimov's picture; but he had not recognized him bundled up in an overcoat and a fur hat, standing in the darkness on his doorstep.

In the living room, the two men struggled to overcome a formidable language barrier. The Russian kept repeating a single word: it sounded to Friberg like "asool." Friberg was bilingual in English and Finnish—his parents had emigrated to America from Finland, settling in the heavily Finnish community of Westminster, in north-central Massachusetts, where he was born—but he spoke no Russian. The KGB man in turn spoke no Finnish and only broken English.

Finally, Friberg handed the Russian a pencil and a piece of paper, and Klimov wrote the letters "asyl."

Now there could be no mistake. Major Anatoly Klimov of the KGB was trying to write the word "asylum" in English.

Friberg, alone in the house—his wife was on a visit to the States—had suddenly acquired a Soviet defector and his entire family. Not merely a defector but a KGB walk-in, the dream of every CIA officer. There was no talk of Klimov's remaining as an agent-in-place, reporting to the CIA from inside the KGB; the Russian, frightened for his life, gave Friberg two hours to get him out of Helsinki. After that, Klimov warned, the KGB would notice his absence and try to block his escape.

The Russian also told the CIA man his true name. It was not Klimov, he revealed. It was Anatoly Mikhailovich Golitsin.

When Golitsin walked in, Frank Friberg had been working for the CIA for ten years. The station chief was a man of medium build, with blue eyes and brown hair—an ordinary-looking man but for a sizable fencing scar on his left cheek, earned at Harvard. He had worked for the agency under commercial cover in Sweden and traveled all over Europe, posing as a sales representative for a manufacturer. In 1957, the agency had sent him to Finland under diplomatic cover. He had been promoted to chief of station earlier in 1961.

Thus, at the age of forty-nine, Friberg toiled in the shadows in an unglamorous agency outpost, a station that gained what importance it had by virtue of its geographic location on the periphery of Soviet power. The defection of Anatoly Golitsin was the major event of his espionage career, and years later, he had no difficulty recalling every detail.

"I knew he was a good-sized catch," he said. "We hadn't had one of his stature since Deriabin in 1954.[1] We'd been in touch with Golitsin," Friberg added. It was, after all, the height of the Cold War, and the CIA was always alert for potential Soviet recruits. "We had someone dealing with him on visa matters, to get a better assessment of

[1] Peter Deriabin, a KGB major, had defected in Vienna that year.

him. We knew he was KGB, but he was a hard-liner, and we thought there was no chance of getting him to defect. In fact, we thought he would be the last one to defect."

Now Golitsin explained his motive to Friberg. He said he was fed up with the KGB. He had been feuding with his boss, V. V. Zenihov, the KGB resident in Helsinki. "Golitsin was a CI [counterintelligence] officer," Friberg explained. "His task was to work against the principal enemy, the U.S.A., England, and France. He told me, 'Zenihov just doesn't understand CI. And now my defection serves him right.' He wanted so much to get even with the KGB that it dominated his entire existence.

"He said he had planned this far in advance, a year to a year and a half before he actually took the step. He didn't even tell his wife until six months before, and they agreed to wait until their daughter could come to visit them. She had been in school in Moscow."

The CIA station chief had to move fast. There was an eight-o'clock flight for Stockholm that night. Friberg telephoned Stephen Winsky, a young CIA officer, who sped to the house, picked up the Golitsins' passports, returned to the consulate, and stamped in American visas. That was easy for Winsky to do; his cover was embassy vice-consul.

"As we were getting ready to leave for the airport," Friberg said, "Golitsin ran to the side of the driveway near the street and dug a package out of the snow." Golitsin told him that the package, which he had buried before ringing Friberg's doorbell, contained documents that he had managed to take when he left the Soviet embassy. But Golitsin kept the package with him constantly, and he never showed the contents to the station chief.

On the way to the airport, Friberg rendezvoused with Winsky, who handed him back the passports. Golitsin was growing increasingly nervous. "We got him out in a little over two hours," Friberg said. "I got tickets on the commercial flight. I took him out under the name of Klements, using his Russian passport with the U.S. visa. No one questioned it, because it was so close to his 'real' name, Klimov."

Friberg had, of course, alerted CIA headquarters in Langley, Virginia, where the word of the impending arrival of a high-ranking Soviet defector was electrifying, and badly needed, news. Only eight months earlier, the CIA, after riding high in the fifties under the avuncular, pipe-smoking spymaster Allen W. Dulles, had been devastated by the spectacular failure at the Bay of Pigs.

The CIA's bungled operation on the beaches of Cuba had not only failed to overthrow Fidel Castro but ended in the death of 114 Cuban exiles and the capture of most of the rest of the almost 1,500-man brigade. It had proved a vast embarrassment to President John F. Kennedy, after only three months in office. Kennedy had inherited the covert operation from his predecessor, Dwight D. Eisenhower, but he had given the go-ahead for the Cuban invasion and took responsibility for its failure. The setback put Kennedy at a terrible disadvantage at his summit meeting in Vienna in June with Soviet leader Nikita S. Khrushchev, who bullied the young President.

Only three weeks before Golitsin appeared on Frank Friberg's doorstep in Helsinki, Kennedy had replaced Dulles with John A. McCone, a millionaire businessman from California. Richard M. Bissell, Jr., the architect of the Cuban invasion, who headed the CIA's Directorate of Plans, still lingered on as the DDP, but was soon to be replaced by his deputy, Richard M. Helms.[2]

Although headquarters eagerly awaited the defector's arrival, a series of misadventures lay ahead for Friberg and the Golitsins as they set out for Washington. They made the 8:00 P.M. flight to Stockholm, only to discover that they would have to shuttle to another airport, north of the Swedish capital, for the connecting flight to New York. Golitsin, petrified at the possibility of being grabbed by the KGB, refused to set foot in another international airport. The next flight out originated in Helsinki, and Golitsin feared the KGB might be aboard.

While the station chief pondered his next move, he and his charges went to ground in a safe house in Sweden for the better part of two days. Finally, Friberg arranged to borrow the American air attaché's plane to fly Golitsin and his family to Frankfurt. Meanwhile, the CIA's Office of Security dispatched a three-man team, headed by Stanley C. Lach, to guard the defector. By the time Golitsin reached Frankfurt, the OS men, although unseen by Friberg, were discreetly in place.

In Frankfurt, Friberg and the Golitsins boarded an Air Force plane

[2]The Directorate of Plans became the Directorate of Operations in 1973. Inside the CIA, both the directorate and its chief, the deputy director for plans, were known as the DDP, later the DDO. In recent years, CIA officials have tended to refer to the Directorate of Operations, more logically, as the DO and to its chief as the DDO. To make matters even more confusing, the Directorate of Operations is also known as the Clandestine Services, or as some prefer, the Clandestine Service.

for the States. But it was an unpressurized World War II Liberator bomber, and after half an hour, at 8,000 feet, Golitsin's daughter, who was sensitive to the altitude, began to choke. Friberg ordered the plane back to Frankfurt, where he booked a commercial flight on Pan Am to London and New York. There was another day of delay while the CIA arranged a new passport for Golitsin under yet another alias.

Friberg and the Golitsins then flew to London. No sooner had they landed than British security agents swarmed over the plane, investigating a rumor that a bomb was aboard. Friberg managed to persuade the British to leave the Golitsins on the plane as all the other passengers were evacuated. The airliner eventually took off for New York, but the defector's odyssey, and Friberg's, was not over yet. A dense fog had rolled in over New York, and the flight was diverted to Bermuda. More CIA security agents were rushed to the island, where Golitsin remained overnight.

The next day, Friberg and the Golitsins finally flew to New York. "He'd had enough of planes by that time," Friberg said. "We went to Penn Station and took the train to Washington."

A familiar face was waiting. "We were met at Union Station by Steamboat Fulton, a case officer who knew Golitsin. His real name was Robert. He had worked with me for two years in Helsinki. He had met Golitsin at a couple of diplomatic receptions." The Russian and his family were whisked to a safe house in northern Virginia. Friberg, exhausted, checked into the Key Bridge Marriott.

The station chief's job was simply to get Golitsin safely out of Helsinki and away from the KGB. But inevitably, during their seemingly endless four-day journey to Washington, the two men talked. Golitsin's English, although still halting, was improving with practice.

What Golitsin said was only a tiny blip on the screen, but it was a harbinger of things to come. In Bermuda, Golitsin indicated that Golda Meir, then Israel's foreign minister and later prime minister, was a KGB agent. "He said an Israeli VIP had been in the Soviet Union in 1957, and he had got the impression this Israeli was a KGB agent. He came up with Golda Meir, because that was the only Israeli who had been there about that time."

Friberg understandably concluded that Golitsin had a tendency to see spies everywhere, although he was, perhaps, not as vigilant as the KGB man who served as security chief of the Soviet embassy in Helsinki. "Golitsin told me the head of security was suspicious of a cat that kept coming through the ironwork grille on the windows. The guy thought somehow the cat was being used to penetrate their security."[3]

The Helsinki station chief noticed something else during the four days he traveled with Golitsin. "He would sometimes confuse names. For instance, he gave me the name of a fairly prominent Finn whom he confused with a hard-line Finnish Communist. They had exactly the same last name, Tuominen. Poika Tuominen was scheduled to be premier of Finland after the Soviets invaded in the winter war in 1939, but he couldn't stomach it and he defected to Sweden. Erikki Tuominen had been head of the Finnish security police and he was a Communist. He was ousted around 1949, as a Soviet informant. Golitsin was saying that Poika was the bad one. Well, it was Erikki."

From the start, Golitsin proved difficult to handle. "He was stubborn," Friberg said, "and he did not like to be disagreed with. He insisted he didn't want to meet with anyone who spoke Russian. He was inordinately afraid of anyone who spoke Russian."

Clearly, Friberg had private misgivings. But once Golitsin arrived at the safe house in Virginia, the Russian was treated royally. As befit a source of major importance, senior officials came to call. Early in Golitsin's debriefing, McCone's deputy, General Charles P. Cabell, arrived, accompanied by John M. Maury, Jr., the chief of the Soviet Russia (SR) division.

The Soviet division initially took charge of Golitsin, as was normally the case when the agency got a Soviet defector. But from the start, the debriefing of Anatoly Golitsin was closely monitored by James J. Angleton, the chief of the CIA's Counterintelligence Staff, who had full access to the tapes and transcripts. Eventually, in fact, the defector was turned over by the Soviet division to Angleton—a decision that was to have enormous consequences for the CIA and the future of American intelligence.

The reason for Angleton's consuming interest in Golitsin was evident. It was the primary job of the counterintelligence chief to prevent any KGB moles from burrowing into the CIA. When a Soviet defector

---

[3]On the other hand, the suspicious Soviet security man may have been on to something. The CIA did experiment with implanting microphones in cats, so that the household pets could be used to eavesdrop on the agency's unsuspecting targets. The CIA's scientists realized that machines cannot easily discriminate among sounds, tune out background noises, and listen only to conversation. But they reasoned that a cat, if properly trained, could do so.

arrived at Langley, the first question put to him was always the same: did he know of any penetrations inside the CIA?

If the KGB had succeeded in planting a mole at a high-enough level within the CIA, the agency's secret operations would be known in advance by Moscow. The CIA, without realizing it, would be controlled by the KGB. This was the nightmare that Angleton and other CIA officials feared the most.

And Golitsin fed into their fears. Friberg recalled, "He said he had seen some material at KGB headquarters that could only have come from a very sensitive area of the agency. From someplace high inside the CIA."

The implication was plain, and frightening. If Golitsin was right, the KGB had an agent inside the CIA. Pressed for a name, a description, a clue—anything—Golitsin could only provide tantalizing fragments.

The mole, he told his CIA interrogators, was someone of Slavic background whose name might have ended in "-sky." He had been stationed in Germany. His KGB code name was Sasha.

And there was something else, Golitsin said. The mole's true last name began with the letter K.

Chapter 2

The Principal Suspect

■

In the James Bond movies, the armourer who outfits the fictional spy with his exotic gadgetry is known simply as Q.

In real life, if anyone inside the CIA came close to the description of the American Q, it would almost certainly have been S. Peter Karlow. Karlow had served with distinction in the Office of Strategic Services, the wartime forerunner of the CIA. After the war, he joined the new Central Intelligence Agency. For Karlow and so many others who had fought a secret war in the OSS, the pull of the new CIA—a place to continue the same clandestine struggle in the Cold War—was almost irresistible.

Although not trained as a scientist or engineer, Karlow had always been drawn to technical problems. He realized that the fledgling intelligence agency lacked the sophisticated equipment needed to support its spies. Bugs, cameras, tape recorders, radios—all were huge and bulky. In particular, the CIA lacked state-of-the-art eavesdropping devices. Something would have to be done, Karlow realized, to bring America's espionage organization into the modern age.

With that goal in mind, Karlow had approached the agency soon after it was created in 1947. The CIA's leaders found his arguments persuasive. "I said that during World War II, we had mostly relied on British tools. Why is it that we, as the world's greatest technological society, couldn't make our own?" Karlow suggested a crash program to develop high-tech gadgetry.

"I was set up as chief of the Special Equipment Staff. We got into problems such as bouncing sound off a windowpane. In those days, we couldn't do it. The state of technical equipment for surveillance was pathetic. Case officers were being sent abroad with little or no technical training. It was an exercise in frustration."

Karlow's efforts to improve the CIA's technical capabilities ran into the usual bureaucratic obstacles until 1949, when he received help from an unexpected quarter. On a visit back to CIA headquarters, Peter Sichel, the chief of the Berlin base, later to become famed as a wine expert and producer, asked the agency's technical people to make up hollow bricks that could be used as dead drops, the hiding places that spies often use to communicate with their agents.[1]

"The technical people asked what German bricks looked like," Karlow recalled. "We should have known exactly the size and shape of German bricks. Sichel hit the ceiling." The incident proved Karlow's broader point—that the CIA needed better technical support for all of its clandestine operations. "And that's when Helms said, 'Go to Germany and set up a lab.' " At the time, Richard Helms was chief of Foreign Division M, which became the agency's Eastern European (EE) division.[2]

Karlow was delighted. Although born in New York City, he had spent part of his childhood years in Germany and spoke the language fluently. Soon after New Year's of 1950, he reported in to the CIA station in Karlsruhe, south of Frankfurt. Within six months, he had set up his laboratory in what looked like an innocent group of row houses in Höchst, a suburb of Frankfurt.

"Dick sent me to Germany to see what was needed to send agents into Eastern Europe," Karlow said. At the time, the Eastern European division was attempting to infiltrate agents into Soviet-bloc countries. The CIA's Soviet Russia (SR) division mounted a parallel operation to parachute agents into Soviet territory. "We dealt with guns, locks, paper. We made the tools you needed to send people into denied areas," Karlow said. "Clothing with correct labels, identity papers, union membership cards, employment documents, ration cards."

[1]The Berlin base chief came from a family of generations of winemakers from Mainz, near Frankfurt. He left the CIA in 1959, after serving as station chief in Hong Kong, and became perhaps best known as the producer of Blue Nun wine.
[2]To avoid confusion, Foreign Division M (FDM) will be referred to here by its later and better-known name, the Eastern European or EE division.

The CIA got many of its documents from refugees from the East who had turned in their identity papers. Karlow altered the documents, making what he called "new originals." For cover purposes, the CIA designated Karlow's staff of forgers and printers as the "7922d Technical Aids Detachment of the United States Army." The unit also manufactured documents, using the same German paper stock that the Eastern European countries imported and used. "For documents, we had to know when they changed paper color, rubber stamps, and so on. We aged documents by walking on them with our bare feet, carrying them in our back pockets. It was all stage-prop stuff. That's what I did. Stage props."

Some of the problems confronting Karlow seemed insoluble. For example, there were times when the CIA's agents in the field needed to develop a roll of film without access to a darkroom. Could it be done? Karlow went to the Polaroid Corporation, whose founder, Edwin H. Land, helped to develop the U-2 spy plane and its cameras for the CIA. Karlow outlined the problem, and the Polaroid technicians came up with a simple answer. "They said to take the two chemical packs that come with Polaroid film, go into a dark area, and run the strip of undeveloped film between the packs. It worked!"

Not everything did. In 1952, according to Peter Sichel, "we got the order to steal a MiG from the Russians." The priority request had come to the CIA from the Air Force, which badly wanted to acquire the latest-model MiG fighter plane, the MiG-15. To do the job, the CIA recruited an agent who was an experienced pilot but had never flown a MiG.

"The agent was a Czech with a withered hand," Karlow said, "and we promised him hand surgery."

Karlow was assigned to provide technical support for the scheme. The CIA's plan was to steal the MiG-15 from East Germany and fly it across the border to a West German airfield, where the U.S. Air Force had a plane hidden and a crew ready to take the MiG apart, load it aboard, and fly it to Wright-Patterson Air Force Base, in Ohio. "We found a vulnerable East German airfield, but the Czech agent would have to cut through electrified barbed wire. We designed noiseless cutters that would allow him to get through without being electrocuted or causing the wires to twang when they were cut. On each side of the cutter blade, we put screw clamps that held the wire in place as it cut. We also equipped him with a silenced Luger pistol."

To help train the Czech agent, Karlow was asked to build a mock MiG cockpit. At first Karlow had to guess where the various handles and levers would go. "Then they gave me more data, and we changed the handles. We had to know what the cockpit looked like, because our agent would have thirty seconds to fly it out."

But first the agent was taken to an airfield in the British zone of Germany "and tested on a Vampire that he had never seen before." The agent took off and flew the plane successfully.

The plot to steal the MiG was ready to go, according to Karlow, when General Walter Bedell Smith, the director of the CIA, called the case officers in charge back to Washington. "Beedle" Smith asked where the pilot had been trained for the mission. "When told that he was trained at an American air base in Germany," Karlow said, "Smith canceled the operation. Nobody had stopped to consider that stealing a Russian plane might start World War III. If the pilot were caught, the first thing he would be asked is where he was trained. It would tie it right to the United States."

Karlow spent six years in Germany, returned to headquarters, and was assigned to work for Helms in a psychological warfare unit of the Eastern European division. Later, after the Hungarian revolt of 1956, he was named deputy chief of the Economic Action Division, another psywar unit in the Directorate of Plans.

Three years later, he finally had a chance to push for miniaturization of cameras, transmitters, and other spy equipment. "Why can't we have a transmitter in the onion in a martini?" Karlow asked.[3] His pleas were heard, and that year Karlow organized and, with the title of secretary, headed the CIA's Technical Requirements Board.

The board worked on methods to bug electric typewriters so the words being typed could be captured electronically from some distance away, and it helped to develop a tiny transmitter that could be placed behind the dashboard of a car to enable it to be followed at a distance.

But the CIA's technical boffins worked hardest of all at playing

[3]Karlow was speaking figuratively. But a microphone disguised as the olive in a martini was actually displayed at a Senate wiretap hearing in February 1965. What appeared to be a green olive stuffed with pimiento was really a tiny transmitter that could pick up a conversation whether or not it was submerged in gin and vermouth, the senators were told. The "toothpick" sticking up from the olive acted as an antenna.

catch-up with the KGB: they were trying desperately to reproduce an unusual, highly sophisticated bug that the Soviets had used against the United States with devastating effect. The bug employed a technology that had not been encountered before, and CIA scientists were having trouble figuring it out.

In 1945, the Soviets had presented to Ambassador Averell Harriman in Moscow a carved replica of the Great Seal of the United States. The hollow wooden seal had decorated the wall of four U.S. ambassadors before the listening device it concealed was discovered by the embassy's electronic sweepers in the early 1950s.[4]

"We found it and we didn't know how it worked," Karlow recalled. "There was a passive device inside the seal, like a tadpole, with a little tail. The Soviets had a microwave signal beamed at the embassy that caused the receptors inside the seal to resonate." A human voice would affect the way the device resonated, allowing the words to be picked up. "Technically it was a passive device, no current, no batteries, an infinite life expectancy."

The effort to copy the Soviet bug that had been discovered inside the Great Seal was given the code name EASY CHAIR by the CIA. The actual research was being performed in a laboratory in the Netherlands in two supersecret projects code-named MARK 2 and MARK 3.

Unknown to Karlow and the CIA, British intelligence had succeeded in replicating the Soviet bug, which MI5, the British internal security service, code-named SATYR. In his book *Spycatcher,* former MI5 official Peter Wright said he first thought the device was activated at 1,800 megahertz, but then tuned it down to 800 MHz and it worked.[5] But, according to Karlow, the British did not share their secret with the CIA.[6]

Karlow's work on EASY CHAIR was to have unexpected conse-

---

[4]The United States kept the embarrassing discovery secret for almost a decade. But in late May 1960, after the Soviets shot down the CIA's U-2 spy plane, Washington tried to counter international criticism by going public with the Soviet eavesdropping device. Henry Cabot Lodge, the U.S. ambassador to the United Nations, opened up and displayed the Great Seal and its tiny bug at the UN Security Council.

[5]Peter Wright, *Spycatcher* (New York: Viking, 1987), pp. 19–20.

[6]In his book, Peter Wright indicated that he had perfected SATYR by 1953 and shared the device with U.S. intelligence. But Karlow says the CIA was not told. "It's obvious Wright knew about SATYR, and I didn't," Karlow said. "It was still a requirement to me in 1959. We had no indication there was a working model of SATYR."

quences. When Anatoly Golitsin dug his package out of the snowbank in front of Frank Friberg's house in Helsinki, one of the papers it contained was a KGB technical document warning that the CIA was working on an eavesdropping system to match the Soviet bug.

"Golitsin said it was a KGB requirements circular that came from headquarters in Moscow to Helsinki," a CIA officer recalled. "The document said to be on the alert for any information about the joint American-British research effort. It was detailed enough to lead the CIA to conclude that this referred to the project we were working on with the Brits." Although the eavesdropping device had not yet been perfected, the document said, the system was a potential threat. The KGB seemed to know about EASY CHAIR.

And EASY CHAIR was a project of the Technical Requirements Board. The Counterintelligence and Security staffs of the CIA immediately swung into action. To the agency's sleuths, it seemed logical to start at the top. They zeroed in on the secretary of the board.

If Peter Karlow had not existed, James Angleton would have had to invent him. "Sasha," Golitsin's mole, had spent time in Germany. Karlow had run the laboratory in Höchst. Sasha had a Slavic background, and a name that might have ended in "-sky." When the CIA's investigators pulled out Karlow's file, they discovered that his name at birth was Klibansky, and that his father at times had claimed to have been born in Russia. And Sasha's name, according to Golitsin, began with a K.

To top it off, there was the apparent leak from the CIA's eavesdropping and countereavesdropping unit. By January 15, 1962, wiretaps had been secretly installed at Karlow's home on Klingle Street in Northwest Washington. In the thick, secret CIA dossiers that began to build as the counterintelligence and security staffs hunted for the elusive Sasha, one phrase appeared repeatedly in the documents dealing with Karlow. He was, the CIA files made clear, the "principal suspect."[7]

It did not stop with Karlow. On the basis of Golitsin's vague and

[7]For example, a memo labeled "Espionage" from Sheffield Edwards, director of the CIA's Office of Security, to J. Edgar Hoover, director of the Federal Bureau of Investigation, begins: "Mr. Peter Karlow, principal suspect in the subject case . . ." Memorandum, Edwards to Hoover, February 19, 1963.

fragmentary information, the CIA's Counterintelligence Staff and the Office of Security began searching through the files of all CIA officers in the Clandestine Services whose names began with the letter K.

More than one loyal CIA officer was to find his career sidetracked—or ended—merely because he had the misfortune to have a name beginning with the eleventh letter of the alphabet.

Within three weeks of Golitsin's arrival at the safe house in northern Virginia, the mole hunt that was to corrode the CIA for almost two decades had begun.

Peter Karlow had not intended to become a war hero. He was a student on a full scholarship at Swarthmore College in the summer of 1941. "I saw war coming and wanted to get into intelligence," Karlow said. He filled out several applications, and in July 1942 he was commissioned an ensign in the U.S. Navy and assigned to the OSS. By February 1944, he was stationed on Corsica, working with PT Boat Squadron 15, a Navy unit that supported OSS operations.

The OSS maintained a fifteen-man radar intercept station, known as a listening post (LP), on Capraia, a small island north of Elba. The intercept station was a vital link, because it was used to spot German planes flying in low to bomb the U.S. air base on Corsica. "The LP was manned by OSS uniformed guerrillas, all Italian-speaking Americans," Karlow said. "The Germans attacked, landed a raiding party, and destroyed the radar set and other equipment."

As the duty officer that day, Karlow's job was to get the LP operating again. By this stage of the war, Italy had declared war on the Nazis and joined the Allies. "I ran around trying to find replacement equipment and a boat to bring it in. There was no U.S. boat available, so I got hold of an Italian PT boat. I rounded up the Italian crew from the local bars and found the captain and we went out. We reached the island, made contact with the radar detachment, unloaded the equipment, and got out."

But the Germans had planted trip mines in the shallow harbor of Capraia, rigged to go off after a ship passed over them a certain number of times. As Karlow's boat edged gingerly out of the harbor on February 20, one of the mines exploded in ten feet of water. The ship blew up.

"I was standing on the port side, the mine was on the starboard side. I was blown out into the water." In the explosion, Karlow smashed his knee on the torpedo tube. Italian fishermen pulled him out of the sea, but he developed gangrene from the polluted water. He was taken to a field hospital in Corsica, then flown to Sardinia, where surgeons amputated his left leg above the knee.

Of the twelve-man crew—ten Italians, including one officer; Karlow; and one British officer who went along as an observer—all but Karlow and two enlisted men died. Karlow was the sole surviving officer.

At the age of twenty-two, he had given his left leg for his country. Karlow was fitted with an artificial limb, and learned to walk again, to swim, drive a car, and live a close-to-normal existence. Indeed, so determined was he to overcome his disability that few who met him in later life even realized he had lost a leg in the war.

Back in Washington in the fall of 1944, Karlow was greeted by General William J. "Wild Bill" Donovan, the head of the OSS. And Donovan, who later pinned a Bronze Star on Karlow for the action at Capraia, had good news. "When I reported back to the OSS buildings on E Street, Donovan came out, put his arm around me, and said, 'Peter, welcome back, I've got a job for you.' Then he was gone in an instant. That's the way he was—he moved fast but took a personal interest in his men."

The job was to serve as a member of Donovan's personal staff for the rest of the war. Then, in 1946, Karlow was assigned to write, with the help of Kermit Roosevelt, a classified history of the OSS in World War II. The study was later declassified and published.[8]

In the new CIA, Karlow's vision and his technical skills won him steady advancement and the support of the influential Richard Helms. It was to Karlow that Helms turned in 1961 after the agency was rocked by the failed invasion at the Bay of Pigs.

Helms, then the deputy director for plans, called Karlow in and gave him a special assignment. President Kennedy, Helms said, wanted to establish a single place within the government to handle foreign policy crises; he had ordered Dean Rusk, the Secretary of State, to set up an operations center at the State Department, with an

---

[8] *War Report of the OSS,* with a new introduction by Kermit Roosevelt (New York: Walker and Company; Washington, D.C.: Carrollton Press, 1976). As Karlow had done, "Kim" Roosevelt, grandson of President Theodore Roosevelt, moved from the OSS into the CIA. He ran the CIA operation in Iran in 1953 that overthrew Mohammed Mossadegh and restored the Shah to the throne.

officer assigned from each military service and agency of the government involved in national security. Karlow would be the CIA representative. "In the summer of 1961," he said, "I reported to the State Department."

It was a prestigious post, representing the CIA in a presidentially created center within the State Department, but it was outside the agency, and it was not the job that Karlow wanted. What he hoped for, he had told Helms, was to be appointed chief of the CIA's Technical Services Division, which developed and controlled all of the agency's gadgetry, from exotic weaponry to wigs, from voice alteration devices to the latest bugs and eavesdropping gadgets. By background and experience, Karlow felt he was qualified to run TSD, a post that would truly and finally make him the American Q. Helms had been noncommittal, but Karlow came away from the meeting with the impression that he might yet get the TSD job after his tour at the State Department.

Within six months he would instead become the prime suspect in the CIA's frantic search for a traitor within its ranks. In the prevailing climate of suspicion, bordering on panic, the agency's highest officials would succumb to the fear that Peter Karlow, winner of a Bronze Star, was a Soviet mole.

And no one would tell him.

Chapter 3

AELADLE

For its code names, the CIA uses combinations of two letters, known as digraphs, to indicate geographic or other subjects. Soviet defectors or agents-in-place were given the digraph AE, followed by a code name. Anatoly Golitsin was christened AELADLE.[1]

From the start, AELADLE was trouble. Some of his information, it is true, was to prove valuable to the CIA. But Golitsin made it clear to his handlers that he considered himself a man of supreme importance who was almost alone in fully understanding the nature of the Soviet menace. He had little patience for dealing with underlings.

To a degree, all defectors are troublesome. Cut off from their homeland, their culture, their language, and often their families, Soviet and other defectors from Eastern Europe frequently had understandable psychological difficulties in adjusting to their new environment. In some cases, they were unstable, or impulsive to begin with, or they might not have taken the usually irrevocable and often dangerous step of changing sides in the Cold War. Their motives were varied. Many were seeking a way out of failed marriages. Others left for ideological reasons. Some were frustrated in their careers—the motive that Golitsin gave—and still others were simply attracted to the affluent lifestyle of the West. More often than not, defectors came over for a

---

[1]For a new identity to enable Golitsin to start life in America, the CIA also gave Golitsin the name John Stone. His British code name was KAGO.

mixture of these or other reasons. And almost none were free of complaints, problems, and demands.

Having said that, by all accounts Anatoly Golitsin was in a class by himself. Early on, he demanded to see President Kennedy, who declined. Golitsin also demanded, unsuccessfully, to deal directly with J. Edgar Hoover.

Although blocked in his efforts to gain access to the Oval Office, Golitsin wrote a letter to President Kennedy and insisted that it be delivered to the Chief Executive. To pacify Golitsin, the CIA assigned its most celebrated Russian-speaking operative, George G. Kisevalter, to meet with the defector. A huge man, well over six feet, built like a linebacker, Kisevalter was nicknamed "Teddy Bear" inside the CIA. Born in St. Petersburg, the son of the Czar's munitions expert, Kisevalter had the deceptively innocent face of a friendly bartender. His appearance and demeanor concealed a quick mind, combined with an encyclopedic memory and a distaste for pretension in any of its forms. Among the Soviet division's field operators, Kisevalter was first among equals. He was the CIA case officer who handled the agency's two premier spies: Lieutenant Colonel Pyotr Popov of the GRU (the Soviet military intelligence service), who was the first Soviet intelligence officer ever recruited by the CIA, and GRU Colonel Oleg Penkovsky, whom Kisevalter had personally met and debriefed during Penkovsky's three trips to the West in 1961.[2]

Howard J. Osborn, then head of the Soviet division, called Kisevalter in to give him his delicate assignment. "They didn't want the letter to go to the President," Kisevalter said. "Golitsin was a loose cannon; nobody knew what he would say or do. It was embarrassing to have him write to the President. They sent me to accept the letter; I was authorized to promise to deliver it to the President." But Kisevalter's real mission was to find out what was in the letter "and if it was not innocuous, to stop it."

Kisevalter met Golitsin at an unmarked CIA building on E Street, across from the State Department. Golitsin was already seated at a desk when the CIA man arrived, and he sat down across from the

[2]Kisevalter's prestige within the agency was so great that it probably saved him from becoming a suspect himself. His name, after all, began with K, he had a Slavic background, and he had served in Germany.

defector. "I was acting friendly," Kisevalter related. " 'Let's speak Russian,' I said. 'Let me see your letter.' " Golitsin handed it across the desk.

"The letter said, 'In view of the fact that the President who has promised me things through his brother, Robert, may not be President in the future, how can I be sure the United States government will keep its promises to me for money and a pension?' " Kisevalter glared at Golitsin.

"I said, 'You S.O.B. You're a first-class blackmailer. This is *shantazh*! [the Russian word for blackmail]' "

Shaken by Kisevalter's reaction, Golitsin changed his mind and demanded the letter back.

Oh, no, Kisevalter said. You want it delivered to the President, I'll deliver it. Kisevalter grinned as he recalled the moment. "Golitsin jumped up on top of the desk and then jumped down on my side and we began wrestling for the letter. I let him win."[3]

Anatoly Golitsin had first come to the attention of the CIA seven years before he defected in Helsinki. In 1954, when the KGB officer Peter Deriabin had defected in Vienna, he had named Golitsin as someone who might be vulnerable to recruitment by the CIA. At the time, Golitsin was a young counterintelligence officer working in Vienna. Deriabin was said to have told his debriefers that Golitsin had an exaggerated idea of his own importance and was disliked by his colleagues.

The two KGB men were to meet again, under unusual circumstances. For security reasons, the CIA goes to great lengths to keep Soviet defectors apart in the United States. But sometimes things go wrong. "Golitsin's safe house was out in the woods," George Kisevalter recounted. "He needed a haircut, so they took him into town. Golitsin is walking down the street in Vienna, Virginia, toward a barber shop on Maple Avenue and Deriabin comes out of the barber

---

[3]Although the President did not see Golitsin, his brother, Attorney General Robert Kennedy, did meet with him. George Kisevalter heard the tape of part of the conversation between Robert Kennedy and Golitsin. "I needed a translator for Bobby Kennedy," Kisevalter said. "His Boston accent was impossible to decipher. Golitsin was claiming, 'I was made promises in the name of the President.' Robert Kennedy said he would tell his brother."

shop and greets him like a long-lost friend. The security people almost died.''[4]

According to biographical details released by the CIA and by British intelligence, Anatoly Golitsin was born near Poltava, in the Ukraine, in 1926, but moved to Moscow seven years later. At the age of fifteen, while a cadet at military school, he joined the Komsomol, the Communist youth organization. In 1945, the year World War II ended, Golitsin joined the Communist Party and transferred from an artillery school for officers in Odessa to a military counterintelligence school in Moscow. He was graduated in 1946, joined the KGB, and while working at headquarters attended night classes to earn a college degree in 1948. He took advanced intelligence courses for two years, then worked for about a year in the KGB section that dealt with counterespionage against the United States.

He was posted to Vienna by the KGB in 1953, under diplomatic cover as a member of the staff of the Soviet High Commission. He targeted Soviet émigrés for a year, then worked against British intelligence. When he returned to Moscow in 1954, he attended the KGB Institute for four years and earned a law degree. For a year, he worked in the KGB's NATO section. Then, in 1960, he was assigned to Finland.[5]

"He caused trouble for the KGB before he ever defected," according to Don Moore, a former senior FBI counterintelligence official. Tall, white-haired, genial, and shrewd, Moore headed the FBI's Soviet counterintelligence operations for seventeen years. Golitsin, Moore said, had wanted to reorganize the KGB, "and he tried the same thing

---

[4]After the chance meeting, Golitsin and Deriabin wanted to see each other, so the CIA arranged a meeting in a motel between Deriabin, Golitsin, and Golitsin's wife, Irina. The CIA bugged and taped the meeting, but didn't learn much. According to Kisevalter, Golitsin asked Deriabin, "How much are you getting?" Irina Golitsin "complained we lost everything we owned" and Deriabin angrily reprimanded her for voicing such material concerns.

[5]These details of Golitsin's background are set forth in his book, *New Lies for Old,* in the introduction signed by four American and British intelligence officers who had worked closely with Golitsin: Stephen de Mowbray, of MI6, the British external spy agency; Arthur Martin, the Soviet counterintelligence chief of MI5, the British internal security service; Vasia C. Gmirkin of the Soviet division of the CIA; and Newton S. "Scotty" Miler, who was chief of operations of the CIA's Counterintelligence Staff under James Angleton. See Anatoliy Golitsyn, *New Lies for Old* (New York: Dodd, Mead, 1984), pp. xiii–xvi.

with us. He would have liked to have run the FBI, the CIA, and the NSA, too, if we'd let him."

When Moore met Golitsin for the first time, it was just after the CIA's U-2 spy pilot Francis Gary Powers, who had been captured and jailed by the Russians, was traded for the imprisoned Soviet spy Rudolf Abel on a bridge in Berlin on February 10, 1962. Abel, a full colonel in the KGB, was an "illegal," a spy who operates without benefit of diplomatic cover. He had worked as an artist and photographer in Brooklyn. Arrested after his alcoholic assistant turned himself in to the CIA, Abel had been serving a thirty-year sentence in the Atlanta Federal Penitentiary.[6]

As the FBI's top counterspy against the Soviets, Moore wanted to meet Golitsin, the defector who had so impressed the CIA. Moore asked Sam Papich, the longtime FBI liaison man at the CIA, to accompany him to a hotel in downtown Washington that the agency had chosen as the site for the secret meeting. "The CIA brought Golitsin to a room in the Mayflower," Moore said. "He was stocky, gruff, shorter than I am, about five foot nine or ten. He was convinced we didn't release Abel for Powers unless we had doubled Abel. We hadn't. 'When he gets back over, the KGB will turn him,' Golitsin said."

Moore, who respected Abel as a clever, case-hardened professional, knew there was no chance in the world that Abel would ever become a double agent and work for American intelligence as the price of his release. But in the Mayflower meeting, the FBI man had gained some insight into Golitsin's conspiratorial thinking. Not only was the Russian convinced that Abel had been doubled against the Soviets, but he was sure that the KGB would discover this and play him back against the CIA.

"His messages to you—give them to me and I will tell you what they mean," Golitsin told Moore.

"How can you tell?" Moore asked, playing along.

---

[6] I interviewed Moore in his home in northern Virginia. At one point, he led me down to the basement, where he showed me a black-and-white sketch hanging on the wall, entitled "Smith's Bottom, Atlanta." It portrayed a group of poor black women hanging out wash from the back porches of their row houses on a laundry line strung across their yards. The artist was Rudolf Abel. "He could see the scene from his prison windows," Moore said. After the spy trade, a prison official presented the sketch to Moore as a souvenir.

"Oh, I can tell."

Remembering the encounter, Moore smiled and said: "That was typical Golitsin."

For the CIA's Soviet division and the Counterintelligence Staff, however, the problems of handling Golitsin were less significant than assessing the substance of his information. Golitsin might have an overblown idea of his own importance, he might demand to see the President and J. Edgar Hoover, but that could be managed. After all, a previous defector, Michal Goleniewski, had provided what proved to be extremely valuable information to the CIA, even though he eventually became persuaded that he was the czarevich, the Grand Duke Alexei, son of Czar Nicholas II, and, as such, the last of the Romanovs and heir to the crown of Imperial Russia.[7]

Two years before Golitsin's defection in Helsinki, the CIA station in Bern, Switzerland, received a series of letters, fourteen in all, from someone who appeared to be a Soviet-bloc intelligence officer. The letters were signed "Sniper." Late in 1960, Sniper defected in West Berlin and identified himself as Michal Goleniewski, an officer in the Polish intelligence service.

The information he provided in his letters enabled the British to arrest Gordon Lonsdale, a KGB agent posing as a Canadian jukebox salesman in England, who had recruited Henry Frederick Houghton and his spinster girlfriend, Ethel Elizabeth Gee, both of whom worked at the Portland Naval Base, near Southampton, a center for antisubmarine research. MI5 had trailed Lonsdale to suburban Ruislip, where two Americans, Morris and Lona Cohen, who were living in England under the names Peter and Helen Kroger, used a high-frequency transmitter to send the naval secrets to Moscow.[8] The Cohens, too, were arrested, and all five went to prison.[9]

[7]In the mid-1960s Goleniewski began writing open letters to CIA director Admiral William F. Raborn and to Richard M. Helms, Raborn's successor, which appeared in fine print as paid advertisements in the *Washington Daily News*. In the ads, Goleniewski explained that he was the czarevich. All of this was very awkward for the CIA.
[8]As Peter Kroger, Cohen had become well known in London's antiquarian book trade, operating from a room in the Strand. The Cohens had been in contact with Rudolf Abel in New York, but disappeared in 1950, turning up four years later in England.
[9]The FBI established that Lonsdale was really Conon Trofimovich Molody, who was born in Moscow but brought up in Berkeley, California, by an aunt who passed him

Goleniewski has also been credited with providing the information that led the British to unmask and arrest George Blake, an MI6 agent working for the Soviets who had served time in a North Korean prison camp, then worked for British intelligence in Berlin.[10] Goleniewski is said to have provided additional leads that led to the arrest in 1961 of yet another top Soviet agent, Heinz Felfe, the head of Soviet counterespionage for the West German Federal Intelligence Agency (BND). Felfe was a key subordinate of the BND's chief and founder, the reclusive ex-Nazi general Reinhard Gehlen.

Since this deluge of counterintelligence information had come from a single Polish defector only a year before Golitsin's arrival, the CIA was understandably eager to hear every scrap that Golitsin, an actual KGB defector—not merely an officer of a satellite service—could summon up from his memory. Beginning, of course, with his warning of a mole inside the CIA itself.

But his charges went far beyond that. Other Western services, he warned, were a Swiss cheese of Soviet penetration, being nibbled away from within by KGB moles. In time, Golitsin claimed that, in addition to the United States, the Soviets had penetrated the intelligence services of Britain, France, Canada, and Norway.

In the beginning, the Soviet division interrogated Golitsin, as was the normal practice when the agency acquired a KGB defector. But there was constant friction. Golitsin, for example, clashed bitterly with Donald Jameson, one of the officers in the division who spoke fluent Russian and specialized in working with Soviet defectors. By October 1962, it was clear that Golitsin had become totally disenchanted with his handlers. For one thing, the division had declined to

---

off as her son. In 1938, at age sixteen, he returned to Moscow. On April 22, 1964, he was exchanged at the Heerstrasse checkpoint in West Berlin for Greville Wynne, an MI6 agent who had served as a courier for Oleg Penkovsky.

[10]So extensive was the damage done by Blake to British and U.S. intelligence that he was sentenced in 1961 to forty-two years in prison, one of the longest sentences ever given in British legal history. In 1966, he escaped from Wormwood Scrubs prison to Moscow, where he took a Russian wife, Ida, fathered a son, Mischa, and was given a dacha by the KGB. In 1989, Blake asserted what Western intelligence had long suspected—that he had betrayed Operation Gold, the Berlin tunnel the CIA and MI6 had dug in 1955 to wiretap Soviet and East German communications in East Berlin. The tunnel operated for more than a year, until April 1956, but it harvested little information of value. Blake apparently had told the Soviets about it before the excavation began.

accede to his demand that he be given millions of dollars to run counterintelligence operations against the Soviet Union.

"Golitsin said to me and to others that he wanted ten million," Jameson recalled. "He said NATO was incapable of protecting itself from Soviet penetration. The only way it could be protected would be to create a special security service that he would run, reporting essentially to nobody. To do that he wanted this sum, ten million. The money was to ensure his independent control over this thing."[11]

According to Pete Bagley, who was in charge of counterintelligence for the Soviet division, the decision was finally made to turn Golitsin over to James Angleton, the CIA counterintelligence chief. "Jim got Golitsin about October of '62, around the time I was coming into the division," Bagley said. "Golitsin's demands exceeded what the division could do for him. He wanted to see the President. I suppose we could have recruited Jack Kennedy, but he had other jobs to do. As a last resort he [Golitsin] was turned over to the CI staff. And also because his statements were all about penetration, not only of the U.S., but of Britain, France, Norway. And CI staff was responsible for liaison with those services."

It was finding the mole supposedly burrowing inside the CIA itself, however, that became the primary preoccupation—obsession might be a more apt word—of James Angleton. The debriefings of Golitsin were intense, and went on for months. As the investigation grew and spread far beyond Peter Karlow to include literally dozens of suspects, the demands on Angleton's staff, and that of the Office of Security, were overwhelming. By 1964, Angleton realized he needed more manpower just to handle the "Golitsin serials," as he called the burgeoning files created by the debriefings of the KGB man.

Angleton brought in Newton S. Miler, who was then the CIA station chief in Ethiopia, to help run the mole hunt. It was not his first assignment for Angleton; he had worked on the CI staff, dealing with Soviet counterintelligence, from 1958 to 1960.

A tall (six foot one), tough-looking man, with a deliberate manner, "Scotty" Miler had blunt, thick features and the face of a county

---

[11]Jameson remembered Golitsin asking for $10 million. Other former CIA officers thought the figure was even higher. According to one published account, the defector, in his meeting with Robert Kennedy, had asked for $30 million, a request that the Attorney General turned down. See David C. Martin, *Wilderness of Mirrors* (New York: Harper & Row, 1980), p. 109.

sheriff or a motorcycle cop, which was deceptive, because he was a thoughtful man with a good deal more depth than his roughhewn appearance might suggest. The son of a meat-packer in Mason City, Iowa, Miler had joined the Navy's V-12 program during World War II at Dartmouth, where he graduated with a degree in economics in 1946. He joined the Strategic Services Unit (SSU), a forerunner of the CIA, which sent him to China. When the agency was created by Congress in 1947, Miler was absorbed into it. He worked as a case officer overseas for thirteen years, in Japan, Thailand, and the Philippines.

When Angleton brought Miler in from Addis Adaba, he assigned him the title of deputy chief of "special investigations," the euphemism that Angleton gave to the mole hunt. The work was carried out by a unit of the Counterintelligence Staff known as the Special Investigations Group, or SIG.[12] While the term "special investigations" included other, unspecified "sensitive matters," Miler said, "the main thing we were doing was the search for penetrations. That was the primary thing."

By 1990, many years after he had retired from the CIA, Scotty Miler was living in Placitas, New Mexico, in a home that he and his wife had built in a remote area of the rolling, dry hill country north of Albuquerque. He had long since tried to put the mole hunt behind him. But, once found, he was willing to talk about it, and about the nature of counterintelligence, at length, and in considerable detail. He chain-smoked constantly as he talked.

Was it really true that Golitsin tried to identify the mole by a letter of the alphabet? As was his style before responding to most questions, Miler took a drag on his filter cigarette, paused, and looked off into the distance for a moment. "Yes," he replied. "He said the man's name began with the letter K."

But Golitsin had offered more detail than that, Miler continued. "He said Sasha had operated primarily in Berlin. But also in West Germany, and other areas of Western Europe. He did not know whether Sasha was a [CIA] contract officer or a staff officer. He also

[12]The SIG dated back to 1954, when the CI Staff was created. Initially, according to CIA records, the name of the mole-hunting group was the Special Investigation Unit. But no one ever referred to it that way. "We always called it the Special Investigations Group," Miler said. Eventually that became official; the name was changed to the Special Investigations Group (SIG) in 1973.

said the penetration had a Russian or Slavic background.[13] He gave other indications of operations that had been compromised. So we began going through the files, who was involved in what and where. Putting the pieces of the jigsaw together."

But Golitsin, according to Miler, did not confine himself to the clues about the elusive Sasha. He also provided other indications that the CIA might harbor a mole. Golitsin told the CIA of a visit to the United States in 1957 by V. M. Kovshuk, the head of the KGB's American embassy section.[14] As the name implied, the section's target was the U.S. embassy in Moscow.

"Golitsin said Kovshuk would only have come to meet a high-level penetration in the United States government, possibly in the agency. Golitsin was able to identify a photo of Kovshuk." Checking its files, the FBI confirmed that Vladislav Mikhailovich Kovshuk, using the name Vladimir Mikhailovich Komarov, had indeed been assigned to the Soviet embassy in Washington for ten months, from early in 1957 to the fall of that year.[15] Moreover, Golitsin warned, the KGB—knowing that he had defected and that he knew of Kovshuk's mission to America—would attempt to deflect the CIA from the true purpose of the visit.

It might seem entirely plausible that there could be other explanations for the visit to America of the mysterious V. M. Kovshuk. As a specialist in running operations against Americans, he might, for example, simply have wanted to travel to the United States, to increase

[13]There was, Miler explained, a certain ambiguity to Golitsin's claim that the mole had something Slavic in his background. It could mean that "the person himself had a Slavic background, or it could also mean he worked in Soviet operations," Miler said. "In the early days of the mole hunt, because Golitsin had said Sasha had a Slavic background, we confined the search to case officers with Slavic backgrounds. But his [Golitsin's] bona fides had not yet been established, and there was a question of whether he had his information right, so you had to look beyond Slavic case officers. The interpretation we put was he [the mole] had himself a Slavic background but you couldn't rule out the other interpretation."

[14]The section was a unit of the American department of the KGB's Second Chief Directorate, which watches Soviet citizens and foreigners in the Soviet Union.

[15]The FBI takes clandestine photographs of known or suspected Soviet intelligence officers in the United States, and in any case has copies of photos of all Soviet embassy employees from the visas they must obtain to enter the country. Golitsin would have been shown an FBI "mug book" in order to identify Kovshuk/Komarov. In Washington, "Komarov" moved into an apartment building on upper Connecticut Avenue. He had the title of first secretary at the Soviet embassy.

his knowledge of the country that was his target. A Washington assignment was also attractive for obvious reasons. Even for a ranking KGB official, a trip to the West was a plum, a chance to get out of the oppressive atmosphere of Moscow and see the world, and, not incidentally, to shop for luxuries unavailable in the Soviet Union.

But to the CIA counterintelligence officers, prompted by Golitsin, the Kovshuk trip took on a much more sinister connotation. It could, after all, mean a mole. That possibility could not be ignored. To the trained counterintelligence mind, every fragment, every detail, no matter how tiny or trivial, may have possible significance in unraveling a larger deception by the enemy. Sometimes, of course, the CI officers turn out to be right. Sometimes they are wrong. Often, they never know.

On just such gossamer threads, the Counterintelligence Staff gradually wove the full-blown theories of a penetration—or worse yet, penetrations—of the CIA that were to consume the agency over two decades.

And no one was better at spinning and weaving the most intricate patterns, at detecting the complex plots of a clever and relentless Communist foe, at perceiving the delicate strands and synapses that might be invisible to the less experienced eye, than the chief of the Counterintelligence Staff himself, James Jesus Angleton.

Chapter 4

Molehunter

In the early 1950s, Tom Braden was a young assistant to Allen W. Dulles, the CIA's deputy director for plans, the head of the agency's clandestine arm. As Braden recalled it, he and his wife were in their bedroom one evening when Braden relayed some office gossip.

"Beedle doesn't like Allen," he told her. Mrs. Braden understood the remark; it meant that General Walter Bedell Smith, the formidable director of the CIA, did not care for Dulles, the famed World War II spymaster who was eventually to succeed him as director. Braden thinks he added some comments about how the dreaded Smith, whom Winston Churchill compared to a bulldog, was mistreating Dulles.

"The next day," Braden said, "Dulles called me in. He asked, 'What's this about Bedell and me?' "

Adopting an innocent expression, Braden professed not to know what Dulles meant. "I might have given him a less than candid answer," Braden admitted. "He repeated the conversation word for word, and I didn't deny it the second time. It was so accurate."

"You'd better watch out," Dulles warned him. "Jimmy's got his eye on you." Braden said he drew the obvious conclusion: James Angleton had bugged his bedroom and was picking up pillow talk between himself and his wife, Joan.[1] But Braden said he was only mildly

---

[1]Braden, who recounted the incident to friends, later heard that "Angleton denied that story about the bug. He never denied it to me but to friends of mine who knew

surprised at the incident, because Angleton was known to have bugs all over town.

"Angleton would come into Allen's office first thing in the morning and report what his bugs had picked up the night before. He used to delight Allen with stories of what happened at people's dinner parties. One house he bugged was Mrs. Dwight Davis. Her husband had been Secretary of War in the Coolidge cabinet.[2] In the early 1950s she was a much-sought-after Washington hostess, a dowager lady who had senators and cabinet members to her table. Jim used to come into Allen's office and Allen would say, 'How's the fishing?' And Jim would say, 'Well, I got a few nibbles last night.' It was all done in the guise of fishing talk."

Braden said he had personal knowledge of these conversations in Dulles's office, because "I was present and heard this, and not just on one occasion. Angleton would report that people said this, and people said that. Some were derogatory remarks about Allen, which Allen enjoyed. I presumed that they came from a bug.

"It seemed to me scandalous. Everybody assumed he bugged CIA staff officers too, not just dowager ladies. I think most people assumed he was doing it." At a bugged dinner party, Braden said, "some senator or representative might say something that might be of use to the agency. I didn't think that was right. I think Jim was amoral."[3]

Angleton and liked him. Angleton said to tell me that the story was simply not true." But was it true? "Yes," Braden replied, "that's what Angleton did." Braden left the agency four months before Angleton became the first chief of the newly created, centralized Counterintelligence Staff on December 20, 1954. But prior to that date, Angleton headed one of several smaller covert staffs then in existence and designated with the letters A through D. "He was there," Braden said. "He was doing the bugging while I was there. Titles didn't matter much in those days."

[2]Although Secretary of War, an Army major general, and an investment banker, Dwight F. Davis was better known as the man who donated the Davis Cup to international tennis. He was himself three times national doubles champion. He died in 1945. His second wife, Pauline, the Washington hostess, was the daughter of President Theodore Roosevelt's Secretary of the Navy. Mrs. Davis died in 1955.

[3]Braden served in the CIA for five years, from 1949 to 1954, rose to a division chief, and later became well known as a newspaper columnist, television host (of CNN's *Crossfire*), and author. As chief of the agency's International Organizations division, he channeled CIA money to a broad range of anti-Communist cultural groups overseas, and, through the AFL-CIO, into labor unions in Europe. Later, a book he wrote about his large family, *Eight Is Enough* (New York: Random House, 1975), became the basis for a television series in the 1970s and 1980s.

Robert T. Crowley, a former CIA officer who had worked with Angleton, said the CI chief did not arrange wiretaps on his own. "Jim didn't have the resources to do anything like that," he said. "If the director approved, OS [the Office of Security] would do it. Jim would be the beneficiary. He would get the take. But Jim had no technical support of his own."

Nevertheless, stories such as Braden's—and they are legion— helped to make Angleton a sinister and mysterious figure inside the CIA, and in the tight social circles in Washington in which he moved.

His nicknames reflected this. In the CIA, his agency pseudonym— used in cable traffic—was Hugh Ashmead. But his colleagues referred to him variously as "the Gray Ghost," "the Black Knight," "the Orchid Man," "the Fisherman," "Jesus," "Slim Jim," or, less flatteringly, "Skinny Jim" or "Scarecrow."[4] In the dull bureaucracy of Washington, and even in the secret intelligence bureaucracy, few officials had such colorful sobriquets.

But it was more than that. James Angleton's hobbies, his background, his style, his whole life, fit the popular conception of what a CIA chief of counterintelligence *ought* to be like. The image and the man were made for each other; James Angleton could have stepped right out of Hollywood's Central Casting.

There was, for example, his legendary skill as a fly-fisherman, his well-documented prowess as a grower of, and expert on, orchids, his avocation as a collector of semiprecious gems. To his many admirers,

---

[4]Despite a widely believed myth to the contrary, one name that Angleton was *not* known by was "Mother." The first use of that term occurred in a two-part series in the *National Review* in 1973 written by Miles Copeland, a former CIA officer, that described in fanciful terms a spooky agency character named "Mother," who resembled Angleton. Miles Copeland, "The Unmentionable Uses of a CIA," *National Review,* September 14, 1973, and "There's a CIA in Your Future," October 26, 1973. In his book *Without Cloak and Dagger* (New York: Simon & Schuster, 1974), Copeland elaborated on his conceit, describing "Mother" flanked by two greyhounds in an office at CIA styled like a hunting lodge with a twenty-foot-high beamed ceiling. Then author Aaron Latham wrote a novel about Angleton entitled *Orchids for Mother* (Boston: Little, Brown, 1977). Copeland confirmed that his use of the name "Mother" was entirely fictional: "You are right about my use of 'Mother' as a nickname for Jim Angleton. This name, along with a lot of other things I've said in books and articles, was hokum to ease problems I was having in getting past the mental defectives who used to be in charge of clearing manuscripts of loyal alumnae [*sic*]." Letter, Miles Copeland to author, October 10, 1990. Copeland, seventy-seven, died January 14, 1991, in Oxfordshire, England.

these were not accidental interests; rather they were extensions of his brilliance as a counterintelligence officer. The same patience that was required to land a brook trout in a mountain stream was necessary to reel in a Soviet spy, a false defector, or a double agent of the KGB. It took years, as well as great patience, to grow an orchid, and this too was pure Angleton. One cannot see him in his black homburg bowling with the boys for relaxation. In the same way, the gemstones that he found in the caves and crannies of the Southwest, polished to perfection, and fashioned into cuff links or other gifts for his friends, these, too, were akin to the nuggets of counterintelligence information that he could pan from the river of cables, reports, and debriefings that crossed his desk. The key fact that when placed in context would shine as brightly as any topaz. Or so his admirers saw it.

And the fisherman, like the spycatcher, must understand lures. Angleton studied them carefully. One of his fishing partners was Sam Papich, a tall, tough Serb from Butte, Montana, who had worked in the copper mines like his father before him and who was the FBI liaison man with the CIA for nineteen years. The two men were close, J. Edgar Hoover's ambassador to the CIA and the chief of the CI Staff.

"Jim had the hands of a surgeon, and he made beautiful trout flies," Papich recalled. "Sometimes we'd go fishing together. Jim would walk up and down for quarter of a mile studying the water, vegetation, the insects. Then he'd decide what to do. He could give you a lecture on the life of the mayfly from the larval stage up until time it's a fly. I'm a trout fisherman, too, but he was a master at it. He usually released the fish he caught. To him, it was the challenge."

If Angleton fished for trout with Hoover's man, at the same time quietly strengthening his lines into the bureau, the flowers, too, were intertwined with his life as a counterspy. Merritt Huntington, the owner of Kensington Orchids, in suburban Maryland, knew Angleton for years and admired him both as a spy and as a horticulturist. "Angleton was a typical spook, America's number one spook, a real patriot," he said. "He used orchids as a cover. He had a brilliant, photographic memory. His knowledge of orchids was very extensive."

He used orchids as a cover? "Yes," Huntington said, "he would travel as an orchid-grower. He knew every orchid-grower in Europe. We always knew when big shots from Israel were coming, because Jim would need a bunch of orchids. Cut flowers for the Israelis."

"He was a breeder. He bred and named a couple of orchids. He named one for his wife. A cattleya called 'Cicely Angleton.'[5]

"Jim used to sit for hours and talk about orchids. He never talked about his work. I knew who he was, but he never talked politics. He could disappear for six months, but when he was around he would call. He was never without his trench coat."

Angleton was once quoted as saying that of all the orchids, "the lady slipper is my favorite because it's the hardest to grow."[6]

Sam Papich talked about the flowers, too, and the gemstones. "Jim would often send an orchid to a lady he met; he'd meet a lady, and next day she'd get an orchid, not from the flower shop, but from Jim's nursery. His clothes were usually rumpled. But all the women liked him. He made them all feel very important and beautiful. He wasn't a BS artist but he had a knack of bringing up subjects that were interesting and made people feel at home.

"He went to Tucson and collected stones and made beautiful jewelry. He made rings, bracelets, necklaces." Papich paused. "He had tremendous intellectual curiosity. He worked hard. He did most of his work at night."

It was somehow fitting that a mole hunter should be a nocturnal creature, a man who preferred to work in the dark. And Angleton's physical appearance was part of his mystique—tall, thin to the point of looking emaciated, dressed in black, conservative clothes.

"He always wore three-piece suits," recalled former FBI counterintelligence man Don Moore. "He didn't even take off his coat and tie to play poker."

A CIA officer who knew Angleton well described him this way: "He

---

[5]"Wait a minute," Huntington offered, "and I'll look it up for you in the registry of the Royal Horticultural Society. That's the international registry for plants. It's in London. The RHS volumes are published every five years." He rummaged around for a moment, got out the latest volume, and opened it. "Let's see, yes, 'Cicely Angleton' is the name of a cattleya registered with the Royal Horticultural Society in London. It was registered in 1973. Yep, here he is: 'James Angleton, 4814 33d Road, North Arlington, Virginia.'" *Cattleya,* a genus of orchids native to tropical America, is named for William Cattley of Barnet, England, the nineteenth-century patron of botany. With their large, bright flowers, cattleyas are the most popular of orchids. There are about sixty species.

[6]Aaron Latham, "Poet, Florist, Angler, Spy," *Washington Post,* May 20, 1987, p. C1. Latham had interviewed Angleton shortly after he was dismissed as CI chief in December 1974.

was about six feet, with a hawk nose, dark shadows under his eyes, rather pale skin. Like someone who hadn't been in the sunlight very much. He was slightly stooped over. He would have been tall if he stood straight. Fairly large ears, graying hair, parted in the middle and combed straight back." Angleton wore thick horn-rimmed glasses, but his most interesting feature by far was his extraordinarily wide mouth, set in an angular jaw. Oddly, it almost made him resemble one of the fish he might have pursued, perhaps a bass, or a pike. It was a mouth that often wore a small, mysterious smile, the smile of a man who had a secret he would not share.

"He had a large office in Langley," Angleton's colleague recalled, "a desk covered with objets d'art, dark furniture. A little spooky? Not necessarily, but Jim did nothing to dispel that. Jim always looked buried behind a pile of documents all covered with restricted-access labels. He was soft-spoken but his voice carried conviction. He was definite about everything he said. And what he said was the voice of God."

Despite a serious bout with tuberculosis, the counterintelligence chief chain-smoked cigarettes. "He must have smoked three or four packs a day," a colleague remembered. "I've been in a car with him and he could hardly breathe. He'd turn on the air conditioner to try to get his breath."

And he drank. Espionage is a stressful profession, and a lot of CIA officers have problems with alcohol. "Jim would go to lunch about twelve-thirty, and have plenty to drink," one former colleague remembered. "He came back and was very voluble. He never did any work after lunch."

Angleton was a poet, or at least he had been deeply involved in poetry at Yale, an admirer of T. S. Eliot and Ezra Pound, and this aesthetic side, combined with the enormous secret power he wielded, made him a unique figure in the CIA and added to the ominous shadow he cast. For it was precisely this blend of poet and spy, of art and espionage—a craft with a suggestion of violence always present just below the surface—that added to the hint of menace in Angleton's persona. As a literary intellectual, he must have appreciated the delicious dramatic irony that he embodied.[7]

[7]In a British television interview, Angleton once referred to "a wilderness of mirrors," a phrase taken from T. S. Eliot's poem "Gerontion" and applied, as an apt descrip-

In a city in which information is power, secret information is the most valuable of all. And it was the belief within the CIA that Angleton possessed more secrets than anyone else, and grasped their meaning better than anyone else, that formed the basis of his power. Angleton understood this very well, and he cultivated an aura of omniscience.

"Angleton would walk around with his briefcase," George Kisevalter recalled. "He'd say, 'I have incredible material here from the bureau.' 'What is it?' 'I can't discuss it here.' If you can't discuss it in the DDO, where can you discuss it? It was ridiculous." But Kisevalter knew that Angleton's power rested on secrecy. "The key was knowing things and keeping the information to himself."

On one occasion, the CI chief buttonholed Kisevalter in an elevator at CIA.

"You've got to see this film," Angleton said. "It bears out my thinking."

"What film?" Kisevalter asked.

"The Manchurian Candidate."[8]

The secrets that Angleton did not share not only enhanced his power within a secret agency, they gave him the advantage in bureaucratic infighting. Secrecy served as an unassailable fallback position in any argument.

A CIA case officer who had worked closely with Angleton understood this. "When I was sent to London, Angleton was one of those who approved," he said. "You weren't going to go unless Jim also anointed you. But as time went on I just began to think that his conclusions were wrong. I'd listen to all his convoluted theories and say, 'But Jim, that is not in accord with the facts.' Jim would say, 'There are certain things I can't tell you.' I always felt it was because he couldn't justify his case."

Although wary of Angleton, Tom Braden understood the wellsprings of his power. "Angleton had the charm of Sherlock Holmes,"

---

tion of counterintelligence itself, by author (and later CBS correspondent) David C. Martin, who used it as the title of his book about Angleton's search for KGB spies, *Wilderness of Mirrors* (New York: Harper & Row, 1980).

[8]The plot of *The Manchurian Candidate,* a 1962 film based on a novel of the same title by Richard Condon, supposes that the North Koreans have brainwashed an American prisoner of war and programmed him to return to the United States and assassinate a presidential nominee.

he said. "The detective. Someone who knew something you didn't."

If Angleton cloaked himself in an air of mystery and intrigue, if he was the most sharp-witted merchant in the bazaar of CIA secrets, there was one truth he could not escape for all of his power. His job was unenviable.

It was James Angleton's *job* to suspect everyone—and he did. That is the road to insanity, and there are those former colleagues who thought that he was indeed mad at the end. But these are clinical conclusions that should not be lightly or casually rendered, even by those who knew and worked with him. It is much easier to conclude that somewhere along the line, a lifetime of suspicion had corroded his judgment.

But it should also be said that suspicion is a necessary evil, or at least a necessary function, in an intelligence agency. The CIA and its operations are obvious targets for penetration by opposition intelligence services. Thus, there must be, within the CIA, a mechanism for defending against Soviet penetration of CIA operations and of the agency itself. That effort is called counterintelligence.

Practitioners of CI argue endlessly, in Talmudic fashion, over the precise and best definition of their art. From their debates, however, some general agreement has emerged. Perhaps the most succinct definition has been offered by Raymond G. Rocca. A tall, thin, scholarly man with gray hair and a goatee, he served as Angleton's deputy both in the OSS in Italy and in the CIA. "Counterintelligence," he said, "deals with the activities of other intelligence services in our own country or against our country abroad. In other words, CI is precisely what it says: counter intelligence. The term defines itself."

Scotty Miler, who, like Rocca, served as Angleton's deputy, agreed. "The goal of CI is to protect your institutions and operations from penetration, including deception," he said.[9]

Since Miler was Angleton's deputy chief of the Special Investiga-

[9]In its final report in 1976, the Senate Select Committee on Intelligence, headed by Senator Frank Church, D., Idaho, defined counterintelligence as "an intelligence activity dedicated to undermining the effectiveness of hostile intelligence services." It defined counterespionage as an aspect of counterintelligence that attempts "to detect and neutralize foreign espionage." "Foreign and Military Intelligence," Book 1, *Final Report of the Select Committee to Study Governmental Operations with Respect to Intelligence Activities,* United States Senate, 94th Congress, 2d Session, April 26, 1976, pp. 163, 620.

tions Group (SIG), it was his job, of course, to ferret out the penetration in the CIA, whose existence the CI Staff did not doubt once Golitsin had defected and warned of "Sasha." And a major task of counterintelligence, under any definition, was first and foremost to detect and apprehend any mole or moles inside the agency.

The CI Staff was responsible not only for identifying Soviet agents planted inside headquarters in Langley, but for protecting CIA operations in the field from KGB penetration. If a case officer in the field proposed to recruit an agent, the geographic division responsible for the country involved would check the CIA's files for any information about the person. The CI Staff would request such "traces" from the files of other U.S. intelligence agencies; in rare cases it might discreetly request information from other, friendly intelligence services. The name traces might result in information that would discourage a planned recruitment.

There is a shibboleth in the intelligence world that case officers fall in love with their agents. The case officers want to believe in the people they have recruited and the information the agents provide. The CI Staff are professional skeptics. They are paid to doubt.

Robert Crowley, a former clandestine operator for the CIA, an iconoclast, and a man of great wisdom with a gift for metaphor, compared the role of the Counterintelligence Staff to that of a credit manager in a a large company. "The salesmen, who are the case officers, want to advance their careers by racking up big sales. They're aggressive, work on commission, and are eager for new business. The credit manager takes a hard look at the customer, checks his balance sheet and his credit reference, and says: 'Don't ship.' Naturally, the salesmen don't like it."

For this reason, there was an inbuilt tension between the CI Staff and the operating divisions of the Directorate of Operations, or Clandestine Services. The divisions divided the world into geographic areas. Although the names of the divisions have changed over time, the CIA's clandestine directorate has traditionally had a Soviet division and other geographic divisions for Europe, the Middle East, Africa, Asia, and Latin America.

In theory, a division chief outranked a staff chief, but the division chiefs were reluctant to test their power against Angleton's, because they knew his was greater.[10] Angleton made up for whatever rank he lacked on the organization chart by his close bond with the CIA directors under whom he worked, in particular Dulles and Richard Helms. Like the two directors, Angleton had served in the OSS, and those roots ran deep in the agency.[11] The CI chief was a charter member of the Ivy League "Old Boys" who ran the CIA like a private club well into the 1970s. By wartime service, social background, schooling, and temperament, the Ivy Leaguers were drawn together and, with some exceptions, were the key decision-makers in the agency. They were comfortable with each other.

Beyond the natural friction between the geographic divisions—the operators—and the CI Staff chief, a larger issue lurked just below the service: the mole hunt. As the search for traitors intensified in the early 1960s, the atmosphere of mistrust, particularly within the Soviet division, which bore the brunt of the investigations, became pervasive. No one knew where suspicion would strike next.

And this, of course, raised a puzzling, troublesome issue inside the CIA. Any organization rests on trust, perhaps the more so in a secret agency engaged, at times, in dangerous work. Yet the counterintelligence function is a necessary check against penetration by an opposition service. How can the two needs be reconciled? What would happen over time to an agency that simultaneously required institutional trust and institutional suspicion?

It is unlikely that these questions ever surfaced within the CIA during the era of the mole hunt. The Clandestine Services and the CI Staff were run by hard-eyed men (and very few women) who were busy dealing with day-to-day practical problems. The search for penetrations coincided with the height of the Cold War, a time of maximum activity by the CIA. And if anyone did take the time to ponder these

[10]The divisions and the CI Staff were subordinate to the Directorate of Plans (which became the Directorate of Operations in 1973). The CI Staff, therefore, was a staff of the DDP, the deputy director for plans (the DDO since 1973), and not of the Director of Central Intelligence (DCI), which is the formal title of the director of the CIA.

[11]So close were Dulles and Angleton that after Dulles died in 1969, his sister, Eleanor Lansing Dulles, asked Angleton to give away his pipes to Dulles's best friends in the secret world. Don Moore, the Soviet counterintelligence chief for the FBI, who had worked for many years with both the CIA director and Angleton, got two of Dulles's favorite briars. "I chose them because they came in a leather case that had the initials 'A.W.D.' on the side," Moore said.

philosophical questions, he would not have dared to raise them with the Scarecrow.

James Jesus Angleton was born in Boise, Idaho, on December 9, 1917, eight months after the United States entered World War I. His father, James Hugh Angleton, had served in the Army in Mexico under General John J. "Black Jack" Pershing, chasing Pancho Villa, and had married a seventeen-year-old Mexican woman, Carmen Moreno. (Angleton was baptized a Catholic and named Jesus after his maternal grandfather.) James had a younger brother and two younger sisters. The family lived in Boise, and later in Dayton, Ohio, where the senior Angleton was an executive of the National Cash Register Company. In 1933, when James Angleton was a teenager, his father took the family to Italy, where he had bought the NCR franchise, and in time he became president of the American Chamber of Commerce in Rome.[12] The Angletons lived well, much of the time in a palazzo in Milan.

James Angleton spent his summers in Italy and attended Malvern College, a British preparatory school. In 1937, he entered Yale, where he served on the editorial board of the Yale literary magazine, and with E. Reed Whittemore, Jr., who was to become a well-known poet, he launched *Furioso,* a poetry journal that had a considerable impact. While a student at Yale, Angleton also came to know, and admire, Ezra Pound.[13] Angleton was graduated from Yale in 1941, and in 1943, while serving in the infantry, he was recruited by the OSS. Sent to London, he worked in counterintelligence for the first time in the X-2 section, where his boss was his former Yale professor Norman

[12]For biographical details on Angleton, see Tom Mangold, *Cold Warrior: James Jesus Angleton: The CIA's Master Spy Hunter* (New York: Simon & Schuster, 1991), the first comprehensive biography of the counterintelligence chief; Robin W. Winks, "The Theorist," an illuminating chapter on Angleton and his intelligence career, in Winks, *Cloak and Gown: Scholars in the Secret War, 1939–1961* (New York: Morrow, 1987), pp. 322–438; and Seymour M. Hersh, "Angleton: The Cult of Counterintelligence," *New York Times Magazine,* June 25, 1978.

[13]Pound, the controversial poet and Fascist sympathizer, was, like Angleton, a native of Idaho. He moved to Italy in 1924, and during World War II he broadcast propaganda, directed at Allied troops, for the Mussolini government. Indicted for treason and brought back to the United States for trial, he was judged mentally incompetent and confined to St. Elizabeths Hospital in Washington for twelve years. He returned to Italy after his release and died there in 1972 at the age of eighty-seven.

Holmes Pearson. That same year, Angleton married Cicely d'Autremont of Tucson, Arizona, the daughter of a wealthy Minnesota mining family; Angleton had met her while she was a student at Vassar.

Angleton rose rapidly in the OSS, and after the Allied landing, he was sent to Rome, where, by the end of the war, he had become chief of counterintelligence in Italy. One of his jobs was to help the Italians rebuild their own intelligence services. The extensive contacts he made in Italy during the war were to serve him well when he joined the CIA in 1947.

The following year, he was involved in the CIA's massive effort to influence the 1948 Italian elections. The agency poured millions into the operation to defeat the Communists and support the Christian Democrats, who won.

But Angleton's primary interest, his real love, was counterintelligence, and in 1954 he was authorized by Dulles to set up and head the CI Staff. Part of the Angleton mystique was that he was seldom seen, even by members of his own staff. So reclusive a figure was Angleton that during his reign as CI chief, a standard joke arose about him in the agency. In a crowded elevator at headquarters, if the door opened and closed and no one could be seen getting on or off, the other riders would look at each other, nod knowingly, and say: "Angleton."

And, in truth, the CI chief preferred the seclusion of his office, Room 43 in the C corridor on the second floor of the headquarters building. From that power base, Angleton was to become the dominant figure in CIA counterintelligence for twenty years.

But under Dulles, he added another string to his bow. In an unusual arrangement, he was placed in charge of the "Israeli account," so that operations and intelligence involving the Mossad, or the other Israeli spy agencies, were channeled solely through Angleton.

If Angleton did not trust the pro-Arab case officers in the CIA's Near East division, there is evidence that he also distrusted Jews as biased in favor of Israel. George Kisevalter tells of a revealing incident that took place in 1970, when he was teaching a senior intelligence course at "Blue U," the CIA's school for spies in Arlington, Virginia.[14] In the course, Kisevalter was explaining the workings of foreign intel-

---

[14]"Blue U" was the informal name given to an eight-story two-tone-blue office building, designed with an unusual concave front, at 1000 North Glebe Road in Arlington, a northern Virginia suburb of Washington. Courses were given there in locks and

ligence services to a class of CIA, military, and foreign service officers who were preparing to go overseas. He wanted an expert on Israeli intelligence, so he asked for John Hadden, who had recently completed a six-year tour as CIA station chief in Israel. "I sent a request in writing to Hadden," Kisevalter said. " 'Office of Training requests you deliver lecture on Mossad.' Angleton initialed it. Hadden delivered a gorgeous lecture on the Mossad. At the next course for senior officers I requested Hadden again. Angleton said 'No, come see me.' So I did. Angleton said, 'I won't allow this. We are not going to do it in-house.' "

"I protested. I asked, 'Why not?' Angleton replied: 'How do you know how many Jews are in there?' 'What difference does it make?' I asked. 'Are you going to throw them out of the agency?' I went to Jocko Richardson, who was chief of training. Richardson said, 'What the hell's the matter with him?' But there was no lecture on the Mossad."

For Angleton, counterintelligence remained the major concern, and even the Israeli account was a means to that end. John Denley Walker, who succeeded Hadden as station chief in Israel, said, "Angleton was indeed in charge of Israeli affairs, but his major interest was CI. He wanted Israeli intelligence to spot possible Soviet plants among Jewish émigrés from the Soviet Union."

Once Golitsin arrived on the scene, talking of a mole, and with specific, albeit fragmentary, clues to his identity, the search for penetrations became Angleton's overriding goal. In Golitsin, Angleton had found a soulmate. Here at last was a man, fresh from the KGB, who played a precise counterpoint to Angleton's fugue.

To Angleton and his large CI Staff, it made perfect sense to assume that the KGB had succeeded in planting a mole or moles inside the CIA. Logically, in the presumption of moles in the agency there was an analogy to the argument that life must occur elsewhere in the universe. Those who posit the existence of extraterrestrial beings point to the statistical improbability that in the boundless expanse of space, life should exist only on the planet Earth. In much the same fashion, the CI Staff argued that the intelligence services of other nations—

---

picks, flaps and seals (how to open letters clandestinely), and photography, among others.

notably the British—had been penetrated by the Soviets. Why should the CIA be exempt? Just as the federal government has its massive radio telescope in Green Bank, West Virginia, listening for radio signals from other worlds that may or may not exist, so the CIA's Counterintelligence Staff watched and waited and listened for the faint sound of burrowing moles. It was only sensible to assume they were there.

Angleton also had personal reasons to press the search for penetrations with such ferocity. He had been taken in by the supreme mole of the century, Kim Philby, and he was not about to make the same mistake twice.

Harold Adrian Russell "Kim" Philby had joined MI6, the British Secret Intelligence Service, in 1940, and by the end of the war he had risen to chief of the Soviet section of MI6, which meant that Moscow knew everything of importance that the British secret service was doing or planning to do against the Soviet Union. In 1949, Philby was assigned to Washington as the MI6 liaison with the CIA. Angleton dined regularly with Philby at Harvey's, a downtown restaurant in the capital also much favored by J. Edgar Hoover. The CIA's ace counterintelligence chief never once suspected that the man sitting across the table and exchanging secrets with him was in fact a dedicated Soviet agent from the start.

In May 1951, Philby's recent houseguest in Washington, Guy Burgess, fled to Moscow with Donald Maclean, a fellow official of the British foreign office, and Philby was suspected as "the third man" who had tipped off the two Soviet spies. But the British could not prove their case against Philby, and were reluctant to press charges against a member of Britain's Old Boy establishment. It was not until late January 1963 that Philby, realizing the net was closing in at last, bolted from Beirut to the safety of Moscow.[15]

To Angleton, the Philby debacle was a humiliating experience, and it had an enormous, wrenching impact upon him. Although much has been made of the effect of Philby's treachery on Angleton, there were

[15]Like George Blake, Philby took a Russian wife, Rufa, was given the rank of general in the KGB, and lived comfortably in an apartment in Moscow, where he was interviewed by author Phillip Knightley four months before Philby's death in May 1988. See Phillip Knightley, *The Master Spy: The Story of Kim Philby* (New York: Alfred A. Knopf, 1989).

at least two cases in the CIA itself, never publicly disclosed by the agency, that convinced the CI chief that he had reason to be concerned about turncoats.

One was the mysterious affair of Bela Herczeg, who had been born in Hungary and served in the OSS and then in the CIA as a case officer in Vienna and Munich. Herczeg vanished in 1957, and Angleton was certain that he had defected to the Mossad. The CIA case officer's disappearance was doubly embarrassing for Angleton, since the counterintelligence chief handled Israeli affairs for the CIA.

Herczeg, who was Jewish, had gotten out of Hungary before World War II and come to the United States. He was down South training as an Army paratrooper in 1943 when Nicholas R. Doman, an OSS officer in charge of operations against Hungary, spotted his name on a list. Doman, who had met Herczeg in Hungary before the war, was looking for agents; he cut orders to have him brought to Washington and recruited him into the OSS. He sent Herczeg to Bari, Italy.

"He was being trained as part of a team of agents to be dropped into Slovakia," Doman said, "but he got sick, and it saved his life. He never made the jump. All but two or three of the team were mopped up by the SS and executed."

After the war, Herczeg was assigned to a U.S. intelligence team that was tracking down Nazis. He interrogated Ferenc Szálasi, the notorious Fascist Prime Minister of Hungary, who was executed. Herczeg later joined the CIA and worked for the agency from 1952 to 1957 in Austria and Germany. But friction soon developed between him and his superiors.

George Kisevalter remembered Herczeg. "I had met him in Vienna when he was stationed there, working against the Hungarians. We had dinner once in a restaurant around the corner from the CIA station on the Mariahilfer Strasse. He was an ex-Hungarian, socially prominent, a fine horseman. A big, burly individual. He insisted I try the *fogas,* a wonderful fish from Lake Balaton, he said. He was on leave in West Germany around 1957 and defected to the Israeli service.

"In 1958, Joe Bulik, a case officer, comes to see me in Berlin on official business from headquarters. He says, 'Angleton wants me to ask you whatever you know about Herczeg. He's gone.' Angleton knew he'd gone over to the Israelis. Angleton wanted to know did I know how he went, and where. I knew nothing. There was nothing much I could tell Bulik. Angleton was upset, of course. It's a friendly service, but people don't just switch intelligence services."

Angleton's deputy, Scotty Miler, also said that Herczeg had defected to the Israeli intelligence service. "The Mossad admitted this to the agency," Miler said. "It was, of course, of especial concern to Angleton, since he handled Israeli affairs. And also there were worries about Soviet penetration of the Mossad. Angleton briefed me about the case in general terms, just so I'd be aware of it."

I tracked down Bela Herczeg in Budapest in 1990. He was seventy-eight and in poor health, but he confirmed that he had vanished from the Vienna station more than forty years before. He denied he had gone to work for the Mossad, however. "I disappeared," he said. "I never got in touch with the agency." He declined to say why he had vanished, although he made a veiled reference to "policy differences" with his CIA superiors. "I did not work for the Israelis," he said.

While Angleton was scouring the world looking for him, Herczeg had returned quietly to the United States, he said, where he worked as a money trader in New York, then as a Toyota salesman for several years in Coral Gables, Florida. He moved back to Hungary around 1982.

Nicholas Doman, who remained in touch with his old OSS colleague, said Herczeg had in fact gone to Israel, and then to Australia "after he quit the agency." But he said Herczeg had never spoken of working for the Mossad. "He was generally frank with me because of our OSS connections. He never told me that." He confirmed, however, that Herczeg "had a falling-out with the CIA and he had always bitterly complained about the agency."

If Angleton was upset by the Herczeg affair, which the agency managed to keep secret, he had even more cause for alarm in the case of Edward Ellis Smith, the first CIA man ever stationed in Moscow. Smith, who was born into a solid Baptist family in Parkersburg, West Virginia, and grew up there, was graduated from the University of West Virginia in 1943, during World War II. He joined the Army, served in Europe during the war, and earned three Bronze Stars for valor. After the war, he worked in Washington in G-2, the Army intelligence branch, and learned Russian at the Naval Intelligence School. In 1948 he went to Moscow for two years as an assistant military attaché. By September 1950, he was back in Washington, assigned now to the CIA.

In 1953, the CIA's Soviet division arranged for the first time to send a man to Moscow. With his knowledge of the Russian language, intelligence training, and previous posting in the Soviet capital, Smith, then thirty-two, was an obvious choice. He left the Army, and the agency dispatched him to Moscow under diplomatic cover, as an attaché in the Foreign Service.

Smith had a specific assignment. A year earlier, Pyotr Popov, the GRU lieutenant colonel, had contacted the agency in Vienna. He was being run for the Soviet division by George Kisevalter. Popov, code-named GRALLSPICE, was the CIA's first asset inside Soviet intelligence. The acquisition of an agent-in-place within the GRU, the Soviet military intelligence service, was a major event at Langley. To provide support for the Popov operation, a special unit was created inside the Soviet division, designated SR-9.[16] It was Edward Ellis Smith's task to select dead drops in Moscow to allow the CIA to communicate with Popov, in the event that he was sent back to GRU headquarters from Vienna.[17]

"Smith was looking for drop sites and setting up for Popov," Kisevalter confirmed. "His selection of dead drops was terrible. Popov did not like the sites Smith chose. 'They stink,' he complained. Smith, thank God, didn't know it was Popov he was setting up for."

On a trip back to Moscow, Popov had checked out the dead drops selected by Smith. When he returned to Vienna and met with the CIA at a safe house, he was upset. "What are you trying to do, kill me?" he asked. Popov complained that the drops were inaccessible; it would have been suicide to use them.[18]

[16]At the time, the division was called the Soviet Russia division (SR), hence SR-9. Later the name was changed to the Soviet Bloc division (SB). There were other changes and consolidations. In recent years, the division has been known as the Soviet/East European division (SE).
[17]Dead drops are hiding places where an agent can leave rolls of film or documents to be retrieved at a later time by a case officer. The drop sites must be easily accessible but not so obvious that a janitor or children playing in a park would stumble upon them by accident. Typically, the CIA used spaces behind radiators in building lobbies, or hollow bricks, or a nook behind a loose stone in a wall.
[18]Popov's complaints about the dead drops are described in an autobiography by Peer de Silva, the CIA officer who ran the support operation for the GRU agent. But de

Smith was fired by the CIA, but the case, although hushed up, involved a good deal more than the discontent over the drop sites. According to Kisevalter and other former CIA officials, Smith was sexually compromised by his maid, who was a "swallow," a female agent of the KGB.

"The KGB called him 'Ryzhiy,' the redhead," Kisevalter said. "That was their crypt. He had light red hair, reddish. Not flaming red. The redhead's girl was Valya, the maid. He was bragging about his maid making good martinis, and we didn't like it one bit. They [the KGB] forced one meeting with Smith. We don't know what he gave them at the first meeting. They were setting up for a second meeting. They attempted to make other meetings."

But Smith, realizing he was in deep trouble, confessed to his superiors that he had fallen into a KGB "honey trap." According to Pete Bagley, who was later in charge of counterintelligence for the Soviet division, "Smith reported the approach by the KGB in 1956 and was brought back and they questioned him and were not happy with his answers and they fired him."

No word of the disaster in Moscow leaked out. The CIA was able to keep the lid on the fact that the first officer it ever sent to Moscow had been ensnared by the KGB. The agency, however, had not heard the last of the Smith case, as will be seen.

Edward Ellis Smith moved to San Francisco and built a distinguished career as a bank executive, author, and Soviet expert, his indiscretion in Moscow a secret that remained buried in the past. His books included a study of the Okhrana, the czarist secret police, and a biography of Stalin's early years.[19] Ironically, Smith concluded that Stalin had been a czarist police agent inside the Russian revolutionary movement.

Smith was elected to the board of governors of the exclusive Commonwealth Club in 1972. Ten years later, a few minutes after midnight on Saturday, February 13, 1982, Smith was killed in Redwood City by

---

Silva did not identify Smith as the man who chose the drop sites. Peer de Silva, *Sub Rosa: The CIA and the Uses of Intelligence* (New York: Times Books, 1978), p. 69.
[19]See Edward Ellis Smith, *"The Okhrana": The Russian Department of Police* (Palo Alto: Hoover Institution, 1967), and *The Young Stalin: The Early Years of an Elusive Revolutionary* (New York: Farrar, Straus & Giroux, 1967).

a hit-and-run driver in a white Corvette that witnesses said roared through a red light at high speed. Police said Smith carried a briefcase containing notes for a book with references to the CIA and the KGB, but a police spokesman said there was no reason to think that the death was anything but accidental. "There's nothing clandestine involved," he said. The next day, the driver, Donald Peck, thirty, who had served two prison terms for burglary, turned himself in. A witness said Peck was drunk, but no blood-alcohol tests were available, since he had waited a day to surrender. He later pleaded no contest to hit-and-run driving in return for dismissal of vehicular-manslaughter and drunken-driving charges. On November 3, Peck was fined $750 and sentenced to one year in jail.

The CIA's Counterintelligence Staff had been dismayed by the KGB's entrapment of Edward Ellis Smith. "The problem was more serious than we ever resolved," said Scotty Miler. "He admitted he had been compromised. But he did not make full admission of what he might have given the Soviets."

To James Angleton, the Smith case only proved the point. The agency had already been penetrated, its first man in Moscow compromised. The counterintelligence chief did not need to be convinced there were moles. The problem was to find them.

Chapter 5

The Moscow Station

Paul Garbler knew there would be a lot of drinking at his bon voyage party in 1961. For one thing, it was an exciting moment in the history of the CIA: he had just been chosen as the first chief of the Moscow station.

For another, the host of the party was the legendary William King Harvey, whose Falstaffian figure attested to his fondness for booze. Behind his ample back, Harvey was known as "the Pear," for his shape. A crew-cut former FBI agent, Harvey was a colorful, tough character who always packed a gun, drank three martinis for lunch, and had a disconcerting habit of falling asleep at meetings.[1] It was Harvey, over drinks one night in Berlin seven years earlier, who had persuaded Garbler, a Navy pilot, to resign his commission and join the CIA. "And when you were drinking with Harvey, you were drinking a lot," Garbler recalled.

In less than a decade, Garbler had risen from a case officer in Berlin, where he had served under Harvey, to the man selected to head the most important field station in the CIA. Garbler had every reason to be proud of his achievement.

The other guests at Harvey's party were Richard M. Helms, then

---

[1]Within the agency, Harvey became notorious for slumbering through staff meetings. At one such meeting at the CIA station in Frankfurt, Harvey started nodding off as usual, and gradually his jacket opened, exposing his gun in its holster. Someone wrote a sign and placed it on his potbelly: "Fattest gun in the West."

the assistant deputy director for plans; Thomas H. Karamessines, a senior official of the DDP; Eric Timm, chief of the Western European division; and James Angleton. It was this small group of senior agency officials who had made the decision late in 1960 to establish the CIA's first station in the Soviet capital.

Garbler's principal mission, indeed the major reason for the decision to open the Moscow station, was to provide a means of clandestine communication with the agency's premier spy in the Soviet Union, Colonel Oleg Penkovsky of the GRU. "What we had up to then was singletons going into Moscow under various kinds of cover," Garbler explained. There was no station, he said, and therefore no chief of station. "I was the first legitimate COS in Moscow."

So there was a great deal to celebrate. "Everybody drank a lot of booze. It got pretty wild. Helms left early. Angleton backed me into a corner. He said, 'I've been working with FBI. We've got a couple of cases where the source has returned to the Soviet Union and we want to maintain contact. I'll let you know details tomorrow and you tell me if you can handle it.' The next day Angleton told me where the dead drop was." Garbler agreed to run Angleton's agent in Moscow.

Garbler, a tall, rugged, and handsome man, had the face of a Western cowpuncher but had been born in Newark, New Jersey, and grew up in south Florida, where his father was a successful builder. Garbler joined the Navy a few months before Pearl Harbor, and while training as an aviation cadet in Jacksonville he met Florence Fitzsimmons, an attractive Army nurse from Bayside, Queens. They were married in the midst of the war. Florence served in the Italian campaign, landing at Salerno with the Fifth Army and working her way up through Italy. Paul was a dive-bomber pilot flying from carriers in the Pacific, so they did not see each other for two and a half years, until the war ended. Garbler flew in the first and second battles of the Philippine Sea and at Chichi island, and won three Distinguished Flying Crosses and eight Air Medals.

After the war, the Navy sent Garbler to Washington to learn Russian and receive training in intelligence. He shipped out to Seoul, South Korea, in 1948, and served as President Syngman Rhee's personal pilot. He was in Korea in June 1950 when the North Koreans invaded.

The Navy sent Garbler back to Washington, and a year later he was assigned to the CIA and trained as a spy. In 1952, although still in the

Navy, he began a three-year tour in Berlin base for the CIA. Using the alias Philip Gardner, Garbler took over as the case officer handling Franz Koischwitz, a principal agent whose target was the Soviet military establishment at Karlshorst, in East Berlin. It was while in Berlin that Garbler accepted Harvey's invitation to leave the military and join the CIA.

He returned to headquarters in 1955 and was sent to Stockholm the following year as deputy chief of station. By 1959, he was back in Washington, working in the Soviet division, an assignment that helped to put him on the short list for chief of the Moscow station.

On November 30, 1961, Garbler reported in to the American embassy in the Soviet capital, under cover as the assistant naval attaché. In Moscow, Garbler's small CIA station operated under the handicap of massive KGB surveillance of embassy employees. The station was so clandestine that even the distinguished American ambassador, Llewellyn E. Thompson, a kindly but shrewd career diplomat, was not sure which members of his staff might be spooks. Because of KGB bugs, sensitive conversations inside the embassy had to take place in "the bubble," a secure room-within-a-room.

"Tommy's first question in the bubble after I arrived," Garbler recalled, "was, who was here for the CIA other than me?" There were not many names that Garbler could provide; the station was so small that Garbler had only a few officers on his staff.[2]

Within a few months, he was joined by his wife, Florence, who taught at the Anglo-American school and helped him in his espionage work. "She had no operational training or tasks. But she accompanied me on some visits to help screen me. If I had to empty a drop in Gorky Park, I'd have no reason to be there. But if Florence was with me, we'd be strolling around together, I'd point things out to her, and eventually we'd sit on a bench. That would be the dead drop. Or marking a signal site with chalk at a theater, she would screen me from the view of casual passersby. She was a big help to me."

[2]In most stations, the CIA is housed in one area of the embassy. For security reasons, the handful of CIA officers in Moscow were scattered around the building. Garbler had to arrange meetings with them through an elaborate system of signals. "Making contact in the embassy with station officers was a lot like setting up a clandestine meeting with an agent in, say, Paris. I used different signals and signal sites with each officer. In Moscow it sometimes took two days to meet a station officer. All the meetings were in the bubble."

The month after Garbler arrived in Moscow, Anatoly Golitsin defected in Helsinki. Garbler had no reason to pay much attention to that at the time, since he was concentrating on his primary mission of monitoring clandestine contacts with Oleg Penkovsky, whom the CIA regarded as its most important asset inside the Soviet Union.[3]

"We were able to do quick brush contacts with Penkovsky at social affairs," Garbler said. "For example, an embassy official would give a cocktail party, Penkovsky was invited. On his trips to the West, Penkovsky had been shown photographs of people who might give him something or take his film. He would know that somebody was going to brush him at this party. One or two times we did this. At different locales, including Spaso House, the ambassador's residence."

Garbler met Penkovsky only once. "It was at a reception at Spaso House. Penkovsky did not have my picture, and did not know who I was." Garbler, living his cover as assistant naval attaché, was in uniform at the reception. As far as Penkovsky knew, he was having a pleasant chat with an American naval officer; he had no idea he was talking to the chief of the CIA station.

Oleg Vladimirovich Penkovsky, the CIA's most celebrated spy, was born in 1919 in Ordzhonikidze, in the northern Caucasus, the son of a White Russian army officer who was killed battling the Bolsheviks at Rostov during the Russian civil war. Young Oleg was raised by his mother, who, to protect her son's future, claimed that his father had died of typhus.[4] Oleg went to artillery school in Kiev. After the Soviets attacked Finland in 1939, Penkovsky's rifle division was sent to the front. Assigned to duties in Moscow the following year, Penkovsky met Vera Gapanovich, the daughter of a powerful Soviet general.

[3]Golitsin defected only two weeks after Garbler got to Moscow. "I heard about it," Garbler said. "A cable from headquarters arrived. It said that there had been a defection in Helsinki and the KGB was digging through the city, looking for the guy. We used to make occasional shopping trips to Helsinki, and the cable said it wouldn't be good to go at this time. I replied I wasn't planning to go to Helsinki."

[4]The family was divided. Penkovsky's great-uncle, General Valentin Antonovich Penkovsky, had joined the Red Army. He was caught in Stalin's purges, jailed but not executed, and fought with valor against the Nazis in World War II, becoming the wartime commander for the Far East military district. He rose high in the Soviet military and earned three Orders of Lenin. He met his nephew Oleg once in Moscow and, in a secret reunion over tears and vodka, promised never to report Oleg's White Russian father.

When the Germans attacked the Soviet Union in 1941, Oleg was sent to the Ukraine, where he earned eight decorations but was hit by shrapnel, was knocked unconscious, and lost four teeth. In the hospital back in Moscow, Penkovsky met General (later Marshal) Sergei S. Varentsov, who had been injured in a jeep accident.

Varentsov took a liking to the young artillery officer, and made him his aide on the spot. And he soon had an assignment for Penkovsky. Varentsov's daughter, Nina, the apple of his eye, had married a Jew, a Major Loshak, who got in trouble with the authorities for selling cars and parts on the black market. He was arrested in Lvov and sentenced to be shot. The marshal sent Penkovsky to intercede, but he arrived too late. "After her husband had been executed," said George Kisevalter, the CIA case officer who handled Penkovsky, "Nina Varentsov pulled a pistol from an officer and blew her brains out. Penkovsky spent his own money to give them a decent burial. When he reported back to a tearful Varentsov, the marshal said, 'You're like a son to me. You did everything you could. You did what I would have done.' "[5]

The episode cemented the personal bond between the powerful marshal and his young aide. Varentsov got Penkovsky into the prestigious Frunze Military Academy and persuaded him to go into intelligence work. Penkovsky married Vera Gapanovich, and his star was on the rise. In 1955, he was sent to Turkey as the acting GRU resident in Ankara. Six months later, a GRU general, Nikolai Petrovich Rubenko, whose real name was Savchenko, arrived in Ankara to take over as the resident. Tension soon developed between Penkovsky and his bullying boss, a much older man. Penkovsky also disliked a rival GRU officer in Ankara, Nikolai V. Ionchenko, later an adviser to Ho Chi Minh in Hanoi.[6]

[5]Many details of Penkovsky's background and his espionage career for the CIA were provided to the author by George Kisevalter in a series of interviews at Kisevalter's home near Washington. Kisevalter had been told of these events by the Soviet spy in the course of many hours of debriefings during the GRU colonel's three trips to the West in 1961. Kisevalter's account went beyond the version published in *The Penkovskiy Papers* (New York: Doubleday, 1965), a memoir ostensibly written by Penkovsky and smuggled out of the Soviet Union but in fact prepared with material provided by the CIA from the spy's debriefings in the West.

[6]The trouble came to a head when the GRU resident received an order from Moscow. As George Kisevalter recounted it, "A cable came in—lay off operations because the Shah of Iran was paying a state visit. Every hostile intelligence service in world will

Penkovsky returned to Moscow in 1956 and was preparing to be sent to India when the KGB at last unearthed the fact that his father was a White Russian army officer. He was eventually cleared but downgraded and assigned to a selection board for GRU trainees. By this time Penkovsky was becoming increasingly frustrated in his career. In November of 1960, he was transferred to the State Committee for Science and Technology, which meant that he would deal with foreign businessmen and officials and be able to travel abroad. But even before this opportunity presented itself, Penkovsky had already reached a momentous decision.

Three months earlier, in August 1960, Penkovsky made the first of four attempts to offer his services to the West. The GRU colonel was returning home from summer leave in Odessa when his train stopped in Kiev, so that cars from another train from the Caucasus could be attached. As he walked on the platform, he noticed two American college students speaking Russian. In Moscow the next day, Penkovsky spotted the same two students in Sokolniki Park, followed them toward the Hotel Ukraina, and approached them. He handed them a package and begged them to deliver it to the American embassy.

"They took the package," Kisevalter said. "The Marine guard lectured the students, don't take things from Russians. I was at headquarters when the package came in by courier. My God, we grabbed our heads and went crazy. Everything was typed in Russian. The first letter was an invitation to dance. 'I'm an intelligence officer. My people are suffering. Khrushchev will plunge the world into a third world war. I want to offer my services. I realize this letter is not enough. On page three and four you'll find a sketch of a dead drop and a signal site elsewhere to indicate a message has been placed. I want

be there, don't get caught. Despite the orders from Moscow, Ionchenko wanted to keep a meeting with a Turkish agent who had U.S. Air Force maps. Penkovsky called Turkish security and they nailed Ionchenko, who was expelled. They shot the Turk. Penkovsky was assigned to escort Ionchenko out. Rubenko made life so impossible that Penkovsky cabled Moscow, using KGB channels. This hit the central committee. Khrushchev called in both Rubenko and Penkovsky. The general was censured and thrown out of the GRU. Penkovsky was rewarded for vigilance and reassigned."

But he was a marked man for having opposed his boss, a general. It took the intervention of Marshal Varentsov to get Penkovsky a new assignment to the Dzerzhinsky artillery school in Moscow for a nine-month course in missiles.

precise instructions of how I can securely deliver to you a package which contains all details of the entire Soviet arsenal of rocketry, conventional and nuclear.' "

Kisevalter was animated as he spoke of what was surely one of the most electric moments of his espionage career. Penkovsky's letter, he said, "contained a most unbelievable list of incoming candidates for the military-diplomatic academy, which is their highest intelligence school, and backgrounds of the candidates, their assignments after graduation, and languages." It was an intelligence bonanza such as the CIA had never seen.[7]

"But we didn't have assets in Moscow," Kisevalter lamented. "We didn't respond to Penkovsky's letter." Incredible as it may seem, the CIA did not have anyone in the Soviet capital who could reply to Penkovsky's overture. There was no CIA station in Moscow.

"About October of 1960, we get a cable from MI6," Kisevalter said. "It reports that two British businessmen said some nut named Penkovsky in civilian clothing had wined and dined them in Moscow. Penkovsky asked them to take a package to the American embassy. They refused. 'Will you take my card?' They agreed. It listed Penkovsky's office on Gorky Street. On the back he wrote, 'Please call this number,' his home number, 'at ten A.M. on any Sunday from a pay booth.'

"Another month goes by and we try to get a guy into Moscow. We had no one Russian-speaking there. We had no one to run, no agents, so there was no one there. We sent one of our people in as an assistant supply officer." The CIA man moved into America House, a Moscow apartment building catering to foreigners but staffed by Soviets.

"Meanwhile, we're trying to figure out about Penkovsky. We don't understand how a military intelligence officer could walk around Moscow in civilian clothes." Eventually, the CIA learned the answer: Penkovsky had been assigned to the civilian scientific committee.

About this time, a Canadian diplomat, William Van Vliet, recently

---

[7]Of the names on the list, Kisevalter said, "one quarter were to be especially trained as illegals. These were starred. One French-speaking agent going to Lebanon, one English-speaking agent going to Israel, and so on." To confirm the validity of Penkovsky's list, ten CIA case officers were assigned to analyze all that the agency knew about the GRU officers. File traces were run, and the CIA was able to identify about forty of the sixty names on the list. "We had photos of about twenty-five," Kisevalter said. "Those with no record had never been outside the USSR."

returned from Moscow, flew to Washington from Ottawa to see Kisevalter. In all likelihood, Van Vliet was acting for the Royal Canadian Mounted Police (RCMP), then in charge of that country's counterintelligence. Penkovsky, Van Vliet said, had approached him and James Harrison, another Canadian official, at the National Hotel in Moscow and turned over his business card and a sealed envelope that Penkovsky said contained drawings of Soviet ballistic missiles. Once again, Penkovsky asked that the package be delivered to the Americans. Harrison, Van Vliet told Kisevalter, was greatly distressed that Canada had been ensnared in what appeared to be an American spy operation. "I thought he was going to have apoplexy," Van Vliet said.

The Canadians kept the package overnight, Kisevalter related. "Then they called Penkovsky, called him back, and said, 'Here, take your package.' " The documents were returned to Penkovsky unopened.[8]

Penkovsky had now made three attempts to communicate with the CIA, and had nothing to show for it. What happened next would have discouraged a less persistent spy. "Our guy is now in place in Moscow," Kisevalter said. "We sent him a message for Penkovsky—'Please don't contact anyone else, don't deliver the package for your own security, be patient, we will contact you.' The case officer knows he's surrounded by Soviets in America House and starts drinking heavily. He doesn't find a phone booth until eleven A.M., an hour late, and then he improvises. The message he gave Penkovsky was a senseless garble. He was drunk. He now teaches school in West Virginia."

In April 1961, Carlton B. Swift, Jr., the CIA operations chief in London station, the millionaire scion of the meat-packing family, reported that a British businessman, Greville Wynne, had met Penkovsky in Moscow. "Penkovsky took him to parties," Kisevalter said. "When it was time for Wynne to leave, Penkovsky pulls out an envelope and says please deliver these to the American embassy in London."

[8]Official documents released by the Canadian government early in 1991 placed the date of Penkovsky's approach at the National Hotel as January 9, 1961. Blair Seaborn, the Canadian chargé d'affaires in Moscow, had approved the decision to rebuff Penkovsky. He was later overruled by a new ambassador, Arnold Smith, who arranged to put Penkovsky in touch with MI6, according to the documents. See Dean Beeby, Canadian Press, "We Nearly Did It Again," *Ottawa Citizen,* March 1, 1991, p. A2.

MI6 had already recruited Wynne, who traveled frequently to the Soviet Union and Eastern Europe, to serve as Penkovsky's courier. He took the envelope back to London. And finally, later in April 1961, the CIA had its first face-to-face meeting with Oleg Penkovsky, who traveled to London as the leader of a Soviet trade delegation. Kisevalter and another case officer, Joseph J. Bulik, flew to London and met with Harold Shergold and Michael Stokes of MI6 in what now became a joint British-U.S. operation. They set up in London's Mount Royal Hotel, near Marble Arch, where Penkovsky's delegation was being wined and dined on another floor by a group of British steel executives. Kisevalter sent a note to Penkovsky asking him to come to Kisevalter's room, using an interior fire escape.

"We waited. There was a knock on the door. There's Penkovsky, in civilian clothes. 'We're the ones you wrote to,' we said." To prove it, the CIA officers showed Penkovsky a copy of his original letter.

"Penkovsky took off his jacket," Kisevalter continued. "From under the lining he removed a package and handed it to us. 'You don't know much about me,' he said. He then told his life story. 'Do you have time?' he asked. We had time."

It was the first in a series of intensive debriefings of Penkovsky that summer in England and France. From London, the CIA-MI6 team followed Penkovsky to Birmingham and Leeds, meeting with him clandestinely seventeen times in fifteen days in the three cities.

During one of these meetings, Penkovsky made a startling proposal: in the event that war was imminent, he would, if the CIA and MI6 wished him to do so, hide miniature atomic bombs at strategic locations around Moscow to destroy the Soviet capital.

"He had twenty-nine critical places in Moscow," Kisevalter said. "He described each of the locations, all significant from a military point of view. The primary headquarters of the Moscow military command, an emergency secondary military headquarters, underground in an abandoned Moscow subway, the headquarters of the artillery command. We let him continue, rather than cut him off, because for us it was useful to get a list of these strategic locations.

"He wanted us to provide the bombs, each small enough to fit in a suitcase. His idea was to go around town in a taxi with the bombs in suitcases and put them in garbage cans or alleys or other places to conceal them." How would the nuclear weapons have been triggered? "They would have been time bombs," Kisevalter said. "All would be triggered to go off at the same moment. Giving him a chance to get away." Penkovsky's scheme to launch World War III with a taxi and suitcases struck the CIA and MI6 officers as impractical, but they did not want to discourage his cooperation. "We told him we didn't have such weapons available," Kisevalter recalled, "but if and when we had such bombs and if a need arose, we would be in touch." Kisevalter smiled. "And we got the twenty-nine locations."

In Leeds, a Keystone Cops episode nearly resulted in Kisevalter's arrest. "Headquarters said I had to go to England as a Scotsman, Mr. McAdam. I registered in a hotel in Leeds. It was pouring cats and dogs. I had just met Penkovsky on the street. 'Can we talk?' I asked. 'Yes, I'm free for two hours.' We went to my hotel. There were a lot of people in the lobby. 'I'll go in, you follow me,' I said. I go through the revolving door into the lobby. He doesn't come in. I think maybe he's misunderstood me. I go out through the revolving door. As I go out, he comes in. Everybody in the lobby is looking over their newspapers. Who are these clowns?"

Matters rapidly got worse; Kisevalter walked back inside into the arms of the police. "I got arrested in the lobby. Detained, anyway. The police said, 'Mr. McAdam, what are you doing? This is the Queen's own.' Queen's own? I had no idea what they were talking about. Turns out it was the census, every ten years, and if you are traveling during that period, you have to register with the police, and I hadn't. There was no way I could fill out the form. I didn't even know my 'father's' name in Scotland. I went to MI6 and they nearly died laughing and then they filled out the form."

Before leaving England, Penkovsky was given a sophisticated camera, fabricated by MI6 technicians, to photograph documents. It looked like a Minox but was specially designed for its task, and used extremely sensitive film.[9]

In July, Penkovsky returned to London with a delegation of Soviet technical experts. He handed over a large group of films and documents to Wynne, and met with the four-man CIA-MI6 team again.

The joint MI6-CIA team worked out procedures for Penkovsky to

---

[9]The camera had a fixed f-stop of f8 and a fixed shutter speed of $\frac{1}{100}$th of a second. Penkovsky was instructed to use a light source of between 60 and 100 watts. He was told that 17.5 by 21 inches was the maximum-size document that could be photographed in one shot. Any document bigger than that required two frames.

continue passing secrets when he returned to Moscow. His contacts would be Wynne and Janet Ann Chisholm, who had once been Shergold's secretary and was the wife of the MI6 station chief in Moscow, Roderick "Ruari" Chisholm. She was flown in from Moscow and met Penkovsky so he would know what she looked like.

Penkovsky was given a CIA communications plan code-named Yo-Yo 51, which consisted of a one-time pad in Cyrillic that he would use to decipher coded messages broadcast to him in Moscow by shortwave radio from Frankfurt.[10] In Penkovsky's case, the CIA broadcast a dummy tape with "cut numbers," a form of altered Morse code. The dummy tape sounded like Morse, but was really a continuous but apparently meaningless stream of dots and dashes. Penkovsky was instructed to don earphones and listen at midnight on Saturday and Sunday on a $26 Sony radio that Kisevalter had bought for him. A five-number group, Penkovsky's call number, would be broadcast at midnight, followed by a dummy group, the last three letters of which would tell him how many real coded groups to expect in the message that followed. If the KGB was listening, the message would sound no different from the dots and dashes that preceded it; only Penkovsky could decipher the text with his one-time pad.

Penkovsky brought with him a long shopping list from Soviet officials. First on the list was a request from the chief of the GRU, Ivan Alexandrovich Serov, who had also formerly headed the KGB. "Penkovsky says Serov wants a garden swing, he wants bees for rheumatic treatment," Kisevalter said. "And Penkovsky brought with him outlines of many women's feet for shoes for wives of the top brass. 'How do you expect to get this stuff home?' I asked. 'Wynne's going back with ten suitcases. The swing can go by boat—we have a boat on the Thames.' So we had a shopping expedition. We had to get a present for Varentsov's birthday—Khrushchev would be there. At Harrods, I got a sterling-silver rocket that dispatched cigarettes and cigars. Just the thing for the marshal. And a watch, but we didn't have a cleared engraver, so we couldn't engrave it. And a sixty-year-old bottle of

[10]A one-time pad is a tiny booklet containing groups of random numbers that an agent uses to decode the messages received. The only other copy is retained by the intelligence service that is controlling the agent. As the name implies, each page of the pad is used only once, then destroyed. Sometimes the pads are made of edible paper. Because only two copies of the pads exist, it is impossible to break the code.

cognac, which we got by having [CIA] case officers scouring France. They did find a cleared dentist, who replaced Penkovsky's missing teeth."

As busy as Penkovsky was, leading his double life, he found time while in London to visit the grave of Karl Marx in Highgate. "He found it covered with garbage," Kisevalter said. "He photographed it, reported to Moscow what a bunch of lemons were in our embassy here, they weren't even taking care of the grave. He was commended."

In September, Penkovsky flew to Paris and stayed for almost a month, meeting with Kisevalter, Shergold, and the two other team members in a British safe house near the Etoile. He returned to Moscow on October 16, 1961. He was never to visit the West again.

With Penkovsky back in Moscow, it had been arranged that he would make contact in an emergency through a dead drop, a hiding place behind a radiator in the lobby of an apartment building at No. 5-6 Pushkin Street. Penkovsky would leave his message in a matchbox, which he would wrap in wire and hang on a hook behind the radiator. The drop, according to Kisevalter, was to be used only in extraordinary circumstances, "for a warning, in the event of a planned surprise attack by the Soviets, or in case of a drastic change in operational procedure. Suppose Penkovsky was unexpectedly transferred out of Moscow, for example. He had to have some way to get word to us." If Penkovsky left anything in the drop he was to signal the CIA by marking a circle in charcoal on lamppost No. 35 near a bus stop on Kutuzovsky Prospekt. The lamppost was checked each day by Captain Alexis H. Davison, the assistant air attaché and embassy doctor, who had been recruited by the CIA for that single task. Davison could do so without attracting attention; he drove by the lamppost every day on his normal route commuting between his home and the embassy.[11]

Late in 1961, the CIA decided to check the drop, even though it had not received a signal from Penkovsky. Headquarters wanted to make sure that the door to the lobby was unlocked, the drop accessible, and everything in working order.

[11]In addition, Penkovsky was instructed to telephone Hugh Montgomery, Garbler's deputy chief of station, at Moscow 43 26 87 to alert him to the chalk mark. "There was no voice conversation," Kisevalter said. "After three rings, Penkovsky would hang up."

The agency persuaded John V. Abidian, the embassy's security officer, to perform that risky task. Although a State Department employee, Abidian needed little persuasion. "The job was there and needed to be done," he said.

A tall, darkly handsome New Englander with striking features, Abidian was particular about his appearance. "I had a mania for having a decent haircut," Abidian said. When he had arrived in Moscow the previous year, he had gone to great lengths looking for a good barber. "I finally found one. Near the barber there was a bookshop. It just so happens that the lobby on Pushkin Street was near the bookshop, around the corner. I was able to get my haircut while I knew surveillance was sleeping, or smoking. Then I went into the bookstore in one door and went out the other door." Abidian turned the corner and slipped into the lobby, a dimly lit place with a pay phone along one wall. "I remember the stairwell, the radiator on the right side, a very small lobby." Abidian double-checked, just in case Penkovsky had left something hanging behind the radiator. "But there was nothing there. It was late afternoon, and dark in the lobby." Although Abidian does not remember doing so, he may have lit a match to inspect the drop. "I put my hand down as far as I could—it would take a very skinny hand to get down further."

Since the drop appeared to be empty, Abidian duly reported this back to the CIA. He recalled checking the Pushkin Street drop again, at least once. But, ducking from the barber shop to the bookstore to the dead drop, Abidian was confident that he had not been observed by the KGB.

Six weeks after Penkovsky returned to Moscow from Paris, Garbler was in place in the Soviet capital. Although busy with the Penkovsky case, he was developing other assets for the Moscow station. One was a diplomat of another country who was cooperating with the CIA. Garbler invited several guests, including the diplomat, to his apartment one night to view a film. In the darkness, he slipped a small device to the man which had a sharp point at one end and a hollow container for a message.

"It was to be planted near a pole on the highway and used as a drop," Garbler said. "The man didn't plant it. He claimed he had been under surveillance and decided he'd better not." Garbler asked for the device back, and the diplomat returned it to him a week later at another film night in the station chief's apartment.

Garbler put it in his pants pocket and then under his pillow that night. He shipped it back to CIA headquarters, where it was analyzed by the Technical Services Division. To his horror, "TSD told me it was radioactive," Garbler said. "The Soviets had apparently broken into the man's embassy safe and planted an isotope in the device." Garbler was told this had been done to make it easier for the Soviets to find it.

"I thought back on the fact that for six hours I had it in my pants pocket, near my vital organs," Garbler related, "not to mention under my pillow." The episode left no permanent ill effects but impressed Garbler on the lengths to which the Soviets would go to counter the CIA.

Meanwhile, he waited for a signal from Angleton. Although Garbler had agreed, at the farewell party at Bill Harvey's house, to handle the counterintelligence chief's agent in Moscow—one did not lightly say no to Angleton—Garbler and the CI official were not the warmest of colleagues. It went back to an incident in 1956 when Angleton had visited the Stockholm station. At the time, Garbler was the deputy COS.

Angleton met with Garbler and Paul Birdsall, the chief of station. The counterintelligence chief made some small talk; he was enjoying the weather, having a nice time in Stockholm. Then he stood up, took off his jacket, removed a belt, and from a hidden compartment inside it extracted a code pad.

"I'd like to send a message," Angleton announced.

"Does it have to do with something happening in Sweden?" Garbler asked politely.

"Sure."

"We're responsible for what happens here. Would we know what you're reporting?"

"No way." Since Angleton traveled with his own codes, they could not be read by the local station. Garbler turned to Birdsall. "Paul," he said, "I don't think we should let him send the message. Let him send it by Western Union if he wants to." Birdsall, a mild-mannered Harvard man who had no stomach for confrontation, overruled his deputy and told Angleton to go ahead and send the message.

Now, after several months in Moscow, Garbler received an eyes-only message from Angleton at headquarters. The CI chief had set up a communications procedure for his agent. When the dead drop, located in Gorky Park, was ready to be cleared, the agent would send an innocuous postcard to an accommodation address abroad. Angleton would be informed when the postcard arrived and would send a code word to Garbler in Moscow, a signal to unload the drop.

When the signal came, Garbler, accompanied by his wife, Florence, went to Gorky Park. The drop was a hollow rock. If it was there, that meant there was a message inside. The rock was where Angleton had said it would be. After making sure they were not under surveillance, Garbler picked it up and walked away.

Back at the embassy, Garbler opened the rock and found a long message inside, encoded in a series of five-digit groups. That created a problem for the station chief. In sending code, the procedure was to spell out the digits in letters. The number "6," for example, became "six," and then the text was encoded again. Even though the agent's code used only numbers under ten, Garbler estimated that each group of five digits would require three or more groups of five letters, spelled out. But this would create an unusually long message.

From the length of the material in the rock, Garbler calculated it would take several "operational immediate" messages to send the entire contents to Angleton. Since all traffic went through the Soviet telegraph system, this extraordinary traffic would alert and possibly alarm the Soviets. Was World War III coming? Garbler cabled Angleton, outlining his dilemma and asking for instructions. Did the counterintelligence chief *really* want the message by cable? The reply came back: "Send as agreed."

The communications room had feeble air conditioning and was hot and stuffy. Garbler, stripped down to his undershirt, sat in the commo room for four hours, painstakingly using one-time pads to reencode the contents of the rock. He had sent four operational messages when headquarters cabled him: "Stop! Send rest by routine precedence," the lowest and least urgent level of communication.

Garbler never knew the identity of the agent, or what the message in the rock said, and he never heard another word from Angleton. But the Moscow station chief may have hoped that, having serviced Angleton's agent, the CI chief might forget, or at least forgive, the incident in Stockholm. As the first chief of the Moscow station, Garbler's future seemed bright, and Angleton was not a good man to cross.

Garbler never confided in John Maury, the chief of the Soviet division, that he had agreed to unload Angleton's rock. The counterintelligence chief had made it clear when he approached Garbler that the operation was to be handled with the utmost secrecy.

And Garbler may have had another sound reason for not telling his division chief. He knew that Maury was not one of Angleton's admirers. The head of the Soviet division, an affable, pipe-smoking Virginia gentleman not normally given to harsh judgments, had made his view on that subject graphically clear, on more than one occasion.

"Maury used to say of Angleton," Garbler remembered, "that if you cut his head off, he won't stop wiggling until after sunset."

Chapter 6

Contact

■

Early in June of 1962, Yuri Ivanovich Nosenko, a thirty-five-year-old KGB officer serving on the Soviet disarmament delegation in Geneva, approached an American diplomat and asked for a private talk. The diplomat notified the CIA station in Bern, the Swiss capital, and Pete Bagley, an officer specializing in Soviet operations, immediately left by train for Geneva.

There, Bagley and Nosenko met at a CIA safe house. Nosenko, apparently very nervous, drank during the interview. He told Bagley he had been drinking before the meeting as well.[1] The encounter proceeded with some difficulty; Bagley spoke little Russian, and Nosenko's English was limited. A Russian-speaking CIA man was clearly needed on the scene.

Headquarters was alerted. As soon as the cable from Switzerland arrived in Langley, George Kisevalter was told to fly to Geneva. Not

[1]The amount of alcohol flowing at this and subsequent meetings in Geneva later became an issue in the Nosenko case. "It was not a boozing party," Bagley said. "He wasn't drunk at any of the meetings." But Nosenko later claimed he had been drunk during his conversations with the CIA. John L. Hart, a CIA witness to a House committee, said Nosenko had "four or five" Scotch and sodas before the meetings and that the Russian blamed alcohol for his having given answers that exaggerated his importance in the KGB. ". . . At all these meetings I was snookered . . . I was drunk," Hart quoted Nosenko as saying. *Investigation of the Assassination of President John F. Kennedy,* Hearings, Select Committee on Assassinations of the U.S. House of Representatives, Vol. II, 1978, p. 491.

only was Kisevalter fluent in Russian, he had handled the agency's two most important Soviet cases, first Pyotr Popov, then Penkovsky. He was the logical choice to meet Nosenko.

It was a time of intense activity inside the CIA. Six months earlier, Anatoly Golitsin had defected in Helsinki, and his warnings about "Sasha," a penetration of the CIA whose name began with the letter K, had launched the secret mole hunt in Angleton's counterintelligence staff. Wiretaps were in place on Peter Karlow, who remained unaware that he was the principal suspect. In Moscow, Paul Garbler continued to monitor contacts with Penkovsky, who was still transmitting Soviet military secrets to the West, although he was increasingly nervous that the KGB might have discovered his espionage activities.

Now, Yuri Nosenko had offered his services. He was, in time, to become the most controversial defector in the history of the CIA.

"Bagley met the plane and took me to the safe house," Kisevalter said. "Nosenko would be coming over." But first, certain preparations had to be made. "We bugged the place," Kisevalter said. "I put in hidden microphones hooked up to a tape recorder." That done, Kisevalter and Bagley settled down to wait.

It is doubtful that the CIA, had it tried, could have found two more disparate officers to assign to the same case. In style, personality, background, and appearance, the two men were a study in contrast.

George Kisevalter was a big, shaggy sheepdog of a man, irreverent of authority, street-smart, a field operator at heart, and, deep down, resentful of the clubbish atmosphere of an agency that would, he felt, deny him top rank because he would always be an outsider, a foreigner at birth, born in czarist Russia.

Kisevalter, the older of the two officers, was born in St. Petersburg in 1910. His father, the Czar's munitions expert, had been sent to Vienna in 1904 to oversee production of shells for the war with Japan. There he met a French woman from Dijon, a schoolteacher who returned to Russia and married him. When World War I broke out, the senior Kisevalter was sent to the United States to oversee a munitions plant near Chester, Pennsylvania, that was manufacturing three-inch shells for the Czar.

After the Russian revolution, he took his wife and child to New York, where he made aircraft pontoons. The Kisevalters became U.S. citizens. Their son, George, was graduated from Dartmouth with a bachelor's degree in 1930 and, a year later, with a master's degree in civil engineering.

Fresh out of Dartmouth, Kisevalter went to work for the New York City Parks Department, where he helped to build the Children's Zoo in Central Park.[2] After that, Kisevalter joined the Army. When World War II broke out, the Army, learning that Kisevalter spoke Russian, sent him to Alaska as a liaison officer with Soviet pilots who were ferrying some twelve thousand warplanes to the Soviets through Fairbanks. In Alaska, the planes were refitted with Soviet markings, red star decals on both sides of the fuselages. Halfway through the war, Kisevalter ran out of red stars, and, improvising, bought a supply of Texaco decals from the local gas station. "I bought the stars," he said, "we put them on, and said to the Russian pilots, 'Go ahead and fly Texaco.' They did."

At the end of the war, Kisevalter was serving in G-2, Army intelligence in Germany. For two years, he worked with General Reinhard Gehlen, who had headed Foreign Armies East (Fremde Heere Ost), the branch of the German general staff that gathered intelligence on the Soviet Union. Kisevalter debriefed Gehlen, whom the CIA was to set up as head of West German intelligence, "on everything he knew about the Soviet army."

Then Kisevalter left the Army and intelligence work for Nebraska, where for five years he grew alfalfa.[3] Kisevalter's farm-belt career was short-lived. In 1951, he joined the CIA, establishing the reputation that led him, a decade later, to the safe house in Geneva.

Tennent Harrington "Pete" Bagley had arrived in Switzerland by a more conventional route. Bagley was handsome, cultivated, buttoned-down, and ambitious, with a quick, analytical mind and social and family credentials rooted in the Navy and Princeton. Then thirty-six, he had been born in Annapolis, the son of a vice-admiral. Two brothers also became admirals, one serving as vice-chief of naval opera-

[2]Kisevalter's zoo phase gave rise to tales, still believed by some inside the CIA—but untrue—that he had designed the bear cages at the Bronx Zoo.
[3]Kisevalter, even in 1990, talked enthusiastically about the virtues of alfalfa. "We would heat it with gas drums, grind it into a powder, and extract vitamin A," he reminisced. "Mixed with corn, it is invaluable for poultry as chicken feed. Vitamin A is the vital thing a chicken needs. Chickens used to taste fishy because they were fed cod liver oil. But chickens that are fed alfalfa meal don't taste fishy. It's excellent for dogs and cats too. Alfalfa is no longer needed, of course; now they use synthetic vitamin A for chickens."

tions, the other as commander of U.S. naval forces in Europe. His great-uncle Admiral William D. Leahy had served as President Franklin D. Roosevelt's wartime chief of staff.

Instead of following family tradition, Bagley joined the Marines on his seventeenth birthday in 1942. After the war, he attended Princeton, but he got his bachelor's degree at the University of Southern California, and a doctorate in political science at the University of Geneva, Switzerland. He joined the CIA in 1950, worked in Vienna for four years in the early fifties—that was when he escorted Soviet defector Peter Deriabin back to Washington—and was near the end of a four-year tour in Bern, where he had handled the Goleniewski letters, when Nosenko made contact in Geneva.

Kisevalter and Bagley did not have to wait very long. "About two days after I arrived in Geneva," Kisevalter said, "Nosenko walks in one afternoon. He's in his thirties, nice-looking, brown hair, about five-ten, fairly muscular. He's very nervous, and starts drinking."

The KGB man offered to sell information to the CIA for 900 Swiss francs, claiming he needed the money to replace KGB funds he had spent on a drinking bout. Later, Nosenko admitted he invented this story; he said he feared that an offer to give away information for nothing would be rejected as a provocation, as had sometimes happened in the past when KGB officers, acting under instructions, approached the CIA.

Nosenko was not talking about defecting. "He wanted to go back home," Kisevalter said. "His daughter, Oksana, had a serious asthmatic condition, and the Kremlin clinic to which he had access told him the Soviets didn't have the medication that was needed. We called back to headquarters. There was none in the U.S. Finally, we found that there was some in Holland. We hired a pilot who flew to Geneva with the medication. Two years later, he claimed it saved her life."

Belting straight Scotch, Nosenko began talking, disclosing information that he hoped would establish his bona fides with the two CIA officers. Early on, he revealed that Boris Belitsky, a prominent correspondent for Radio Moscow then being run as an agent by the CIA under the code name AEWIRELESS, was actually a double agent under KGB control. The revelation stunned Kisevalter, because he knew that only two years earlier, Belitsky had passed a CIA lie-detector test in a London safe house with flying colors. "The polygraph operator said Belitsky was absolutely okay," Kisevalter recalled. "He said, 'He could sing 'The Star-Spangled Banner' through his asshole.' "

Armed with that kind of unqualified reassurance, the CIA had been taking Belitsky's information at face value.[4] The correspondent had been recruited in 1958 at the Brussels World's Fair by George Goldberg, a CIA man who had been born in Latvia and spoke fluent Russian. By 1962, AEWIRELESS was being run by two case officers, Goldberg and Harry F. Young.[5] To prove his point, Nosenko was able to name both CIA men to Kisevalter and Bagley.

"Belitsky was in Geneva covering the disarmament meetings," Kisevalter recounted. "Nosenko said, laughing, 'You're not going to do anything about Belitsky because if they find out anything, I'm dead. If they even find out I'm here, I'm dead.' "

For a time, Goldberg and Young were not told that their agent had been doubled, lest by a slip of the tongue or even by intonation or manner they tip off AEWIRELESS to the fact that the CIA now knew he was under KGB control.

Boris Belitsky, by 1962 already a leading correspondent for Radio Moscow, was a slightly balding man of medium build who dressed like an English gentleman and spoke excellent English with an American accent. His father had been an overseas official of Amtorg, the Soviet trade agency, and Boris was educated in New York City.[6]

Geneva was getting crowded. While Kisevalter and Bagley were meeting with Nosenko, Bruce Solie of the CIA's Office of Security, who was working closely with the Counterintelligence Staff in the mole hunt, flew in, hoping to ask Nosenko about penetrations. Kise-

[4]There were doubts about Belitsky in some quarters, however, despite his remarkable performance in London. For example, the reports officer in the Soviet division who handled the take from the Russian concluded he was a plant. Within the division, Belitsky remained a controversial asset.

[5]Young left the CIA in 1965, became a history professor at the University of Indiana, and later wrote *Prince Lichnowsky and the Great War* (Athens, Ga.: University of Georgia Press, 1977), a book about Karl Max Furst von Lichnowsky, the German ambassador to London who tried to prevent the outbreak of World War I.

[6]By 1989, Belitsky was deputy chief of Radio Moscow's department that broadcast to Great Britain and North America. Belitsky spent considerable time in England and was a well-known figure on British television. In 1965, he came up with a wildly improbable explanation of Britain's 1963 "Great Train Robbery." The $7.8 million heist, Belitsky said in a broadcast from Moscow, had been carried out not by common criminals, but by the British secret service to finance its clandestine operations.

valter, fearing too many cooks, said he would do the asking, and he kept Solie out of the safe house.

Kisevalter and Bagley knew nothing of Anatoly Golitsin's warnings about moles in the CIA and his specific allegations about "Sasha." Both CIA officers, however, said they remembered Solie passing along questions for Nosenko.

"Solie gave me a whole shopping list of what to ask," Kisevalter recalled, "including several questions about Sasha. I met him in a bistro, an outdoor café, more than once. I told him whatever Nosenko had said on the subjects he was interested in."

According to Bagley, Nosenko said he had no information about a KGB mole in the CIA named Sasha. Nosenko's interrogators pressed him as well on the matter of Vladislav Mikhailovich Kovshuk, the official of the KGB's Second Chief Directorate who had served in Washington in 1957 under the name of Vladimir Mikhailovich Komarov. Golitsin had claimed that Kovshuk was of such senior rank that he could only have come to the United States to meet a high-ranking penetration.

Could Nosenko shed any light on the Kovshuk mission? Nosenko said he could, that Kovshuk had been sent to Washington to contact a KGB source code-named ANDREY. But Nosenko described ANDREY as a low-level source, a noncommissioned officer who had worked at the American embassy in Moscow, had since returned to the United States, and lived in the Washington area.

Even as Nosenko revealed the truth about AEWIRELESS, George Goldberg was meeting secretly with Belitsky in another safe house in Geneva, still blissfully unaware of what was going on. Belitsky passed what he claimed was classified information to Goldberg during a total of eighteen hours of debriefings in Geneva over a period of several days.

Goldberg was finally told his agent had been compromised. Even after Nosenko's disclosure, the agency continued to run Belitsky, in part because the CIA considered it valuable during the Cuban missile crisis that October to see what kind of skewed information Belitsky was passing.

But AEWIRELESS may have provided good information for two or three years after he was recruited. According to Goldberg, "Belitsky didn't report his CIA recruitment [to the KGB] until 1961 or 1962." He knew this, Goldberg said, because "Nosenko said Belitsky told him he was recruited by the CIA in England in 1961"—three years *after* his apparent recruitment by Goldberg in Brussels.

As Nosenko continued to talk, he revealed other even more unsettling information: the case of the handsome Armenian. The KGB, he revealed, had followed someone from the American embassy in Moscow and had observed him checking a dead drop in an apartment lobby. "The Soviets called him the handsome Armenian," Kisevalter said. "But they knew his name. Nosenko also told his name. Abidian."

Kisevalter immediately suspected, correctly, that the emergency drop of the CIA's most important agent had been compromised. He assumed that the hiding place that Nosenko was talking about was the Pushkin Street drop that had been set up for Oleg Penkovsky. As the case officer handling Penkovsky, Kisevalter knew the significance of Nosenko's disclosure, and was dismayed. Since the emergency drop in the building lobby on Pushkin Street had never been used, Kisevalter concluded the KGB did not yet know it was meant for Penkovsky. But the drop was now contaminated; the KGB knew its location. Kisevalter said nothing to Nosenko, of course, but in dispatches to the CIA from Geneva, he warned headquarters that the drop had been detected.

"Abidian was cockier than he should have been," Kisevalter said. "He wanted to look at this place at night. An apartment lobby. But Abidian, unbeknownst to him, was under heavy surveillance. It was very dark. The lights were out or dim. They saw the Armenian nosing around. He was lighting matches, looking for the dead drop. That made it twice as suspicious. He came back and said, 'Yes, it's there.' "

"The KGB elaborately staked out the lobby for six months. Workmen building false walls. Nosenko told me they watched it for six months. I asked him, 'What happened?' Nosenko replied, 'They ran out of powder.' In Russian, it means there were no results, the troops ran out of gunpowder. In other words, after a while they got tired of staking it out."[7]

---

[7]Bagley insisted that Nosenko did not mention the dead drop in these initial meetings in Geneva in 1962 but only at a later meeting in 1964, by which time Penkovsky had been arrested. Kisevalter was equally adamant that Nosenko had revealed the KGB's knowledge of the drop in 1962. Nosenko himself appeared unable to resolve the matter. Former CIA officer Donald Jameson, who discussed the question with Nosenko in June 1991, said Nosenko remembered that the drop had been under KGB

Nosenko also warned the CIA men that the walls of the American embassy in Moscow were honeycombed with forty-two microphones. "And he told us enough to find them," Kisevalter said. Golitsin had also spoken of microphones in the embassy; eventually the State Department announced that forty had been found.[8]

As Nosenko talked about eavesdropping in the Moscow embassy, his own words, of course, were being picked up by Kisevalter's concealed microphones and tape-recorded. The two CIA officers held a series of meetings with Nosenko in the safe house over a period of several days. Kisevalter, because he was fluent in Russian, conducted the questioning. Bagley, although his Russian was limited, took notes. All of this was an elaborate charade; Nosenko undoubtedly assumed he was being taped, but the note-taking was designed to reassure him that he was not.

As Nosenko's story emerged, it became clear that he was a product of the Soviet elite. His father, Ivan Isiderovich Nosenko, was Nikita Khrushchev's minister of shipbuilding. Yuri Nosenko was born in Nikolayev, a river port near the Black Sea, not far from Odessa, on October 30, 1927. His father was a self-made man who worked in the Odessa shipyards, studied at night, and became an engineer. His mother, the daughter of an architect, had more of an upper-class, intellectual background. In 1934, Nosenko's father moved the family to Leningrad, where he supervised a shipbuilding plant. Five years later, the family moved to Moscow, where the father had risen to minister of shipbuilding at the time of his death in 1956. But the senior Nosenko's career had been dealt a devastating blow two years earlier when Khrushchev scrapped the huge naval fleet that Stalin had ordered built. Two keels had already been laid for aircraft carriers. The construction program made little sense; the ships would have been

---

surveillance twenty-four hours a day. "But he said, 'I honestly don't remember whether I mentioned it in '62 or '64. It was something I knew about before '62, and logically I would have mentioned it, but I don't recall.' " There was no conflict, however, over the substance of Nosenko's disclosure; both Kisevalter and Bagley agreed that Nosenko said that the KGB had spotted Abidian at the drop.

[8]The microphones looked like wheels from a roller skate, and were painted gunmetal gray. In the center of each, a tube about the size of a drinking straw projected outward to just behind the plaster to funnel the sound to the microphones. In some cases, pinholes had been made in the plaster to enhance the transmission of sound. The State Department announced the discovery of the microphones on May 19, 1964. Presumably, they had been uncovered some time earlier.

obsolete, and no match for the U.S. Navy. Khrushchev's cutback left Ivan Nosenko with little to do. His father, Yuri Nosenko said, was so depressed that he spent the last months of his life on a couch, able only to sleep and sigh.

But his son, with a high official for a father, had risen rapidly inside the Soviet intelligence hierarchy. In 1942, during World War II, Yuri Nosenko was sent to a naval preparatory school, and then to the naval academy, where he proceeded to shoot himself in the foot to avoid military service, according to a former CIA official.[9] He was nevertheless able to switch to Moscow's prestigious Institute of International Relations, and was recruited into the GRU, which sent him to the Far East as a Navy intelligence officer. In 1953, he joined the KGB and took a wife, Ludmilla, the daughter of a prominent Communist family.

Nosenko claimed to Kisevalter and Bagley that he now held the rank of major in the KGB. He also said that after joining the KGB, he was assigned to the Second Chief Directorate, which is responsible for internal security and operations against foreigners in the Soviet Union.[10] More specifically, Nosenko said he was put to work in the First Department, which was responsible for surveillance of the American embassy and recruitment of its personnel. In 1955, he said, he was transferred to the Seventh Department, specializing in tourists. He said he was transferred back to the First Department in 1960 and then in 1962 was bounced back to the Seventh Department, the tourist section. He traveled to London in 1957, as a security officer escorting a group of Soviet athletes, and to Cuba in 1960.[11]

[9]Leonard V. McCoy, "Yuriy Nosenko, CIA" (Fort Myer, Va.: *CIRA Newsletter*, Volume XII, No. 3, Fall 1987, published by Central Intelligence Retirees' Association), p. 19. Nosenko gives a different version of the incident. In 1991 he told Donald Jameson, another former CIA official, that he shot himself in the left hand while playing with a pistol and was soon afterward dismissed as a naval cadet. Nosenko claimed the shooting was accidental.

[10]Nosenko was on temporary duty in Geneva to keep an eye on the members of the Soviet disarmament delegation. Normally, he was assigned to the KGB's Second Chief Directorate, and would seldom have had reason to travel outside the Soviet Union. "After Golitsin defected," Kisevalter said, "the Soviets said that any group of five or more traveling abroad will have a watchdog from the Second Chief Directorate. Nosenko told us that."

[11]For additional details about Nosenko's background, see Gordon Brook-Shepherd, *The Storm Birds: Soviet Post-War Defectors* (London: Weidenfeld & Nicolson, 1988), pp. 179–83, and *Investigation of the Assassination of President John F. Kennedy,*

Nosenko offered no explanation of what had impelled him to contact the CIA, other than his story about the missing Swiss francs, which he later admitted was untrue. But whatever his motive, he had more information to impart. The KGB, he revealed, had penetrated British intelligence in Switzerland. Nosenko had a rather personal reason for knowing about this, according to Kisevalter. "It came about this way. Nosenko is playing around with a British secretary in Geneva who worked for MI5.[12] Yuri Ivanovich Guk, a KGB man who is in Geneva, runs into Nosenko. They are good friends. Nosenko tells Guk, 'She'd be a good piece of tail.' 'For chrissakes, Yuri,' Guk says, 'stay away from her, she's in British intelligence. What will happen when *our* man in MI5 reports back to Moscow that you're fooling around with her?' We didn't tell the British," Kisevalter said resignedly, because they would have insisted on knowing the source. "What could we say without blowing Nosenko inside out?"

But the CIA did share news of another British penetration. A year earlier, Anatoly Golitsin had spoken of a Soviet spy in the British Admiralty. The ensuing investigation had narrowed the field of suspects, but had not pinpointed the mole. Now, Nosenko provided additional details that enabled the British, three months later in September of 1962, to arrest William John Vassall, a thirty-eight-year-old clerk in the Admiralty.[13]

In 1954, Vassall had been sent to Moscow as clerk to the naval attaché, who reported his work satisfactory despite "an irritating effeminate personality." Although his fellow employees called him "Vera" behind his back, apparently hardly anyone except the KGB realized he was a homosexual who could be blackmailed. In a statement to Special Branch, Vassall remembered being plied with brandy

---

Hearings, Select Committee on Assassinations of the U.S. House of Representatives, Vol. II, 1978, pp. 439–43.

[12]MI5, the British security service, is responsible for internal security but does have representatives abroad, although far fewer than MI6, the British secret intelligence service. MI5 is roughly equivalent to the FBI and MI6 to the CIA.

[13]Members of the Counterintelligence Staff discounted the value of Nosenko's leads in the Vassall case. "Golitsin gave us information on Vassall," Angleton's deputy, Scotty Miler, said. "Nosenko's information put the final nail in the coffin. They almost had him. He would have been caught anyway."

and photographed naked in bed with "two or three" male friends, he was not quite sure how many, in "several compromising sexual actions." The Russians used the photos to force him to spy, both in Moscow and later in London. When he wanted to get in touch with his Soviet contacts in London, he was told, he was to draw a circle on a tree with pink chalk.

According to Kisevalter, what Nosenko knew was that "the man was in the Admiralty and that he was a homosexual. He explained to me how he found out. A Soviet case officer had returned home from England and received awards in Moscow. There was so much fanfare—and jealousy—that everybody speculated that man had had a big hit. Nosenko learned why, he picked it up in the corridors."

Kisevalter questioned Nosenko in an effort to learn more about how much damage had been done by Edward Ellis Smith, the CIA's first man in Moscow, who had been ensnared by his KGB maid and fired. Nosenko, according to both Kisevalter and Bagley, confirmed that Smith had been compromised. In fact, Nosenko said, since he had worked in the KGB section that targeted the American embassy, he had personally handled the Smith case. "Nosenko was running the girl, Valya," Kisevalter said. It was Nosenko who revealed that the KGB had code-named Smith "Ryzhiy," for his red hair.

The KGB, as Kisevalter related it, forced one meeting with Smith and tried to set up another one. "Nosenko said Smith was reluctant to come to a second meeting. Nosenko asked the girl, 'Is he coming to the meeting?' Nosenko said she replied that 'he [Smith] was acting like Hamlet' about whether or not to come to the meeting."

There were other disclosures. Golitsin had warned the CIA that a Canadian ambassador to Moscow was a homosexual. Now, Nosenko confirmed that the gay ambassador was John Watkins, a distinguished academic who had served in Moscow in the mid-1950s. According to Kisevalter, Nosenko told how Watkins and the Canadian foreign minister, Lester Pearson, had attended a dinner party at Nikita S. Khrushchev's dacha in the Crimea in 1955. As the vodka flowed, the Soviet leader began needling Watkins. "Khrushchev was plastered and made wise remarks about Watkins," Kisevalter continued. "He said, 'Not everybody here likes women.'" Among the guests was General Oleg Mikhailovich Gribanov, head of the KGB's Second Chief Directorate, which targeted foreigners in the Soviet Union.

"Gribanov was running Watkins and was ready to blow his stack," Kisevalter said.[14]

Nosenko also described the KGB's operations in Geneva, an important intelligence base because of the frequent international meetings held there, many under the auspices of the United Nations units headquartered in that city. "Nosenko told us how many case officers they had in Geneva, how they operated in Geneva, the computers they used for surveillance. They monitored all police channels. And he told us they had a system of using rental cars in Geneva to avoid their own cars being spotted."

In his meetings in the safe house in Geneva, Nosenko also revealed that the Soviets had penetrated a CIA operation against a KGB officer. The operation had begun when a woman agent working for the CIA in Vienna confessed to her handlers that she was having a dangerous love affair. "She had fallen in love with a Soviet KGB officer whom she met in the Soviet Union," Kisevalter said. "She told us of the love affair. The officer left Moscow and went by ship from Odessa to Piraeus to meet the girl in Vienna. The idea was to compromise the KGB officer. But since Nosenko knew of it, it meant the Soviet officer was under control." To Kisevalter, the case was yet another disclosure that "helped prove Nosenko's bona fides."

One of Nosenko's allegations was too hot to handle, even for the CIA. According to Kisevalter, Nosenko told him that the Soviets "had the goods" on columnist Joseph Alsop, "a homosexual, and they have photos and if he gets out of line they can blackmail him if he doesn't write what they want. 'There is a sword over his head,' Nosenko said. So I went to Tom K. [Thomas H. Karamessines, at the time the CIA's assistant deputy director for plans]. He said cut it out of the tape and don't write it up. Because Alsop was a good friend of the President. He told me to cut it out of the tape, and I did."

[14]When the Royal Canadian Mounted Police (RCMP) later interrogated Watkins, who had retired from the foreign service, he said he was gay and had engaged in homosexual liaisons in the Soviet Union, but denied he had given secrets to the KGB or favored the Soviet Union, either as ambassador or later as assistant undersecretary for external affairs in Ottawa. The interrogation of Watkins began in Paris, where he was living, and continued in London and Canada. It was winding down when on October 12, 1964, he died suddenly of a heart attack in his Montreal hotel room in the presence of his two RCMP interrogators. The CIA had little doubt, but no proof, that he had been compromised. For a detailed account of the Watkins case, see John Sawatsky, *For Services Rendered* (Ontario, Canada: Penguin, 1986), pp. 172–83.

Alsop, one of Washington's most influential syndicated columnists, was not only a friend of President Kennedy but of many other prominent political figures. Urbane and erudite, he was also an art collector, art historian, and author. Whether or not the Soviets thought they could bring pressure on him, their efforts could hardly have been a success—Alsop was a hard-line anti-Communist and severe critic of the Soviets in all of his writings.[15] He constantly warned that the Soviets were ahead of the United States militarily, and that Washington faced a "missile gap." He died in August 1989 at his Georgetown home at the age of seventy-eight.[16]

Nosenko also talked about the KGB's "litra" system, the use of certain chemicals in secret operations. "Nosenko said Soviet counterintelligence used litra to mark people's mail or their location," Kisevalter said. "An embassy employee is waiting for a light to cross the street. A nice old lady is standing next to him, also waiting to cross. She presses a button on a vial and a little stream of liquid hits his shoes. Later on, dogs—collies and shepherds—follow the man, they can pick up his trail."[17]

[15]It was not only the Kremlin that took notice of Alsop's sexual preference, whatever it might have been. The Eisenhower White House as well was interested in the columnist's private life. In December 1959, on the eve of Eisenhower's state visit to India, his press secretary, James C. Hagerty, took a colleague of Alsop's aside during a reception at the White House. Hagerty was enraged. "I'm taking Alsop off this trip," he told the correspondent. "Did you see that piece he wrote? I'm going to lift his White House pass. He's a damn fairy. The FBI knows about him."

[16]Friends of Alsop, even those who knew him for a long time, could shed little light on the subject. Tom Lambert, a foreign correspondent and colleague of Alsop's on the *New York Herald Tribune,* said he had heard the story about Alsop and the Russians. "I heard the Russians had the pictures, that they caught him with some young man," Lambert said. Lambert was covering the Korean War for the Associated Press when he first met Alsop, and although he knew the columnist well for some forty years, he had no idea whether Alsop was gay. "If he was, Joe certainly never spoke of it." Don Cook, the *Trib*'s correspondent in Paris for many years, said, "My own guess is he [Alsop] was really pretty asexual. He was so self-centered he just couldn't fit a relationship with a woman into his life. I don't know how active he was pursuing women, but he certainly didn't pursue men. And he was married for several years to Susan Mary Patten." But, Cook added, he didn't really know.

[17]As Kisevalter explained it, litra was a precursor of the "spy dust" that the KGB employed to track Western diplomats and journalists and their contacts. The disclosure by the United States in August 1985 that the Soviets were using the spy dust caused a furor at the time. The chemical, nitrophenylpentadienal (NPPD), was an invisible powder that the Soviets sprinkled on the steering wheels or doorknobs of American diplomats—presumably including CIA officers in the Moscow station—so

As the conversations with Nosenko in Geneva neared their end, the CIA men worked out a plan for future meetings. "He agreed to recontact," Kisevalter said. "He insisted that there be no recontact in the Soviet Union," where surveillance by his own KGB officers made such an attempt highly dangerous. "Five or six agents, Russians working for the CIA, had been lost as a result of recontact in the Soviet Union," Kisevalter said.

"Now we had to set up a commo plan for Nosenko. Before I left Geneva, I contacted the OS [Office of Security] and got some high-security addresses and cable routes in New York. The address we used was in Manhattan. A person who was an agency asset. With these commo plans, I made arrangements with Nosenko to recontact us from anywhere in the free world to the New York address by cable or mail." Nosenko was instructed to sign his message "Alex."

"Three days after he sent the cable, we'd meet at seven P.M. under the marquee of a movie house with a name that began with the highest [closest to the letter A] letter in the alphabet in the city the cable was sent from."[18]

And so they parted. "We gave Nosenko a bolt of cloth, for his wife to make a dress. We had done that before with other walk-ins. He said thank you for the medicine, and yes he had memorized the address in New York."

Kisevalter and Bagley were taking no chances on losing the record of Nosenko's debriefings. "We left Geneva on different planes," Kisevalter said. "One of us took the notes and one took the tapes."

Both Bagley and Kisevalter returned to Langley believing they had pulled off a major coup—a KGB officer was spilling secrets in profusion, and, rare among Soviet intelligence officers, had agreed to re-

that tiny traces would be left on the hands or clothing of Soviet citizens with whom they came in contact. U.S. government scientists analyzed and tested the substance for six months and concluded early in 1986 that in the levels used by the Soviets, the spy dust "does not pose a health hazard." The tests also found that luminol, a second tracking chemical used by the KGB, was not dangerous to humans.

[18]If Nosenko chose to recontact the CIA by letter or postcard, the procedure varied slightly, since there was no way to judge how long it would take for the mail to reach Manhattan. So if Nosenko recontacted by letter or card, he was instructed to date the letter several days later than the day on which he actually mailed it. The meeting would take place three days after the false date he wrote on the letter.

main as an agent-in-place of sorts. While he had ruled out any contact in Moscow, he had agreed to an eventual recontact with the CIA. While it is always vastly more desirable from Langley's viewpoint for an agent-in-place to continue to feed information from within the KGB, Nosenko met the CIA halfway; he would be back, which was preferable to what happened in the case of most walk-ins, such as Golitsin, who insisted on defecting to the West immediately. Defectors could be debriefed and milked for all they knew, but there came a time when they wound down and ran out of information. To the CIA, an agent-in-place, even one on a hold button like Nosenko, was a far better asset.

The two case officers were excited about the take: AEWIRELESS, the revelation that Boris Belitsky had been doubled against the agency and would not, after all, be singing "The Star-Spangled Banner" in the unusual manner suggested by his polygraph operator; the case of the handsome Armenian, and the grave danger that Kisevalter felt it posed for the Penkovsky operation; the microphones in the walls of the American embassy in Moscow; the penetration of British intelligence in Switzerland; the information that was to lead to the arrest of William John Vassall, the clerk in the British Admiralty; the new detail about the sexual compromise of Edward Ellis Smith, the CIA's first man in Moscow; the Soviet penetration of the CIA's efforts to turn the supposedly lovestruck KGB officer in Vienna; the KGB's rental cars and other tradecraft in Geneva; the litra system—the list was impressive.

Bagley was walking on air as he reported to James Angleton on his meetings in Geneva with Nosenko. Angleton greeted him with all the enthusiasm of a father whose small son had triumphantly dragged home a dead alley cat.

There was room in Angleton's pantheon of defectors for only one god. Anatoly Golitsin had predicted this; he had warned that other defectors or agents would be dispatched to deflect from his warnings of a mole in the CIA. To the counterintelligence chief, Nosenko had done just that by his explanation of Kovshuk's visit to Washington, and by his insistence that he knew of no Soviet agent code-named Sasha working for the CIA.

"When I came back I thought we had a genuine one," Bagley said. "I was enthusiastic about Nosenko. Angleton said, 'Before your next meeting I'd like you to see the file on another defector. Golitsin.' I read the file, and I came out and said, 'There's something wrong. I think we've got a bad one.' "

Later, it was said that Angleton had used all of his formidable powers of persuasion to influence Bagley and convert the younger man to his view. It did not happen in precisely that way, according to Bagley. "There was no Svengali," Bagley said. But it was Angleton who had turned him around? "No," Bagley replied. "The information turned me around."[19]

A hairline fault had opened within the CIA that in time was to become a cataclysmic earthquake. From that moment on, a faction within the CIA, led by Angleton, with Bagley at his side, was to hew to the unshakable conviction that Yuri Ivanovich Nosenko was a plant under KGB control. The "war of the defectors" had begun.

But in a real sense, the war was not about the conflict over the bona fides of Anatoly Golitsin and Yuri Nosenko, although that was the battleground on which it was so bitterly fought. The war was really about moles.

[19]As Bagley was later to testify to a House committee, "Alone, Nosenko looked good to me . . . seen alongside [Golitsin] whose reporting I had not seen before coming to headquarters after the 1962 meetings with Nosenko, Nosenko looked very odd indeed." *Investigation of the Assassination of President John F. Kennedy,* Hearings, Select Committee on Assassinations of the U.S. House of Representatives, March 1979, Vol. XII, p. 594.

Chapter 7

Closing In

■

Peter Karlow still had no idea yet that both the CIA and the FBI now suspected that he was Sasha, the elusive Soviet mole whose true name, according to Anatoly Golitsin, began with the letter K.

Karlow was reporting to work at the State Department each day as the CIA's representative in the operations center. By early in 1962, the entire, massive security apparatus of the United States government had targeted Karlow, who had become a goldfish in a bowl. The case was considered so important that J. Edgar Hoover, the FBI director, had been alerted, and CIA director John A. McCone was being kept fully informed of the progress of the highly secret investigation.

The first inkling Karlow had that something might be wrong had initially caused him only a vague sense of unease, as one might experience in the stillness before a summer storm. It had occurred, that tiny harbinger, late in 1962 when he was told to report to an unmarked CIA building at 1717 H Street in downtown Washington. There two FBI agents were waiting.

"They were two routine-looking dark suits," Karlow remembered. "White shirts, dark ties, brown hair. The two agents asked me about a German forger whom I'd worked with. He was an ethnic German who had grown up in Russia, but he had made his way through the lines to Germany during the war. They told me he wanted to defect to the Soviets. They said this particular guy, the old forger, who was living in Bethesda, had an aunt who was urging him to return to the

Soviet Union. I knew that was the last thing he would do. The forger was working as a private engraver in Washington—I had seen him from time to time. Ostensibly, they wanted me to assess the chances he would redefect. I told them there was no way he was going back. I knew this was a cock-and-bull story. He had nothing to gain by going back.

"I realized something was wrong, but I didn't know what. My reaction was, how could the two FBI agents be so far off the mark, and why me? Looking back on it, it was a pretext interview to have an excuse to meet me." The FBI agents wanted to get a closer look at the man they had been told might be a Soviet spy. But at the time, Karlow did not dwell on the incident. He wrote an "eyes-only" memo to Richard Helms, the DDP, reporting on his odd FBI interview, and put it out of mind.

A few weeks later, another small blip crossed Karlow's radar screen. Two other FBI agents showed up at Karlow's home on Klingle Street in Northwest Washington, where he lived with his wife, Libby. "They said there was a suspicious couple down the street who are German, but may be spies for a hostile country. Could they use my garage to set up listening equipment? The next morning my phone sounded tapped." Karlow, after all, was a technical expert for the CIA, and knew the signs. "There was a slow response on the dial tone, because the tap puts additional drain on the line. The phones were just not behaving right."[1]

By now, Karlow knew he was the target of some sort of investigation, but he was not overly worried. He still hoped that after his tour at the State Department ended Helms would appoint him head of the Technical Services Division. Perhaps the FBI visits were simply part of an unusually thorough security vetting for that sensitive post.

Even so, the weird encounters with the FBI were unnerving. Karlow was getting jumpy. He looked out the window one morning and saw a man working on a telephone pole outside his home. "I called the phone company and they said, 'There is no work order for your street.'"

Soon afterward, a fourth strange incident took place. "A company

---

[1] At the time, Karlow said, "my wife was chairman of a Smith College benefit in honor of Helen Hayes and the phone calls were pouring in. In retrospect, it amused me to think of all the conversations that the FBI had to monitor."

arrived to clean our furnace for free, courtesy of Washington Gas Light. I told them I'd just had it cleaned. They cleaned it anyway."

Backstage, inside the security apparatus, a hidden drama was unfolding. A number of factors had combined to make Karlow the prime suspect in the mole hunt almost immediately after Golitsin's arrival in Washington. There was, first, the document the Soviet defector had brought out; it suggested the KGB knew about the CIA's attempt to copy the Soviet bug that had been discovered inside the Great Seal in the American embassy in Moscow. And that in turn had led the sleuths to focus on Karlow, whose Technical Requirements Board was working on EASY CHAIR, the effort to develop the device. Since, in addition, Karlow's name began with the letter K, he had served in Germany, and his name at birth sounded Slavic—elements that seemed to fit Golitsin's profile of Sasha—the CIA's investigators were sure that the mole was within their grasp.

On January 9, 1962, only a little more than three weeks after Golitsin defected, Sheffield Edwards, the director of the CIA's Office of Security, decided that the Karlow case was of sufficient gravity that the FBI would have to be alerted and its help enlisted.[2] That would have been a natural enough decision by Edwards, since the security chief was widely considered to be Hoover's man inside the CIA. By January 15, government records show, "installation of [deleted] coverage on the Subject" was in place, a clear reference to the wiretaps on Karlow.[3]

Three days later "the FBI was formally advised of the agency concern that KARLOW could be identical to the [deleted]," an obvious reference to Sasha.[4]

On February 5, Sheffield Edwards met with Sam Papich, Hoover's liaison to the CIA, and briefed him and another FBI agent on the Karlow case. Ominously, Edwards told the FBI men that "certain meetings . . . had been held in the recreation room in the basement of

[2]CIA Memorandum for the Record, January 13, 1975. What happened inside the CIA and the FBI can be pieced together from heavily censored secret documents declassified and made available many years later by the CIA, and additional material obtained from the FBI under the Freedom of Information Act. This account draws in part on those materials.
[3]FBI Headquarters memorandum, January 15, 1962.
[4]CIA Memorandum for the Record, January 13, 1975.

the home of the Subject." The CIA security chief was right, although the irony escaped him; Karlow and his wife had hosted a German beer and wurst party in their basement to mark the tenth anniversary of the agency's Technical Aids Detachment that Karlow had set up in Germany on orders from Richard Helms. The guests were all present or former CIA technical people.

According to a CIA memorandum of Edwards's meeting with Papich, the FBI was informed that "Subject is still at the Operations Center, Department of State, but that plans are being made for a transfer of the Subject." The CIA, Edwards told Papich, "desired that the FBI conduct a full covert investigation of the subject." The CIA "would give any and all assistance possible."

There is always an inbuilt tension between the two agencies in cases of suspected espionage. The CIA, as an intelligence agency, wants to assess damage, and if possible, to make operational use of what it learns. The FBI, as an arm of the Justice Department, wants to put spies in prison. These two objectives conflict, a point that the CIA tried to finesse as it asked the FBI for help in the Karlow investigation. At the meeting, the FBI representatives noted that "the general aim of the FBI was, of course, prosecution if a criminal case can be established." The CIA, Edwards smoothly assured the FBI agents, had an "open view" in regard to criminal prosecution, although "the primary interest of this Agency, of course," was to determine whether Peter Karlow was a Soviet spy, "and if so what Agency information has been compromised by Subject."

Four days later, on February 9, "Mr. Papich advised that the matter had been brought to the attention of Mr. Hoover and a decision made that the FBI would investigate the Subject case in full."[5]

Not satisfied with the pace of the FBI probe, the agency urged that the bureau conduct a "pretext interview" of Karlow. J. Edgar Hoover did not at all like to be told how to run the FBI, especially by the CIA. On March 6, Hoover frostily advised McCone, the CIA director, that the FBI had decided to conduct a "discreet investigation" of Karlow's "background and present activities." Hoover added: ". . . accordingly, we do not intend to approach him for interview at this time." But

[5]The account of the February 5 CIA-FBI meeting and Hoover's agreement to conduct a full investigation of Karlow are from "CIA Memorandum to File, February 14, 1962." The signature on the document was blanked out by CIA censors, but it is almost certainly that of Sheffield Edwards, the director of the CIA's Office of Security.

during the course of the FBI investigation, Hoover added, "Karlow will be appropriately interviewed" and the CIA advised of the results.[6] Karlow was placed under heavy surveillance, his every move closely watched for one year.

When Karlow traveled to Philadelphia, carrying a large box, FBI agents trailed him, hoping this might be the big break in the case. He was seen entering a building and emerged three hours later without the box. To the watching FBI agents, Karlow's actions appeared sinister, the more so because they were unable to peer inside the building. The FBI surveillance report described the problem:

"Observation at 1127 South Broad by a special agent of the Federal Bureau of Investigation revealed that this was a three-story row brick structure. . . . It is noted that nothing can be observed within the business establishment inasmuch as Venetian blinds extend across the entire window in the front of the store and are kept tightly closed." If the FBI men thought that Karlow had delivered a box full of CIA secrets to a Soviet installation, they would have been disappointed to learn the truth. Karlow had gone to Philadelphia to be fitted for a new artificial limb to replace the one he was wearing. "It was my leg man," Karlow explained. "And the sign right on the front of the building said 'B. Peters & Company, Orthotics and Prosthetics.' " He paused, and added: "My leg was in the box."

There is a strong streak of nativism among many counterintelligence and security officials, a presumption that what is alien may well be traitorous, and at the very least, un-American. So when the CIA's Office of Security, the CI Staff, and the intelligence division of the FBI began digging into Karlow's background, they found enough alarming material to reinforce their natural xenophobia.

To begin with, Karlow's name at birth, and until he was sixteen, wasn't Karlow, it was Klibansky. Not only did his original name begin with the letter K, it was Slavic as well. It takes little imagination to picture how the same sleuths whose suspicions were aroused when a war hero carried his artificial leg in a box to Philadelphia would have reacted to the discovery of his family's Russian-sounding name. This was, after all, the era of J. Edgar Hoover.

And in fact, when Karlow was finally confronted by the FBI and

[6]Memorandum, Hoover to McCone, March 6, 1962.

interrogated, more than a year after the CIA had launched the secret investigation, the bureau's agents questioned him repeatedly about his father's background and nationality, and about the conflict over his father's birthplace in various documents that Karlow had filled out.

Sergei Klibansky was born on April 18, 1878, in Frankfurt, Germany. He was a singer and voice coach, and by age thirty was the youngest director of a major Berlin music conservatory. Karlow's mother, Ferida Weinert, came from an affluent family that owned a textile mill in Silesia. In 1910, Sergei and Ferida Klibansky came to New York, where Karlow's father had been offered a position as a singing instructor.

"They were adopted by a very fast social set," Karlow said, "patrons of the opera, people like George Washington Hill. Then the war broke out." The Klibanskys remained in the United States.

They became naturalized American citizens in 1921, the same year that their son, Serge Peter, was born. His father, although German, had sometimes claimed to have been born in Russia. "In World War I, it was better to be a Russian than a German," Karlow said. He speculated that his father, moving in a musical world, may also have thought it was better for his career to be a Russian. Whatever the reasons, Sergei Klibansky could not have divined that his minor rewriting of his past was, almost half a century later, to cause major difficulties for his son.[7]

Sergei's career prospered. "He taught stars at the Met, Geraldine Farrar and others," Karlow said. And in the roaring twenties, the Klibanskys lived a glittering life among the international set, plying the Atlantic first class on ocean liners and dividing their time between Berlin and an apartment on Manhattan's West Side. "My parents went back to Germany every year or two. By the time I was fourteen, I'd crossed the ocean fourteen times. I was in grade school in Berlin for a year, in the first grade."

It all came crashing down in the Depression. "My father had everything on ten percent margin," Karlow said. Early on the morning of

[7]When Karlow was born on March 5, 1921, his birth certificate listed his father's birthplace as Russia. But the following month, in April, his father correctly listed Germany as his country of birth on his naturalization papers. The FBI went to the trouble of confirming this by locating Sergei Klibansky's birth certificate in Frankfurt am Main.

September 17, 1931, while Karlow, his older sister, and his mother slept in the adjoining room of their apartment, his father went into the kitchen and turned on the gas oven. Within a few moments, at the age of fifty-three, he was dead.

Peter was graduated from McBurney Prep in 1937, the same year that the family legally changed its name to Karlow. He won a scholarship to Swarthmore, and when war came, joined the Navy and the OSS. In 1947, when the newly created CIA heeded Karlow's arguments for developing more sophisticated spy gadgetry, he joined the agency. He ran the Special Equipment Staff, tinkering with bugs and other espionage devices, until Richard Helms sent him to Germany in 1950 to set up his lab outside Frankfurt.

In 1952, while stationed in Germany, Karlow married Elizabeth "Libby" Rausch, who had joined the agency not long after she was graduated from Smith College, and had been sent to Höchst to work in Karlow's technical detachment. She later worked in counterintelligence in the Soviet division in Frankfurt and Munich, but left the agency around the time their first child was born in 1953. Karlow's mother also worked for the CIA for a time, in the Office of Training and later as a part-time language instructor in German and Italian.

Karlow returned to headquarters in 1956; his jobs in the Eastern European division and as deputy chief of the Economic Action Division followed. In 1959, he organized and became secretary of the Technical Requirements Board, the CIA unit that, among other projects, was attempting to copy the bug in the Great Seal. In the summer of 1961, Helms sent him to the operations center at State. Six months later, Golitsin defected, and Karlow, who had risen to senior positions in the CIA, was suddenly, and without his knowledge, suspected of being a Soviet spy and a traitor to his country. In the climate of the time, it seemed to matter not in the least that he had nearly died defending it.

In the summer of 1962, Karlow went to see Helms and asked out of the State Department. "I asked to be relieved because my career was going nowhere. The job I wanted was chief of the Technical Services Division. Helms didn't turn me down, but didn't offer the job either." To Karlow, Helms seemed to leave the door open. "But Helms said, 'In the meantime, clean up some things for me. Go back to the Economic Action Division.' " The CIA's deputy director for plans did not spell things out, but Karlow felt that Helms was tacitly suggesting that some of the unit's operations, if not the entire division, be phased out. It was a delicate mission, since Karlow had worked in the division several years earlier. Now he would be coming back to wield the ax for Helms. It was not a role likely to make him very popular with his former colleagues in the division.

When Karlow reported in to his old shop, he found himself confronted with a zany agency operation that might have come straight out of a novel by Evelyn Waugh. The target was the West African nation of Guinea. "A businessman from Brooklyn was being paid to buy a freighter and import products from Guinea, to show the Guineans the beauty of the free market," Karlow recalled. "He had managed to buy a shipload of bananas from Guinea. They were green with black spots. He was trying to sell them to Gerber, the baby-food company. Someone from Gerber didn't think they were just what they wanted. He ended up selling the shipload of bananas to Poland at a loss, which the agency paid for."

Not only did Gerber not want green bananas with spots for its baby food, there was a small fiscal problem as well. "There was one hundred thousand dollars unaccounted for in that Guinea trader operation. I recommended that the operation be closed down, which the people in the division thought I was doing out of malice. But I found there were already three major American companies established in Guinea. I questioned the premises of the operation."

By early fall, Karlow had wound up his work in the Economic Action Division and was marking time. "I was on ice. I had no reason for knowing I was under suspicion. I felt there was a lingering vendetta against me by the EAD people. So when my career started to go badly I thought maybe it was a result of this internal feud."

Still, when the strange visits from the FBI and the furnace cleaners began occurring, Karlow was briefly encouraged to think his fortunes were improving. They might be checking him out for the Technical Services Division job after all.

By Christmas, however, Karlow had received devastating news. He had been turned down for the position of chief of TSD. "I blew my fuse and went to see Helms," Karlow said. Having worked with Helms for years, Karlow decided he knew him well enough to call on the deputy director for plans at his home. On a Sunday evening early in the new year, Karlow drove to Helms's house on Fessenden Street, in Northwest Washington.

Confronting the DDP, Karlow demanded to know what was going on.

" 'Okay,' Helms said, 'you'll hear on Monday.' " Helms did not elaborate, but Karlow left that evening feeling that at least some sort of new assignment was in the offing. And sure enough, on Monday, Karlow got a call from Howard Osborn of the CIA's Office of Security. "Osborn said they'd cleared it with Helms that I should work on a sensitive security case." He would be doing the work, Karlow was told, in the Washington Field Office of the FBI in the Old Post Office Building on Pennsylvania Avenue.

"I called Helms, who was out of town. I reached Tom K., his deputy, who said yes, go ahead and do that."[8] What Karlow did not realize was that *he* was the sensitive security case.

On Monday, February 11, Karlow reported in to the FBI field office. Two agents, Aubrey S. "Pete" Brent and Maurice A. "Gook" Taylor, were waiting.

"They said to me, 'You have the right to remain silent.' "

The words struck like a thunderbolt.

Now Karlow knew that his worst suspicions were true. The man on the pole, the pretext interview about the German forger, the furnace cleaners, the slow dial tone on his telephone—everything he had tried not to face was now a reality.

For Karlow, a veteran of American intelligence for twenty-one years, the moment was surreal. Like a character in a Kafka novel, he groped to find out what he was being accused of and why. The FBI agents would not tell him.

"What is this about?" Karlow demanded. Silence. That, the agents said, would emerge in their meetings. Karlow asked if he was entitled to counsel. And if so, how could a lawyer who was not in the CIA be cleared?

Karlow asked the agents to let him make a telephone call to Lawrence R. Houston, the agency's general counsel, who was also a close

[8]Thomas H. Karamessines, then the CIA's assistant deputy director for plans, was universally known inside the agency as Tom K.

friend. He reached the CIA attorney. "I asked him, 'Who shall I get as a lawyer? Can you assign me one of your people?' He couldn't. He advised me to answer the questions, and if I couldn't to say nothing and call him back. Larry was in a double position—he was a friend, and he was the agency's counsel."

So, without benefit of a lawyer, Karlow's interrogation began. It was to last five days.

Karlow again asked the agents to explain the subject of the interrogation. Was it about him? If so, he would be glad to help in any way. He had nothing on his conscience. But the agents would not reveal their purpose.

In the classic "good cop, bad cop" ploy, one agent was friendly, the other hostile. The atmosphere in the room grew tense. "You're playing games and wasting time," Karlow snapped at one point. If there was something wrong, something that had been misinterpreted in his background, he was anxious to get it cleared up.

Stone-faced, the agents told Karlow to come back the next day. On Tuesday, Karlow said, the interrogation went this way:

FBI: What is your name?
PK: Serge Peter Karlow.
FBI: Is that how it was always spelled?
PK: You mean, on my birth certificate, it's Sergei.
FBI: That's two different names.
PK: No, it's the same name. In Germany, for example, it would be spelled Sergei. In France, Serge.

The FBI men questioned Karlow in endless detail about members of his family, every place he had lived, every school he had attended, every job he had held. Karlow pointed out that all of this information was on the record; since he had worked for OSS and the CIA for more than two decades, with frequent review for security clearances, it was all in the files.

We want to get it all straight, the FBI agents replied. And on they went for hours, examining Karlow's entire life in microscopic detail. "I asked again and again what the purpose was, we could save time if they stopped playing games. No reaction."

On Wednesday, it was back to his family. What were the names of his father's parents? If his grandfather's name was Michael, why had he sometimes listed it as Misha? Karlow explained the names were the same, it was like John and Jack.

The FBI agents pounced again.

FBI: What was your grandmother's maiden name?
PK: Von.
FBI: No, it was Vou.

Karlow was incredulous. "I laughed when I realized what had happened. They'd found my father's birth certificate in Frankfurt and couldn't read Gothic. In the zigzag, handwritten old German, which was dropped between the wars, the letter 'u' has a line over it. Without a line, it's an 'n.' There was no line over the 'u' but the FBI couldn't read it."

More detailed questions about schools, and political groups Karlow had joined at Swarthmore. Then back to his father. Was he born in Germany, or Russia?

The agents began questioning Karlow about people he had known over a lifetime, every name he had listed on the Personal History Statement he had filled out when he joined the CIA, every name he had mentioned in agency memos, former CIA employees, even that of Richard Helms. "They went alphabetically through everyone I knew. Friends, colleagues, relatives, and for each they asked, 'Was he a homosexual?' 'Did you know Jones? Was he a homosexual? Did he make any advances to you? Is Helms a Communist?' I said, 'I'm not going to answer that, it's too ridiculous.' "

On Thursday, the FBI men began interrogating Karlow in detail about CIA operations to penetrate the Soviet Union. "They were particularly interested in my knowledge of bugging devices."

The agents pressed Karlow on the code name for the CIA project to replicate the bug in the Great Seal. Karlow refused to yield up the name EASY CHAIR. "The FBI asked if I gave the Soviets any information on American knowledge of this gadget. My answer was no. The total of my information was that R&D work was continuing and involved a technician in Holland."

At CIA, Karlow had also worked on the development of "a non-detectable car bug that could be quickly planted. The idea was to take a tiny unit and plant it behind the dash of a car. It would allow you to follow the car and listen to conversation at a discreet distance. It would be powered by self-contained batteries." In the course of his research, Karlow had visited an electronics laboratory at Montauk, on the tip end of Long Island, that was conducting similar research for the FBI. As a result, Karlow was also aware of the bureau's own efforts to eavesdrop on cars.

Now Karlow's interrogators turned to that subject. "They asked me about the bugging of automobiles that were supposed to have been delivered to the Soviets in Mexico City. I knew about it."

It had been a joint operation. "The FBI and the CIA had bugged four Fords which were to be delivered to the Soviet embassy in Mexico City in 1959. To install the bugs, the FBI stripped the cars down to the chassis, so the bugs were theoretically not findable, yet the Soviets knew right away. So the FBI pointed the finger at me. The FBI said, 'You were the guy who leaked that information to the Soviets.' It was nonsense, of course."

The FBI seemed fully aware of the operation involving the Brooklyn businessman who had tried to off-load the CIA's spotted bananas on the Gerber baby-food company. "They insisted on knowing the name of the agent—the businessman—and the extent of the money unaccounted for, which was over a hundred thousand dollars."

The FBI agents pressed Karlow repeatedly on how many times he had been to East Berlin. Karlow thought two or three times, at most, and always on CIA orders.

The agents appeared convinced that the CIA harbored homosexuals. They kept coming back to that subject. "The FBI asked about why there were so many 'queers' in the CIA's German stations in the early 1950s."

Next, the agents grilled Karlow about secret inks. When Karlow was in Germany, headquarters had asked for secret writing inks for use in Eastern Europe and sent along two samples. "We had them analyzed and found one was aspirin and one was vinegar. Both can be used. We ran an investigation and found that the best stuff around for secret writing was being used by the Russians. I said we needed something better than aspirin. We came up with secret writing formulas in Germany."

The FBI wanted to know about Karlow's formulas. Why had he developed the new inks?

"They seemed to be trying to put an interpretation on it that I was

coming up with secret writing methods that were better than anything
Washington had but that I was also giving them away to the Russians."

Karlow was told to come back on Friday. He was to be "flut-
tered"—given a lie-detector test.

On Friday morning, facing the polygraph, Karlow again demanded
an explanation.

> PK: Now will you tell me what this is about?
> FBI: Yes, we will. You're under direct suspicion of being a Soviet spy,
>   a Soviet agent working in the CIA.

"I couldn't believe it. I laughed and said, I thought I had done
something serious, like leaving a safe open." But Karlow's bravado
masked a terrible realization. "I knew right there my career was over.
'This ends my career,' I told them. 'If you want my badge, you're
welcome.' "

Stunned by the accusation, outraged and angry, stricken by what it
meant to his future, Karlow pressed the FBI agents for details. "What
was I supposed to have done and where? The FBI said, 'We ask the
questions—you'll have plenty of time to find out.' "

Karlow was wired to the polygraph machine. The operator
strapped a corrugated rubber tube around his chest, a pneumograph
that would expand and contract to measure his respiration rate. An
inflatable pressure cuff, called a cardiosphygmomanometer, was
wound around Karlow's arm, to record his blood pressure and pulse.
Finally, the most scary object of all, a pair of metal electrodes were
attached to his palm with surgical tape. The device, a psychogalva-
nometer, would measure Karlow's galvanic skin response (GSR) to
electric current. The reading would vary with how much he perspired
as he was questioned. All of these instruments were hooked up to a
recording device that would measure his responses as squiggly lines on
a roll of moving graph paper.

"The polygraph cuff was making my arm turn blue. They kept
pushing on how many times I had been in East Berlin. Was my Soviet
case officer so-and-so? It was a woman's name, I'm not sure of what
name it was, I think they said Lydia." From the line of questioning,
it appeared that the FBI believed that Karlow had met with "Lydia"

in East Berlin. "They asked about addresses in East Berlin. They wanted to see my reaction, did I know those addresses. I said no to all of them."

The most dramatic moment of the lie-detector test was now at hand.

"You are supposed to answer questions yes or no," Karlow explained. "They asked, 'Do you know Sasha?' I said yes, and the needle jumped. Because I was thinking of Sasha Sogolow. In Berlin in the 1950s, Sasha to me was only one person—Sasha Sogolow. A big booming Russian type. He'd always say, 'I'm Russian and a Jew and they [the Soviets] love me.' He'd go with a case officer to meet an agent. He'd be the 'chauffeur.' And he'd come back and say, 'The KGB chauffeur was Colonel so-and-so.' I would meet with Sasha Sogolow often. He was in Berlin. We fixed him up with a fake driver's license.'"⁹

Karlow could see the flurry of excitement among the FBI agents when he reacted to the name Sasha. He was not sure why. "I was thinking of Sasha Sogolow. But that wasn't the Sasha they were thinking of," as Karlow later learned.

"They never asked any motivational questions. I finally said, 'Why would I want to be a Soviet spy? I've got a great wife, two gorgeous children, and a good job.' " The FBI agents did not answer his question.

It was Friday afternoon before the polygraph test was over. Karlow had been grilled for five days.

"Afterward, I went tearing over to Houston's house in George-town. 'What's going on?' Larry said, 'Well, it's a difficult case.' " The CIA general counsel, Karlow said, asked him to "write a report of everything you can think of" that might have caused his security problem.

"Monday, I went steaming into Helms's office. He greeted me, as usual, as 'Sergeyevich.' Helms always called me Sergeyevich [son of Sergei]. This time I said maybe the humor of the nickname is no longer appropriate under the circumstances."

Helms, too, asked Karlow to write a report "of everything I could think of." Having been accused as a Soviet spy, and a traitor to his country, Karlow was now being asked by the agency's senior officials

⁹Sogolow, who was born in Kiev, joined the CIA in 1949 and served as a CIA case officer in Germany and in the Soviet division at headquarters. He died in 1982.

to provide the reasons, a twist that, again, could have been crafted by Kafka.

"Helms said, 'Consider yourself under Larry Houston's authority.' I said, 'Well, this means the end of my career. So this is goodbye.' But I told Helms, 'I'm going to do everything I can to get this cleared up.' "

Karlow had one more stop on his rounds. He went down to the second floor, to the Counterintelligence Staff, and called on James Angleton.

Angleton, chain-smoking as usual, sitting stooped over his desk, had a warning for Karlow. He spoke deliberately.

"This is a very uncertain and highly dangerous situation," he said. "There is more that goes on here than I can possibly explain to you. It has to do with a Russian defector."

Angleton leaned forward and added: "Please don't discuss this with anyone."

It was dizzying. Not only had Karlow been accused of high treason, and then asked to explain why, he was now being ordered to remain silent. The counterintelligence chief had made it clear: the fact that Karlow had been accused as a mole, his career destroyed, and his life all but ruined was a CIA secret.

Chapter 8

Roadshow

By the fall of 1962, Anatoly Golitsin had worn out a succession of case officers in the Soviet division; it was one reason he was turned over to James Angleton.

"The division got tired of him," said Scotty Miler, Angleton's former deputy, in explaining the decision. According to another former CIA officer, the feeling was mutual. "Golitsin was furious at the Soviet division. They were pushing him hard. He'd run out of gas and they kept pushing him."

As Pete Bagley, the former Soviet division counterintelligence officer, noted, yet another reason for the switch was the nature of what Golitsin was saying; there were moles not only in the CIA, the Soviet defector charged, but in other Western services as well. And it was the CI Staff that had responsibility for liaison with those foreign services.

Since Golitsin alleged that British intelligence had been penetrated, Angleton some months earlier had invited Arthur Martin, a senior MI5 counterintelligence officer, to visit Washington and interview the former KGB man. Martin was not only impressed with Golitsin, he eventually persuaded him to come to England.

According to a veteran CIA officer who had served in London, "The real romance began in England. The man who started it all was Arthur Martin. He became infatuated with Golitsin's ideas. Arthur took the entire family over to England—Golitsin, his wife, and daughter. He said to Angleton, 'I guarantee this man's security.'" Angleton may not have bargained for Golitsin's departure, but it would have been awkward to say no, given the long-standing, if sometimes strained, "special relationship" between U.S. and British intelligence. And Angleton did not want to cross Golitsin; if he stood in Golitsin's way, he might risk losing him for good.

In Britain, Golitsin acquired his British code name, KAGO. He was handled by Martin; Peter Wright, later to achieve worldwide fame by selling MI5's secrets in his book *Spycatcher;* and Stephen de Mowbray, an MI6 officer. Golitsin arrived in England in March 1963, shortly after Harold Wilson had become the leader of the opposition Labor Party.

It was a time of enormous political upheaval in England, and spies were at the root of the trouble. In January, Kim Philby had confessed in Beirut to being a Soviet agent, and then fled to Moscow, providing dramatic public confirmation of what the British government had consistently denied—that he was a Soviet mole in MI6. The government of Prime Minister Harold Macmillan was reeling from the Profumo scandal, in which it was revealed that Christine Keeler, a call girl, had shared her favors with John D. Profumo, the secretary of state for war (who was married to actress Valerie Hobson), and with Captain Eugene Ivanov, the assistant Soviet naval attaché, who was in reality an agent of the GRU. It mattered not that Profumo would hardly have been interested in discussing military secrets in bed with Keeler, who in turn would supposedly whisper them to Ivanov. It was a marvelous scandal, involving a naked swimming party at Cliveden, Lord Astor's estate (where Profumo first glimpsed Keeler *au naturel*), "society doctor Stephen Ward," another call girl named Mandy Rice-Davies, and, of course, the cabinet minister and the spy. Fleet Street fulfilled to the maximum its solemn obligation to keep the British public informed; the London newspapers overlooked no detail of the Profumo scandal.

But all of this threatened to be topped when Anatoly Golitsin blew into town. With the encouragement of his British counterintelligence handlers, he concluded that Harold Wilson was a Soviet mole.

Scotty Miler confirmed that Golitsin had dropped this bombshell after arriving in Britain. "Golitsin would not tell us what he told the British. But yes, that was what Golitsin said, that Wilson was a Soviet agent."

Golitsin appears to have reached this startling conclusion about the leader of the British opposition party by a chain of reasoning that was, to say the least, indirect. Shortly before Golitsin's arrival in England, Hugh Gaitskell, then the head of the Labor Party, had died prematurely. Some six weeks earlier, Gaitskell had called on the Soviet embassy in London about a visa for a pending trip to the Soviet Union. He was offered, and drank, a cup of coffee.

Peter Wright has said that Arthur Martin told him Gaitskell had died of a mysterious virus diagnosed as lupus, a tropical disease rare in temperate climes. Wright said that he went to Porton Down, Britain's chemical and biological warfare laboratory, to investigate whether the KGB might have poisoned the British political leader. He also consulted with Angleton, who sent him a translation of an obscure Soviet scientific paper which reported that the Russians had developed a chemical to induce lupus in experimental rats. But Wright concluded that Gaitskell, not being a laboratory rat, would have had to have ingested an enormous quantity of the chemical to have contracted the disease, unless, of course, the Soviets had developed a more powerful drug since the publication of the Soviet paper seven years earlier.[1]

When Golitsin learned of the suspicions in MI5 over Gaitskell's death, he put it together with gossip he said he had heard inside the KGB before he defected, rumors that the KGB's Department 13, its gruesomely named Department of Wet Affairs, was planning to assassinate a Western leader in order to get its own agent in place as his successor. Wilson had been elected Labor's leader on February 14, less than a month after Gaitskell's death. To Golitsin, it was all clear.

The British had very likely implanted the idea of Wilson's treachery with Golitsin, according to another former CIA officer. "I think the British tried out a lot of ideas on him. 'Would you think it possible Wilson was a spy?' they asked, and they linked it to the Gaitskell business. Golitsin when he came to us was a very ignorant man, but

---

[1]Peter Wright, *Spycatcher,* pp. 362–63. Other published accounts say that a postmortem examination of Gaitskell showed he was not a victim of lupus, the full name of which is lupus erythematosus, but of "an immune complex deficiency," the symptoms of which had begun a year before his death on January 18, 1963, and many months before he drank the celebrated cup of coffee at the Soviet embassy. See David Leigh, *The Wilson Plot: How the Spycatchers and Their American Allies Tried to Overthrow the British Government* (New York: Pantheon, 1988), pp. 82–83.

he learned. He sucked things up. He would say, 'That's very likely.' 'I think I heard something about this.' He picked up these ideas and embroidered them."

Golitsin's speculations were to have repercussions in England for more than a decade. Harold Wilson was elected Prime Minister in 196 ₹, and some time afterward, according to Peter Wright, Angleton made a special trip to London to see Edward Martin Furnival Jones, MI5's counterespionage chief, to warn him that "Wilson was a Soviet agent."[2] Angleton would not name his source, but the allegation was filed by MI5 under the code name OATSHEAF. Wilson was defeated in 1970 but reelected to a second term as Prime Minister early in 1974. It was then, according to Wright, that unnamed colleagues in MI5 tried to enlist him in a plot to leak information from the files of the security service to the press in order to oust Wilson from office. Wright said he refused to participate in the attempted coup against the Prime Minister.

That may be, but it is clear that MI5 extensively investigated both Wilson and his associates. Beginning in 1953, Wilson had made several trips to the Soviet Union, representing various British business interests. These visits had not escaped the notice of British intelligence.

According to Don Moore, who headed Soviet counterintelligence for the FBI at the time, "Golitsin's theory was anyone who spent a lot of time in the Soviet Union had to have been recruited. Wilson spent time in the Soviet Union. But you must differentiate between Golitsin's theories and what he knew. What he knew was solid and useful. His theories were something else."

MI5 investigated two of Wilson's political supporters, Rudy Sternberg and Joe Kagan, both Jews of Central European origin who had come to England and made their fortunes. Sternberg, an Austrian by birth, imported fertilizer and other products from East Germany. Kagan, a Lithuanian, was a raincoat manufacturer from Huddersfield whom MI5 suspected of leaking secrets he had gleaned from Wilson to a Soviet intelligence officer in London. After only eighteen months in office during his second term, Wilson suddenly resigned in March 1976. His decision, according to the British journalist David Leigh, came after a "blazing confrontation" with Sir Michael "Jumbo" Han-

---

[2]Peter Wright, *Spycatcher,* p. 364.

ley, the head of MI5, in which Wilson correctly accused the security service of plotting against him.[3]

Did MI5, spurred by Golitsin and Angleton, ultimately succeed in driving a British Prime Minister from power? The picture is fuzzy, but enough evidence has emerged to suggest that something very much like that may have happened. The story gained enough currency that, thinly disguised, it was even turned into a television drama.[4]

But quite aside from the Wilson plot, Golitsin's trip to England in the spring of 1963 was even more memorable for helping to trigger Britain's own mole hunt, which became much more highly publicized than the CIA's search for traitors, although it was ultimately to prove as inconclusive.

The first tallyho in the British mole hunt had sounded earlier in the year after Philby's dramatic escape to Moscow. On a trip to Washington in January 1963, not long before Golitsin's departure for England, Arthur Martin met with the FBI's Don Moore and Anthony Litrento, a street-smart agent who was the bureau's leading expert on Soviet illegals. Martin announced portentously that he had just received word that Philby had confessed in Beirut.

Moore recalled Litrento's reaction. " 'Do you have him in custody?' Tony asked. 'I don't know,' said Martin. 'If you don't, he'll be gone tomorrow,' said Litrento. And by God he was."

In the wake of the Philby disaster, Golitsin told the British that he had heard talk in the KGB of a "Ring of Five," a group of Soviet spies inside British intelligence. The first four members of that notorious group were easy enough to identify. All had gone to Cambridge University, where they were presumably recruited. Guy Burgess and Donald Maclean had fled to Moscow in 1951, Kim Philby had followed suit early in 1963, and Anthony Blunt, a former MI5 officer, was already under suspicion as the fourth man.[5] But who was the fifth man?

---

[3]David Leigh, *The Wilson Plot,* p. 234.

[4]In 1988, American public television broadcast a British TV play starring the late Ray McAnally as Harry Perkins, a blue-collar Yorkshireman who becomes Prime Minister of England and the target of schemers in the security service who plot to overthrow him. The play, *A Very British Coup,* was, of course, fictional, but it was obviously modeled on MI5's efforts against Harold Wilson.

[5]Blunt, an art expert and curator of the Queen's paintings, confessed in 1964, in exchange for immunity from prosecution, but had been suspected and questioned by MI5 for many years before that. Prime Minister Margaret Thatcher confirmed Blunt's

Arthur Martin and Peter Wright were convinced at first that the mole was Graham Mitchell, the deputy director of MI5. Later, the two counterintelligence officers decided the mole was none other than Sir Roger Hollis, the director-general of MI5.

The former CIA officer who served in the London station had no doubt of Golitsin's key role in all this. "The British mole hunt was a direct result of Golitsin," he said. "Golitsin said there was a mole at a high level in British intelligence. Graham Mitchell was the first person Golitsin fingered."

MI5 secretly installed a closed-circuit television camera and wiretaps in Mitchell's office and observed him for weeks. As a suspect, he was given the code name PETERS. During the investigation, Arthur Martin, the British equivalent of Angleton, flew to Washington to coordinate MI5's mole hunt with the FBI and the CIA.

"Arthur came over," said a former high-ranking U.S. intelligence official who met with Martin. "It was very hush-hush. He would only talk one-on-one. At the time they were analyzing Graham Mitchell. Mitchell was under surveillance and would sometimes sit with his head on his desk. Arthur thought that meant he was a spy, sitting and thinking, 'Oh my God, they know about me.' For chrissake, the guy was just taking a nap after lunch!"

Mitchell, fifty-seven when he became the target of his own security service, was an upper-class Englishman, educated at Winchester and Oxford, who limped from an encounter with polio but was a superb yachtsman and chess champion. He had worked closely with Hollis in MI5 during the war, and when Hollis became the director in 1956, Mitchell was appointed as his deputy.

After fifteen months, the mole hunters had come up empty-handed. Mitchell retired, and his case was closed, for the moment. But the problem remained; was there a mole in the house? If not Graham Mitchell, might it be the director himself?

To investigate these sensational suspicions, a joint MI5-MI6 unit, the oddly named FLUENCY committee, was created, with Arthur Martin as its chairman.[6] Its members toiled in secrecy for five years but

---

identity, and his espionage for the Soviets, in a statement to Parliament in November 1979. Blunt was stripped of his knighthood and died in 1983 at the age of seventy-five.
[6]Intelligence code names, like tropical storms, are usually chosen in order from a

failed to prove that their own boss, Roger Hollis, or his former deputy, Graham Mitchell, was a Soviet spy.

Hollis, who was a month younger than Mitchell, was the son of the bishop of Taunton, and also Oxford-educated. In his youth, he had spent several years working for a tobacco company in China in the 1930s before joining MI5, a fact that gave the mole seekers endless grounds for speculation and suspicion. Shanghai was known to be a nest of Communist spies between the wars. Perhaps Hollis had been recruited in China by the Soviets. Perhaps, like Philby, he was a long-term Soviet penetration agent in British intelligence. But none of this could be proven.

In 1965, Hollis retired, but the investigation only intensified. He was given the code name DRAT, which may have unintentionally reflected the frustration of the mole hunters over their inability to prove their case.

It never seemed to end. Mitchell was hauled out of retirement, interrogated, and cleared again. In 1970, MI5 renamed its counterespionage arm K Branch, and the mole hunters were placed in a new section designated K7. That same year, Hollis was brought back for interrogation at a safe house in London as Peter Wright, in another building, listened in on headphones.

Both the CIA and the FBI were informed of the progress of the British mole hunt. "We were kept reasonably well privy to what they were finding," the CIA's Scotty Miler said, "because it had a direct bearing on the security of U.S. intelligence. We were aware the British investigations were going on. Angleton worked with [Maurice] Oldfield, Wright, Hanley, Dick White, whoever was in charge."

The difficulty was, MI5 wasn't finding very much. Sir Roger Hollis died of a stroke in 1973, along with his secret, if he had one. In 1981, when the fact of the Hollis investigation became public, Prime Minister Margaret Thatcher made a statement in Parliament gingerly clearing Hollis.[7] Graham Mitchell died in 1984, by which time his private ordeal as PETERS had also become public knowledge.

---

prepared list. As a rule, therefore, they have no particular relevance to their subject matter.

[7]While the investigation "did not conclusively prove his innocence," Mrs. Thatcher said, leaving herself an escape hatch, ". . . no evidence was found that incriminated him, and the conclusion reached . . . was that he had not been an agent of the Russian intelligence service." Statement to Parliament by the Prime Minister, March 26, 1981.

If no fifth man could be positively identified, some of the mole hunters had nevertheless believed that he was John Cairncross, a former MI6 officer who had confessed years earlier to having been a Soviet agent during World War II. Cairncross was allowed to resign and not prosecuted. But it was an unrepentant Anthony Blunt who had named Cairncross to MI5 interrogators, and there was doubt that Blunt would have revealed the name of a high-level spy. Moreover, Cairncross left the government after he fell under suspicion in 1951. In 1990, he denied that he was the so-called Fifth Man, but a year later he said that he was.[8]

The Soviet defector Oleg Gordievsky, who had been named the KGB resident in London, added a postscript to the British mole hunt in 1990. He reported that two of the KGB's senior British specialists—who were presumably in a position to know the identity of their agents in England—had dismissed the reports about Hollis as untrue.[9]

Anatoly Golitsin had succeeded in turning British intelligence upside down, and in the process helped to create a cottage industry of mole hunters in England, whose books have been published, and

[8]Most of the details of Britain's long-running mole hunt have surfaced because of the work of British journalists, academics, and authors. The suspicion of Hollis was first publicized by Chapman Pincher, a leading British journalist specializing in intelligence, in his book *Their Trade Is Treachery* (London: Sidgwick & Jackson, 1981), and a later work, *Too Secret Too Long* (New York: St. Martin's Press, 1984). As it later emerged, Pincher's source was the former MI5 mole hunter Peter Wright, who had been introduced to Pincher by Victor Rothschild, of the banking family, also a former MI5 officer. Then Wright himself wrote about the search for penetrations, as well as other matters, in *Spycatcher*. Anthony Blunt was identified by Mrs. Thatcher only after the publication of Andrew Boyle's book *Climate of Treason,* published in the United States as *The Fourth Man* (New York: Dial, 1979), which pointed to Blunt without naming him. Blunt's career was chronicled in depth in John Costello's *Mask of Treachery* (New York: William Morrow, 1988), which nominated Guy Liddell, a former deputy director of MI5, as the unknown Soviet mole. Rupert Allason, a Conservative member of Parliament who writes under the name Nigel West, is the author of several informative books dealing with the period, including *Molehunt: Searching for Spies in MI5* (New York: William Morrow, 1989). British historian Christopher Andrew and the Soviet defector Oleg Gordievsky kept the controversy going by naming Cairncross as the Fifth Man in their book *KGB: The Inside Story* (New York: HarperCollins, 1990). Cairncross, then seventy-six and retired in France, denied it. "I am not the Fifth Man," he said (*Washington Post,* October 18, 1990, p. A38). But in 1991, Cairncross reversed himself. "I was made one of the five during the war," *The Mail* quoted him as saying. "I hope this will finally put an end to the 'Fifth Man' mystery." (*New York Times,* September 23, 1991, p. A8.)
[9]Andrew and Gordievsky, *KGB,* pp. 7–8.

eagerly read, on both sides of the Atlantic. If he was a boon to publishers, he was, in the end, less valuable to British intelligence.

But a major reason that Golitsin's charges could not simply be ignored was the awful truth of the Philby case. Philby had, after all, at one time been head of the Soviet section of MI6. That being so, it was surreal, but not impossible, to believe that even the head of MI5 could have been a traitor.

Although Golitsin is sometimes credited with providing leads that confirmed Kim Philby's role as a high-level Soviet mole, Philby had fled to Moscow weeks before Golitsin's arrival in London. Golitsin, it is true, had warned CIA in 1962 of moles in the British intelligence services, but by that time, Philby had already been under suspicion for more than a decade. As a result, Golitsin's contribution to the Philby case, if any, remains marginal at best.

But whatever high drama surrounded Golitsin's sojourn to England took an unexpectedly farcical turn in July 1963. It began when the London *Daily Telegraph* learned of the presence in England of an important Soviet defector. John Bulloch, a reporter for the newspaper, attempted to check the story with the government, thereby alerting British officials. Next, a "D notice" was issued on the evening of July 11 requesting that the press refrain from mentioning the defection.

A peculiarly British institution, the D notice system has no equivalent in the United States. Under it, the Defence, Press and Broadcasting Committee, a joint government-press group, issues advisory warnings to the British press that news about certain kinds of information—military secrets, intelligence, codes, and communications intercepts, for example—may be protected under Britain's Official Secrets Act. The notice, therefore, can be disregarded at the risk of breaking the law.[10]

What was unusual about the D notice issued in this instance, how-

[10]As the system worked in 1991, eight standing D notices dealing with broad categories of defense and intelligence information had been issued to the British news media and were kept in a "black folder" by each news organization. In the past, D notices were frequently issued to try to prevent the publication of specific stories. Although that can still be done, no specific D notice had been issued in more than ten years. British journalists and writers often consulted the secretary of the committee, Rear Admiral William A. Higgins, about whether a contemplated article or book might violate the law. So, while the system had evolved and changed, the D notice machinery remained very much in place.

ever, was that it named the defector—or purported to—thereby alerting all of Fleet Street to the story. But the notice, in what appeared to be a half-baked attempt at throwing the hounds off the scent, gave the defector's name as "Anatoli Dolnytsin."

On Friday, Tom Lambert, the *New York Herald Tribune* correspondent in London, learned the name, now circulating among British reporters. When the newspaper's Washington bureau sought to check further, the CIA urgently requested that the story be killed. It was too late to stop the flood tide. In London, John Bulloch and his editors decided to go with the story, despite the D notice, and published it on July 13, using the defector's altered name as it had been given in the notice.[11] The other London papers wrote the story as well, and the wire services spread it around the globe.

In Washington, CIA officials were thunderstruck by the British leak. They angrily accused the British of deliberately floating the story by means of the D notice in order to divert attention from the Profumo sex scandal. Dismayed and angered by the uproar in London, Golitsin packed his bags and took the first available flight back to Washington. British security officials immediately suspected that the original leak to the *Daily Telegraph* had been "put out by the Americans" to force Golitsin back to Langley.[12]

The entire episode did nothing to strengthen relations between MI5 and the CIA. But the upshot was that James Angleton had his prize defector back in his hands.

Before Golitsin captivated Arthur Martin and helped to launch the mole hunt in England, he had warned his CIA handlers of penetra-

[11]The British intelligence services, as part of their apparent attempt to sow confusion, may have chosen the name Anatoli Dolnytsin not only thinly to mask Anatoly Golitsin's true identity but in the hope that the press would assume the defector was Anatoly A. Dolnytsin, who had been stationed in the Soviet embassy in London for three years until September 1961. The *Daily Telegraph* reported that this Dolnytsin might be the defector, which seemed logical until a Soviet embassy spokesman announced two days later that the staff member in question was a protocol clerk who had not defected and was, at that very moment, back in Moscow at his desk in the foreign ministry. Embarrassed British intelligence officials later put it about that an error had led to the release of the false name, Dolnytsin, in place of the defector's true name. The explanation was implausible, since the real Anatoly Dolnytsin had not defected.

[12]Gordon Brook-Shepherd, *The Storm Birds: Soviet Post-War Defectors* (London: Weidenfeld & Nicolson, 1988), p. 172.

tions inside French intelligence as well. The French security services were a fertile ground for his charges. The word "byzantine" does not do justice to the complex and checkered history of the French spy agencies.

French intelligence had a reputation for dirty tricks and even criminal activity long before the French secret service blew up the *Rainbow Warrior,* a Greenpeace ship, in New Zealand in 1985, killing a photographer. The ship, which had planned to protest French nuclear tests at a South Pacific atoll, was sunk by the French external service, the Direction Générale de la Sécurité Extérieure (DGSE). The service acquired that name under President François Mitterrand, but it had been known before that as the Service de Documentation Extérieure et de Contre-espionnage (SDECE). Most French people know it better as "la Piscine," or the swimming pool, the nickname for its headquarters in northeast Paris.[13]

To American intelligence officials, the SDECE was known in short-hand as "S-deck." The French spy agency was involved in the 1950s and 1960s in a series of murders in Algeria of supporters of the independence movement. The agents recruited by French intelligence officers around the world were traditionally known as "honorable correspondents," but many were anything but honorable, including gangsters, ex-convicts, and mercenaries among their ranks. One unit of the SDECE, the Service Action, functioned as a hit squad.

The Direction de la Surveillance du Territoire (DST) is responsible for internal security and counterintelligence, and is roughly equivalent to the FBI. Its headquarters, too, are in Paris, at 7 Rue Nelaton not far from the Eiffel Tower.

Golitsin warned that Soviet moles had burrowed into the French secret service and the French government, possibly even into the cabinet of President Charles de Gaulle. The warning was taken seriously enough that President Kennedy sent a letter to de Gaulle to alert him to the charges. De Gaulle dispatched General Jean-Louis de Rougemont, of the Deuxième Bureaux, the French military intelli-

[13]The DGSE headquarters is located.in a ten-story office building with a checkerboard exterior at 141 Boulevard Mortier, part of the complex formed by the old Tourelles military barracks. The headquarters is just to the south of the Georges Vallerey public swimming pool—named for France's 100-meter 1948 Olympic swimming champion—which is on the Avenue Gambetta where it intersects the Rue des Tourelles. The spy agency's location close by the swimming pool explains its nickname.

gence service, as a special envoy. He flew to Washington, met with Golitsin, returned to Paris, and reported to the Elysée Palace. As a result of his mission, the head of the SDECE, General Paul Jacquier, and the director of the DST, Daniel Doustin, sent a joint team of debriefers to Washington to meet with Golitsin, to whom the French gave the cryptonym MARTEL.

Golitsin claimed that there was, within the SDECE, a ring of half a dozen Soviet spies, code-named SAPPHIRE. He seemed to have considerable knowledge of the organization and operations of the French service.

"Golitsin was a pro-French Soviet," said a former CIA officer familiar with the defector's charges. "He had a kind of affection for the French, although he'd never lived there. He had a large list of twenty-five or thirty leads, not names, but very thin leads. And he kept talking about how a senior KGB official had referred to their agents in France as sapphires, in other words, a collection of jewels."

The allegations about SAPPHIRE did not improve the already rather brittle relations between the French service and the CIA. The agency's counterintelligence officers were dismayed at the thought that CIA secrets shared with the SDECE might have seeped back to Moscow through the French. As the French CI officers continued to debrief Golitsin, the impression grew within the CIA that French intelligence was shot through with Russian spies.

"The whole French thing was a mess," the former CIA man said. "Some of the leads pointed to personalities in S-deck who'd been involved in operations with us and about whom there had been some suspicion, but no proof. Jim [Angleton] weighed in against these people, and it caused a lot of friction. Golitsin was saying there were moles in the Elysée, in the French government, and in French intelligence, who could influence French policy."

From Angleton's vantage point, the French services did not seem to be moving aggressively to weed out Golitsin's supposed nest of spies. The CIA suspected the French were more interested in covering up the potential political scandal than in finding and punishing the moles.

But in France, Golitsin's allegations did lead to accusations against two prominent political figures, Jacques Foccart and Louis Joxe, and a diplomat, Georges Gorse. Foccart, who became a member of de Gaulle's inner circle during the general's exile in London during World War II, was a member of the French cabinet and a high-level adviser to de Gaulle on intelligence affairs when he fell under suspicion as a result of Golitsin's warnings. In the press, Foccart was accused of having organized the *barbouzes,* the bearded ones, a shadowy group of criminals who carried out the terrorist attacks in Algeria, and of being the Soviet mole described by Golitsin. Foccart denied the charges, sued several newspapers, and won. He continued to serve as a minister under de Gaulle and then under President Georges Pompidou.

Louis Joxe, the second Frenchman to fall under the long shadow cast by Golitsin, had served as ambassador to Moscow in the early 1950s and held a high post in the French government under de Gaulle. As the minister in charge of Algeria, he had been instrumental in settling the conflict there and establishing Algerian independence in 1962, a fact that made him unpopular among the right wing and may have also explained why he became a target of the French mole hunters. But as in the case of Foccart, when the smoke had cleared, there was no evidence against Joxe, who continued to enjoy the trust of de Gaulle.[14] The diplomat investigated by the French mole hunters, Georges Gorse, had served on missions to the Soviet Union and as ambassador to Tunisia.

Golitsin also said that aside from extensive penetration of the French government, the KGB had a highly placed spy in NATO, who was able to give Moscow instant access to classified documents, even those marked "Cosmic," the highest category. The information Golitsin provided has been credited with unmasking Georges Pâques, a Soviet spy inside NATO headquarters, which was located at the time in Paris. When arrested in August 1963, Pâques was deputy head of the press department. He was convicted of treason and sentenced to life imprisonment, a term later reduced to twenty years.

As the French writer Thierry Wolton has pointed out, Pâques could not have been the spy inside NATO whom Golitsin described. Golitsin defected in December 1961 and Pâques did not go to work for NATO until October 1962.[15] However, Pâques had passed secrets to the Soviets for many years and had previously worked for the defense ministry, where he had access to NATO documents.

[14]Officials in the SDECE itself also fell under suspicion as a result of Golitsin's charges. Among them were Colonel Leonard Houneau, the deputy chief of the spy agency, and Georges de Lannurien, a high-ranking official.
[15]Thierry Wolton, *Le KGB en France* (Paris: Bernard Grasset, 1986), p. 123.

If not Pâques, who was the spy in NATO? Almost two decades later, although not as a direct result of Golitsin's information, a Soviet spy in NATO was unmasked. He was Hugh George Hambleton, a Canadian economics professor who had worked for NATO from 1956 to 1961. In 1977, the FBI caught and "turned" a KGB illegal, a Czech named Ludek Zemenek, who had entered the United States from Canada and was using the name Rudolph A. Herrmann. He agreed to act as a double agent for the FBI. He revealed to the FBI that one of his contacts was Professor Hambleton, whom the Canadians chose not to prosecute. But Hambleton, who held dual Canadian-British citizenship, unwisely flew to London in 1982, where he was promptly arrested, convicted, and sentenced to ten years in prison.[16]

For many years a dramatic story has circulated inside American intelligence agencies of a spy, in addition to Pâques, who jumped out the window to his death while being questioned as a result of information supposedly provided to the French by Golitsin. Despite the persistent reports to the contrary, however, the files of the CIA do not reflect that Golitsin provided the information that led to the spy's capture.

There actually was such a spy. Colonel Charles de Jurquet d'Anfreville de la Salle "was an agent of the Rumanian secret service and then of the GRU," according to Marcel Chalet, the former head of the DST.[17] Colonel de la Salle was a retired top air force officer, a hero of a joint French-Russian air wing in World War II. In part as a result of his wartime experience, he remained sympathetic to the Soviets. In May 1965, at the Brasserie Lipp, the famed café on the Left Bank, de la Salle's girlfriend introduced him to Ion Iacobescu, a spy for the Rumanian secret service, who had a cover job at UNESCO. De la Salle had contacts in electronics firms and was recruited by the Rumanian, to whom he passed along data about French military aircraft. In time, de la Salle was run jointly with the Rumanians by Vladimir Arkhipov, a Soviet diplomat in Paris who was really an officer of the GRU.

Facing a recall to Bucharest, Iacobescu defected to England and turned in de la Salle, who was arrested in Paris in August 1969. When

[16]For the most detailed account of the Herrmann-Hambleton case, see John Barron, *KGB Today: The Hidden Hand* (New York: Reader's Digest Press, 1983).
[17]Letter, Marcel Chalet to author, July 19, 1990.

questioned at DST headquarters, de la Salle confessed to spying for
the Rumanians. He made no mention of the Russians. He asked to
return to his apartment to get a file, and two DST officers accompanied him to his home at Ivry-sur-Seine, a Paris suburb. "Going up to
his apartment," a former FBI counterintelligence agent said, "a
French officer asked him about his Soviet connections. 'I didn't know
you knew about that,' de la Salle replied. He went to get a drink or
left the room for a minute and jumped out of the kitchen window,
landing on a DST car." De la Salle's death was listed as a suicide. The
defector who turned him in was Iacobescu, not Golitsin.

For the most part, Golitsin's sweeping charges of Soviet infiltration
of the French secret service and of the de Gaulle government had few
visible results. In 1968, however, the French connection erupted into
a major scandal.

At its center was Philippe Thyraud de Vosjoli, who had served as
the SDECE's liaison officer in Washington from 1951 until he resigned
abruptly in October 1963. De Vosjoli had escaped from Nazi-occupied
France during World War II. He made his way over the Pyrenees to
Spain and joined de Gaulle's Free French intelligence service in London.

In Washington, de Vosjoli, whose SDECE code name was LAMIA,
established close relations with the CIA, and with its director of
counterintelligence, James Angleton. But as the questioning of Golitsin proceeded, the case began to drive a wedge between the two
intelligence services. The S-deck team would obtain fuzzy descriptions
of moles from Golitsin, then comb its files in Paris to try to find names
to fit the defector's leads. The French would then try out the names
in the next session with Golitsin in Washington. "The problem," de
Vosjoli wrote, ". . . lay in the fact that each session with Martel
[Golitsin's French cryptonym] was also attended by American representatives, and each time our people dropped a name in front of
Martel, that person automatically became suspect to the Americans."[18] De Vosjoli said his contacts with American intelligence began
to dry up. "The word seemed to be out not to take any chances with
the French."[19] In the meantime, during 1962 de Vosjoli set up a

[18]P. L. Thyraud de Vosjoli, *Lamia* (Boston: Little, Brown, 1970), p. 307.
[19]*Ibid.*

French spy network in Cuba, which was feeding information to him in advance of the Cuban missile crisis.

In December, de Vosjoli was called back to Paris by the SDECE and, by his account, ordered to set up a network to obtain military and nuclear secrets in America. De Gaulle, increasingly isolated from the United States, wanted his own nuclear weapons, the *force de frappe.* Moreover, de Vosjoli asserted, he was accused of having fed false information to France reporting that the Soviets had introduced offensive missiles in Cuba, a fact he said the French refused to believe. Golitsin's charges, according to de Vosjoli, were seen by his superiors as part of an American plot to embarrass France.

Dismayed by this turn of events, de Vosjoli resigned on October 18, 1963, with a stinging letter to General Jacquier, his chief. Claiming that he feared for his life, he went into hiding.

He later told his story to the novelist Leon Uris, who based his best-selling novel *Topaz* on the affair.[20] In France, the SDECE regarded de Vosjoli as a double agent who had "defected" to the Americans. U.S. intelligence officials do not deny they protected him when he resigned.

"De Vosjoli asked for asylum," a former FBI counterintelligence agent said. "S-deck suspected he was already working for Jim Angleton. That may not be far from the truth. Of course he would have worked closely with Angleton, that was his job. Somewhere along the line his allegiance was transformed. He came to realize his own service was unreliable. It stirred up a storm. There was a long inquiry in France."

According to a retired CIA officer, "De Vosjoli tried to argue the Angleton case with S-deck. He told them that the agency thinks Golitsin is a reliable defector, and gradually he became the advocate of Angleton and Golitsin, in the view of the French. Later on, Golitsin

[20]Leon Uris, *Topaz* (New York: McGraw-Hill, 1967). In the novel, Golitsin is "Boris Kuznetov," and de Vosjoli is "André Devereaux." The following year, de Vosjoli told his story in *Life* magazine. He appeared on the cover of the issue of April 16, 1968, photographed from the rear, wearing dark glasses and a homburg that made him look not unlike James Angleton. In the movie version of *Topaz,* directed by Alfred Hitchcock and released in 1969, a French spy for the Soviets goes out the window to his death and lands on a car. This scene, which in some respects closely paralleled the death of Colonel de la Salle, may have helped to reinforce the belief in U.S. intelligence circles that Golitsin was somehow linked to the de la Salle case.

went over and dealt personally with the French. Met with them on some islands in the Caribbean or somewhere. But that was years later."

Angleton's deputy, Scotty Miler, said that the order to gather American secrets was what precipitated de Vosjoli's break with the French service. "De Vosjoli defected from S-deck when he was instructed to begin spying on the United States," Miler said. "Golitsin's information had uncovered Pâques and some others. De Vosjoli suspected there was a Soviet penetration in the French service who had influenced them to target S-deck against the U.S. De Vosjoli said he would have no part of that."

A French official with knowledge of the affair insisted that de Vosjoli's fears for his safety were justified. "De Gaulle decided to kill de Vosjoli and sent Service Action to kill him. De Vosjoli was tipped off and escaped to Mexico." Later, he moved to south Florida.

In time, the mole hunt spread to Canada as well. Golitsin had only vague leads to Soviet penetration of the Canadian intelligence service, but the Mounties eventually—and with prompting from the CIA—focused on their own chief of Soviet counterespionage, Leslie James Bennett.

The son of a South Wales coal miner, Bennett had worked in British communications intelligence, and while in Istanbul after World War II, he had met Kim Philby. He emigrated to Canada in 1954, joined the RCMP Security Service, and rose to a position of power that roughly paralleled that of James Angleton in the CIA.[21]

During the 1960s, a number of Canadian operations against the Soviets went sour, and Bennett, in an investigation code-named Operation Gridiron, was placed under surveillance for two years. According to one former CIA officer who knew Bennett well and was familiar with the case, "Golitsin was shown Bennett's file, or information about him, and he said, 'Yes, I think he's a Soviet agent.' That was a very powerful factor."

Equally important were the suspicions of Bennett voiced by one of

[21]At the time, the RCMP was responsible for counterintelligence and counterespionage in Canada, much as the FBI is in the United States. In 1984, responsibility for security and intelligence was transferred from the RCMP to the new Canadian Security Intelligence Service (CSIS). Although the CSIS had some liaison officers stationed overseas, Canada had no formal external intelligence agency.

Angleton's officers, Clare Edward Petty, who was a member of the SIG, the mole-hunting arm of the Counterintelligence Staff. Petty's reason was labyrinthine. Bennett had asked the CIA to place surveillance on a Soviet KGB man stationed in Canada who was traveling to South America. Soon after, Heinz Herre, the liaison man in Washington for the BND, the West German intelligence service, visited Bennett in Ottawa and mentioned he had recently taken a trip to South America. According to Petty, Bennett remarked that Herre might have run across the KGB man, who was there at the same time. At that, Petty said, "Herre turned white as a sheet," or so Bennett reported back to the CIA. "Bennett had the feeling that Herre was guilty, that maybe Herre and the KGB man had met or traveled together."

The CIA, Petty said, "gets hot and bothered and puts Herre under surveillance. A few months later, in the summer, Herre goes to Jackson Hole on vacation and two KGB guys go on the same trip." As Petty saw it, the KGB was trying to frame Herre by sending its officers out wherever Herre was traveling. "It was to make Herre look bad. This technique had happened two or three times with different members of the Gehlen organization." Leslie James Bennett, Petty decided, was part of the KGB plot. "We would not have known anything about Herre's South America trip if Bennett had not informed us," Petty said.

It was a dizzying, mind-bending exercise, but according to the former CIA man familiar with the episode, "The Herre incident is what triggered the Bennett case. Jim Angleton played a powerful role. He said push on, press forward. Angleton used all his devious methods to charm the Canadians with long lunches and lots of booze."

Bennett was an easy target in part because he was a civilian in a paramilitary organization. He almost always wore the same old tweed jacket with suede elbow patches, and he had long hair, which annoyed the spit-and-polish Mounties. With the CIA, the British, and the French busily conducting their own mole hunts, it was almost as if Canada did not want to be left out. By 1970, Bennett had become the target of the RCMP mole hunt.

The Canadian surveillance teams feared that Bennett was using carrier pigeons to communicate with the KGB. They trailed him repeatedly from his home to a wooded area where he removed a wire cage from his car trunk. The watchers dared not get close enough to see what Bennett was releasing from the cage, but they feared the worst. It was a hilarious example of how far afield suspicion can lead counterintelligence sleuths; in fact, Bennett was trapping black squirrels in his garden and, kindly, releasing them far from his home.

Undaunted, the Mounties tried to spring a clever trap of their own, informing Bennett that a Soviet defector was coming to Montreal for a meeting. It wasn't true, so if the KGB showed up at the meeting site to learn the identity of the defector, it would mean that Bennett had tipped off the Russians, since no one else had been told of the notional meeting. The mole hunters were foiled by a blizzard that hit Montreal that night; in the blinding snow, no one could tell if the Soviets had turned up or not.

The RCMP finally confronted Bennett in 1972, subjecting him to a harsh interrogation that proved nothing. Although Bennett passed a polygraph test and maintained under oath that he was never a Soviet agent, he was forced out after eighteen years and moved to Australia.[22]

The former CIA officer who knew Bennett said, "This was a Canadian tragedy. A terrible thing was done to this man. He was fired and his wife left him. His life was virtually ended at that point. He was completely innocent."

When Golitsin flew back to Washington from London, after the D notice disaster had surfaced him, he requested and got a private audience with John McCone, the director of the CIA.

"He told McCone a number of things," a former CIA officer said. "One thing he said was that Wilson was a spy and Gaitskell had been murdered by the KGB. And other fantastic things. McCone was astonished. He sent off a cable to Hollis." The CIA director asked what on earth was going on.

McCone's cable went to Archibald B. Roosevelt, the London station chief, and was taken around to Leconfield House, on Curzon Street, then MI5's headquarters, by Cleveland C. Cram, the deputy chief of station.

"Hollis sent back a cable saying, in effect, it's all a lot of baloney," the CIA officer continued. "Hollis said, 'We have no evidence to

[22]In 1977, a Canadian journalist, Ian Adams, wrote a best-selling novel entitled *S, Portrait of a Spy* (Agincourt, Ontario: Gage Publishing, 1977), about a Soviet mole inside the RCMP. Because of the apparent similarity to his own case, Bennett sued Adams and his publisher and won.

support these things.' But Angleton kept pounding on the theme that Wilson was a spy.''

By then, Hollis himself had become a suspect inside MI5, and the British mole hunt was careening out of control. Golitsin's roadshow had been brief, but the effect on British intelligence was devastating, and would reverberate for years.

In the CIA, the hunt was gathering momentum.

Chapter 9

CHICKADEE

In Moscow in 1962, Oleg Penkovsky was passing detailed information to the West on Soviet rocket strength and strategic planning, information that was to assist President Kennedy that October in his handling of the world's first nuclear confrontation, the Cuban missile crisis.

At the CIA's Langley headquarters, Penkovsky's top-secret information on Soviet missiles was given a special code name, CHICKADEE. The "bigot list"[1] that controlled who had access to CHICKADEE material was highly restricted, as befitted data flowing from what one official study called "the single most valuable agent in CIA history."[2]

The CIA designated with the code name IRONBARK all material from Penkovsky that dealt with subjects other than Soviet missile

[1]"Bigot list" is the CIA term for a list of persons with access to a specific sensitive operation or to a type of special intelligence.

[2]Anne Karalekas, "History of the Central Intelligence Agency," Book IV, *Final Report of the Select Committee to Study Governmental Operations with Respect to Intelligence Activities, United States Senate* (Washington: U.S. Government Printing Office, 1976), p. 58. Other studies have disputed the value of Penkovsky's reports, arguing that they were not crucial in shaping U.S. policy during the Cuban missile crisis. For example, one analysis by a former CIA Soviet specialist said that while Penkovsky provided a "tremendous amount" of important military information, he "had not been aware" that the Soviets had placed medium- and intermediate-range missiles in Cuba. Raymond L. Garthoff, *Reflections on the Cuban Missile Crisis* (Washington, D.C.: Brookings Institution, rev. ed., 1989), p. 63.

strength.[3] Together, CHICKADEE and IRONBARK were among the most closely guarded secrets of the United States government.

Penkovsky passed his rolls of film, containing photographs of secret Soviet documents, to both Greville Wynne and Janet Ann Chisholm, the attractive, dark-haired wife of the MI6 station chief in Moscow. Sometimes, Penkovsky met Chisholm in a park while her small children played nearby, and on at least one occasion he handed her films concealed in a box of candy. Usually, Penkovsky would meet Chisholm on a Friday or Saturday near the Arbat, a boulevard in the center of Moscow. She would follow him to a side street, where he would pass the films.

But there were growing signs that Penkovsky's spying had been detected. As early as January 1962, while meeting Janet Chisholm, Penkovsky spotted a small brown car driving slowly by and moving the wrong way on a one-way street. Two weeks later, the same car appeared at another meeting with Chisholm. By July 5, when he met Wynne at the Peking restaurant, the KGB surveillance had become unmistakable. At the airport the next day Penkovsky told Wynne he would, as a soldier, continue to do his job for the West, despite the obvious and increasing dangers.

Penkovsky attended a reception at the British embassy on September 6. Then he seemed to disappear off the screen.

Paul Garbler was nervous. The CIA's premier agent in the Soviet Union had vanished.

"We were really sweating, because we hadn't seen or heard from Penkovsky," Garbler recalled. Then, on November 2, the signal came. A chalk mark appeared on lamppost No. 35 on Kutuzovsky Prospekt, the lamppost that was checked daily by Captain Alexis Davison, the assistant air attaché. And, as prearranged, the telephone rang three times in the apartment of Hugh Montgomery, the deputy chief of station.

To the CIA, the signals meant that Penkovsky had placed something in the dead drop behind the radiator in the lobby of the apartment building at No. 5–6 Pushkin Street. Just to be sure, Garbler got

[3]The British, who were jointly running Penkovsky with the CIA, used the designation ARNIKA for all of his data. They did not distinguish between the missile material and the other kinds of information he was providing.

in his car and drove by the lamppost on Kutuzovsky Prospekt. There could be no question about it; the chalk mark was there.

Perhaps because Penkovsky had not been seen for almost two months, perhaps because Garbler knew the drop was to be used only in case of emergency—whatever the reason, the station chief had a sense of foreboding. But the drop would have to be cleared.

For that task, he selected Richard C. Jacob, a twenty-four-year-old CIA case officer from Egg Harbor, New Jersey, listed on the embassy rolls as an "archivist." For Jacob, it was the moment of truth. He was a spy in Moscow, which might be glamorous on paper, but now he was facing the real thing, a mission that might be dangerous.

Garbler took pains to prepare him. "I spent about an hour in the secure room with the young guy being sent out to clear the drop," Garbler recalled. "I can't explain why I took him into the bubble and spent that much time with him getting him ready, other than instinct. It was my gut that made me go through everything and tell him what to do if anything happens."

"What do you mean if anything happens?" Jacob had asked nervously.

"The message has to be in a matchbox," Garbler replied. "Hold it in your hand until you get out on the street, and if you're jumped, drop it, try to drop it in the gutter, the sewer if you can. Don't have it."

Jacob nodded, and Garbler went on, "They'll try to sweat you. Don't admit anything about clearing a drop. Demand to call the embassy."

When Jacob arrived at the Pushkin Street drop, the KGB was waiting. He had walked straight into a trap, just as Garbler had feared.[4]

Penkovsky had been arrested two weeks earlier, on October 22, and was under Soviet control when the signal appeared on the lamppost. Analyzing what had happened, the CIA concluded that Penkovsky, under duress, had revealed both the location of the drop and the chalk signal to activate it. At that point, if the Soviets had not already suspected it, they would have realized that the drop where Abidian

---

[4]Jacob managed to get rid of the matchbox as he was detained by the KGB. He was taken to a police station, and, as instructed, insisted on calling the embassy. He was released after Richard Davies, an embassy officer, was dispatched to prove to the KGB that Jacob had diplomatic immunity.

had been observed was for Penkovsky.[5] The KGB then activated the drop by marking the lamppost, and the CIA fell into the trap.

While under control, Penkovsky—or the KGB—sent another, extraordinary signal, the meaning of which was debated inside the CIA for years afterward. According to Garbler, Penkovsky had been told that if he learned the Soviets were about to unleash a nuclear missile attack against the United States, he was to go to a pay phone, call Captain Davison, and blow three times into the mouthpiece. "It meant that this was it. The balloon was going up. And he did it."[6]

There were several possible explanations, Garbler said. Penkovsky may have revealed the signal to the KGB, "and they may have done it to shake us up." Could Penkovsky have disclosed the signal to his captors, but dissembled about its meaning? "It could be," Garbler said. Knowing he was doomed, Oleg Penkovsky may have tried to strike a last blow against his country by triggering a nuclear Armageddon. If so, it would have been consistent with his earlier offer to plant miniature nuclear bombs in various locations around the Soviet capital.

Penkovsky's contact Greville Wynne was arrested in Budapest on November 2, brought to Moscow, and imprisoned in Lubianka. Both men were placed on trial in May 1963, and pleaded guilty.[7] Penkovsky was convicted of high treason and sentenced to death. On May 16, TASS announced he had been executed. Wynne was sentenced to eight years in prison, but traded for the Soviet spy Gordon Lonsdale the following April.

On May 13, after the conclusion of the Penkovsky trial, Richard

[5]John Abidian, "the handsome Armenian," was unaware he had been observed at the drop, or that Yuri Nosenko had revealed that fact to the CIA, until he was interviewed by the author on January 13, 1990. A pleasant man living in retirement in Belgium, Abidian had served in Rio de Janeiro and Paris after Moscow, held a top State Department security post in Washington, and then for nine years was NATO's director of security in Brussels. The CIA never told him that on his one espionage mission for the agency, he had been seen by the KGB.
[6]The Pushkin Street drop could have been used to warn of a Soviet attack, but it could also have been used for other emergency messages as well. The telephone call, silent except for Penkovsky blowing three times into the receiver, would obviously provide a quicker warning of a nuclear attack than would a message left in the dead drop.
[7]The CIA must have taken a special interest in the translator for the court. It was Boris Belitsky, the Radio Moscow correspondent who was run by the CIA as AEWIRELESS but who in reality, as Yuri Nosenko had revealed to the agency in his secret debriefing in Geneva a year earlier, was a double agent under KGB control.

Jacob and four other Americans were declared *persona non grata* and expelled from Moscow.[8]

The Penkovsky case, despite its apparent success, had ended in spectacular failure, the announced execution of the Soviet colonel, and the expulsion of ten Westerners.

But why did the CIA send an officer to the Pushkin Street drop if five months earlier, in Geneva, as George Kisevalter maintained, Yuri Nosenko had revealed that John Abidian, "the handsome Armenian," had been spotted at the drop? The answer is not clear, but Kisevalter maintained that he had immediately reported Nosenko's warning to headquarters.[9]

After Penkovsky's arrest, Kisevalter, furious that the operation might have been endangered, said he complained bitterly that Abidian, who was not even a CIA officer, had been sent to check the drop.[10] He said he voiced his complaint to Joseph J. Bulik, the chief of SR-9, the headquarters unit in charge of operations in Moscow, and the official in charge of the Penkovsky case. Back at Langley, Kisevalter said, "I talked to Bulik in the halls one day at headquarters, in late '62 after Penkovsky was wrapped up. I said, 'Why didn't you tell me the Armenian went to this particular drop?'

"I raised hell about it," Kisevalter said. "Bulik confirmed that the drop checked by the Armenian and the Penkovsky drop were one and the same. Bulik told me, 'Well, we figured it was safe to use him [Abidian] because his tour was up and he's been transferred out of Moscow.' Yes, the horse was already out of the barn."

[8]Besides Jacob, the other Americans expelled were Hugh Montgomery, the CIA's deputy chief of station under Garbler; Captain Davison, the lamppost checker; Rodney W. Carlson, a CIA case officer listed as an "assistant agricultural attaché"; and William C. Jones III, an embassy second secretary. One of the telephone numbers Penkovsky had been given in case he needed to contact American intelligence was of an apartment occupied successively by Jones and Montgomery. Five British officials, including Roderick Chisholm, the MI6 station chief, were also expelled. Both Chisholm and his wife, Janet Ann, had been named in the trial.
[9]Pete Bagley, insisting that Nosenko had not revealed the KGB's knowledge of the drop until 1964, said, "The idea that we would have gone ahead and let Penkovsky use a drop that had been compromised was incredible on the face of it. It is not likely that it would have been used."
[10]Since the KGB had, some months earlier, given up its stakeout at the Pushkin Street location—that fact had also been revealed by Nosenko in Geneva—the failure of CIA headquarters to warn the Moscow station that the drop had been discovered by the KGB did not lead to Penkovsky's capture. But it caused unnecessary international embarrassment for the CIA and for the United States.

In the event, no one ever told the Moscow station chief that the drop was contaminated. Garbler didn't know. Why hadn't headquarters told him? "I don't know," Garbler said. But he added that Bulik, the head of SR-9, was notoriously secretive and extremely careful about what he told anyone, even close CIA colleagues.

Had he been informed that the KGB knew the location of the drop, Garbler said, he would never have sent Richard Jacob to clear it. And he would have tried to warn Penkovsky that the drop could no longer be used. The Soviets would not have caught a CIA case officer in the act of conspiring with Oleg Penkovsky.

The long and short of it was that headquarters told the chief of the Moscow station almost nothing about what was happening in the Penkovsky operation. It was only years later that Garbler would find out the startling reason why he may have been kept in the dark.

CHICKADEE was over, but in the fall of 1963 Garbler was plunged into a new crisis. In the annals of the CIA, the case has become known as "the Cherepanov papers."

Aleksandr Nikolaevich Cherepanov was an officer of the KGB's Second Chief Directorate, whose targets included foreigners and diplomats. The trouble began, according to Paul Garbler, when an American couple came to the embassy with a package of documents. Garbler recalled the pair. "One was a librarian, they were both from Indiana, and they had been dealing with a guide who was taking them to libraries in Moscow. The guide's name was Cherepanov." He had handed them the package with a plea that it be taken to the American embassy.

The couple went to the consulate on the first floor of the embassy on Tchaikovsky Street. They turned the papers óver to an American officer who gave them to Malcolm Toon, the counselor for political affairs under Ambassador Foy Kohler.

"The agreement I had," Garbler said, "was that if we got a walk-in, I would be notified as soon as possible and certainly within a few hours. It was not until the day after the papers arrived that I was called into the bubble by Toon and Walter Stoessel, the deputy chief of mission. Kohler was out of town and Stoessel was the chargé."

The two diplomats told Garbler about the papers and argued they were probably a provocation. They pointed out that in Warsaw the week before, someone had handed a U.S. military attaché a diagram showing the location of missile sites. The attaché was accused of espionage and expelled.

Garbler could hardly believe his ears. Documents, apparently removed from the KGB's files, had made their way to the embassy and the diplomats wanted to return them to the Russians. " 'We've decided to give the stuff back,' they said. 'Okay,' I said, 'but don't give it back until I can review the documents and photograph them.'

"The papers were about an inch thick," Garbler continued. "They gave them to me reluctantly. They said, 'You can look, but we've made an appointment to give them back.' So I took the papers off to my little hutch on the tenth floor and photographed the documents. I had a couple of hours—they had an appointment at the foreign ministry at noon."

The documents, seemingly from the American department of the KGB's Second Chief Directorate, went into great detail about the drinking and sexual habits of a number of employees of the U.S. embassy. "They were doing surveillance, and it was dirty stuff. Such as 'The assistant military attaché drinks and we're going to catch him in the act.' The papers showed them in the posture of blackmail. If I were the KGB I would not use that kind of information as a provocation. I would use missile information. I thought the material was authentic."

Garbler went back downstairs, returned the papers to Stoessel, but asked to meet with him again in the bubble. Garbler insisted that the embassy keep the papers. "I said, 'Walter, you're making a mistake.' I assumed the stuff had to have come out of the KGB files. I said, 'This isn't the kind of stuff they would use in a provocation. This is the kind of stuff that would come from a KGB man who wants to get in touch with us.' Toon joined us, and I argued that if the papers were returned, it would take the KGB no more than an hour to find the source. I said, 'In effect, what you're doing is killing this man.' "

Toon's reply infuriated the station chief. "Mac said, 'Well, you guys kill people every day in your organization, so what difference does it make if you kill one more?' Toon said, 'Besides, it's too late, we've already returned them.' "

Garbler leaped to his feet. "Is the officer taking material back still in the building?" he asked.

"Probably not," Toon replied.

"It was now eleven-fifty A.M." Garbler said, "and the appointment at the foreign ministry was at noon. I left the secure room, went to the nearest window that overlooked the courtyard, and saw the fellow standing by the car getting ready to leave. I went to the elevator, and it was slow coming up. I ran down the nine flights of stairs and went out in the courtyard."

Tom Fain, the American consul, was about to depart for the foreign ministry. Garbler grabbed the papers from his hands and went back up to Stoessel. "I said, 'Walter, I'll risk my life and career on this. Don't give these papers back. A man's life is at stake.' "

Stoessel refused to budge; the Cherepanov papers had to go back to the Russians. Garbler, outranked, had no choice but to give in. "I said, 'Okay, you're wrong, wrong, wrong, but if this is what you want to do, I guess you must.' I went downstairs and gave the papers back to the officer, who was still in the courtyard. He thought I was a lunatic."[11]

The papers went back to the KGB, but, thanks to Garbler, the CIA at least had copies. And sooner than it expected, the CIA was to hear more about Cherepanov.

With Penkovsky shot, and the CHICKADEE and IRONBARK material cut off as a result, Garbler's tour in Moscow was coming to an end. Not long after the confrontation over Cherepanov, however, an event took place that was to change the world—and directly affect the mole hunt secretly under way at CIA headquarters.

Lee Harvey Oswald had arrived in the Soviet Union in October 1959. He left, after more than two and a half years, in June 1962, about six months after Garbler arrived in Moscow. In Dallas, on November 22, 1963, Oswald, firing his rifle from the sixth-floor corner window of the Texas School Book Depository, assassinated President John F. Kennedy.

---

[11]Walter Stoessel died in 1986. Malcolm Toon, who later returned to Moscow as the U.S. ambassador from 1976 to 1979, remembered the incident, but said he could not recall the details; he had indeed worried about a possible KGB provocation, but had not objected to the CIA's copying the documents before they were returned.

Chapter 10

"Give Me Your Badge"

O nce he had been interrogated by the FBI, Peter Karlow knew his career in the CIA was finished.

What he did not know was that Sheffield Edwards, the CIA's director of security, had been out to get him, evidence or no evidence. The fact that there was none did not deter Edwards in the least. In January 1963, three weeks before the FBI interrogation, the CIA security chief called in the bureau's representatives to discuss Karlow, who was still regarded as the "principal suspect" in the mole hunt.

"Individuals present at the conference," Edwards wrote in the wonderfully stilted language of officialdom, "recognized the distinct possibility that a definite case cannot be made against [Karlow] since there is a possibility that [Karlow] is not identical to [Sasha]. The Director of Security indicated that this Agency desired that the other areas of a personnel and/or security nature in the . . . case be fully developed during the interview with [Karlow] since it is the opinion of the Office of Security . . . that [Karlow] whether or not he is identical to [Sasha] should be terminated from Agency employment."[1]

Nothing could be clearer. If the CIA could not prove Karlow a mole, it would find some other reason to fire him. Karlow's continen-

[1] CIA Memorandum to File, January 25, 1963. The document was heavily censored by the CIA before its release, but the words that can, from the context, logically be assumed to be missing have been inserted by the author.

tal manner and educated airs obviously annoyed Edwards, a former
Army colonel, a slender man of military bearing who kept his gray
hair close-cropped. His dislike for Karlow was transparent and
permeates the secret memos he wrote at the time, many of them heavy
with sarcasm. At the meeting, Edwards fretted that Karlow might not
agree to the FBI interview. "However, the general opinion of individuals at the conference," the security chief concluded, "was that
[Karlow], who appears to have a very high regard of his own intellect,
will, whether he is [Sasha] or not, go ahead with the FBI interview."[2]

On February 19, the week after the FBI interrogation, Karlow
called on Edwards. It was a nasty confrontation.

"You're a traitor!" Edwards barked. "It's just a question of
whether we fire you or let you resign."

"And you are a fool," Karlow rejoined.

After a further exchange of pleasantries, the CIA security chief
informed Karlow that a decision would be made in a week on whether
he would be permitted to resign without prejudice.

Karlow protested that he was innocent. It was obvious, he added,
that Edwards did not believe him. "He was not disabused of this fact,"
Edwards wrote.[3]

Two days later, Karlow sent a memo to Richard Helms, as the
deputy director for plans had requested. "I wish to help the FBI in any
way that I can," he wrote, "both to resolve the case and to clear my
name. I have nothing to confess and nothing to conceal. I realize that,
through an incredible error . . . I have come so deeply under suspicion
of treason that my career in CIA is ended." Karlow added: "I intend
to fight any suspicions or allegations of disloyalty or indiscretion in
any way that I can, inside and outside CIA and the government, until
any personal implication or blemish on my record is removed."[4] He
attached a statement explaining the conflict over his father's birthplace in the forms he had filled out over the years, an inconsistency
that the Office of Security had now seized upon, along with minor
security violations by Karlow—he had once left classified waste in a
coffee can, for example—as the club to drive him from the CIA.

The next day, Karlow once more called on Helms, whom he re-

[2]*Ibid.*, p. 2.
[3]Memorandum, Edwards to Hoover, February 19, 1963.
[4]Memorandum, Karlow to Helms, February 21, 1963.

garded as his friend. This time, he told Helms he was planning to resign. Helms, the quintessential bureaucrat, and a man of icy composure, smoothly noted that the case was now out of his hands and under the jurisdiction of the FBI. But Karlow, Helms thought, ought to try to correct "certain discrepancies" that had been found in his personal records.

Karlow did not realize that mole suspects have no friends. In his own memorandum to the files, Helms wrote that he had urged Karlow to clear up any contradictions in the FBI records, or "he was running the risk of having his children live under a cloud as far as any type of government employment was concerned, including a commission in the armed services." Helms added: "I went down this track, because it seems to me that the only leverage one has on Karlow to get any possible admissions from him is to make him concerned not so much as to his own future, but that of his children and other members of his family." Helms concluded: "I gave him no solace. . . ."[5]

At this point Karlow was not trying to save his job. All he could do was to keep battling to clear his name. "When I was finally accused on the fifth day of the FBI interrogation," Karlow said, "I felt relief. There was no way they could prove I was a Russian spy. The accusation was so preposterous. But I didn't want to leave with a cloud over my head."

Karlow kept pressing his accusers for specifics. If he was a Soviet spy, which he knew he was not, what was he supposed to have done, when, and where? He pushed Lawrence Houston, the agency's general counsel, for details of his supposed crimes.

"Finally, they came up with two dates. On January 6, 1950, and August 24, 1951, I was supposed to have been in East Berlin being briefed by my [KGB] case officer," the mysterious "Lydia."

But Karlow was able to find records demonstrating that he was elsewhere on both dates. As it happened, Karlow had a book inscribed, "To my dear friend Peter Karlow, Rouen, the 6th January, 1950"—the very day Karlow was accused of being in East Berlin—which had been given to him by one of France's World War II heroes, Captain Jean L'Herminier. "He was captain of a submarine, the *Casabianca,* that landed one hundred and four French Moroccan commandos on Corsica the night before the island's liberation in 1943."

[5]Richard Helms, Memorandum for the Record, February 25, 1963.

Karlow had something in common with the French hero; the captain had lost both legs in the war.

Karlow had met L'Herminier at the Philadelphia Naval Hospital, where both men had been sent for treatment and to be fitted with artificial limbs. A member of the hospital staff asked Karlow if he spoke French, because there was another patient who spoke no English. Karlow went to the room. "I saw a photo of the sub on the side of the bed and immediately knew in whose presence I was," Karlow remembered. The two men became good friends.

At the end of December 1949, Karlow sailed on the *Ile de France* for Le Havre, en route to Germany to take up his new post in Karlsruhe, where he had been sent to set up the technical laboratory for Richard Helms. "We celebrated New Year's Eve on the *Ile de France*," Karlow remembered. From Le Havre, Karlow took the boat train to Paris, and then another train to Rouen, where he stayed overnight and visited L'Herminier. The Frenchman gave Karlow the book, which was entitled *Casabianca,* and written by the former captain to describe the exploits of his famed submarine during the war.

And, as it happened, Karlow was also able to reconstruct where he had been on the other date questioned by the CIA. On August 24, 1951, Karlow, his mother, and his future wife, Libby, were staying in Berchtesgaden at the Berchtesgadener Hof Hotel. "It was when I proposed to my wife. They found our names in the hotel registry."

Karlow was never told how the CIA came up with the two specific dates. But he was incredulous at the reaction of the agency's Office of Security when, after considerable time and effort, he produced the evidence indicating he was not in East Berlin on the dates in question. Karlow spoke with Robert L. Bannerman, the deputy director of the Office of Security, who was to succeed Sheffield Edwards as director. "Bannerman said, 'You must be a high-level spy because you're so well documented.' " When Karlow was *not* well documented, when the multitudinous application forms he had filled out over the years differed slightly, this was taken as evidence of his guilt. It was an impossible Catch-22.

On March 12, Karlow wrote another memo to Helms. A new CIA team was reviewing his case, but two of its members were from Edwards's staff. Since Edwards "believes me guilty," how could he get a fair hearing? "I am at home on admin leave," Karlow told Helms, "but my 'cover' vis-à-vis my friends in CIA is wearing thin. This case has dragged on far too long already."[6] Helms wrote back a terse note suggesting Karlow take up his problems with Houston.[7]

Three weeks later, however, on April 3, Karlow was able to get a telephone call through to Helms, who reported the conversation in a classified memorandum to the CIA's deputy director, Lieutenant General Marshall S. Carter. Karlow, Helms said, "felt a web had been woven around him based on circumstantial evidence and that he was finding it extremely difficult to untangle the web and come to grips with the exact nature of his alleged derelictions."[8]

By now, however, the web had completely enveloped Karlow. Two weeks later, General Carter brought down the ax. "I have come to the decision that we can no longer employ Mr. Karlow with the Central Intelligence Agency and that he should be authorized to resign," Carter wrote.[9]

But Karlow had already offered to resign. He knew he was powerless to stop the glacial movement of the bureaucracy. But he was able to win one concession. Houston wrote a memorandum for the record stating that the CIA and FBI investigation of Karlow's "security case" had not shown "that he was involved . . . in any way." But the memorandum also noted that the case "remains open in the FBI." It was the best Karlow could do; he gave a copy for safekeeping to a former high CIA official as insurance that it would not be "lost" in the agency's files.

"My name was dragged into this through no action of mine," Karlow said. "Like a chimney pot falling off a rooftop. There was absolutely nothing I could do about it. So I resigned." At age forty-two, Karlow's career in the CIA had ended.

Years later, Karlow could still remember the anger, frustration, and despair he felt during those days in the spring and early summer of 1963. "It was a very difficult period. It was demoralizing, trying to figure out what happened. I had to explain to my family that I wasn't a Russian spy. To my wife, my mother, and my sister."

On July 5, 1963, Karlow left the CIA headquarters building for the last time.

[6]Memorandum, Karlow to Helms, March 12, 1963.
[7]Memorandum, Helms to Karlow, March 12, 1963.
[8]Memorandum, Helms to Carter, April 3, 1963.
[9]Memorandum, Carter to Houston, April 18, 1963.

He met in Lawrence Houston's office on that day with Robert Bannerman, Edwards's deputy in the Office of Security.

"Bannerman said, 'Give me your badge.' "

Karlow wore his laminated plastic identification badge on a chain around his neck. He took it off and handed it to the OS man. "Bannerman escorted me out of the building." Karlow's white Packard convertible was waiting in the parking lot.

Karlow said he did not have any "sentimental thoughts" of the past as he walked out of Langley headquarters that day with Bannerman. "I never had any attachment to that building," he said. "I still believed in a small agency, confused, scattered around the city, hard to find. The headquarters building was Dulles's dream. Things changed after we moved there. It was impersonal after that. I didn't have any feeling about the building."

But as the two men walked through the vast lobby, Karlow pointed to the inscription on the marble wall: "And ye shall know the truth and the truth shall make you free. John VIII-XXXII."

He looked at Bannerman, and said, "I hope you read it sometime."

Chapter 11

―――――

AEFOXTROT

■

George Kisevalter had greased the line.

The address in Manhattan that he had given to Yuri Nosenko before they parted in Geneva in 1962 belonged to an agency asset. If anything came in to that address from abroad, signed by "Alex," it would mean that Nosenko was trying to recontact the CIA.

But Kisevalter did not trust even the best communications arrangements. He tested the link from time to time. They might never again hear from Nosenko, but if he did send a cable, a postcard, or a letter to the Manhattan address, it had to work.

"We had the line greased. I would send a cable to COS, Copenhagen. 'Send cable to following address in New York.' I sent periodic messages from Copenhagen, Geneva, and other places to keep the line activated. And to time it—how soon would we know the message had arrived?" The timing was important, because the CIA was to meet Nosenko, in whatever city he was, under the movie marquee beginning with the highest letter of the alphabet three days after he sent the cable to the New York address.

At Langley, there had been changes since Nosenko's first meeting with the CIA in June 1962. Howard Osborn, who had replaced Jack Maury as chief of the Soviet division, had in turn been succeeded in 1963 by David E. Murphy. In the fall of 1962, Pete Bagley had come back from Switzerland and joined the division as a counterintelligence officer. Having been shown the Golitsin file by Angleton, he was now persuaded that Nosenko was a plant, a dispatched agent of the KGB.

Late in January 1964, Yuri Nosenko returned to Geneva with the Soviet disarmament delegation. "A cable came in to New York," Kisevalter said. "I found out within hours. I flew to Geneva and Bagley flew in separately."

"Bagley met him [Nosenko] under the marquee of the movie theater in Geneva.[1] He gave Nosenko a note with the address of the safe house. We went to a different safe house from the one we used in 1962."

And so the first of half a dozen meetings in the new safe house began. Nosenko did not know, of course, that one of the two CIA case officers he was meeting with—Pete Bagley—now believed him to be a Soviet plant.

It was only two months after the Kennedy assassination. Lyndon Johnson was in the White House, and the Warren Commission, which Johnson had appointed to investigate the murder of President Kennedy, was about to begin hearing the first of 552 witnesses.

The tragedy in Dallas was on everyone's mind, but what Nosenko now told Kisevalter and Bagley staggered the two CIA men. He had, he assured them, personally handled Lee Harvey Oswald's case when the former Marine arrived in Moscow and asked to remain in the Soviet Union.

"Oswald came up almost immediately," Kisevalter recalled. "We questioned Nosenko about every detail on Oswald." What Nosenko told the two CIA men was that the KGB had decided it had no interest in Oswald. And Nosenko added that he was the official who ordered that Oswald be told he would have to leave when his visa expired.

When Oswald then attempted suicide, Nosenko continued, his decision to order Oswald to leave the Soviet Union was overruled by other officials outside the KGB who had decided it would be best, under the circumstances, to let Oswald stay. According to Kisevalter, when Nosenko was asked why the Soviets had reversed themselves, he replied: "Because he tried to commit suicide. There would only be adverse publicity if he tried it again." As Nosenko later explained it

---

[1]Bagley was not sure of the movie theater marquee he stood under in Geneva that night, but "I think it was ABC. There was such a theater in Geneva at the time."

to a congressional committee, the Soviets concluded that if Oswald did succeed in killing himself, the reaction in the press would harm "the warming of Soviet-American relations."[2]

After Kennedy was shot, Nosenko said, General Oleg Gribanov, Nosenko's boss as head of the Second Chief Directorate of the KGB, had ordered Oswald's file rushed from Minsk by military plane. Nosenko said he had examined the KGB file on Oswald and found it to be a routine record of Oswald's stay in Minsk, with references to his wife, Marina. There was, Nosenko said, no indication at all that the KGB had ever approached Oswald for operational purposes.

The two CIA officers in Geneva quickly relayed Nosenko's account to Langley headquarters. As might be imagined, the KGB man's statements caused great controversy within the CIA and later created a problem as well for the Warren Commission, which had to decide whether to give credence to his story.

In the 1964 Geneva meetings, Nosenko also ranged over a wide variety of other subjects. The recent capture of Oleg Penkovsky also loomed large on the minds of his questioners. Nosenko provided the first account of how Penkovsky was caught.

According to the KGB man, Penkovsky's downfall had begun almost by chance. George Kisevalter summarized Nosenko's story. "Penkovsky had one weakness that all Soviet intelligence officers have who work for the army," he said. "They do not appreciate the lengths to which the KGB can go. Internal surveillance is directed against the Russians. In Leningrad [now St. Petersburg], there is an excellent KGB school for surveillance. A Seventh Directorate School. Leningrad is a cosmopolitan city, with a variety of ethnic types. The candidates for the school are chosen from Leningrad or elsewhere, then assigned to Moscow. If they came from Moscow, there's a chance they would be spotted by friends or relatives, so they select them from Leningrad."

In Moscow, Kisevalter explained, the KGB maintains "light surveillance" even on the wives of diplomats. One of the women being watched was Janet Ann Chisholm, the wife of the MI6 station chief. "One person trained in Leningrad and now in Moscow says, 'I think

[2]*Investigation of the Assassination of President John F. Kennedy,* Hearings, Select Committee on Assassinations of the U.S. House of Representatives, March 1979, Vol. XII, p. 490.

this woman reacts to a Russian.' 'Who's the Russian?' 'I don't know. He disappears.' So they assign a more experienced officer. They watch Janet Ann Chisholm.

"From ballet school she walks to get the bus. She walks by a commission shop, where Soviets bring icons and other objects for sale. She browsed in the store and she'd see Penkovsky walk by. She would leave and would follow him to the end of the block where there was an arcade with shops, and steps going down. Out of sight, he could pass films without looking at her. It was an alternate to the park.

"There were eleven meetings with Chisholm, all told, at the park or the arcade. The park was near the British residences. It was a very small, triangular park. Three streets led into it and he could come from any direction, and drop candy or cassettes into her shopping bag.

"When the KGB spotted her, an artist is called in and the two KGB guys describe how the man was dressed. They dress a guy like Penkovsky. They tell him, 'You are to walk in front of the woman, but don't turn your head so she can see your features.' They inserted him in front of Ann and she turned to follow him.

"Now the Sovs are sure that Chisholm is in contact with the as yet unknown Soviet. They call out the brigades, little girls bouncing balls, helicopters to read invisible X's on top of embassy cars, an army of surveillance agents. They spot Penkovsky being followed by Ann and locate who he is and where he lives. It's an apartment house on an island in the middle of the Moscow River.

"It presents surveillance problems. The closest apartment house is half a mile away on the other side of the river. The KGB said, 'We've got to get him out of there,' to search Penkovsky's apartment. Penkovsky often goes for lunch at a fast-food shashlik place near Gorky Street. He goes to lunch as usual and has violent stomach pangs. Penkovsky has been poisoned.

"A friendly old gentleman happens to be next to him and says, 'I'm a doctor.' The doctor happens to have an ambulance around the corner which takes Penkovsky to the Kremlin Polyclinica inside the Kremlin. They pump his stomach while the KGB searches the apartment. They find nothing. This was September-October, after the last meeting with Penkovsky. The KGB searched carefully so as not to tip off Penkovsky they had been there.

"The reason they didn't find anything is that Penkovsky had a desk

drawer he had built with a trick way to open it. All of his spy para-
phernalia was in the desk drawer."

The KGB, according to Nosenko's account, now decided to place
Penkovsky and the apartment under round-the-clock surveillance.
"They checked on the people upstairs," Kisevalter continued. "A big
steel trust executive. They got his boss to call him in and give him a
trip to the Caucasus with his wife. For many years of service to the
state, fulfilling the plan, et cetera. 'Who, me?' the guy says. But the
steel executive is pleased. Then the boss says, 'I have a newly married
nephew coming to Moscow. You know how it is to get permission for
an apartment. Can I have the key while you're gone?' The executive
was hardly in a position to say no.

"The 'nephew' and his 'wife' move into the apartment. There are
geraniums all over in window boxes. Penkovsky's wife, Vera, and
Galina, the daughter, are visiting Varentsov. They are out at the
marshal's dacha. Penkovsky is alone in his apartment. The KGB is
watching with binoculars from their LP [listening post] across the
river. They relay word to the 'nephew,' Penkovsky is doing something
in his desk. On a signal from the LP, down comes a huge pot of
geraniums on a cable. It has a hidden camera that is silent. The
pictures are developed and they see on the film how to open the desk
drawer. *Again* they poison him, go in, and this time they find the
material in the desk, the one-time pad, the camera. It was Nosenko
who told me this story."

During most of the Nosenko debriefings in 1964, Kisevalter said,
Serge Karpovich, a CIA case officer, was present. "He was working
for Bagley, who wanted his own man along, and was concerned I
would not go along with him on Nosenko's bona fides, which Bagley
did not believe." To bug the sessions, Kisevalter said, "Karpovich was
trying to use electric wave pulsation recording. You use ordinary
household current to bug a room. It didn't work worth a damn. So we
just brought in an ordinary tape recorder."

As in 1962, Nosenko had a lot of other cases and more information
to impart. He revealed that the KGB had an important source in Paris
who was transmitting American and NATO military secrets to the
Soviets. He did not know the name of the spy. But he disclosed that
the KGB had a portable X-ray machine that could read combination
locks, a device that, as it turned out, had been used to penetrate a vault
in Paris that held the secrets.

Ten months later, in the fall of 1964, Robert Lee Johnson confessed to the FBI that while an Army sergeant stationed in Berlin in 1953, he had contacted the KGB, which recruited him as a spy. Johnson in turn recruited his best friend, Sergeant James Allen Mintkenbaugh. Johnson was later assigned to the Armed Forces Courier Center at Orly Airport, a heavily guarded communications center for top-secret and other highly sensitive material. In the fall of 1962, he used the KGB X-ray device to read the combination of the vault. Seven times, he removed secret documents and drove to a rendezvous with KGB agents, who photographed the material so that Johnson could replace it in the vault before dawn.

Nosenko, Kisevalter said, described a bizarre group of KGB technical experts who had developed and worked with the hazardous X-ray machine. "He told us about the KGB squad called 'the toothless ones,' so called because they had been exposed in their training to radiation by the very instrument used in Paris to read the combination of the lock. The X-ray machine had two parts which had to be put together. There were about fifteen in this high-tech group. They all had false teeth, metal teeth, I think. One of the toothless ones came to Paris to show Johnson how to use it."[3]

In the Geneva safe house, Nosenko also talked about Aleksandr Cherepanov, the KGB man whose controversial packet of papers Paul Garbler had managed to copy, only three months earlier, before diplomats in the American embassy in Moscow had insisted on giving them back to the Soviets. The papers had contained reports of KGB surveillance of American diplomats.

"When we asked him about the Cherepanov papers," Kisevalter recalled, "he said, 'These are my operations.'" The case officers pressed Nosenko. If Cherepanov was a legitimate KGB officer, what was his motive for turning over the papers to the couple from Indiana who brought them to the embassy?

[3]According to Kisevalter, Nosenko's leads enabled the FBI to identify Johnson, but not to arrest him, since the bureau lacked proof of his espionage. Back in the United States, and employed at the Pentagon, Johnson went AWOL in 1964 after his wife threatened to expose him as a Soviet spy. When FBI agents called on her to investigate his disappearance, she told them the truth, and implicated Mintkenbaugh. Johnson surrendered in Reno, Nevada, late in November and confessed. He and Mintkenbaugh pleaded guilty in 1965 and were each sentenced to twenty-five years in federal prison. Johnson died in prison in May 1972 after being stabbed by his son, Robert, who was visiting him at the federal penitentiary in Lewisburg, Pennsylvania.

"Cherepanov resented being treated by the KGB as a stooge," Kisevalter said. "He and another officer signed off to destroy papers at the KGB. He managed to keep the material from going in the burn bag."

Paul Garbler, if Nosenko's account was accurate, was correct in fearing that Stoessel and Toon, by returning the papers, had sealed Cherepanov's fate. Nosenko not only claimed that the operations described in the papers were his, he said he had participated in a nationwide manhunt to track down the errant KGB man. "Nosenko went north chasing Cherepanov," Kisevalter said. "But they caught him in the south. They nailed him on the Iranian border and executed him."

During the clandestine meetings with the CIA officers, Nosenko provided the first hint that he was toying with the idea of defecting to the West. "We talked about his future," Kisevalter said. "He was expecting a letter from his wife. 'By mail?' I asked. 'No, from Guk. He's coming from Moscow.' " Yuri Ivanovich Guk was the KGB colleague whom Nosenko had talked about in 1962; it was Guk who Nosenko said had warned him to stop seeing the British secretary who worked for MI5 in Geneva.

"Guk brings the letter," Kisevalter continued. "Nosenko comes early one day and reads it to me alone. He's upset. It was an intimate, sentimental letter with news of his family. He's saying, 'They may not send me out again. Maybe I should stay.' He said, 'Maybe I'll never see her again.' " To Kisevalter, Nosenko was struggling with his emotions and the pull of his family.

Even so, the case officers were stunned, "stupefied," as Bagley put it, when on February 4, Nosenko dropped a bombshell. He said he had decided to defect, because he had received a cable recalling him to Moscow. He asked for the protection of the CIA.

"He said, 'I've been ordered home,' " Kisevalter recalled. "Bagley ran for the cable room and told headquarters of the recall." Despite Bagley's conviction that Nosenko was a KGB plant, he urged that Langley agree to take him. Nosenko's information about Oswald was so potentially explosive it overrode the CIA officer's objections. Recalling Bagley's action, Kisevalter said, "He recommended we accept him in view of the Kennedy assassination, and what Nosenko had said about Oswald. Of course, the answer came back, grab him. If it comes out that we sent him home we're in trouble."

Nosenko had said in 1962 he did not want to defect. He had changed his mind, he said now, because he feared the KGB suspected him, he might never be able to leave the Soviet Union again, and he wanted to build a new life. Much later, Nosenko admitted that his story of a recall cable was false; he said he had made it up to convince the CIA to accept him.

"For reasons best known to the Soviet division," Kisevalter said, on instructions from headquarters "we spent days in Geneva on the organization chart of the KGB, including every individual he [Nosenko] could remember. Had we known he would defect, we would have got that information later."

On February 4, Nosenko was given American identity documents and driven across the Swiss border to Germany in civilian clothes. After a week, he was flown from Frankfurt to Andrews Air Force Base outside Washington, arriving on February 11. "He was kept in a safe house in northern Virginia," Kisevalter said. "A man-and-wife CIA team acted as cook and housekeeper and security." He was christened AEFOXTROT.

For Nosenko, his new life in the United States quickly turned into a nightmare that was to continue not for months, but for years. Angleton and Bagley viewed Nosenko's mission as twofold: to deflect from Golitsin's leads to moles inside the CIA, and to convey a message to the West that the KGB was innocent of involvement with Lee Harvey Oswald, and therefore had no link to the assassination of President Kennedy.

On the face of it, Nosenko's assertion that the KGB had no interest in Oswald seemed to defy logic. As a former Marine, Oswald presumably had at least some information that the KGB might want to know. Moreover, Oswald had been stationed at Atsugi, Japan, a base for the U-2 aircraft. Since 1956, the CIA spy planes had been overflying the Soviet Union to collect intelligence data; and to the CIA it seemed improbable that the KGB would not want to debrief Oswald about the U-2.[4]

---

[4]In 1978, when Nosenko testified to the House Select Committee on Assassinations, he said the KGB was unaware of any knowledge Oswald might have had about the U-2 because it had not questioned him. Asked why Oswald, a radar operator at Atsugi, had not been interrogated about the U-2, Nosenko replied that the KGB "didn't know that he had any connection with U-2 flights." Testifying to the same committee, former CIA director Richard Helms said he found Nosenko's testimony

Yet Nosenko held to his account; the KGB had not debriefed Oswald and had not recruited Oswald. The reason Nosenko gave, in effect, was that Oswald was too flaky for the KGB to want to deal with him. On March 3, 1964, a month after Nosenko defected, he was interviewed by the FBI. He said he had made the decision to turn down Oswald's original request to remain in the Soviet Union because Oswald did not appear "fully normal."[5] When Oswald's file was rushed from Minsk to Moscow after the assassination, Nosenko added, he had read a summary memo in the file written by Sergei M. Fedoseev, chief of the First Department of the KGB's Second Chief Directorate. As the FBI report put it, Nosenko "recalled that it contained the definite statement that from the date of OSWALD's arrival in the USSR until his departure from the USSR, the KGB had no personal contact with OSWALD and had not attempted to utilize him in any manner."[6]

Nosenko had even more surprising news about Oswald for the FBI. From the file, Nosenko said, he knew that Oswald had a gun in the Soviet Union and "it was used to shoot rabbits. NOSENKO stated that Western newspaper reports describe OSWALD as an expert shot; however OSWALD's file contained statements from fellow hunters that OSWALD was an extremely poor shot and that it was necessary for persons who accompanied him on hunts to provide him with game."[7]

But rabbits and spy planes were peripheral to the central problem faced by the CIA as a result of Nosenko's statements about Oswald. Boiled down, it came to this: if Nosenko was a true defector, his information was of great importance because it could be taken as strong evidence that the Soviets had no connection to Kennedy's

---

on this point "quite incredible" and added that he had been unable "to swallow" it.

On May 1, 1960, six months after Oswald arrived in the USSR, the Soviets shot down the CIA U-2 piloted by Francis Gary Powers. Much of the plane remained intact. From that date on, the Soviets had less need to question anyone about the U-2; they had one. *Investigation of the Assassination of President John F. Kennedy,* Hearings, Select Committee on Assassinations of the U.S. House of Representatives, March 1979, Vol. XII, p. 479, and September 1978, Vol. IV, p. 179.

[5] FBI report of March 5, 1964, in *Investigation of the Assassination of President John F. Kennedy,* Hearings, Select Committee on Assassinations of the U.S. House of Representatives, March 1979, Vol. XII, p. 509.

[6] *Ibid.,* p. 512.

[7] *Ibid.,* p. 513.

murder. But if Nosenko was a dispatched agent of the KGB, and not a true defector, did that mean that Oswald was acting for the Soviets when he shot the President?

Richard Helms, the deputy director for plans, fell into that trap. When he testified to the House Assassinations Committee in 1978, Helms, by now a former CIA director, said that if Nosenko fed the CIA false information about Oswald's KGB contacts, "it was fair for us to surmise that there may have been an Oswald-KGB connection in November 1963, more specifically that Oswald was acting as a Soviet agent when he shot President Kennedy."[8]

But if Nosenko was indeed carrying a message, other, less chilling explanations were possible. Oswald had lived in the Soviet Union, and had killed an American president. If he acted entirely on his own, it would not be hard to envision the Soviet leadership panicking after Dallas, and sending someone to reassure the United States that the Soviets had no connection to the assassination. But Helms was right about one thing—it was of "the utmost importance to this Government to determine the bona fides of Mr. Yuri Nosenko."[9]

The questions over Nosenko's authenticity were to split the CIA down the middle, with Angleton, Bagley, and their adherents on one side of the chasm and most of the agency's officials on the other. While many members of Angleton's staff believed, with their boss, that Nosenko was "bad" or "dirty"—the shorthand terms favored inside the CIA for false agents—most officials of the Soviet division, and the agency's leaders, eventually concluded he was what he said he was, a genuine defector. The debate over Nosenko, however, has continued to this day, particularly among former CIA officers.

But in the beginning, the doubters prevailed. There was, to start with, the matter of Nosenko's rank. According to Bagley, "He was a major in 1962 and a lieutenant colonel, he said, when he came out in 1964. Then he admitted he was a captain." But defectors before Nosenko had been known to inflate their rank and puff their importance in an effort to impress their new best friends.

Intriguingly, however, the debate over Nosenko's rank tied in with the Cherepanov papers. Nosenko produced a KGB travel document that he said he had carried in 1963 when he participated in the man-

[8]*Ibid.*, September 1978, Vol. IV, p. 21.
[9]*Ibid.*

hunt for the traitorous Cherepanov, a document that showed his rank as lieutenant colonel. The CIA debriefers raised all sorts of questions about the document—why did Nosenko still have it, why did it show a higher rank than captain, which he later admitted was his true rank? The CI Staff believed that the KGB had provided Nosenko with a phony document to support his claims of higher rank. "Why was he traveling to Geneva with an internal travel document, anyway?" asked Scotty Miler.

"There was an explanation," a former high official of the CIA said. "He *was* a captain. Whenever they sent KGB officers out of Moscow they gave them the temporary rank of major or lieutenant colonel on the temporary ID card. Nosenko's expecting a promotion but he defects before it's finally signed. He thinks of himself as having been promoted."

Nosenko's debriefers turned to the subject of "Sasha." Two years earlier, Anatoly Golitsin had warned of a mole in the CIA with that KGB cryptonym. Peter Karlow, the principal suspect, had been forced out of the CIA, but the gumshoes had been unable to prove that Karlow was Sasha, or even that there was a penetration of the agency. Did Nosenko know of a mole named Sasha?

"We drew a blank from Nosenko on the name Sasha in '62," Bagley said. "In '64 he volunteered the name Sasha and said it was a U.S. Army officer in Germany. You'd think since it was only a year and a half before, he would have remembered that he didn't know about any Sasha." Bagley said that the Army officer's identity was established with the help of a later Soviet walk-in, whom U.S. intelligence code-named KITTY HAWK.

Angleton's deputy, Scotty Miler, confirmed that "some of Nosenko's information was valuable." For example, Miler said, his leads also helped to narrow down the search for the Army officer. "Nosenko knew his Sasha had served in Berlin. He knew the time frame. The FBI located him. Sasha turned out to be an Army major. He was not prosecuted. He confessed and was used as a double. The bureau turned him." The Army officer, who needed money to pay for a German mistress, had been recruited by the KGB in Germany in 1959. He later returned to Washington and provided low-level intelligence to the Soviets during the Cuban missile crisis.

James E. Nolan, Jr., a former deputy assistant director of the FBI for counterintelligence, believed the case had even more ramifications than met the eye. By the time that KITTY HAWK, whom Nolan regarded as a KGB plant, although others do not, had provided additional information that led to the major, "he was no longer in the Army. He was given immunity in exchange for his cooperation. Nosenko's Sasha was used briefly as a double when the Soviets showed some new interest in him. We let it run for a little while."

Nolan said he believed that the Soviets recontacted this Sasha "to build up KITTY HAWK's bona fides, because KITTY HAWK had provided information that led us to the Army major. So recontact would prove the major was indeed a Soviet agent, and thus underscore KITTY HAWK's bona fides."

The case of the Army major, while not very important in itself in the annals of the Cold War, illustrates the complexity of the world of counterintelligence. Golitsin warned of a Sasha in the CIA, Nosenko spoke of a Sasha in the military, who was identified with the help of a third Soviet KGB officer whose provenance remains unresolved to this day.

Nosenko's debriefers questioned him as well, as they had in 1962, about Vladislav Kovshuk, the high-ranking KGB official who had visited Washington in 1957 under an alias. Golitsin had speculated that Kovshuk was so important that he must have come to the United States to meet a mole inside the American government, perhaps in the CIA.

Nosenko repeated that Kovshuk had been dispatched to Washington to meet a KGB source code-named ANDREY. According to Bagley, Nosenko provided enough information to lead U.S. intelligence to a noncommissioned officer who had worked at the American embassy in Moscow, had since returned to the United States, and lived in the Washington area. By most accounts, ANDREY was a sergeant who had worked in the embassy motor pool. "ANDREY knew nothing, and was not prosecuted," Bagley said. Kovshuk did meet with ANDREY near the end of the Russian's tour in Washington, Bagley added. "He made the contact, turned ANDREY over to the residentura, and then left. What was he doing the rest of the time? Nosenko did not know. 'He was hunting for him,' Nosenko said. We asked, 'A chief of section hunting for a source?' Nosenko said, 'It took all that time to find him.' But he was in the phone book in Washington, we pointed out. Nosenko had no answer."

Bagley's comments on Kovshuk's mission capture the flavor of his view of Nosenko, and Angleton's, and of the interrogation that began in 1964. Virtually all of Nosenko's statements and explanations were met with a deep, pervasive suspicion. As a result, nothing Nosenko could say was accepted at face value.

"Nosenko was a plant, is a plant, and always will be," Bagley said.[10] In this fixed view of Nosenko as a KGB plant, the leads the defector provided were either yielding up spent assets, spies whose value was long past, or were designed to deflect from the real mole or moles in the CIA whom Golitsin was trying to uncover.

Golitsin said Sasha was a CIA penetration. Nosenko said Sasha was an Army officer. Golitsin said Kovshuk came to America to meet a high-level mole. Nosenko said Kovshuk came to meet ANDREY, who turned out to be an Army sergeant.

"He was pointing away from the Golitsin leads to penetrations," Bagley said. "My test for defectors is, do they provide current access to previously unknown information? Nosenko didn't." But Nosenko seemed to have revealed a great number of cases. For example, what about his leads to Robert Lee Johnson, who cracked the safe containing NATO secrets in Paris? "Robert Lee Johnson had lost his access and was a burned-out case," Bagley replied.

On April 4, less than two months after the defector had arrived in the United States, the CIA began what its officials euphemistically referred to as the "hostile interrogation" of Yuri Nosenko. Although he had chosen to live in a free society, Nosenko was confined by the CIA for the next four years and eight months. For more than two years of this period, he was isolated in a concrete cell under brutal conditions. Later the conditions improved, but his movements were still restricted. Nosenko, to put it simply, had become a prisoner of the CIA, lost in an American gulag.

Former CIA director Stansfield Turner has blamed Angleton for the decision to imprison Nosenko, a view bitterly disputed by Angleton loyalists. "Angleton . . . decided that Nosenko was a double agent, and set out to force him to confess," Turner wrote. ". . . Angleton's counterintelligence team set out to break the man psychologically."[11]

Responsibility for the decision to incarcerate Nosenko and place

[10]Bagley stated this with utter conviction, and an almost religious faith, during an interview with the author early in 1990, twenty-six years after Nosenko's defection.
[11]Stansfield Turner, *Secrecy and Democracy: The CIA in Transition* (Boston: Houghton Mifflin, 1985), p. 44.

him under harsh interrogation was shared with Angleton by Helms; David E. Murphy, the head of the Soviet division; and Bagley, the division's counterintelligence officer. Murphy minced no words in telling Helms that Nosenko "must be broken" if the CIA was to learn the truth, although the agency's desire for more information, he admitted, "may conflict with the need to break Subject."[12]

When questioned by a congressional committee about his own role, Helms waffled. The decision, he said, "was jointly arrived at." He added: "I don't know who exactly made the final decision. . . . I was a party to the decision. . . . I don't want to duck anything. . . . I was there. It would not have been my final decision to make."[13] In testimony to the same committee, Murphy was asked if he had "primary responsibility for what happened to Nosenko." He replied: "I was responsible for the case."[14]

However, according to Bagley, "The decision to start hostile interrogation was made by David Murphy, Helms, and me. Angleton did agree to the incarceration. It was unthinkable that he didn't. Angleton agreed to the hostile interrogation, along with Helms and Murphy. Angleton never opposed the incarceration."[15]

A former CIA officer who closely studied this period of the agency's history, however, had no doubt that "Angleton was the bottom line on incarcerating Nosenko. Absolutely. Murphy did it? Horseshit! Sure, Soviet division had responsibility for Nosenko, but it could not have happened unless Jim signed off on it, unless he agreed."

The CIA officer then made a startling disclosure: "What Jim really wanted to do with Nosenko was send him back to the Soviet Union.

[12]Memorandum, Murphy to Helms, February 17, 1964, in *Investigation of the Assassination of President John F. Kennedy,* Hearings, Select Committee on Assassinations of the U.S. House of Representatives, September 1978, Vol. IV, p. 87.
[13]*Investigation of the Assassination of President John F. Kennedy,* Hearings, Select Committee on Assassinations of the U.S. House of Representatives, September 1978, Vol. IV, p. 103.
[14]*Ibid.,* March 1979, Vol. XII, p. 531.
[15]For the most detailed examination of Angleton's role, see Samuel Halpern and Hayden Peake, "Did Angleton Jail Nosenko?" in *International Journal of Intelligence and Counterintelligence,* Vol. 3, No. 4 (Winter 1989). The article, although an apologia for Angleton, does demonstrate that other CIA officials were involved. However, the study also quotes Bagley, in a footnote, as saying that the decision was "taken jointly" by the CIA officials involved, "*including Angleton*" (italics added).

Helms would have no part of it. And rightly so. Then the idea arose, let's start this harsh interrogation."

One of the problems faced by later investigators was that it was almost impossible to find traces of Angleton's role in the affair. "I never saw a document he signed off on," the CIA man said, "but he didn't object. Jim's fingerprints were never on anything. He was the artist of all time. Nosenko was confined for three years. But in three years, Angleton never objected. There is no shred of evidence that Angleton ever complained to Helms."

For almost a year and a half, beginning on April 4, 1964, Nosenko was confined under harsh conditions in an attic room of a safe house outside Washington. He had been told that day that he was being taken there for a physical and a polygraph test. He later described what happened. "After finishing the test an officer of CIA has come in the room and talked with a technician. [The CIA officer] started to shout that I was a phoney and immediately several guards entered in the room. The guards ordered me to stand by the wall, to undress and checked me. After that I was taken upstairs in an attic room. The room had a metal bed attached to the floor in the center of this room. Nobody told me anything, how long I would be there or what would happen to me."[16] Some days later, the interrogations began.

Nosenko had no access to television, radio, or newspapers, his food was subsistence-level—for many months it consisted mainly of weak tea, watery soup, and porridge—and he was under constant observation. He was also denied cigarettes. "I was smoking from fourteen years old, never quitted. I was rejected to smoke. I didn't see books. I didn't read anything. I was sitting in four walls . . . I was hungry . . . I was thinking about food because all the time I want to eat. I was receiving very small amount, and very poor food."[17]

Washington is brutally hot in the summer, and attic rooms unbearable. Nosenko told what it was like: "I was sitting in some kind of attic; it was hot, no air conditioning, cannot breathe; windows—no windows, closed over. I was permitted to shave once a week, to take

[16]Affidavit of Yuri Nosenko, August 7, 1978, in *Investigation of the Assassination of President John F. Kennedy,* Hearings, Select Committee on Assassinations of the U.S. House of Representatives, September 1978, Vol. IV, pp. 106–8.

[17]*Investigation of the Assassination of President John F. Kennedy,* Hearings, Select Committee on Assassinations of the U.S. House of Representatives, March 1979, Vol. XII, pp. 524–25.

showers once a week. From me were taken toothpaste, toothbrush. The conditions were inhuman. . . ."[18]

As the days marched by, Helms had a problem: what, if anything, to tell the Warren Commission, which was pressing to complete its report. Helms met with former Chief Justice Earl Warren, the commission chairman, and informed him that the CIA had been unable to establish Nosenko's bona fides and could not vouch for the truth of his story. The commission never questioned Nosenko, and its final report, issued on September 27, contained no reference to Nosenko.

It is doubtful that Helms remembered to tell the former Chief Justice, whose Supreme Court promulgated strict standards to protect the rights of criminal suspects, that Nosenko was confined in an airless attic. But as bad as it was, Nosenko's quarters and the conditions under which he was held were luxurious compared to what awaited him. While the Russian was locked up in the attic, the CIA's Office of Security was constructing a special prison cell for him on the Farm.

All CIA trainees go through courses at the Farm, a school for spies in Virginia near Colonial Williamsburg. The CIA base is under military cover as the "Armed Forces Experimental Training Activity, Department of Defense, Camp Peary." Armed guards protect the installation, which stretches over ten thousand acres along the York River. The heavily wooded site is, of course, closed to outsiders and surrounded by a chain link fence. During World War II, it was a prisoner-of-war camp for captured German soldiers.

Blindfolded and handcuffed, Nosenko was taken there in August of 1965 and placed in a twelve-by-twelve-foot windowless concrete cell in a house deep in the woods on the CIA base. Nosenko was watched day and night by a television camera. To occupy his mind, he secretly made a chess set from threads, but it was seen and confiscated by the guards. In an effort to keep track of time, he also fashioned a calendar out of lint from his clothing.

He was desperate for something to read. He was given toothpaste, but it was taken away when he tried, under a blanket, to read the writing on the tube. Nosenko was held, interrogated, and polygraphed in this cell for more than two years.

More than a year went by after Nosenko arrived at the Farm before he was allowed to get any fresh air and exercise. He was taken from

[18]*Ibid.,* p. 525.

his cell for thirty minutes a day to a fenced-in exercise pen, from where he could only see the sky.

It was "deplorable," Helms later told congressional investigators, but the CIA was in a position where it risked criticism for holding Nosenko too long, but would have been "damned the other way" if it had not "dug his teeth out to find out what he knows about Oswald." The cell on the Farm, Helms tried to persuade the House committee, was therapeutic for Nosenko, almost a Virginia branch of Alcoholics Anonymous. "Mr. Nosenko, at the time he defected and before, was a very heavy drinker. One of the problems we had with him during his first period of time in the United States was he didn't want to do anything except drink and carouse. We had problems with him in an incident in Baltimore where he starting punching up a bar and so forth. One of the reasons to hold him in confinement was to get him away from the booze and settle him down and see if we could make some sense with him."[19]

Nosenko was convinced he was given drugs, including "hallucination drugs," during his confinement. The CIA has denied this, claiming that Nosenko was given only necessary medications.[20] Helms testified that he turned down a request to administer "truth drugs, such as, I believe, sodium pentothal." Another CIA witness said the proposed truth serum was sodium amytal.[21] In his memoir, Stansfield Turner said Nosenko was given "one or more of four drugs on seventeen occasions."[22]

[19]Ibid., September 1978, Vol. IV, p. 31.
[20]According to CIA records, however, Nosenko was given Thorazine, a powerful drug used to control psychotic disorders and manic depression. Other drugs administered were Zactrin, also known as Zactirin, a mild tranquilizer and aspirin combination no longer produced; Donnatal, an antispasmodic drug for indigestion; tetracycline, a common antibiotic; and antihistamines and cough syrup. Nosenko told a congressional committee in 1978 that he had been given a hallucinogenic drug, and speculated more recently that it was LSD. Investigation of the Assassination of President John F. Kennedy, Hearings, Select Committee on Assassinations of the U.S. House of Representatives, September 1978, Vol. XII, pp. 521, 525, and 543; and Tom Mangold, Cold Warrior: James Jesus Angleton: The CIA's Master Spy Hunter (New York: Simon & Schuster, 1991), p. 188.
[21]Investigation of the Assassination of President John F. Kennedy, Hearings, Select Committee on Assassinations of the U.S. House of Representatives, September 1978, Vol. IV, p. 116, and September 1978, Vol. II, p. 532.
[22]Turner, Secrecy and Democracy, p. 45. When questioned by the author, Turner said he did not recall the source of this information in his memoir. However, since Turner did not identify the drugs in his book, his assertion that Nosenko was given drugs

Other psychological pressures were applied. For example, just before he was flown to the Farm, Nosenko was told by his CIA interrogators that he would be held for more than ten years. While confined, Nosenko was polygraphed three times. But the first two lie-detector tests were rigged, designed to break Nosenko and persuade him to confess that he was a dispatched agent of the KGB. The first time, the CIA man giving the lie-detector test was instructed to tell Nosenko he had flunked, regardless of the outcome. Nosenko was also told that the polygraph could read his brainwaves, which was not true. The results of a second polygraph—actually a series of polygraphs over ten days—suggested Nosenko was lying about Oswald, but the CIA later said the test was invalid. And small wonder; Nosenko was wired to the machine for seven hours for one test, and while his interrogators took their lunch breaks, he was left strapped to the chair so he could not move. One such "lunch break" lasted for four hours. The polygraph operator also harassed Nosenko, warning that there was no hope for him, and that he might well go crazy. Nosenko passed a third polygraph, which included two questions about Oswald, and the CIA considered this test to be the only one that was valid.

Bagley personally handled the Nosenko interrogation by closed-circuit television that linked the special prison on the Farm to Langley headquarters. Three interrogators on the scene questioned Nosenko.

Bagley contended that the CIA had not, at the outset, planned to incarcerate Nosenko for so long. "We expected it to be ten days, two weeks, to confront him with the holes in his story." Why, then, had it lasted more than four and a half years? "He dug himself deeper with new contradictions," Bagley said. "He clearly had not held the jobs he claimed. And he said he had participated in operations against the U.S. embassy that he didn't take part in. His statements were designed to hide something."

Guided by Bagley, the interrogators pounced on any conflicts in Nosenko's story. For example, Nosenko had claimed that in Geneva in 1962, he personally participated in the operation against Edward Ellis Smith, in which the CIA's first officer in Moscow had been sexually compromised by his KGB maid. Smith's entanglement with

---

seventeen times is not necessarily in conflict with the CIA's official position that Nosenko was given only normal prescription drugs, no truth serums.

the KGB swallow was discovered in 1956.[23] Nosenko said he had been transferred to the Seventh Department, handling tourists, in 1955. "During the hostile interrogation of Nosenko," Bagley said, "he was confronted with the fact that he said he handled Smith, but how could he have handled Smith if he was already transferred to the tourist department? 'Who's Smith?' Nosenko asked. Upon which we played back the tapes of the '62 meeting in Geneva in which he talked about Smith. The tapes were loud and clear. He listened to them, and he said"—here Bagley grimaced, imitating Nosenko—" 'Mr. Bagley got me drunk.' "

It was, of course, entirely possible that Nosenko was puffing when he claimed to have entrapped Smith, but he surely would have known of the operation. The successful ensnarement, in bed, of the CIA's first man in Moscow would undoubtedly be the subject of considerable corridor gossip, and much snickering, inside the Second Chief Directorate. And it was also possible that the maid had been planted on Smith as early as 1955, before Nosenko transferred to the tourist branch. As with so much in the world of counterintelligence, almost every event can have an explanation that is either sinister or innocent, depending on one's viewpoint.

James Angleton, for example, made much of the fact that the premier FBI source in New York City, a KGB officer code-named FEDORA by the bureau, had vouched for Nosenko's bona fides. This, Angleton believed, proved that FEDORA himself was a plant, since the FBI source had assured the FBI that Nosenko was a real KGB defector.

It was a line of reasoning for which an undergraduate in a beginning college course in logic would be flunked. In the first place, Nosenko might be a real defector; the comments of the FBI's Soviet asset in New York would then be accurate. But even if Nosenko was assumed to be a plant, as of course Angleton believed, there were several alternative explanations for FEDORA's statements, including the obvious possibility that the Soviet source in New York had not been told by the KGB that Nosenko had been sent. Or if Nosenko was real and FEDORA a plant, FEDORA might still support Nosenko to shore up his own credibility. The permutations and combinations were, in fact,

[23]The KGB prefers to call an agent used as a seductress a "sparrow." The CIA uses the term "swallow." The reasons for these ornithological differences are not clear.

endless. FEDORA's comments about Nosenko really proved nothing about either man.

A former high-ranking FBI official disputed Angleton's conclusion that FEDORA had vouched for Nosenko in the first place. "FEDORA was simply reporting overhearing a conversation about Nosenko in which two Soviets at the UN mission, probably both KGB, were saying, 'Oh, it's terrible about Nosenko.' " He pointed out that the *New York Times,* on February 11, had carried a front-page article from Geneva reporting Nosenko's defection. It would have been read, of course, by Soviet diplomats in New York. "FEDORA wasn't confirming Nosenko's bona fides at all. He was reporting a conversation, and he had no knowledge of whether what he overheard was true. But to the Scotty Milers and other people in Angleton's shop, the information from FEDORA was just what they were looking for."

Angleton had one reason to doubt FEDORA that was more persuasive. "FEDORA said a cable had been received from Moscow about Nosenko's defection," a former CIA counterintelligence officer said. "We ran all sorts of NSA tests and couldn't find any evidence such a cable existed." The National Security Agency, the nation's code-breaking arm, might not be able to read the Soviet code, but from information provided by FEDORA, it could perform traffic analysis that might indicate whether a cable was sent on the date, and at the time, that he said it was. NSA was not infallible, however, and it could not always pinpoint a particular message.

FEDORA, code-named SCOTCH by the CIA, was Aleksei Isidorovich Kulak, a KGB officer under cover at the United Nations, first as an employee of the secretariat and then as a scientific attaché in the Soviet mission to the UN. He began feeding information to the FBI early in 1962, only a few months after he arrived in the United States to begin work on November 29, 1961, as a consultant to the UN Scientific Committee on the Effects of Atomic Radiation. Kulak, then thirty-nine, married and accompanied by his wife in New York, was a short, stocky man whose name, of course, meant "wealthy farmer" in Russian. "We called him Fatso," said an FBI man who worked the case.[24]

---

[24]FEDORA was later erroneously identified in some published reports as Victor M. Lessiovski, a KGB officer who held a high rank in the UN. Lessiovski was rumored to be the KGB resident in New York City. FEDORA told the FBI that Lessiovski was indeed a top KGB agent, an important man, but not the resident. A short, plump man

Kulak was no run-of-the-mill KGB man. He was a spy who specialized in collecting scientific and technical secrets. He had a doctorate in chemistry and had worked as a radiological chemist in a Moscow laboratory.[25] As winter turned to spring in 1962, Kulak had walked into the FBI office on Manhattan's East Side one day and offered his services. He said he was disgruntled about lack of progress in his KGB career. The Soviet system, he said, had not recognized his abilities. But either Kulak or the FBI building might have been watched by the Soviets. Eugene C. Peterson, who served fifteen years in FBI counterintelligence, and became chief of the Soviet section, agreed that if FEDORA was genuine, he was taking a chance in the way he made the initial contact. "It was risky," he said. "It raised questions."

Peterson, a tall, husky, balding man with clear blue eyes and a skeptical, streetwise face, added: "FEDORA provided a paucity of CI information. He did not identify any penetrations." Mostly, he said, FEDORA identified who was who in the KGB residentura in New York.

J. Edgar Hoover had total faith in FEDORA, but it was always possible that the doubts at the working level never got up the line to Hoover. And the doubts did exist. "There were questions, right from the start," Peterson said. "And certainly for the last four to six years."

On the other hand, a former high-ranking CIA official insisted that FEDORA had provided the United States with valuable information. He was convinced that the KGB man was a valid source, for several reasons. "There were a whole series of things," he said. "His attention to details about surveillance and countersurveillance. You surveil the individual and when he comes to the meeting you see if he is taking precautions, whether he is worried about being followed. FEDORA was worried about surveillance. If he walks out of his office and goes straight to the safe house, you know something is wrong. Then, there

who walked his wife's pet poodle every night near their home in Manhattan, Lessiovski served as personal assistant to UN Secretary-General U Thant of Burma for eight years. The KGB man moved in the highest social circles in Manhattan. He was so well connected, in fact, that when Pope Paul VI visited New York in 1965, it was Lessiovski who arranged for Jacqueline Kennedy to meet the pontiff. The former First Lady was amused that she had been introduced to the Pope by the KGB. Lessiovski left New York in 1971 and returned to the Soviet Union.

[25]Although a consultant, Kulak was an employee of the UN secretariat for two years, attached to the Office of the Undersecretary for Special Political Affairs. He held the highest professional rank at the UN below that of a director.

was his willingness to disclose information about KGB officers. Which he did. They don't like to give away identities of officers."

Above all, the CIA man said, FEDORA had revealed to the United States what the KGB had tasked him to collect in the area of science and technology. "He gave us their S&T requirements. A KGB wish list. Identifying factories where military equipment was being manufactured. Everything he wanted was military. Tanks, missiles, everything. He was a very useful source, given the paucity of our access in those days."

To make Kulak look valuable to the KGB, the FBI provided him with "feed material," genuine U.S. secrets cleared by the CIA and other American intelligence agencies and passed to FEDORA for transmittal to Moscow. "It was low-grade stuff," the CIA man said, "but not phony."

The periodic clandestine meetings between Kulak and the FBI were videotaped. "I saw videos of FEDORA being debriefed," the CIA official related. "Chunky guy, typical Russian. These were New York FBI agents debriefing him, in English. With a big bottle of Scotch from which all were drinking."

In February 1963, Kulak left the UN secretariat and switched over to the Soviet mission to the United Nations. In 1967, Kulak told the FBI he had been recalled to Moscow on normal rotation. When he returned in 1971, again as a scientific attaché, he resumed his relationship with the bureau. But FEDORA's position, if he was a true agent-in-place, became more and more tenuous. News accounts, including one by Seymour M. Hersh in the *New York Times,* suggested that the FBI had penetrated a Soviet diplomatic mission in the United States. Hersh reported that one of the reasons that President Richard Nixon had established the secret White House plumbers unit was ostensible concern that "a highly placed Soviet agent of the KGB . . . operating as an American counterspy would be compromised" by the Watergate inquiries.[26]

[26]Seymour M. Hersh, "The President and the Plumbers: A Look at 2 Security Questions," *New York Times,* December 9, 1973, p. 1. To test whether FEDORA was in jeopardy as a result of the published reports, a former FBI counterintelligence agent said, the CIA gave one of the news stories to a low-level analyst. Within a few hours, he claimed, the analyst had pinpointed Kulak as the likely FBI source. But Hersh's story did not indicate whether the KGB man was based in New York or Washington. It did say that the source had been a double agent "for nearly ten years," but other

In 1971, during the furor over the Pentagon Papers, the classified history of the Vietnam War leaked to the *New York Times* by Daniel Ellsberg, Kulak reported that a set of the papers had been delivered to the Soviet embassy. The CIA scoffed at the report. In a meeting with David R. Young, one of the chiefs of the White House plumbers, CIA director Richard Helms said he discounted the report because "we know the fellow who has been giving us these reports and we have our doubts about them."[27]

In all, Kulak/FEDORA served two years in New York with the UN secretariat, beginning in 1961, and then two tours with the Soviet mission between 1964 and 1977, with a four-year break in between when he was called back to Moscow.[28] Despite the doubts about Aleksei Kulak, KGB walk-ins are hard to come by; over this sixteen-year period, the FBI paid him approximately $100,000.

"In 1977 when FEDORA was getting ready to go back for the last time," Peterson said, "we pointed out the articles that had been published. We told him, 'Your life is in jeopardy.' 'Oh, I can handle that,' he said. My own view is that if he wasn't a plant, he would have been executed."

After passing information to the FBI for more than a dozen years, Kulak/FEDORA returned to Moscow for the last time in 1977 and was subsequently seen there by the CIA, alive and well. That, of course, did not prove he was genuine. It either meant that Kulak was a true spy for the United States who had escaped detection, or a double agent for the KGB all along. "He would have been under surveillance in Moscow," Peterson said, "and when he met with the CIA, they would have moved in and rolled him up."

In 1978, the writer Edward Jay Epstein revealed the code name

---

Soviet diplomats had been assigned in this country for that long. Told that the FBI had been concerned that his story might unmask FEDORA, Hersh laughed. "The source came from high up in the FBI," he said.

[27]David Young, "Memorandum of Conversation, July 21, 1971," in *Statement of Information Submitted on Behalf of President Nixon,* Hearings, House Committee on the Judiciary, May–June 1974, Book IV, p. 107.

[28]Oddly, Kulak's name varied slightly on each tour. In *Permanent Missions to the United Nations,* the official diplomatic list of the UN, the name "Alexei Sidorovich Kulak" appears for the first time in January 1964, with the title "First Secretary" of the Soviet UN mission. From January 1968 through May 1971, he drops off the list. He reappears in September 1971, this time as "Aleksei Isidorovich Kulak," with the new title "Counsellor." He drops off the list for the last time in February 1977.

FEDORA, describing him as a KGB officer at the UN collecting data on "science and technology."[29] U.S. intelligence officials were shaken by the disclosure, because the description of the Soviet asset was so specific that they assumed he was a dead man. "We estimated that after the Epstein book, he [FEDORA] was through," a former senior CIA official said. "There is no way he could have survived."[30] But, oddly, nothing happened to FEDORA, as far as the CIA could learn.

Boris A. Solomatin, who served as the KGB's New York resident from 1971 to 1975, during Kulak's second tour in Manhattan, offered one possible explanation. In an interview with the author in Moscow in September of 1991, Solomatin, although declining to refer to FEDORA by his true name, said: "There were circumstances that deflected suspicion. He was a Hero of the Soviet Union during the war, and it diverted suspicion."

The debate over FEDORA's bona fides has never subsided. The CIA accepted him as genuine in 1975 (after Angleton's departure).[31] The FBI has had more difficulty making up its mind, and has flip-flopped back and forth on the question. In 1967, the FBI seemed to accept FEDORA as bona fide.[32]

But a later secret study supervised by James E. Nolan, Jr., the deputy assistant FBI director for counterintelligence, and completed in March 1976, concluded that FEDORA was a plant, a view said to have been modified by the FBI again in the early 1980s. By 1990, the CIA had learned that Kulak had died of natural causes.

At the same time that FEDORA was active, the FBI and later the CIA were receiving information from another Soviet source in New York City, Dimitri Fedorovich Polyakov, an officer of the GRU, Soviet military intelligence. He was code-named TOPHAT by the bureau and BOURBON by the CIA, which preferred liquor over headgear. In intelligence circles, the names FEDORA and TOPHAT became inextricably in-

[29]Edward Jay Epstein, *Legend: The Secret World of Lee Harvey Oswald* (New York: Reader's Digest Press/McGraw-Hill, 1978), p. 20.
[30]The counterspies were almost equally appalled by the apparent origin of the disclosure. It was well known in intelligence circles that Epstein's major source had been James Angleton. The former CIA counterintelligence chief, officials concluded, had deliberately blown FEDORA, whom Angleton considered a plant.
[31]The CIA decision was based on a study by Benjamin Franklin Pepper, an officer in the Soviet division, who concluded that FEDORA was authentic.
[32]Under the cryptonym VUPOINT, an FBI study that year of FEDORA and other Soviet assets suggested that Kulak was a legitimate source.

tertwined, like ham and eggs. In 1966, Polyakov was sent to Burma, and in the early 1970s he was posted to India, where Paul L. Dillon served as his CIA case officer. Back in Moscow after that, he continued to send information to the CIA, using a burst transmitter provided by the agency. The Soviets announced in 1990 that TOPHAT had been caught. They later said he had been executed on March 15, 1988.[33]

But FEDORA and TOPHAT were sideshows. At Langley, it had become increasingly clear that the Nosenko interrogation was a disaster. Moreover, it was one that carried a potential for scandal if the public should learn that the CIA had imprisoned a defector. Whether Angleton and other CIA officials even stopped to consider the catastrophic effect on other potential defectors should the Soviets find out about Nosenko's ordeal is not known.

But something had to be done. In 1967, Helms, by now the director of the CIA, ordered Bruce Solie, of the Office of Security, to review the question of Nosenko's bona fides. On October 28, Nosenko was finally taken from his cell and shifted to the first of three safe houses in the Washington area. Conditions improved considerably, but his movements were still restricted, and he was not a free man.[34] Not until March 1969 did the CIA finally allow Nosenko a two-week vacation in Florida. In a memo to Helms, Howard J. Osborn, the director of the Office of Security, wrote: "Nosenko is becoming increasingly restive and desirous of obtaining freedom on his own. After nearly five years of varying degrees of confinement, this desire, including that for feminine companionship, is understandable."[35]

Bagley clearly saw the potential for scandal. He sent a letter to Angleton warning of the "devastating consequences" if Nosenko was

[33]In his book *Spycatcher,* published in 1987, former MI5 official Peter Wright wrote that TOPHAT had provided information that led to the arrest in 1965 of Frank C. Bossard, a forty-nine-year-old employee of the British Aviation Ministry who was photographing documents about American missile guidance systems on his lunch hour. Bossard was sentenced to twenty-one years in prison. In fact, the FBI intelligence division had misled MI5, wrongly attributing these leads to TOPHAT in order to protect another GRU source in New York, code-named NICKNACK.
[34]In all, from April 4, 1964, to August 13, 1965, Nosenko was confined to a safe house near Washington. From August 14, 1965, to October 27, 1967, he was imprisoned in the cell at the Farm. From October 28, 1967, to December 1968 he was held at three safe houses in the Washington area.
[35]Memorandum, Osborn to Helms, March 24, 1969, in *Investigation of the Assassination of President John F. Kennedy,* Hearings, Select Committee on Assassinations of the U.S. House of Representatives, September 1978, Vol. IV, p. 41.

set free. Taking pencil to paper, he wrote down a list of possible "actions" to handle the Nosenko problem. Option number 5 was "Liquidate the man," number 6 was "Render him incapable of giving coherent story (special dose of drug etc.). Possible aim, commitment to loony bin," and number 7 was "Commitment to loony bin *without* making him nuts."[36]

But Bagley, who had risen to deputy chief of the Soviet division by 1966, never sent his list of chilling options to anyone, and it was obviously not meant to see the light of day. It became public only because in 1976, Angleton's successor as CI chief, George T. Kalaris—with the approval of then CIA director George Bush— named John L. Hart, a former station chief, to conduct another review of the Nosenko case. Hart discovered Bagley's penciled list in the files and told Congress about it.

Bagley, ambushed by Hart, was furious. The options on his list, he said, were "never proposed, it was a thought process: here we sit with this guy and what do about it? These were handwritten notes in pencil, never shown to anyone else, never intended for anyone else."

Had he really contemplated murdering Nosenko? "Of course not," Bagley replied. "I wouldn't permit it and it was not agency policy. There wouldn't be any thought of it. I might add it's my own policy as well. I don't go around killing people. And Hart knew it." But the thought *had* occurred; "liquidate the man" was one of the ghastly options on Bagley's list.

In October 1968, Bruce Solie submitted his report to Helms, clearing Nosenko.[37] On the basis of the report, the KGB man was rehabili-

---

[36]*Investigation of the Assassination of President John F. Kennedy,* Hearings, Select Committee on Assassinations of the U.S. House of Representatives, September 1978, Vol. II, pp. 519, 525, 536. Some of the words in Bagley's jottings were abbreviated but are spelled out here for clarity.

[37]A 900-page summary of the agency's file on Nosenko, prepared by Bagley, later cut by him to 447 pages, and submitted in February 1968, reached an opposite conclusion. It argued that Nosenko had lied on every major point about his KGB background. A decade later, the House Assassinations Committee also concluded that "Nosenko lied about Oswald." But the committee noted that the defector's imprisonment "virtually ruined him as a valid source of information on the assassination." *The Final Assassinations Report: Report of the Select Committee on Assassinations, U.S. House of Representatives* (New York: Bantam, 1979), p. 114. All other CIA studies supported Nosenko's bona fides. In addition to the Solie report, there were two later internal reviews of the Nosenko case, one by John Hart in 1976, while George Bush headed the CIA, and one in the spring of 1981, by Jack J. Fieldhouse,

tated, hired as a consultant by the CIA, and given $137,052 in lost pay and resettlement expenses.[38]

Helms did not have an easy time of it when he tried to explain the Nosenko affair to Congress. Representative Harold S. Sawyer, a Michigan Republican, asked the former CIA director whether he knew that what had been done to Nosenko, holding him without trial, subjecting him to "physical and mental torture," broke the law. Helms wasn't sure; he thought Nosenko's legal status fell into a "gray area." The congressman did not buy it:

Mr. Sawyer: Well, he was a human being, wasn't he?
Mr. Helms: I believe so.
Mr. Sawyer: You know in most states even treating an animal like this will land you in jail.

Helms did not reply.

As for Yuri Nosenko, he summed up his experience succinctly. "I passed through hell," he said. "I was true defector."

---

a CIA officer, undertaken at the request of CIA director William J. Casey. Both reports, as well as Solie's study, concluded that Nosenko was what he said he was—a KGB officer who changed sides and defected to the CIA.

[38]Other Soviet intelligence officers who came over to the West in the years since Nosenko's arrival have said he was, as far as they knew, a bona fide defector. For example, Victor Gundarev, a KGB colonel who defected in Athens in 1986, told me in July 1989: "Nosenko was real. I was a student at the KGB Higher School in 1964. They talked about him as a traitor. Of course it could be a cover story, I don't know." It is true that other defectors might not have valid or detailed knowledge about Nosenko. On the other hand, according to former senior CIA officials, no defector subsequent to Nosenko has provided information that casts doubt on his bona fides.

Chapter 12

Molehunt

By the late summer of 1963, the mole hunt at the CIA was in full cry.

Golitsin's sojourn to England had temporarily slowed it down, but after the defector's abrupt return from London, the search for penetrations gained new momentum. The mole hunt was directed by James Angleton, who now began showing Golitsin classified CIA files so that the defector could comb through the agency's secrets, looking for clues and likely suspects.[1]

In July, the same month that Golitsin returned to Langley, Peter Karlow, the first suspect, had resigned. But nothing had been proved against him. If Karlow was not the mole, then who was? Nor could it be assumed that there was only one traitor in the ranks. The CI Staff did not, in fact, confine itself to searching for a single Soviet agent inside the CIA. The agency might be honeycombed with moles. As the

---

[1] It was very odd indeed to allow a Soviet, and a former KGB officer, to read secret CIA files. In defense of the practice, Scotty Miler, a key former member of Angleton's staff, said that Golitsin was not shown raw files but "sanitized" versions from which some sensitive material had been deleted. However, Miler said that it was only in 1969—after the mole hunt was long under way—that he had been instructed "to sanitize the files," and began doing so. "Up to that time I had not been involved in it," Miler said. "I don't know what happened before."

investigation grew, its target expanded, following a familiar rule of bureaucracy.[2]

To conduct the mole hunt, Angleton had turned to the Special Investigations Group (SIG) within the Counterintelligence Staff.[3] Its chief at first was Birch D. O'Neal, a courtly Georgian with a syrup-thick Southern accent, who had joined the FBI in 1938 and later switched over to the CIA. A portly, florid-faced man, O'Neal, as befitted his position, was extremely secretive. "Nobody had the vaguest notion of what Birch was doing," said a former colleague in the SIG, "to the point where you sometimes wondered whether he did either."

But if O'Neal, then fifty, and already looking toward his retirement, presided over the hunt, the master of the hounds was Scotty Miler, whom Angleton handpicked and brought in from Ethiopia, where he was station chief, to join the SIG and the search for penetrations. Angleton named him deputy chief of the SIG.

Miler, an old Far East hand, slow-spoken and tough, had a natural bent for counterintelligence work. In his view, every possible suspect had to be scrutinized, for a mole could be anyone, anywhere. Every lead had to be followed up meticulously. The security of the agency might depend upon it. And Miler had a system. If a CIA colleague fell under suspicion, he would draw up a list of every questionable item in the man's personal background or arising out of the operations in

[2]The term "mole" as a description of a penetration agent placed inside an opposition intelligence service or government was popularized by John le Carré in his spy novels, and to some extent filtered into the vocabulary of real spies. Most CIA officers prefer the term "penetration." The first use of the word in an intelligence context has been traced to Sir Francis Bacon's history of the reign of King Henry VII, published in 1622: "He was careful and liberal to obtain good intelligence from all parts abroad. . . . As for his secret spials which he did employ both at home and abroad, by them to discover what practices and conspiracies were against him, surely his case required it: he had such moles perpetually working and casting to undermine him." Francis Bacon, *The History of the Reign of King Henry the Seventh,* F. J. Levy, ed. (Indianapolis: Bobbs-Merrill, 1972), p. 243. Bacon, however, appears to have used the word "moles" in the sense of "dissidents" or "opponents"; in the modern usage it means a person reporting back to a foreign intelligence service.
[3]Inside the CI Staff, the SIG was pronounced not as an acronym, but with each letter enunciated. It had always had the responsibility for detecting penetrations in the agency, among its other duties, but the search for moles became its principal function after Golitsin defected.

which he had been involved. Then, one by one, plodding through the files, he would eliminate those points for which, after further investigation, he had satisfied himself there were benign explanations. When this laborious process had been completed, if there were still items left on Miler's list, then the suspect would be marked down as a possible security risk. Not necessarily guilty, but a risk. Agency officials at a higher level would have to decide what to do about the suspect; that was not Miler's responsibility. Sometimes Miler would have dealings with the very people he was secretly investigating, or he would run into them in the halls. It made him feel uncomfortable. It was a difficult job, mole hunting, but someone had to do it.

Half a dozen other CIA officers were assigned to the SIG, including Jean M. Evans, an ultraconservative former OSS counterintelligence officer, bilingual in French, who concentrated on analyzing Golitsin's leads.[4] A spare, slender man of medium height, with thinning hair, Evans wore glasses perched on a sharp nose that gave him a rather birdlike appearance. He seldom talked about himself. A New Englander, with a laconic, Yankee manner, Evans had been an Army colonel before joining the CIA and had worked for the agency in Munich. In Munich, he had headed counterespionage at the CIA's Pullach base, which operated in tandem with General Gehlen's organization.[5] Like Miler, Evans was a meticulous man; no detail escaped his eye. But then, as CI officers are fond of saying, counterintelligence is in the details.

Clare Edward Petty, another member of the SIG, was an Oklahoman, a trim, gray-haired, square-jawed man with a friendly, somewhat professorial air. He had joined the CIA after the war and worked in Germany with the Gehlen organization for eight years. He took pride in having fingered Heinz Felfe of the West German Federal Intelligence Agency (BND) as a possible Soviet spy even before the defector Michal Goleniewski provided the leads that led to Felfe's

[4]Because of Evans's fluent French, Angleton often used him as an intermediary in dealing with Marcel Chalet, the head of the DST, the French internal service.
[5]The CIA had two bases in Munich at the time: the Pullach base at the headquarters of General Reinhard Gehlen, whom the CIA had set up as chief of an independent intelligence organization that became West Germany's BND, and the Munich operations base, headed by David Murphy, which conducted operations independent of the Gehlen organization.

arrest in 1961. Petty joined the SIG in 1966. In time, he was to become its most controversial member, because of the astonishing conclusion he reached about the identity of the senior CIA mole.

One of the SIG's tasks was to analyze a windfall of coded Soviet wireless traffic that had been acquired by Western intelligence during World War II and given the cryptonym VENONA. Only tantalizing bits of the code had been broken. The traffic included code names of Soviet agents in the West, but not their true identities. The SIG pored over the material, hoping for new leads to moles. Birch O'Neal eventually came to be responsible for the VENONA material, and for the collection abroad of "collateral," information such as travel records, shipping schedules, and so on, that might help to decrypt the Soviet traffic.

Another SIG member, Albert P. Kergel, also worked on the VENONA traffic and coordinated closely with the National Security Agency in the search for penetrations. A slender, balding man, well over six feet tall, Kergel was originally from New York State, a historian by training and a graduate of Columbia University whose specialty was the Soviet Union and Eastern Europe. John D. Walker also worked on the VENONA intercepts for the SIG during a brief period between assignments as station chief in Israel and Australia.

There were a few others who came and went: Charles Arnold, a six-foot officer with a Dick Tracy profile and a perpetually worried expression, joined the SIG but quickly became known as a naysayer. "He was the one who'd say, 'You don't have a case,'" a former CIA officer recalled. "Arnold became very skeptical of the whole thing and wrote a lot of papers urging his fellow mole hunters to get back on track." With that sort of attitude Arnold was not destined to last long on the SIG; he soon left the agency and retired to a small town in the Virginia Tidewater. William F. Potocki, part of a husband-and-wife CIA team, also worked closely with the mole hunters. A big, blond-haired career officer from Chicago, he had worked in the Berlin base for Bill Harvey before joining Angleton's staff in 1958.

The SIG's offices were on the second floor of CIA headquarters, overlooking a low roof and just around the corner from Angleton's own office in Room 2C43 on the same floor. Indeed, from his office Angleton could look across the way to the SIG offices in the D corridor, located in a wing at right angles to his own. Just by glancing out the window, he could reassure himself that the mole seekers were hard at work.

The mole hunt was given the code name HONETOL.[6] It was to last almost two decades, and before it petered out, the search for penetrations had investigated more than 120 CIA officers. But the mole hunt was not limited to the CIA.

"We were investigating everyone in the United States government," said a former senior member of the CI Staff. "We had files on people in USIS, Commerce, and other agencies. We had newspaper people. Newspaper cases were in the files."

If the mole hunters ranged far afield, the main arena for their efforts was nevertheless the CIA itself. For it was the agency, obviously, that offered the most tempting target to the KGB.

A mole in the CIA could tell the KGB about the agency's ongoing operations and its plans for future operations. He or she could give the Soviets the names of CIA officers under cover around the globe and of key officials at Langley. And, perhaps even more important, a Soviet mole inside the CIA would be well placed to detect whether the KGB itself had been penetrated.

The real danger, from the CI Staff's viewpoint, was not a low-level Soviet agent at Langley. Because of the compartmentalization that intelligence agencies practice, with varying degrees of success, a low-level traitor would probably have access only to a limited amount of classified material in his or her own section. The real danger would be a mole high enough up in the Clandestine Services to have access to a wide array of CIA operations and plans.

Ideally, the KGB would have liked to recruit the director of the CIA, or failing that, his deputy, or the deputy director for plans, the chief of the Soviet division of the DDO, or the chief of counterintelligence. Recruitments at that level would be rather difficult for the Soviets to achieve. And it would have been an awkward and delicate

[6]Pronounced ha-nuh-toll (the first syllable spoken as in the name Hans), the cryptonym sounded like a cold remedy but apparently was a sort of acronym. A former CIA officer said: "Jim was trying to win over the FBI and particularly Hoover to cooperate in the mole hunt. He came up with the idea of HONETOL because it incorporated the first two letters of Hoover's name with some of the letters of Golitsin's name, Anatoly." According to Miler, the cryptonym was used jointly with the British, who, of course, were hard at work looking for their own moles.

matter for Angleton and his mole hunters to investigate themselves or their own superiors. As a result, the CI Staff tended to look downward, and to concentrate its search for penetrations in the Soviet division, a choice dictated by both logic and discretion.

Because the target of the CIA's Soviet division was the Soviet Union itself, and because the division spent a great deal of its time trying to recruit Soviet intelligence officers, it was reasonable to assume that a high priority for the KGB would, in turn, be the recruitment of a CIA case officer inside the Soviet division. The case officer would have access to a broad range of operations, and beyond his own knowledge he would hear gossip in the corridors about other CIA assets and intelligence successes.

If the mole was not Peter Karlow, no matter; the list of CIA officers whose names began with K was long enough to provide ample fodder for the SIG for years. In July 1964, Golitsin, poring over the CIA's files, triumphantly pointed to a new candidate. This time, he was sure, he had found the penetration.

The officer's name began with the requisite letter. He had a Slavic background, since he was of Serbian descent, and he had served in Berlin. He thus fit Golitsin's mole "profile."

Richard Kovich was known as Dushan to his intimates. He was a seasoned officer who had handled half a dozen of the CIA's most sensitive cases. He supported George Kisevalter in the running of Pyotr Popov, the GRU colonel who was the first major CIA penetration of Soviet intelligence. He was the case officer for Mikhail Federov, whose CIA code name was UNACUTE, a GRU illegal whom Kovich had recruited in Paris. With the knowledge and consent of the Norwegian secret service, he ran Ingeborg Lygren, a Norwegian woman who worked in her country's embassy in Moscow but reported through Kovich to the CIA. And he was the first case officer for Yuri Loginov (code name AEGUSTO), a celebrated KGB illegal whose fate, along with Lygren's, became a major embarrassment to the agency.

In 1964, when his trouble began, Kovich was thirty-seven and had worked for the CIA for fourteen years, having joined the agency straight out of the University of Minnesota. A handsome man of six feet, Kovich was an extrovert with a sense of humor and a self-assurance that often made him speak up when others were silent.

He was born Dushan Kovacevich in Hibbing, Minnesota, the son of Serbian immigrants. His father, who was totally illiterate, ran electric shovels, digging iron ore from the Mesabi Range. It was a tough, polyglot town, where thirty-seven languages were spoken, and Kovich got out by joining the Navy at age seventeen.

The CIA assigned him to the Soviet division from the beginning. He started out with the agency in Japan, targeting Soviets, helped Kisevalter on the Popov case in Austria in 1953, then ran the defector shop in Washington for a while. (At the Farm, Kovich was known for putting the initials KTIP on the blackboard when he lectured to trainees about defectors; it meant Keep Them in Place.) In 1955, operating from headquarters, he supported Kisevalter again for three years on the long-running Popov operation.

By now, Kovich was a "third national officer" for the division, which meant he recruited people in other countries to work in Moscow. One of his recruits was Ingeborg Lygren, the secretary to Colonel Wilhelm Evang, the chief of the Norwegian military intelligence, who had sent her to Moscow in 1956 to work as the secretary to the Norwegian ambassador, Erik Braadland. Evang's service was the Norwegian equivalent of the CIA, and Lygren became Kovich's asset with Evang's blessing. As a NATO ally, Norway was happy to share with the CIA whatever information Lygren might pick up on the diplomatic gossip circuit. For three years, under the cryptonym SATIN-WOOD 37, she reported to Kovich from Moscow.

Per Hegge, a foreign correspondent for *Aftenposten,* the leading morning paper in Norway, remembered Lygren. He had met her by chance at Oslo University in the early 1960s. "She was taking Russian courses, after she had returned from Moscow," he said. "Perhaps she wanted to keep up with her Russian, I don't know." Lygren, he said, was an unlikely spy. "She was a gray mouse, very ordinary-looking, five-seven, maybe forty-five at the time. She grew up in Stavanger in southwest Norway where people have a strong regional accent that makes it very hard for them to pronounce Russian words, and she had a terrible accent."

Once Golitsin got to read Kovich's file, he must have seen the name Ingeborg Lygren and remembered that during the 1950s the KGB had a source in Moscow who was a Norwegian woman. That was it, Golitsin said, the big breakthrough; Lygren was a Soviet spy, and Kovich had run her for the CIA! He had probably used Lygren as a communications channel to his KGB masters, or so Golitsin speculated.

In the career of Dushan Kovich, the CI Staff clearly had discovered a rich tapestry, with threads that led off in a dozen directions. One can almost hear the members of the SIG licking their chops. Here, at last, was Sasha. They were wrong, and their mistake shattered several lives and in the end cost the CIA—and the American taxpayers—a great deal of money, but that is getting ahead of the story.

Angleton was ecstatic. Now the mole hunt was getting somewhere. In the fall of 1964, the CIA decided to tip off the Norwegians, but Angleton did not tell Evang. After all, if Lygren was a mole, her boss might be a supermole, working for the Soviets, hand in glove with Richard Kovich.

Instead, the CIA warned Norway's civilian surveillance police, a hush-hush agency headed by Asbjørn Bryhn, a tough character who had been a hit man in the Norwegian resistance, killing Nazis during the occupation, never sleeping in the same place twice. Alerted by the CIA, the surveillance police watched Lygren for months. Their reports noted that she led a remarkably ordinary life and engaged in no suspicious activities. Nevertheless, acting on the CIA's information, they arrested her in September 1965 and began a series of harsh interrogations.

At the time, Lygren was back in Oslo at her old job, working for Evang in military intelligence. But when the surveillance police arrested her they didn't tell Evang for several days. "She just didn't show up for work one day," Per Hegge said. "Of course, Evang was furious. He and Bryhn didn't speak to each other, even before the Lygren affair. The friction went back to World War II, when Bryhn was living in the woods on the run against the Nazis and Evang was with the Norwegian exiles in London, living well. There was a lot of animosity between London and the groups that were in the woods."[7]

Lygren was imprisoned for almost three months. The Norwegian press had a field day with the case. It looked as though a Russian spy

---

[7]There was more than wartime rivalry involved, according to Hegge. "Bryhn mistrusted Evang, who had been a member of a radical student group, the Mot Dag [Toward the Dawn], and considered him a Soviet mole. This greatly distressed the Prime Minister at the time, Per Borten, of the Center Party, a sort of Harry Truman without the brains, a gregarious man who could not stand the fact that his two intelligence chiefs didn't even speak to one another. And of course the case caused a considerable scandal for his government at the time."

was working in the very heart of Norwegian intelligence. The headlines trumpeted the spy case for weeks. Evang in particular came under heavy fire, but his offer to resign was turned down by the defense minister. One report suggested that Evang had sent Lygren to Moscow to approach the Soviets in the risky role of a double agent.

All the while, the surveillance police were grilling Lygren relentlessly, trying to force her to admit she was a Soviet spy, which she was not. One interrogation report was seized upon by Bryhn's staff as amounting to a "confession." Then, abruptly, in mid-December, the state's attorney decided there was insufficient evidence to prosecute. The case against Lygren was dropped. She was reinstated in her job, but, devastated by her ordeal, she eventually retired and left Oslo.

Parliament named a special panel, the Mellbye Commission, to investigate the war between the two intelligence agencies, and another official board, the Committee of Justice, to probe the Lygren case itself.[8]

Despite the fact that the Norwegian government had dropped the espionage charges against Lygren, Angleton remained convinced she was guilty. In March 1968, Bryhn's successor as head of the surveillance police, Gunnar Haarstad, came to Washington to meet with high officials of the CIA and the FBI. Angleton and his deputy, Ray Rocca, took the Norwegian police chief to a small restaurant in Georgetown for a pleasant lunch that Haarstad said "had very little to do with anything other than flies used when fishing for salmon. The Lygren case was not touched upon at all. . . . However, when we stood up from the lunch table in Georgetown, Angleton took me a bit to one side, removed a piece of paper from his pocket, and asked me to read it." The note Angleton handed to him, he wrote, was a brief summary of Golitsin's information about Lygren. "Angleton wanted the paper back, but by quickly scrutinizing it, I could see that it contained nothing more than what I already knew from before." Haarstad realized that his American colleagues regarded the case against Lygren as "hard as a rock." Haarstad added: "Angleton let me understand, quite cryptically, that he was convinced that Golitsin's information

[8]The Mellbye Commission was headed by Jens Christian Mellbye, a public defender who later became a member of Norway's supreme court. As a result of the Lygren case, the commission became a permanent watchdog body for the country's intelligence agencies.

and judgment were correct, and that it was a mistake for the Norwegian authorities to drop the case against Lygren.'"[9] Despite Angleton's view, a few months later, in July, the Norwegian parliament voted to award Lygren $4,200 as compensation for her unjustified arrest and suffering.

Frustrated in their efforts to nail Kovich over the Lygren case, the mole hunters turned their attention to UNACUTE, the GRU illegal whom Kovich had run in the midst of Lygren's tour in Moscow. Soviet illegals are trained to spy abroad without the benefit of diplomatic cover and immunity. They are difficult to spot, because, chameleonlike, they blend in with the populace of their target country. Typically, they open a small business as cover.

Mikhail Federov—whose true name, Kovich believed, was Alexei Chistov—was a GRU illegal who traveled to Switzerland with a Mexican passport and ended up in France. In Paris, Federov posed as a studio photographer. He had a little shop on the Right Bank where customers could have their portraits made. A short, lean man of military bearing, Federov dressed well, and with his black hair and dark complexion he could easily have passed for a Frenchman or a Spaniard. Certainly no one would have taken him for a Russian. In 1957, he contacted the American embassy and volunteered his services to the CIA. But walk-ins are not always taken seriously. A Mexican photographer claiming to be a Russian spy?

Kovich, overseas on another operation, was told that some screwball had come into the U.S. embassy in Paris claiming he was a Soviet intelligence officer. Kovich hurried to Paris. It took him about seven minutes to conclude that first, Federov wasn't crazy, and second, he was a genuine GRU illegal.

Kovich recruited him. At first, Federov, who was fluent in French and Spanish, wanted to defect. Kovich, following his own "KTIP" principle, worked hard to keep him in place. Finally, Federov agreed. The CIA digraph for France was UN, and Mikhail Federov became, in the agency's files, UNACUTE.

The take was impressive. In April 1958, Kovich met UNACUTE at the Hotel Crillon in Paris. Seven months earlier, in October 1957, the Soviets had stunned the world by launching Sputnik, the first space

[9]Gunnar Haarstad, *In the Secret Service: Intelligence and Surveillance in War and Peace* (Oslo: Aschehoug, 1988), pp. 247–50.

satellite. Now Federov told Kovich that another rocket launch would take place the following month, on May 15. Moreover, Federov added, in late August the Russians would put dogs into canisters and launch them into space.

On May 15 precisely, just as UNACUTE had predicted, the Soviets launched Sputnik III, and a triumphant Premier Nikita S. Khrushchev jibed at the smaller U.S. satellites then circling the earth as "oranges."[10] On August 29, Kovich met with Federov again, this time in a safe house in Berlin. The second launch was supposed to occur, and they were listening to Radio Moscow. Suddenly, the announcer broke in to say that the Soviets had put two dogs into space and parachuted them safely to earth.

Federov chuckled. "What do you think of my information?" he asked Kovich. The CIA man thought it was pretty good. For three years, Kovich ran Federov, but the CI Staff at headquarters was skeptical. UNACUTE, despite a wealth of information that he transmitted to the CIA, was labeled as a probable Soviet plant.

Federov moved around a lot; over a period of three years, Kovich met him in Paris, Nice, Bern, Geneva, and Berlin. Early on, they had met on the French Riviera, and it was there that Golitsin, analyzing Kovich's file, pronounced that the Soviets must have recruited the CIA officer.

In the atmosphere of the time, it was hard to find any Soviet source whom the CI Staff accepted as genuine. Even decades later, these beliefs ran deep. Scotty Miler never changed his mind about Federov. "Federov was a plant who led him [Kovich] on a chase through Europe," Miler said. "There were indications that Federov was out to make a recruitment or reestablish contact with someone who had been recruited."

Perhaps so, but both Kovich and George Kisevalter were convinced that he was a genuine and valuable CIA asset. On one of Federov's trips to the West, Kisevalter recalled, "he went through Berlin and I met him." Kovich had brought Federov to a CIA safe house, and Kisevalter was there, posing as a Frenchman.

"He doesn't know how to drink vodka," Federov said to Kovich. "We'll teach him." Since Kisevalter had been born in St. Petersburg

[10]"Soviet Satellite Weighing 1.5 Tons Fired into Orbit," *New York Times*, May 16, 1958, p. 1.

and had a native Russian's familiarity with vodka, he had some difficulty keeping a straight face as Federov explained that it was necessary to eat something first, a piece of bread or some olive oil, and only then, down the hatch.

"We were trying to find out where the dead drops were in Karlshorst," Kisevalter said. "Federov had buried some documents in a dead drop, not at Soviet headquarters, of course. He had hidden them somewhere near the train station. He told us where to find the documents. A German CIA agent was practically a real mole, digging up the tracks for miles, looking for the drop, but he never found it."[11]

Despite the CI Staff's suspicions, CIA director Allen Dulles considered Kovich's agent so valuable that the agency took an extraordinary step. Soviet defectors or agents often ask to meet the President or the director of the CIA, to reassure themselves of their own importance and to confirm that their information is appreciated at the highest levels of the United States government, but those requests are rarely granted. Federov had asked to meet personally with Dulles. In an unusual move, he was flown in "black," that is, secretly, to Washington, where he met not with Dulles, who was out of the country, but with General Charles P. Cabell, the deputy director of the CIA. According to Kisevalter, Cabell, an Air Force general, "put on his uniform to impress Federov."

It was Kovich who accompanied his prize asset on the flight from Berlin in September 1958. The CIA man had hoped to borrow Dulles's own plane for the trip, but the director was using it on his travels, so Kovich had to scrounge up an Air Force C-54, a four-engine prop plane, for the long trip to Washington. Federov got to see CIA headquarters, met with Cabell, and was hidden in a safe house in northern Virginia for about a week.[12]

After meeting the CIA's deputy director, Federov flew back to Berlin. Some months earlier, in March, Federov had returned to Moscow, but came out again. Now he informed the CIA that he had

[11]Soviet illegals often communicate with Moscow through dead drops. In this case, Federov said he remembered roughly where the drop was but no longer possessed the piece of paper that gave its precise location.
[12]A GRU officer under diplomatic cover could not slip away from his post for such a trip. But as an illegal, Federov could disappear for ten to twelve days and no one would miss him. The CIA had a "window of opportunity" in September when the trip could be scheduled, and it was.

been called back to Moscow once more. In October 1958, he left Berlin and the West for the last time.

UNACUTE was never seen again. After three years as the Russian's case officer, Kovich lost contact. Federov had disappeared. George Kisevalter was convinced that an error by the CIA had led to his capture. "Some jerk in headquarters decided to send a letter to Federov using the Soviet internal mail. It was sent to Moscow by pouch and then remailed in the Soviet Union. They thought the internal mail was too complicated to monitor, but one way the KGB could do it was to spot the guy who mailed it. The letter was intercepted."[13]

Two years after Federov vanished, Kisevalter received information from Oleg Penkovsky suggesting that Federov was indeed a genuine CIA source who had been been detected by the Soviets. It was April 1961 and Kisevalter was meeting Penkovsky in London's Mount Royal Hotel. "Penkovsky tells me, 'I graduated from the rocket academy. One of the generals, General Borisoglebsky, said on graduation

[13]The KGB, Kisevalter added, had successfully trailed at least one embassy officer who had mailed letters in Moscow, with disastrous results. George Payne Winters, Jr., a State Department officer working for the CIA as a "co-optee," was fired because of it, he said. In that instance, the letter, addressed to Pyotr Popov, the GRU colonel working for the CIA, was not supposed to have been mailed. The letter was addressed to Popov at his home in Kalinin. Winters misunderstood his orders and mailed the letter anyway, Kisevalter said; the KGB fished the letter out of the mailbox, and Popov, the first important penetration of Soviet intelligence, was doomed.

According to Kisevalter, it was Popov himself who was able to warn that he had been caught by the mailing of the letter. Although under observation by the KGB in his final meeting with CIA officer Russell Langelle, "Popov slipped him a note. He cut himself deliberately and used a strip of paper to write on, underneath the bandage. In the men's room of the Aragvi restaurant, he slipped off the bandage and passed the note. There were KGB observers behind the wall of the men's room. I translated the message, in which he said he was being tortured and was under control, and how they got him."

Several published accounts have suggested that in Geneva in 1962, Yuri Nosenko said the shoes of the American diplomat who mailed the letter to Popov had been dusted by a maid with a chemical that enabled the KGB, perhaps with the aid of a dog, to trail him to the mailbox. Kisevalter and Bagley, who debriefed Nosenko, agree that although Nosenko talked about the KGB's use of tracking chemicals, he never said anything about spy dust having been sprinkled on anyone's shoes in the Popov affair. The Cherepanov papers also referred to the KGB's use of spy dust, and some members of the CIA's Counterintelligence Staff believed that the references to tracking chemicals by both Nosenko and Cherepanov were somehow part of an effort to imply that these techniques—rather than a mole in the CIA—were responsible for the capture of Popov.

day, hey, let's have a drink. It was May. He, the general, said, life is not a bowl of cherries. Not long ago, he said, I was chairman of a court-martial committee and we condemned a GRU officer to be shot for treason.' "[14]

Although General Borisoglebsky had not disclosed the name of the GRU officer, Penkovsky said the general mentioned that the traitor had been secretly flown to CIA headquarters to meet a high official. Since Federov had been flown in black to meet General Cabell, there was no question that the person Penkovsky was talking about was Federov.

Kovich, too, was later told that Federov had been executed, but that his death had been even more gruesome than Penkovsky had related. The KGB has been known to go to great lengths to discourage Soviet intelligence officers from spying for the West. In the 1980s, Kovich was informed, a Soviet defector to the CIA said that during his training he had been shown a movie of Federov being thrown in an oven alive.

A former CIA officer with knowledge of Federov's fate said, "I know someone who has witnessed films of the execution. One of their favorite ways of doing this was to cremate some guy alive. They'll do it and film it and show it to others and say, 'This is what happens when you go over to your friends at Langley.' "

If Federov had indeed been executed, whether shot or cremated, it would constitute rather persuasive evidence that he was a real agent for the CIA. In 1964, when Kovich fell under suspicion, the mole hunters knew Penkovsky's account of Federov's fate, since Kisevalter had reported it, but it did not slow them down. Kovich's phone was wiretapped by the CIA, and his mail was intercepted.

For there was a third case that Kovich had handled that appeared even more sinister to the CI Staff. In May 1961, only months before Golitsin had defected, the Helsinki CIA station got a Soviet walk-in. Frank Friberg was the station chief, the same COS who later that year found Golitsin on his doorstep in the snow and escorted him to

[14]The story rang true, because General Viktor V. Borisoglebsky was a military lawyer and judge, and a high-ranking Communist Party official who had presided in August 1960 over the trial of Francis Gary Powers, the CIA U-2 pilot who had been shot down over Sverdlovsk earlier that year. Ironically, he also presided over the trial of Oleg Penkovsky in May 1963 and sentenced him to be executed.

Washington. Now, in the spring, Friberg reported the approach of the walk-in who had contacted the embassy.

Kovich, then stationed in Vienna, was dispatched to Helsinki. He met with the Soviet, who said his name was Yuri Nikolaevich Loginov, and who identified himself as a KGB illegal in Helsinki posing as an American tourist named Ronald William Dean. The KGB man said he wanted to defect and go to the United States; he had one foot on the plane. Patiently, following his and the CIA's rule, Kovich persuaded Loginov to remain in place, where of course he could be much more valuable to the West. Then, at some later date, the CIA would spirit him to safety.

Kovich was in Helsinki for about ten days, and while he was there, Loginov kept a scheduled meeting with two other KGB agents, one of whom was none other than Golitsin, using his cover name Anatoly M. Klimov. Loginov met in front of the Astra theater with a KGB man who introduced himself as Nikolai A. Frolov and led him to a parked car, where Golitsin was waiting. A driver took them to the outskirts of the city while Loginov, who was on his initial trip to the West as an illegal, explained some difficulties he had experienced in Italy, the first country he had traveled to after leaving the Soviet Union. Soon after, Loginov met again with his two KGB colleagues and Frolov and Golitsin told him that Moscow Center had accepted his explanations. They gave him a visa to return to Moscow.

Before leaving Helsinki, Loginov reported the meetings to Kovich and agreed to remain as an agent-in-place. The CIA gave him the code name AEGUSTO.

Seven months later, one of first things Golitsin revealed to the CIA was the existence of Yuri Loginov, a KGB illegal who spoke fantastic English. Golitsin had great praise for Loginov's abilities. Since Loginov was now being run by the CIA, it is unlikely, although not impossible, that Golitsin, a defector, would have been told that Loginov had been recruited by the agency. If Golitsin was told, it would have violated all the rules of espionage tradecraft.

But in 1964, Golitsin was shown Kovich's file, and if he saw that Kovich was in Helsinki in mid-May, at the very time that Golitsin met with Loginov, he would have smelled a connection. Golitsin would almost certainly have guessed that Kovich's presence in Helsinki was linked to Loginov.

The story of Yuri Loginov is one of the most controversial in the history of the CIA. It is a case that the agency long attempted to suppress. But the endgame would not be played out for another five years.

Loginov grew up in Kursk, an industrial city south of Moscow, and then in Tambov, the son of a Communist Party apparatchik. During World War II, the family moved to Moscow, where at school Loginov demonstrated his aptitude for foreign languages. In his early twenties he was recruited by the KGB and trained as an illegal. After Helsinki, he traveled to Paris, Brussels, Austria, Germany, Beirut, and Cairo in a series of trips to the West.

By the time Golitsin was shown Kovich's file in the summer of 1964, other case officers, first Edward S. Juchniewicz, then Peter Kapusta, had taken over Loginov's handling. Kovich had become known as a sort of headhunter, an experienced CIA officer on standby who could be sent anywhere in the world to make a pitch to a Soviet. In Berlin, he had married Sara Arthur, a secretary in the Berlin base. Now in 1964, winding up a three-year tour in Vienna, Kovich and his wife returned to headquarters.

He was not promoted, as he had expected to be, and his career seemed stalled. He did not know, of course, that the mole hunters on the second floor had targeted him as the new chief suspect. But he did feel that something was wrong. It was to be more than a decade before he learned officially that he was a suspected Soviet agent. As the CIA would find out in due course, Richard Kovich was not a person to be swept aside and forgotten.

There were others, many others. One of those placed under the counterintelligence microscope was Alexander Sogolow, a large and boisterous Russian-born case officer from Kiev who had the misfortune to be known throughout the agency by the name Sasha.

It was Sogolow whom Peter Karlow had been thinking of when the polygraph operator asked him about "Sasha," making the needle jump and putting Karlow deeper into the quagmire. In Russia, many names have diminutives, affectionate nicknames that friends and family use in place of the more formal given name. For Alexander, the diminutive is always Sasha.

Assigned to headquarters in the early 1960s after a tour in Germany, Sogolow got wind of the fact that the mole hunters in Langley were looking for "Sasha." On a trip to Vienna, he unburdened himself to Kovich, who was then serving in the Vienna station.

"They're going to come after me," Sogolow bemoaned. "I'm in trouble. They say his name is Sasha."

"Hell," Kovich assured him, "relax. There are eighteen million Sashas in the Soviet Union." Ironically, it was the first that Kovich had heard about the search for penetrations back at headquarters. He didn't know that he himself was a suspect.

Sasha Sogolow was born in czarist Russia in 1912, the son of a wealthy Jewish businessman who supplied uniforms for the Russian army. Sogolow used to tell the story of how, when the revolution came, the family fled to Germany, their jewels hidden in a toy cane that was given to him. The family made it safely to Germany, but little Sasha lost the cane. At least that is how Sogolow liked to tell the tale.[15]

The Sogolows immigrated to New York in 1926, where Sasha graduated from City College and St. John's University Law School. It was the Depression, and Sogolow, according to a CIA colleague, "worked for a while selling chicken-plucking machines, until he was beaten up by a bunch of manual chicken-pluckers."[16] During World War II, he was an Army intelligence officer, acting as an interpreter for General Eisenhower and General Patton, and then working for the High Command in Berlin. He joined the CIA in 1949 and was sent to Germany.

Since the Soviet Union was the main target of the CIA, the agency needed Russian-speakers. Like Sogolow, many officers in the Soviet division inevitably had Russian backgrounds, which to the mole hunters made them all the more suspect.

And Sogolow, despite Kovich's ironic reassurances, *was* under suspicion by the SIG. He had a Slavic background and had served in Berlin. It was true that his name did not begin with the letter K, but by now, the CI Staff was not wedded to that detail of the mole profile. The search for penetrations had begun to spread to other letters of the alphabet.

Worst of all for Sogolow, his name was Sasha. On the face of it, it

[15]It made a nice story, but it seemed improbable that the jewels would have been entrusted to a five-year-old. Within the Sogolow family, the accepted version was that the jewels had been smuggled out of Russia in the heel of the shoe worn by Sasha's older sister.

[16]David Chavchavadze, *Crowns and Trenchcoats: A Russian Prince in the CIA* (New York: Atlantic International Publications, 1990), p. 154.

seemed unlikely that the KGB would use the code name Sasha for someone who really was called Sasha. But it was not impossible, and in the atmosphere of the time, the CI Staff was leaving nothing to chance.

"We looked at his file," Miler recalled. "We went over operations he was involved in in Germany, where he had been." The SIG, Miler said, was particularly interested in Sogolow's "proximity" to Igor Orlov, a Russian-born CIA contract agent who had worked for Sogolow in Frankfurt in the late 1950s, and who was emerging as the newest suspect.

As for Sogolow, Miler said, "nothing was found." He was not transferred to a lesser job, Miler insisted, nor placed in the limbo that awaited other targets of the mole hunters in the D corridor. But Sogolow was never to reach the level he had hoped for within the agency.

The SIG also turned its attention to George Goldberg, a tough, street-smart Latvian who got out of Riga with his father just ahead of the Soviet army. The rest of his family, his mother and sister, died at the hands of the Nazis. Goldberg, a stocky, muscular man, drove a taxi in Chicago, went into France on a glider with the 101st Airborne Division on D-day, was wounded in the head, and with blood streaming down his face suddenly found himself staring at the barrel of a 9mm Schmeisser submachine gun.

"They weren't taking prisoners after three days," Goldberg recalled. "I said in German, 'What do you want to shoot me for?' In that moment the young soldier was transformed into a human being. 'You're bleeding to death,' he said. 'Here, hold my gun and let me bandage you.'

"My war lasted three days. I spent the rest of the war in Stalag 4B near Leipzig." Liberated from the German prison camp by the Russians, Goldberg was briefly pressed into service by the Soviet army as a Russian and German translator. He was with the Soviet troops when they linked up with the Americans at the Elbe.

After the war Goldberg worked for Army intelligence, served in Korea, and joined the CIA in 1954. During the 1960s, he was stationed in Munich and Bonn under Army cover. But back at headquarters, the SIG began investigating him, unbeknownst to Goldberg.

"Goldberg had been in Germany," Miler said. "He was also a

defector.[17] He came from the Soviet Union. It was not directly the result of Golitsin's leads, but he was examined in the light of Golitsin's leads to see if there was any connection." Beginning in 1958, Goldberg had recruited and, with Harry Young, run Boris Belitsky, the Radio Moscow correspondent code-named AEWIRELESS, later revealed by Nosenko to be a double agent under Moscow's control.

Was that why Goldberg was a suspect? "His handling of the Belitsky case was one of the reasons," Miler said. "Goldberg had been in Germany. There were other things, operations that went sour."

All during this time, Goldberg was a contract agent, denied the full status as a staff officer that he desired. In 1969, he went to Chicago with the agency's Domestic Operations Division, recruiting foreign students. "By 1970, I should have made permanent staff, because I was acting chief of base in Chicago," Goldberg said. "I might have, but for the trouble." Goldberg was told by the head of domestic operations that his promotion had been blocked "by someone from outside the division." Goldberg, his career thwarted, retired in 1975 to Colorado.

Typical of the targets of the SIG during this period was Vasia C. Gmirkin, a case officer in the Soviet division. Gmirkin's colorful background was unusual even for the division, many of whose officers had roots that reached back to the turmoil of the Russian revolution. He was born in China in 1926, where his father had been the czarist counsel in Urumchi, in Sinkiang province, which borders Russia. Young Vasia grew up speaking Russian and Chinese. When the revolution began, his father returned to Russia to fight with the Cossacks against the Bolsheviks. His unit was pushed back into China. The governor of the province knew and liked him and made him a Chinese citizen and a general. In 1934, Gmirkin's father sent his wife, daughter, and two sons to the safety of Tientsin, near Peking. Soon after, the Soviets marched in, took over, and executed Gmirkin's father. In 1941, at age fifteen, Vasia and the rest of his family managed to get out and immigrate to San Pedro, California. He enlisted in the Navy and returned to China as an interpreter for the Marines. In 1951, he joined

[17]Goldberg was not a defector in the accepted sense of the term. The label "defector" is normally applied to Soviet intelligence officers or other officials from the Soviet Union or Eastern Europe who have sought refuge in the West. Goldberg got out of Latvia before it was overrun by the Soviet army.

the CIA. He worked in Los Angeles for four years and was then transferred to the Soviet division at headquarters. Under State Department cover, one of his jobs for the agency was to escort visiting Soviet farmers around the United States.

Working in Africa and the Middle East, including Baghdad, Gmirkin had some impressive successes, including the recruitment of an opposition intelligence agent. By 1968, he was a branch chief in the Soviet division. But that year, David Murphy, the head of the Soviet division, left to become chief of station in Paris. He was replaced as the Soviet division chief by Rolfe Kingsley, a Yale man and veteran clandestine operator.

By now, virtually everyone of Russian origin in the division was under suspicion, and Kingsley told Gmirkin to clean out his desk; he was through as branch chief. In seventeen years, Gmirkin never got a promotion. He would be recommended by his superiors, and then, he was told, it would be vetoed by the CI Staff.

Gmirkin's final years with the CIA embodied the ironies of an entire era. For Gmirkin, although a victim of the mole hunt, ended up his career as the case officer for Anatoly Golitsin. He served as Golitsin's handler from 1976 until he retired three years later. Although he did not accept Golitsin's theories, he grew personally close to the defector, helped to edit Golitsin's book, and was one of two CIA officers who signed the preface. The other was Scotty Miler.

One of the more bizarre episodes in the annals of the SIG was the investigation of Averell Harriman, whose long and distinguished career included the posts of ambassador to the Soviet Union, under secretary of state, cabinet member, and governor of New York. But to the CI Staff, Harriman was a possible Soviet mole, code-named DINOSAUR.[18]

The investigation of the multimillionaire diplomat began, not surprisingly, with Golitsin. "As a result of Golitsin's allegations," Scotty Miler confirmed, the SIG had decided that "certain things that had occurred when Harriman was active in Soviet affairs ought to be looked at." When Harriman had served in Moscow the Soviets had presented him with the Great Seal of the United States that contained the eavesdropping device. Could that be one reason he was suspected?

---

[18]The SIG used a separate code name for each person it investigated.

"Yes," Miler said, "the fact he accepted the bugged seal was a minor part of it."

But another former member of the SIG was able to shed more light on the matter. "Harriman had been in the Soviet Union early on, helping them build factories and things like that," he said. "Golitsin had a story that a former U.S. ambassador to the Soviet Union had an affair with a Soviet woman, the fruit of which was a son. And that Harriman was still attached to the son and was, as a result of the affair, recruited by the KGB. When this agent, presumably Harriman, went back to the Soviet Union on a visit, they had a play written by a well-known playwright called *The Son of the King* and this was actually produced in Moscow. Harriman attended the premiere and it was so obviously about him that Harriman complained bitterly and got the whole thing taken off the stage.

"Golitsin even came up with an identity for the son. Harriman had written a book in 1956 about a trip to the Soviet Union and acknowledged the assistance of the companion the Soviets had given him, and Golitsin concluded this companion was the son. It's in Harriman's book."[19] In Angleton's *Alice in Wonderland* world, the fantasy of Operation DINOSAUR took on a life of its own.

The investigation was pursued, even though Ed Petty, a member of the SIG, established that Harriman was not in Moscow on the days the play was performed. These were not details that Angleton wanted to hear. DINOSAUR was fed as well by the fact that Harriman had two Soviet cryptonyms in the intercepted VENONA code traffic. "One of them was CAPITALIST," the former mole hunter recalled. "But that proves nothing. It doesn't prove a thing. The Soviets gave crypts to everybody and his brother."

In fact, all of Golitsin's leads, no matter how preposterous, were carefully investigated by the staff of the SIG. Its members were undaunted by the fact that, according to the testimony of John L. Hart, Golitsin, their prime source, had been diagnosed as paranoid. "In the course of his dealings with the Central Intelligence Agency," Hart

---

[19]Harriman did write a book about a trip he took to the Soviet Union in the late spring of 1959: *Peace with Russia?* (New York: Simon and Schuster, 1959). In the acknowledgments, Harriman thanked two senior Soviet officials, Anastas Mikoyan and Georgi Zhukov, and added: "I am grateful also to my numerous guides and interpreters, including Mr. Zhukov's assistant, Vasili V. Vakrushev, who accompanied me throughout my travel and contributed much to its interest."

testified to Congress, "he was diagnosed by a psychiatrist and separately by a clinical psychologist as a paranoid. And I am sure that everyone knows what a paranoid is. This man had delusions of grandeur. He was given to building up big, fantastic plots. . . ."[20]

Perhaps Golitsin's most farfetched view was that the Sino-Soviet split that emerged in the late 1950s was nothing more than a KGB deception. When Angleton proposed to convene a meeting of academics to hear Golitsin's theory, it was immediately dubbed "the Flat Earth Conference."[21] In Golitsin's opinion, the Soviet-Yugoslav split was another massive KGB plot, as was Alexander Dubcek's "Prague Spring," the abortive revolt that ended only when Soviet tanks rolled into Czechoslovakia in 1968. Angleton believed most of these harebrained theories.

At a dinner party, for example, Angleton remarked to the columnist Stewart Alsop that the Sino-Soviet split was merely a KGB invention. Alsop, skeptical, asked for proof. Angleton said he had some, and they arranged to have lunch. "Well, at lunch," said a friend to whom Alsop later related the story, "Angleton produced shards of information that to him indicated a pattern of cooperation between the two countries. For example, Aeroflot, the Soviet airline, still had an agent in Peking, whom Angleton assured Alsop was a KGB man. The Russians were building a railroad on the Chinese border. It was all meaningless to Alsop and reaffirmed his suspicions about Angleton's paranoia."

Don Moore, the veteran FBI Soviet counterintelligence chief, liked Angleton personally but was highly skeptical of the unusual theories advocated by the CIA man and Golitsin. For some reason, Angleton thought that Moore's attitude would change if only the FBI official would socialize with the defector and his wife. Moore declined, but Angleton persisted, bringing up the idea repeatedly. "If you went out with Mrs. Golitsin and Anatoly, you'd have a better opinion," he told Moore. The unlikely foursome never went to dinner, but at some point Moore did meet Irina Golitsin. It did not change his view of her husband's theories.

[20]*Investigation of the Assassination of President John F. Kennedy,* Hearings, Select Committee on Assassinations of the U.S. House of Representatives, September 1978, Vol. II, p. 494.
[21]David C. Martin, *Wilderness of Mirrors* (New York: Harper & Row, 1980), p. 203.

Through it all, the staff of the SIG toiled away, following each of Golitsin's leads, poring through the files, analyzing old cases, hoping that the elusive penetration might yet be caught. And now, in 1964, three years after Golitsin's arrival, the mole hunters thought they had, at last, unearthed Sasha.

Chapter 13

Sasha

He was a little man, no more than five foot five, strikingly handsome, with a flower tattooed on his left hand in the fleshy web between his thumb and forefinger and the letter A, his blood type, tattooed in the same place on his right hand.

He had been a Soviet intelligence officer in World War II fighting against the Nazis, and later a German intelligence officer fighting against the Soviets, so the tattoo of the blood type was understandable, but he never explained the flower to anyone, not even to his wife. His background was equally mysterious. At various times, he had used at least four different names.

To his customers in the successful picture-framing gallery that he and his wife, Eleonore, operated in Alexandria, Virginia, just across the Potomac from Washington, he was known as Igor Orlov. To his wife and friends, he was Sasha. Very few of his customers knew that he had worked as a CIA agent in Germany for thirteen years.

Paul Garbler called him "the little man."

When Garbler had reported in to the Berlin base in 1952 to work for Bill Harvey, he had been introduced to Orlov, who would be his principal agent. In running Orlov, Garbler did not use his real name. He was Philip Gardner.

And Orlov, too, was using an operational name that had been given to him by the CIA. In Berlin, he was Franz Koischwitz.

•   •   •

"Orlov was already recruited and working when I arrived in Berlin," Garbler recalled. Who had recruited him? "That's kind of murky," Garbler said. "By 1952, when I arrived, he had been there for a couple of years as a principal agent for the base. Wolfgang Robinow handled Orlov before me. He was a case officer, born in Germany and spoke German fluently. I took over the little guy from Robinow. He took me to a safe house and introduced me to Orlov." At the time, of course, Garbler did not know his new agent as Orlov, a name he had not yet been given by the CIA. He knew him only as Franz Koischwitz.

"He was little, a china doll of a man, with dark brown hair parted on the side, slicked back. A very natty dresser. He had a wife who was much taller than he was. He was almost obsessively clean. His hands were always well manicured.

"My agent ran eleven whores and a one-armed piano player," Garbler said. "The girls and the piano player worked in a bar in the Soviet sector where a lot of Russian soldiers hung out. The piano player was named Willi. Orlov never told the girls he was working for the Americans, of course."

The primary purpose of the operation, Garbler said, was to try to persuade one of the Soviet military men who patronized the bar to cross over to West Berlin, and then to recruit him. But as a subsidiary target, Orlov/Koischwitz reported any gossip of military or intelligence interest that the women might pick up in the saloon. "If they heard the fifteenth division was moving, they reported," Garbler said. "They gave the little man every single piece of gossip they got."

And Garbler, with Orlov's help, made what appeared to be a Soviet recruitment. "One of the girls, a shapely redhead named named Trudy, brought a Russian enlisted man into West Berlin. We led him to believe he was in touch with a West German university professor, who wanted to know what was going on in the Soviet Union, availability of food, gasoline, et cetera." A CIA contract agent played the part of the professor. The meeting with the Soviet enlisted man took place in an elegant CIA safe house, decorated to look like the home of the professor, whom the hooker introduced as her uncle.

"Wally Driver was the photographer," Garbler said. "When the Soviet came up out of the U-bahn underground station, he was photographed through a peephole in a van. The Russian wore a khaki shirt and jacket, but he was not in uniform. In the house, we were taking pictures as the enlisted man talked with the CIA man posing as the professor, and the whore. Wally Driver put a camera in a cuckoo clock, wrapped it in cotton to silence it, and ran a wire to the professor. The professor was to take the pictures by pressing the button. To conceal the noise from the Russian, our guy had to cough each time he took the picture. We got some real good pictures."

The Soviet enlisted man, according to Garbler, agreed to remain in touch with the "professor." "He did stay in touch. There was communication. He sent at least one letter while I was still there, maybe more.

"It was not all that successful," Garbler admitted, "but looked at then, it seemed fine. It was typical of the wild-ass things we were doing in those days."

Munich, 1947. Eleonore Stirner, then twenty-three, had survived the war and the Allied bombing raids that had badly damaged the city. She remembered people taking shoes off the corpses in Munich after the air raids.

On this winter day in February, she was riding on streetcar No. 8 to Schwabing, a Bohemian section of Munich. "I was delivering food to a professor who was an artist, in his atelier," she said. "I had laryngitis and couldn't speak. Sasha and a tall friend, Boris, got off at the same stop, and it turned out we were going to the same apartment house. They helped me carry the potatoes upstairs to the top floor. The professor whispered, 'They are foreigners, let's invite them in and maybe they have sugar.' That's how I met my husband."

Sasha and Eleonore were married in July, 1948. It was an unlikely match, a former Soviet intelligence officer and the daughter of a Nazi Party member, but in war-torn Germany, Eleonore Stirner was happy to have found a husband. There were not many young men left. "All my friends were dead," she said frankly, "or I never would have married a Russian."

Interviewed in her spacious frame shop and art gallery in Alexandria's Old Town, Eleonore Orlov proved an intelligent woman of boundless energy, her occasional moments of melancholy tempered by a strong sense of humor. She spoke at length about her own past in Nazi Germany, her later dealings with the CIA and the FBI, and the enigma of the man to whom she was married for thirty-four years. Sasha Orlov had died at age sixty in May 1982, leaving his wife and two grown sons, Robert and George.

Eleonore Stirner was born in Munich on March 10, 1923, the daughter of Joseph and Rosa Stirner. "I joined the Hitler Youth at age sixteen," Eleonore Orlov said. "I was head of water sports, canoeing, and so on, for all of Bavaria. It was like the Girl Scouts. It was the only fun we had in life. Everybody liked Hitler." Her father, a six-foot-six SS man, fought in Poland, the Soviet Union, and Italy, where he was captured and held as a POW for two years. "After the war, we lost our apartment because the neighbors saw the black uniform and the boots and threw us out."

Because of her own membership in the Hitler Youth, she was sent to Dachau in 1945, where she served a prison term of five months, working in the fields of the former Nazi concentration camp, weeding and harvesting, and picking the bugs off potatoes. "Polish officers who had been prisoners were in charge," she said. Released in 1946, she was working as a secretary in a medical supply house when she met and married Sasha Orlov.

At the time, he called himself Alexander Kopatzky. He told his wife that he had taken the Polish-sounding name to avoid being sent back to the Soviet Union. He was born, according to Eleonore, on January 1, 1922, in Kiev. He had never revealed his true name to her, she said, although she thought that once, on an official form, he might have listed his parents' name as Navratilov.

He was trim as a gymnast and a man of continental manners, when sober. "He drank a lot of vodka. He kissed ladies' hands. He went to military school in Novosibirsk or somewhere in Siberia. He was definitely an officer. He was very punctual, shined his shoes, did his gymnastics in the morning, he had a neat haircut, short hair all his life, proper dress. And he was a very good shot. Sasha liked to hunt and talked of hunting tigers in Siberia with his father. He was an intelligence officer for the Soviets. In 1944, he was badly wounded in the neck and the calf as he parachuted into Germany. He was captured, nursed back to health in a German field hospital, and recruited as liaison between Vlasov's army and the German army. This was in 1944, a brutal winter."[1]

---

[1] Eleonore Orlov provided me with a one-page biography that Orlov wrote in his own hand. Bearing in mind that Orlov was a spy for three countries, and that the CIA concluded he was a double agent for the Soviets, the dates and details in the document nevertheless appear to coincide with what is known of his background from various

General Andrei A. Vlasov was a Soviet lieutenant general captured with most of his troops by the Germans in July 1942. The Germans allowed Vlasov, who was strongly anti-Soviet, to form a Russian Army of Liberation (ROA), enlisting Russian prisoners of war to join the Nazi war effort and fight the Red Army.[2]

After recovering from his wounds in a German hospital, Orlov joined forces with his captors. By his own account, he served for almost a year as a German intelligence officer before joining General Vlasov's intelligence service. After the war he was imprisoned by the American authorities in Dachau, at the same time that Eleonore was there, although they did not then know each other.

When they did meet, in 1947, Orlov was already working for the CIA in Pullach, outside Munich, where the agency had set up General Reinhard Gehlen and his German intelligence network.

Orlov told his wife very little about his work for the CIA. But according to one former SIG member, in 1948–49, "Orlov had worked in Ukrainian ops in the Munich area for the [CIA's] Munich operations base. He worked for Dave Murphy."

Eleonore Orlov looked back on those early months of their marriage as an idyllic period in her life. The young couple went for picnics in the Bavarian countryside. "I rode my bicycle along the Isar. It was a very happy time."

---

other sources. By Orlov's account, however, he was captured in December 1943, rather than in 1944, as Eleonore remembered the date.

The handwritten biography reads:

Igor Gregory Orlov, born 1-1-1922 in Kiev, Sov. Union. Naturalized Sept. 6, 1962 in Alexandria Va. Naturalization # 8240855.
Military or Government services
August 1941–Dec. 1943 Lt. in Sov. Intelligence Service,
Dec. 43–April 1944, Prisoner of war in German Hospital.
April 1944–March 1945—Lt. in German Intelligence Service, "Staff Valy."
March 1945–May 1945, Intelligence Service ROA (Vlasov Army)
1946–1948—U.S. Intelligence Service
1950–1961—CIA "operatives"

[2]In May 1945, Vlasov and one of his divisions marched into Prague, switched sides, and fought the SS garrison. What happened next is disputed; by some accounts, Vlasov surrendered to the American forces, only to be handed over to the Russians. Other versions claim he was captured by the Soviet army. In 1946, the Russians announced that Vlasov and six other generals had been found guilty of treason and hanged.

THE DEFECTOR:

A previously unpublished photograph of Anatoly Mikhailovich Golitsin, the KGB officer who defected in Helsinki in 1961, touching off the hunt for Soviet moles inside the CIA that lasted for almost two decades. This photo is the first to show Golitsin as a KGB officer before he defected to the CIA. In Helsinki, Golitsin posed as a Soviet diplomat and used the alias "Anatoly Klimov."

THE SUSPECTS:

S. Peter Karlow, a war hero and OSS veteran, was a respected CIA officer and an expert on espionage gadgetry for the agency when he mistakenly became the "principal suspect" in the mole hunt as a result of Golitsin's information. Karlow, investigated and polygraphed by the FBI, then fired from the CIA in 1963, fought for twenty-six years to clear his name.

Karlow receiving a bronze star for valor from General William J. "Wild Bill" Donovan, the director of the wartime OSS, for a daring mission off the Italian coast in 1944. Karlow lost his left leg when his PT boat tripped a Nazi mine and exploded, killing most of the crew.

A Navy dive bomber pilot in the Pacific during World War II, Garbler, below, right, face partially hidden, served as personal pilot to South Korea's President Syngman Rhee, center, before joining the CIA.

© DAVID WISE

Paul Garbler with his Doberman, Magic. The first CIA chief of station in Moscow, Garbler was also suspected as a Soviet spy and exiled to a Caribbean isle. The CIA never told him why. Garbler's innocence was belatedly acknowledged when Congress in 1980 passed the little-known "Mole Relief Act," and the CIA awarded him a substantial settlement.

The CIA sent Garbler to Moscow in 1961 to monitor contacts with Colonel Oleg Penkovsky, the CIA's most celebrated spy in the Soviet Union. But Penkovsky's "dead drop" in Moscow had been discovered by the KGB.

AP/WIDE WORLD

Igor Orlov, the CIA agent whom the agency concluded was Golitsin's "Sasha," the elusive Soviet mole. Orlov operated for the CIA in Germany under Army cover.

Igor and Eleonore Orlov in Munich on their wedding day, July 14, 1948.

Orlov on an idyllic outing near Munich in 1947. He was already an agent of the CIA.

Orlov in Berlin, 1953.

РАЗВЕДКА

<u>I</u> TRADECRAFT — основа конспирации

SECRET — секретно	COVER — маскировка
CONFIDENTIAL — " —	a) NATURAL — естественная
CLANDESTINE — " —	б) ARTIFICIAL — искусственная
	в) PERMANENT — постоянная
	г) TEMPORARY — не постоянная
	(скрыто)

часть работы замаскировано, часть секретно

SECURITY

<u>NATURAL</u>		<u>ARTIFICIAL</u>
STATUT	различные колода наши	STATUT
COVER		SECRET
ACTION		ACTION
LIGHT (поверхностно)		DEEP (глубоко)

COMPARTMENTATION — разгородка

a) HORISONTAL
б) VERTICAL

верт. перегородка

гор. перегородка

<u>I</u>

звенья разрыва

разгородка при помощи: 1. посредников 2. курьеров 3. п/я 4. тайник

при разработке и наблюдении контрразведкой

A ⟷ B   берет 6 недель у A. 120
              B. 120

при точном рассмотре отсюда

$$у A. \quad 120-80-20 = 20$$
$$у B. \quad 120-80-20 = 20 \quad = 400$$

подозрительным

COMMUNICATION — связь

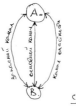

1 MEDIATOR (посредник)	WIESE
2 CURIER	UNWIESE
3 LIVE (п/я)	MOVING
4 DEATH DRAP (тайник)	STATIONARY

сигнализация и пароли и.т.д.

The CIA trained Orlov in espionage tradecraft. Pictured are pages from notes in his handwriting, in Russian and English.

The CIA brought the Orlovs to America, where they opened an art gallery and picture-framing studio in Alexandria, Virginia. The FBI kept the gallery under surveillance for years, but never proved Orlov was a Soviet spy. After his death in 1982, his wife, Eleonore, continued to run the gallery.

"Sasha" Sogolow at the Brandenburg Gate in Berlin. The Russian-born CIA officer became a mole suspect because, to his misfortune, his nickname was the same as the code name of the supposed Soviet mole.

George Goldberg became a suspect after Boris Belitsky, a top Radio Moscow correspondent whom he recruited for the CIA, turned out to be a double agent for the KGB. Innocent, but unaware that he had become a target of the mole hunters, Goldberg was puzzled that the CIA did not promote him.

Goldberg, captured by the Nazis during World War II, was liberated by Soviet troops and pressed into service as their interpreter when the Russians and Americans linked up at the Elbe River in 1945. Goldberg, center, is the man in the wool cap.

Vasia C. Gmirkin, a veteran CIA officer, was one of dozens of officers in the Soviet division who came under suspicion because they spoke Russian. Although he had an outstanding career, he failed to receive a promotion for seventeen years.

Arseny "Andy" Yankovsky. The Special Investigations Group, the CIA's mole-hunting unit, suspected that Yankovsky had betrayed his own agents behind the lines during the Korean War. David Murphy, the chief of the CIA's Soviet division, fell victim to the mole hunters himself because he had helped to recruit Yankovsky into the CIA two decades earlier.

Yankovsky, right, with his older brother Valery, and a tiger they bagged in North Korea about 1942. The Yankovskys were White Russians who fled the Soviet Union and settled in an enclave in North Korea.

Edgar Snow, a CIA officer who married Yankovsky's step-daughter, Nata, was fired by CIA director Allen W. Dulles, along with Yankovsky and another CIA case offi-cer, Vivian L. Parker. Dulles considered Snow's dismissal a "tragedy," and helped him find a job after he was forced out of the CIA.

"Trouble is, it was the wrong woman."
Ingeborg Lygren, an employee of the Norwegian intelligence service, was falsely accused as a Soviet spy because of erroneous information provided by Anatoly Golitsin and James Angleton. The real spy was caught twelve years later.

The CIA mole hunt spread to England as well. There, Sir Roger Hollis, the head of MI5, the British security service, was investigated by British mole hunters for years. Prime Minister Margaret Thatcher said "no evidence" was found to incriminate him.

THE HUNTERS:

James J. Angleton, the reclusive chief of the CIA's Counterintelligence Staff, became obsessed with finding the Soviet mole who he was convinced had burrowed deep inside the CIA.

Poets and Spooks: Angleton helped to found a poetry journal at Yale and his friends included a number of poets. In this rare and previously unpublished photo, Angleton, standing, second from left, is shown during a lighter moment at a private party in Washington in the spring of 1966. Others (standing) are, from left, Ambrose Gordon, poet, professor, and contemporary of Angleton's at Yale; Howard Nemerov, poet and novelist; William R. Johnson, a CIA officer and member of Angleton's Counterintelligence Staff; and (seated), left, John Pauker, poet and official of the United States Information Agency; and Reed Whittemore, poet and Angleton's former roommate at Yale.

Newton S. "Scotty" Miler ran the mole hunt for Angleton and later became his chief of operations. This photo was taken at his home in New Mexico in 1989.

Clare Edward Petty in Helsinki in 1981 in front of a statue of the Finnish composer Jean Sibelius. A member of the CIA's Special Investigations Group that conducted the search for penetrations, Petty concluded that James Angleton himself was the Soviet mole.

THE SOVIETS:

Yuri Ivanovich Nosenko as a young KGB officer before he defected to the CIA in Geneva early in 1964. This photograph, obtained by the author, is the first ever published of Nosenko. A photograph identified as Nosenko and widely distributed by wire services when the KGB officer defected was actually of another member of the Soviet disarmament delegation, V. V. Shustov.

Adolf G. Tolkachev is arrested by agents of the KGB in 1985. For almost a decade, during the Carter and Reagan administrations, Tolkachev was Washington's most valuable spy in the Soviet Union. But an overly suspicious CIA had turned him away three times. The Soviets announced his execution in 1986.

Yuri Loginov, code name AEGUSTO, the KGB "illegal" who passed information to the CIA for six years in the 1960s. When the CIA's Soviet division and Angleton became persuaded that he was a plant, Loginov was betrayed by the agency, arrested in South Africa, and forced to return to the Soviet Union. Later defectors said he had been executed.

The first published photograph of Aleksei Isidorovich Kulak,
code name FEDORA, the KGB officer at the United Nations
in New York who became a legend of the Cold War. Over
a period of sixteen years, FEDORA passed Soviet secrets to
the United States. J. Edgar Hoover considered him his best spy
and the FBI paid him $100,000. The CIA did not trust him.

The first published photograph of TOPHAT, Dmitri Fedorovich
Polyakov, another famous FBI source in New York. The
Soviets announced that TOPHAT, an officer of the GRU, Soviet
military intelligence, had been caught and executed for espionage on March 15, 1988.

THE AGENCY:

During the era of the mole hunt, Richard M. Helms ran the CIA's clandestine directorate and then served as CIA director. A strong supporter of counter-intelligence chief James Angleton, he defended the need for a mole hunt. The possibility of a Soviet spy inside the CIA, Helms said, was "one of the real nightmares" he faced as director.

CIA director William E. Colby fired Angleton in 1974.

George T. Kalaris, James Angleton's successor as CIA chief of counterintelligence. Kalaris commissioned a massive, secret study of the mole hunt and of several controversial spy cases. The mole hunt investigated 120 CIA officers as suspected Soviet spies, destroyed the careers of innocent agency employees, paralyzed the CIA's operations around the globe, and, in its wake, damaged U.S. counterspy operations to the present day.

The roots of the mole hunt reached back to the 1950s, when Edward Ellis Smith, the first CIA man sent to Moscow, was sexually compromised by his maid, a KGB agent. KGB agents forced Smith to meet with them. The CIA fired Smith and hushed up the scandal.

Former CIA station chief Cleveland C. Cram conducted the six-year, classified study of the Counterintelligence Staff and the mole hunt that filled twelve volumes, each 300 to 400 pages long.

TRIUMPH:

Peter Karlow gets his medal. In a
secret ceremony at CIA headquarters
in 1989, Peter Karlow receives the
Intelligence Commendation Medal
from Richard Stolz, then the chief of
the agency's clandestine operations,
who inscribed the photo. Congress
passed the "Mole Relief Act" again
for Karlow, who received close to half
a million dollars in damages from the
CIA, and this medal. Certificate,
below, was signed by CIA director
William H. Webster.

For Peter Karlow, in small recognition for an outstanding professional career of a great gentleman, Dick Stolz, May 26, 1989

The United States of America

To all who shall see these presents, greeting:

This is to certify that the Director of
Central Intelligence has awarded the

Intelligence Commendation Medal

To

Serge Peter Karlow

for especially commendable service

Given under my hand in the City of Washington, D.C.
this 28th day of December 1988

William H. Webster
Director of Central Intelligence

The United States of America

Central Intelligence Agency

Citation

SERGE PETER KARLOW
is hereby awarded the
INTELLIGENCE COMMENDATION MEDAL

in recognition of his more than twenty-two years of devoted service to the Central
Intelligence Agency. He distinguished himself in a series of increasingly responsible
assignments both at Headquarters and overseas. Mr. Karlow demonstrated inspired
leadership, operational wisdom, and good judgment throughout his career, reflecting
credit upon himself, the Central Intelligence Agency, and the Federal service.

The CIA citation, above, right, that
accompanied Karlow's medal recognized his "devoted service to the
Central Intelligence Agency."

At the party on K Street after the
ceremony at CIA headquarters,
among those who showed up to con-
gratulate Karlow was former CIA
director Richard Helms, right. As
deputy director for operations in
1963, Helms did not intervene to prevent Karlow's dismissal.

All of that changed abruptly in 1949, during the Berlin airl
lived a quiet life until one day an American knocked on the d
said, 'We need you in Berlin.'

"In Berlin, he changed his name to Franz Koischwitz. The
cans gave the name to us. I was Ellen Koischwitz. I insisted th
begin with a K because of my linens. My linens said EK, for E
Kopatzky. My mother sent them from Munich."

As Franz Koischwitz, Orlov remained in Berlin for seven ye
didn't work for the CIA in Berlin, but I typed my husband's
reports," Eleonore said. "So I knew the work he was doing."

What Orlov was doing was enrolling women for his networ
went every night to bars, lots of nightspots. Telephone bars,
you can just pick up the telephone and speak to someone at a
across the room. Sometimes he recruited girls at Resi, a telepho
in Hasenheide, a section of Berlin that means 'rabbit's meado'

He was also drinking. Paul Garbler had good reason to rem
that. "Three times," Garbler said, "I had to bail him out
slammer. Orlov was a terrible driver. Used to scare the shit out
driving around Berlin with me. Most Russians are terrible dr
They don't learn when they're little kids, like we do. He would ru
lights, back up in the middle of the street, with cars whizzing ar

"When he talked about something sad, like when one of his girl
the clap, he would cry. His eyes would fill with tears. I never aske
background and he never asked mine."

Tears came to Orlov's eyes again in 1955, when it was time
Garbler to leave Berlin after three years. The CIA man and his a
had their last meeting in a safe house. Orlov presented Garbler
an inscribed book of photographs of Berlin.[3] It was signed, "Fi
Koischwitz with Ellen and Robert June 1955."

A year later, the CIA transferred the Koischwitzes from Berlii

[3]Garbler had it still, almost thirty-five years later. When I interviewed him at his h
in Tucson, where he retired with his wife after leaving the CIA, he walked over
bookcase that covered an entire wall of his study, reached up to a high shelf, and t
it down. It was entitled *Berlin: Symphonie einer Weltstadt* (Symphony of a Metro
lis) and had been published in Berlin in 1955 by Ernst Staneck Verlag. The inscripti
in German, said: "Berlin! Only a tiny stone in the mosaic of your travels through
world. This book may help you when you think occasionally of the city, your wo
and the people you have become acquainted with. With many good wishes we
goodbye to you once again."

Frankfurt, largely because Eleonore had rebelled against their life on the move in furnished rooms, which they switched every few months to preserve security. Their son Robert had been born in 1954. As Eleonore put it, "I wanted out of Berlin. There I was with a baby, and no home. I was like a bag lady."

In Berlin, close to the border and Soviet headquarters, a CIA agent was at risk, Eleonore said. In Frankfurt, deep inside West Germany, there would be no need to move all the time. Moreover, the agency offered to give the Koishwitzes American passports.

"We went to the American consulate to start our citizenship papers.[4] Then we ran into trouble. Franz Koischwitz had been imprisoned for a traffic violation. So the Americans changed our name to Orlov. We had to go to the consulate and swear we were Igor and Eleonore Orlov." Because they had been told they could take only small airline bags on the flight to Frankfurt, she said, before they left Berlin she had given away their few possessions, including her linens monogrammed EK. So it no longer mattered to her whether their new name began with a K.

In Frankfurt, Mrs. Orlov worked for the CIA, screening and translating photocopies of letters intercepted in the mail flowing between the Soviet Union and West Germany. Her husband, she said, "traveled a lot, to Hamburg, Cologne, all over West Germany in a black Opel Kapitan. I know now what he did in Frankfurt. I put it together. We three ladies in the censorship office saw all letters to and from the Soviet Union. My husband visited the people in Germany who wrote those letters to the East. He was trying to recruit people who had contact with Russia."

Eleonore's office was "on an unmarked floor, thirteenth floor of the I. G. Farben building. We looked for letters of intelligence interest, and would put those aside to translate. For example, if someone's aunt in the Soviet Union said they didn't have fish anymore, it might mean a big power plant was being built.

"I even got a letter from Boris Pasternak, a thank-you letter to one of his admirers in Germany for *Doctor Zhivago*. I swindled it, put it

[4] Technically, Eleonore Orlov said, both were stateless persons. "I had German citizenship," she said, "but I lost my citizenship on the day I married Igor, a foreigner. He had no citizenship. I was listed as a 'homeless foreigner,' and had to report to the police every year."

in my pocketbook and kept it like an autograph. No one ever missed it. I put it in my copy of *Doctor Zhivago.*"

In April 1957, the CIA flew the Orlovs to America so that Eleonore, who was pregnant, could have her child in the United States, and to allow the Orlovs to establish a residence to become citizens. First, the Orlovs were taken to Ashford Farm, a CIA safe house on the Choptank River, on Maryland's Eastern Shore.

Later, to have her baby they were moved to another safe house in the Georgetown section of Northwest Washington at 3301 O Street.[5] Her physician at Georgetown University Hospital was Dr. John W. Walsh, who that same summer was caring for Jacqueline Kennedy, whose daughter, Caroline, was born in November.[6]

While waiting for her baby to arrive, Mrs. Orlov said, "a CIA guide took us to the White House, the museums. He tried to give us a taste of America." The Orlovs' second son, George, was born on August 9. "Then back to Frankfurt, and we started a new life with legitimate papers and PX privileges. Sasha got a car and we had a wonderful life."

It was wonderful except for Orlov's relations with his CIA colleagues. In Frankfurt, friction had quickly developed between Orlov and Nicholas Kozlov, another ex-Soviet working for the CIA. Much of the trouble began in 1959 when Orlov went on a trip to Vienna. "For the trip, they gave him elevated shoes to be taller, colored his hair pitch black, and gave him horn-rimmed glasses with no prescrip-

---

[5]Few of the Orlovs' neighbors realized that the CIA operated a safe house in the heart of Georgetown, one of Washington's most elegant residential areas. Real estate records of the District of Columbia list "John M. Boothby" as the owner of the corner house at 3301 O Street from 1947 to 1965, but no trace of such a person could be found. He was not listed at the time in the telephone book, which showed "Cortlandt E. Parker" and later "Samuel S. Ingraham" at that address. Virginia Erwin Page Gore bought the house in February 1965 for $63,000 but never met the seller, "Mr. Boothby." She sold the property a few weeks later to Richard and Lillian Borwick for $75,000. The Borwicks, who were living in the house in 1990, said they were aware that their home had been a safe house used by the CIA. Mrs. Borwick said Mrs. Gore bought the house "from the government." She added: "I knew it was a safe house because every [interior] door had a lock on it. The basement was soundproofed and that's where people were interrogated. There was a single light bulb hanging down from the ceiling." Neighbors told her they saw a lot of foreigners go in and out of the house, she added.

[6]Three years later, Dr. Walsh delivered John F. Kennedy, Jr., at Georgetown.

tion," Eleonore said. When Orlov returned to Frankfurt, he was convinced that his safe had been rifled. "The safe had an outside combination and two unlocked compartments inside and Kozlov had the combination," she said. Before leaving for Vienna, Orlov had put pieces of mica in his part of the safe and found them on the floor when he returned. According to Eleonore, he complained to his superior, Sasha Sogolow—who was later to become a mole suspect in part because of his association with Orlov—but Sogolow dismissed the incident.

The trouble was not over, however, for either Orlov or his wife. CIA security officers investigating the alleged break-in found a postcard in the safe addressed to Eleonore Orlov from an admirer, which her husband had intercepted and placed there. The CIA men grilled Eleonore about the card, accusing her of black market dealings.

"In Frankfurt I had Georgie in the carriage," Mrs. Orlov said. "I met a man in the park. He gave me opera tickets to the Frankfurt Opera House, he was the stage director, and I gave him gin from the PX. This came out in my lie-detector test. The postcard said something like 'If I don't see you I will fall in love with the entire corps of ballet girls.'

"They asked, 'Why did I give him the gin? Did I pay him with cigarettes to make love to me?' I said, 'You're crazy. If I wanted to have a man, I can have one.' I was in trouble because bartering was against the law. I was dismissed from my job."

Eleonore Orlov said she never saw the postcard but that her husband confronted her about it before he left for Vienna. "He was extremely jealous. In Berlin he held a gun to my head several times. Because he smelled cigarettes, and I didn't smoke. I said yes, I was in the subway. I had to sit in the smoking car."

As Mrs. Orlov tells it, her husband's decision to report the alleged break-in of the safe destroyed his relationship with the CIA. "Mr. Sogolow was a good friend of the Kozlovs, so he couldn't possibly do anything," she said. "When he [Orlov] complained about Kozlov, that was the end of our career."

The Orlovs were not told that, however. Igor was promised a new job in the United States, and in January 1961, the Orlovs sailed for New York on the S.S. *America.* On the day before President Kennedy's inauguration, they drove in a snowstorm to northern Virginia. Orlov called a number he had been given to contact the CIA, only to find it had been disconnected.

"Eventually he made contact and was told there was no work for him," Eleonore said. "We had to live. In the summer of 1961 he went to work driving a truck for the *Washington Post*. We had no citizenship papers. We had a green card, but no passports.

"He did not accept the Berlitz course offered by CIA, but we did get some money, about twenty-seven hundred dollars. It was CIA money. I was ready to leave for good. We argued. I said, 'What do you do in this country? What is there here for me? Being the wife of a truck driver?" Mrs. Orlov withdrew $1,800 of the CIA money. "I bought three tickets on the S.S. *Bremen* to go to Germany. I took the children, my books, my feather bed. I went to my mother and she threw me out on the first day. 'I told you not to marry this foreigner. And I know now he's a spy. People here ask me about him.'

"I stayed nine months in Munich, rented an apartment, and Igor sent me every month one hundred dollars. He sold his TV to have money to send me, his typewriter. He only earned sixty dollars a week. I couldn't find a job, I had no papers. Who is Eleonore Orlov? Where did you go to school? What have you done for the last five years?"

In 1962, Eleonore Orlov brought the children back to Washington and rejoined her husband. By 1964, the Orlovs had saved enough money to open a picture-framing gallery on South Pitt Street in Alexandria. A few miles away at CIA headquarters, the mole hunters were closing in.

Scotty Miler had joined the Special Investigations Group in October 1964, and the Orlov case was virtually the first to land on his desk. "Golitsin said Sasha had operated primarily in Berlin, but also in West Germany," he said. "So we began going through the files, who was involved in what and where. Putting the pieces of the jigsaw together. It took three years to focus on Orlov as a candidate, in 1964," Miler said. "Orlov's diminutive was Sasha. He had worked in Germany. There were other people known as Sasha. We started by asking how many people we know were known as Sasha. That's the first layer of investigation. Second, does anyone have a true name beginning with a K? Or an operational name."

Orlov's name did not begin with the letter K, but one can visualize the excitement on the second floor when the mole hunters opened his dossier and saw that before it was Orlov, his name had been Alexander Kopatzky, and then Franz Koischwitz, and that he was called Sasha.

But would the KGB really use a code name that was also a person's nickname? "Unlikely, but not unknown," Miler replied.

After analyzing Orlov's file, and the cases he had handled in Germany, Miler said, the Counterintelligence Staff became "absolutely" convinced that it had uncovered solid evidence against him. Several other former CIA officers interviewed also said they believed that Orlov had been a double agent for the KGB. "He [Orlov] fit the indicators, and his operations went bad," said Pete Bagley.

Within the CIA, it was Bruce Solie of the Office of Security who was given credit for cracking the Orlov case. Solie was the principal officer in OS who had worked on the mole hunt from the start. Tall, thin, and bespectacled, given to long pauses between sentences, Solie grew up on a dairy farm in rural Wisconsin, served as an Air Force navigator in the European theater during World War II, earned a law degree after the war, and in 1951 joined the CIA, where his entire career was spent in the Office of Security.

In addition to the basic profile of Sasha that Golitsin had provided—a name beginning with K, active in Germany, a Slavic background—the defector had provided another fragment of information. Sasha, he said, had given the KGB information about military identity documents that would be carried by agents whom the CIA was sending into the Soviet Union. Solie searched the files but could find no operation that fit Golitsin's description.

But Solie made an interesting discovery: the CIA, more than a decade earlier, had indeed planned to send in an agent with military ID and had been looking for such documents. It was Orlov who had provided them, explaining that he had obtained the documents from a Soviet source. "Orlov came up with three," a CIA officer recalled. "But that wasn't enough. Four were required. So they [the CIA] gave up on it."

Solie went back to Golitsin. Something wasn't right, he said. Golitsin thought about it some more. Maybe, he said, it had been the other way around; that is, Sasha had not passed information to the KGB about identity papers—the KGB had given documents to Sasha to plant on the CIA. To Solie, the case now made sense. Golitsin had originally gotten it backward, but even so, the defector's lead had allowed Solie to pinpoint Orlov. The three documents provided by Orlov, Solie concluded, would have been booby-trapped by the KGB, altered in some tiny detail, so that any agent attempting to use them in the Soviet Union would have been immediately detected.

None of this business about the documents was hard evidence that might stand up in a court of law, but it was enough to allow the agency to ask for a criminal investigation. By mid-1964, the CIA had referred the Orlov case to the FBI.

"It was in the afternoon," Mrs. Orlov said, that the FBI came calling for the first time. "One day early in March of 1965. Six guys rang the bell and said, 'We'd like to search your house. Espionage.' It was after school, about five P.M. Sasha said, 'Can my wife go to a movie with the children?' The FBI agents said okay. He brought me my coat and we went away.

"They were still there when I came back. All the drawers on the floor, every piece of paper photographed. Even from my handbag. I had to leave my purse. They stayed until close to midnight. They said Sasha has to come to the FBI office in the morning after he finished his truck route. They told him to report to the Old Post Office Building in Washington.[7]

"There was no search warrant. At this time we didn't know the word 'search warrant.' The next day an FBI agent, Bert Turner, and another gentleman came to the gallery, where we also lived upstairs, and asked about Berlin, about Germany. They asked me, 'Why do you write to Switzerland so much?' I said, 'This is my aunt.' 'We also know you write to Australia. Who is that?' 'It's my former maid in Germany.' 'And to Montevideo?' 'My aunt, too.' My mother had five sisters. It made me furious. I said, 'Look, it's a free country.'

"They came and came and came every day for days. They asked me to take a lie-detector test and I refused. My husband said, 'They will put you in prison if you don't.' But I didn't. Sasha took an FBI lie-detector test. He passed. He welcomed it.' "

At the FBI, the Orlov case had landed on the desk of Courtland J. Jones, a tall, soft-spoken Virginia gentleman from Lynchburg who had joined the bureau out of law school in 1940. In the fall of 1964,

[7]At the time, the building housed the FBI's Washington Field Office.

when Jones got the case, he was a counterintelligence supervisor at the Washington Field Office.

"The Orlov case was called UNSUB[8] SASHA," Jones said. The FBI had opened the file early in 1962, right after Golitsin's arrival. Each suspect for Sasha, beginning with Peter Karlow, went into the UNSUB SASHA file. "There were five or six serious candidates for Sasha in the file," Jones said, "and maybe some name checks in addition."

Whatever the results of Orlov's polygraph, the FBI agents kept the pressure on. The interrogations at the Washington Field Office continued. The gallery was under constant surveillance. "He was desperate," Mrs. Orlov said, in explaining what happened next.

The *Washington Post* backs up on the rear of the Soviet embassy, and one day in April, Orlov, who was still driving a truck for the newspaper, slipped into the embassy through a rear door. "He came home in the afternoon," Eleonore Orlov recounted, "and said, 'I was in the Soviet embassy and asked for my mother's address. I asked for help because the FBI said they will do something nasty to my mother if I don't say I'm a double agent. And I don't even know if she's living.' "

At first, Eleonore said, it seemed as though Orlov's purpose in visiting the embassy was to find out whether his mother was still alive, or dead and beyond the reach of the FBI. But he quickly made it clear that he had much more in mind. He was planning their escape. "He was so afraid they would arrest both of us. Who would take care of the children? We were living on sixty dollars a week." Her husband revealed, Eleonore said, that he had asked the Soviets for asylum for himself, for her, and their two sons. The embassy had agreed, he said.

"The Soviets told him, tomorrow after school go to the parking lot of a shopping center in Arlandria [a section of Alexandria], not with your car, but in a taxi. In front of the bowling alley there will be a car. You and your wife and children will be picked up." Orlov, she said, ordered her to take the children by taxi to the parking lot the next day; it was not clear, she said, whether he would be there as well.

Eleonore Orlov had no desire to flee to the Soviet Union. "I was frantic," she said. "I called my pastor. He came, he went down on his knees and prayed with me. He said, 'Don't go to the Russians, don't do this.' I called a friend. I asked her, 'If something happens to me,

8In FBI parlance, the term stood for "unknown subject."

will you take care of my children?' I thought I had two choices: to jump from the Wilson Bridge or to go to the parking lot. I was not allowed to bring anything with me, just my driver's license and the car keys."

The next day, Eleonore drove her husband into Washington for another FBI interrogation. She went back to the house. "I went to the basement and discovered one of my cats had given birth to four kittens. That did it. I couldn't leave the house. I just couldn't. So I stayed home. I knew at five o'clock my husband would come home from the interrogation. I just sat there and waited. He came and said, 'Guess what? They let me go. They apologized and said I can go on with my life. Tomorrow we are free. But you did not obey me.' He was very angry. He was even thinking I am working with the FBI. It was a big argument. Very big.

"The FBI had asked him, 'Where were you yesterday?' 'I was in the Russian embassy.' 'Yes, we know.' 'I tried to ask for my mother's address.' If my husband was a Russian spy he wouldn't have to go to the embassy. He would have some way to contact them safer than going in. Maybe he bluffed them [the FBI], but you don't play with your life."

But if Orlov thought his troubles were over, he was wrong. To the mole hunters at Langley, Orlov's visit to the Soviet embassy was final proof that he was a Soviet spy. To his wife, it was the act of a desperate man who feared arrest and hoped to protect his family.

Convinced that Golitsin's Sasha had been run to ground, James Angleton constantly questioned the FBI about the case. "Jim never let it go," said James E. Nolan, Jr., the former FBI counterintelligence official. "He'd ask, 'Have you cracked the Orlov case? What's new on Orlov?' Angleton used the case to keep the bureau on the defensive. "If he had nothing else to throw at us," Nolan said, "he'd beard us about Orlov."

The pressure from the CIA went down the line. Supervised by Courtland Jones, FBI agents kept the Orlovs under surveillance for years.

Suddenly, after Orlov's last interrogation, a parade of new customers began visiting the Gallery Orlov. Some openly identified themselves as FBI agents. They were led by Joseph D. Purvis, the special agent in charge (SAC) of the Washington Field Office. "Mr. Purvis came to have a picture framed with Hoover shaking hands with some guy, with a flag and a big seal in the background," Eleonore recalled. "Then came Mr. Jones. Several FBI agents came.⁹

"Mr. Jones came every year to bring us a basket full of Stayman apples. He sent us Christmas cards for quite a while.

"Mr. Purvis had a gray poodle. It was a toy poodle, he kept it on his arm. The cats would try to jump on the poodle to defend their territory. Once, we framed for Mr. Purvis a portrait of his wife. We framed several pictures of Hoover shaking hands with agents."

Perhaps one of the more bizarre by-products of the entire era of the mole hunt was that great numbers of photographs of J. Edgar Hoover, the director of the FBI, and a symbol of staunch anti-Communism in America for decades, were framed for the FBI by the man whom both Hoover and Angleton suspected to be a Soviet spy, the legendary Sasha.

Another FBI agent, Fred A. Tansey, became a particularly good customer and befriended the family. "He gave us two doors and a finial for the banister, beautiful things he would find for the house. He always found an excuse to visit us."[10]

The FBI agents were there for a reason, not only to keep an eye on the gallery and Igor Orlov, but to gauge the amount of actual business conducted there. James Nolan, who rose to number two in the FBI's intelligence division, confirmed the bureau's motive.

"For a brief period I had the Orlov case," he said. "I got all the receipts [from the FBI men who had pictures framed at the gallery]. That's why the agents were in there all the time. To see how much business they had and whether the shop was a front."

In the spring of 1966, a year after the FBI had searched the Orlovs'

[9]"Over a period of time I took quite a few watercolors and other pictures to be matted and framed," Jones said. He displayed a watercolor of a boater on a river, framed by the Orlovs. Jones spent time at the gallery, he explained, because he wanted to get a firsthand impression of the Orlovs. "I have a strong investigative background," he said. "I always felt the more you know about your opponent, the better. I got to know his boys, I got to know Ellie."
[10]Tansey, who retired in 1980, insisted that he was not on assignment for the FBI when he visited the Orlovs. "My relationship with the Orlovs was strictly with regard to their business," he said. "I was a customer and a friend. I was in the intelligence division at headquarters but had no responsibility for this case." Asked whether he did not worry that his close association with a suspected Soviet spy under investigation by his own division might be misinterpreted, Tansey replied: "I don't comment on things like that."

gallery, there was a new and startling development in the case. A Soviet KGB officer, who came to be code-named KITTY HAWK, contacted the CIA and offered, among other wares, fresh information about Orlov. The KITTY HAWK case was, and remains, one of the most controversial of the Soviet cases during the entire era.

Igor Petrovich Kochnov, who was KITTY HAWK, arrived in Washington late in March 1966 on temporary duty as a Soviet diplomat.[11] About a week later, he telephoned the home in Northwest Washington of Richard Helms, then deputy director of the CIA. Helms was out, and Kochnov got Helms's then wife, Julia, heiress to the Barbasol shave cream fortune. Kochnov said he had information that would be of interest to the CIA.[12]

When CIA officials met with Kochnov as a result of his phone call, he had a suggestion that, on the face of it, was outrageous. He had been sent to the United States, he said, to try to find and contact Nicholas Shadrin, a Soviet defector whose real name was Nikolai Fedorovich Artamonov. In 1959, Artamonov, the youngest destroyer captain in the Soviet navy, had sailed across the Baltic Sea to Sweden in a small boat with his Polish girlfriend, Ewa Gora, who was now his wife.[13] If the CIA would help him fulfill his mission, Kochnov said, his KGB career would skyrocket, and he would work as an agent-in-place for the CIA. Since the CIA protects defectors, often—as in this instance—changing their names, Kochnov's request was bold, to say the least.

But both the CIA and the FBI went along with the operation. Courtland Jones talked it over with Elbert T. "Bert" Turner, who was assigned as Kochnov's FBI case agent. The decision was made, along with the CIA, to put Kochnov in touch with Artamonov and see where it led. "We put him into play and gave him feed material," Jones said. "Turner and I felt it had to be done, and what do we have

[11]Some published accounts have referred to KITTY HAWK as "Igor Romanovich Kozlov," or "Igor Kozlov." But Kochnov never used that name, either in Washington or in his previous posting at the Soviet embassy in Karachi, Pakistan.
[12]There was no mystery to how Kochnov obtained Helms's home telephone number. "I've always been listed in the phone book," Helms said. "My home then was on Fessenden Street."
[13]As it happened, when Artamonov and Ewa reached Stockholm, the CIA officer in the American embassy who received them when they appealed for assistance was Paul Garbler. Garbler, the deputy COS, helped to set in motion the arrangements for their asylum in the United States.

to lose? I was about to go to the Outer Banks on vacation and Bill Branigan, the section chief, called over and one of us said, 'What are we going to call this operation?' Both Bill and I had vacationed on the Outer Banks. I said, "Bill, I'm going to Kitty Hawk tomorrow. Shall we call it KITTY HAWK?' He said, 'Why not?' "

KITTY HAWK, according to several former FBI agents, told U.S. intelligence that Orlov had worked for the Soviets. The KGB man, Courtland Jones said, also told the FBI that Orlov had visited the Soviet embassy, which he had, in 1965. According to another former FBI man close to the case, "KITTY HAWK said that when Orlov went into the embassy, he said he was being interviewed at the time by the FBI, and asked for suicide pills in the event he needed them. And when we asked Orlov about that, he said, no, no, he went to the embassy to ask about relatives."

The KITTY HAWK operation ended in disaster. Kochnov contacted Shadrin, who worked at the time for the Defense Intelligence Agency. Under FBI control, Shadrin pretended to switch loyalties and fed Kochnov information prepared by U.S. intelligence. After several months, Kochnov announced that he had to go back to the Soviet Union, but he turned Shadrin over to other KGB handlers. Shadrin met with the Soviets for several years, once in Vienna.[14] Then in December 1975, he went back to Vienna, accompanied by Bruce Solie, of the CIA's Office of Security, and Cynthia J. Hausmann of the Counterintelligence Staff. On the night of December 20, Shadrin kept an appointment with a Soviet agent on the steps of the Votivkirche, a church on the Rooseveltplatz, not far from the American embassy. He was not seen again.[15]

[14]Although Kochnov's call to the Helms residence had set the KITTY HAWK case in motion, Helms insisted that he had not approved any aspect of the operation. "There was never the slightest intent on my part that Shadrin would go out of the country and meet any Soviet," Helms said. "Whoever manhandled that case, it was not I. I don't recall being asked is it okay to put this guy [KITTY HAWK] in touch with Shadrin. I have no recollection of anyone asking me to make such a decision. It doesn't make sense. I would not have approved it."
[15]The FBI and CIA officials who handled KITTY HAWK do not agree on whether Kochnov was a plant or a genuine agent. James Nolan, the FBI counterintelligence official, who closely studied the case, came away convinced that KITTY HAWK was a fake, in part because he never reappeared as a CIA source. "My view is that if KITTY HAWK was genuine, they [the Soviets] would never have taken him out of the United States," Nolan said. "Or he would have been back here right away. Look, you've got two hundred KGB officers in the U.S., and they can't find Shadrin. He goes and finds

A decade later, the Soviet defector Vitaly Yurchenko provided a postscript to the Shadrin case. Before redefecting to the Soviet Union, Yurchenko told the CIA that KGB agents in Vienna had kidnapped Shadrin. As he struggled in the backseat of a car that was spiriting him out of Austria, Yurchenko said, the KGB agents gave him too much chloroform, and he died.

In 1978, the Orlovs moved their gallery and home to King Street, in Alexandria's Old Town. The FBI's periodic surveillance continued for fifteen years, to no avail.

"We were unable to establish that Orlov was Sasha," Jones said. "Orlov said no, he wasn't, and there you are. What could we do?"

The bureau kept at it, however, not only because of pressure from the CIA, but because the FBI worried that Orlov, even if no longer active as a Soviet spy, might be a "sleeper" agent, to be activated at some unknown time in the future. "In any such investigation," Jones said, "we would consider was he a sleeper, is he going to be contacted by mail, telephone, radio?"

Although Angleton, Miler, and many other CIA officers remained convinced that Orlov was a Soviet agent, that opinion was not universally held, even within the agency. A high-ranking former CIA official familiar with the case concluded: "We did not think that Orlov had ever been under the control of the KGB. My overall impression is we really didn't have a case against Orlov. A lot of suspicions, but no case."

On May 2, 1982, at the age of sixty, Igor Gregory Orlov died of cancer at his home above the gallery. "Two days before he died," his wife said, "one of our former customers, a priest, came in, and asked, 'Can I pray for you?' Igor said it isn't necessary, but if you think it's

---

him in twelve hours, singlehanded. What two big residencies in New York and Washington couldn't do. He's demonstrated he is a brilliant operator in the United States. So he should have come back [to the U.S.], and he didn't. He floated around in Moscow and other places, he was visible, seen, but never so you could talk to him. That ought to tell you after a while that something's wrong. He should have had a red star pinned on him and be sent back here as deputy resident. He wasn't." However, Vasia C. Gmirkin, who wrote a still classified study of the Shadrin case for the CIA's Counterintelligence Staff in the late 1970s, after James Angleton had gone, concluded that both KITTY HAWK and Shadrin were bona fide. By 1990, the CIA had received intelligence that KITTY HAWK had died, of natural causes.

good you can say a few words. The priest said, 'Life is like a river; we people on the banks go into the river and swim a little bit and then we go back to the bank again.' Igor said, 'Yes, you are right. But I would really like to have my ashes in Russia, not in America.' Then he turned to me and said, 'Cremate me and bring the ashes to the Soviet embassy and they know what to do.' I looked at the priest. He said, 'Mrs. Orlov, this is quite natural. All my friends from the East, when it's time to die, they like to be buried in their homeland.'

"The boys were with Sasha all night long. He slipped into a coma and died Sunday morning. Mr. Tansey made the funeral arrangements. There were no services when he died. Monday he was cremated."

Eleonore Orlov did not follow her husband's instructions. "His ashes are upstairs on the mantel," she said. "In a box decorated with a Russian eagle."

Despite Orlov's last wish, and his earlier request for asylum in the Soviet Union, in their thirty-four years together, Eleonore Orlov said, her husband had never expressed any sympathy for the Soviet system, or dropped the slightest hint that he might have worked for the Russians. Rather the opposite, she insisted. "He was very careful in his dealings with anyone of Russian background. He never let anyone in the house. He was afraid to be poisoned by the Russians."

In Berlin, she said, "we were scared to death of the Russians. He was afraid they would kill him. First because of Vlasov, and now because he was working for the Americans. He was poisoned by an East German doctor in West Berlin, poisoned with mushrooms. Not enough to kill him, but perhaps they had planned to bring him over the line to the Russians. It was the time of the *Menschenraub,* the kidnappings on both sides in Berlin."

Why had she never pressed her husband to reveal his true background, his name at birth, for example? Mrs. Orlov smiled and said, "You know the legend of Lohengrin. You know what happened to Elsa."[16] She did ask, once, about the tattoo of the flower on his left hand. "None of your business," he said.

Did Eleonore Orlov believe her husband was a Soviet spy? She did

[16]In Richard Wagner's opera, based on the medieval German story, Lohengrin is a knight of the Holy Grail who rescues Princess Elsa from an unwanted suitor. He is led to her by a swan. She is forbidden to ask his identity, but curious, one day she does, and Lohengrin must leave.

not believe it, she said, nor did she want to believe it. "Deep in my mind I don't know. I asked the FBI to let me talk to Golitsin. They laughed in my face. 'Out of the question.' I'd like to know how he knows about 'Sasha' and the letter K."

Even to entertain the possibility that her husband was a spy hurts her deeply, she said. "For seven years he drove a delivery truck for the *Washington Post* at two A.M. and ran the gallery by day. He worked 2 A.M. to 9 A.M. and then every Monday all day he had to collect from the drugstores and places that sold the paper." If Sasha Orlov had money from spying, she asked, would he have done that?

No, she could not believe he was a spy. "I don't believe he was. There is not a shred of proof. If he did that"—there were tears in her eyes now—"it would be very low. I can't believe a man could lie to his family for thirty years and not help us in our struggle. When we bought the house it was in terrible shape. I worked for a year, tearing off the plaster, stripping it down. I worked as hard as anyone in the gulag. If he let me do that, if he really was a spy . . ." Her voice trailed off.

She composed herself. "If Igor worked for the Russians all his life and took his family for cover, I would not like to sleep at night anymore," she said. "At the end of John le Carré's *A Perfect Spy,* he writes to his wife, I'm sorry. I married you only for cover. I saw the last episode on TV at a friend's home. It came like a mountain of bricks on me. *I said, my God, that could be me.*"

Chapter 14

Trinidad

■

As the first chief of the Moscow station, Paul Garbler had every reason to believe that headquarters was pleased with his performance. He had handled the contacts with Penkovsky as instructed, managed to keep a low profile, and had the wit to copy the Cherepanov papers before they were politely handed back to the KGB.

Midway through his tour, he received word that he had been promoted. Garbler and his wife, Florence, celebrated with champagne and caviar.

In February 1964, as his assignment in the Soviet Union was winding down, Garbler flew out of Moscow to meet with David Murphy, the chief of the Soviet division, who was on a trip to Western Europe. Murphy offered him a top job back at headquarters as deputy chief of the division. But he would start out, temporarily, as chief of operations. Garbler accepted on the spot.

With a few days of holiday on his hands, he went skiing alone in Zürs, Austria, early in March. Although an accomplished skier, Garbler lost his balance and took a spill, suffering a head injury that left him with headaches and partial paralysis on his left side, in his arm and leg. He was taken to a hospital in Wiesbaden, West Germany.

In the hospital, he was visited by Hugh Montgomery, who had been his deputy COS in Moscow but had been expelled the previous year in the fallout over the Penkovsky case. "Montgomery didn't come to Wiesbaden to wish me well," Garbler said. "There was none of that.

I sensed that Hugh was there to see if I was rational, since I had landed on my head. And he said, 'Dave Murphy doesn't want you to go back to Moscow. Why don't you just come home?' I said I walked into the Moscow job and I intended to walk out, not on a stretcher." Garbler soon recovered and returned to his post in Moscow.

In June, he flew back to Langley to take up his new job as operations chief in the Soviet division. But he harbored lingering suspicions about the accident. "I was in good health, I played on the embassy hockey team. I thought somebody had slipped me something." Garbler wondered whether the somebody might have been General Gribanov, the chief of the KGB's Second Chief Directorate, who had the responsibility of watching and compromising U.S. diplomats stationed in Moscow.

"I knew Gribanov had been traveling," Garbler said. "I checked carefully on the movements of General Gribanov. We found he had traveled to Innsbruck and St. Anton, Austria, less than three weeks before I got to Zürs." The CIA was not able to determine what the KGB general was doing in Austria. And there the trail ended; Garbler could not establish that he had been drugged.

And he had other problems to deal with. Almost from the start, things did not go well back at headquarters. Garbler did not slip easily into the role of a gray bureaucrat. He clashed with Pete Bagley, the division's counterintelligence officer. As a former chief of station in Moscow, Garbler did not hesitate to voice his opinions.

Late one evening, there was a flare-up with another officer in the Soviet division over a cable being prepared to alert some thirty CIA stations around the globe. The cable said that the KGB had approached the CIA to work in tandem against the Chinese. Garbler challenged the accuracy of the cable and asked to see the evidence. The officer who prepared it said "the best report came from Rocky Stone in Katmandu." He handed Garbler the transcript of a bugged conversation between Howard E. "Rocky" Stone, the station chief in Nepal, and the KGB resident.

"I read the transcript. The Soviet KGB man says, 'Your Scotch is great, Chivas Regal, the best.' The CIA man says, 'The *zakuski* are wonderful—what about working with us against the Chinese?' The Soviet ducks any response. I was appalled. This was the evidence!"

Garbler went back to the officer. "I asked, 'Is this the best you have?' He said yes. I said, 'That's terrible, there's nothing to it.' He said, 'You haven't been here long enough. That's what Dave wants. Don't make waves.'

"The next day I said to Dave Murphy, 'Do you really want to send this?' Murphy replied, 'It's just possible I made a mistake, you don't belong on my team.' I was out. Pete Bagley had a straight line to be deputy chief and I was looking for a job." In time, as it turned out, Bagley did become deputy chief of the Soviet division.

It seemed to Garbler that there was "something weird" about his rapid fall from grace in the Soviet division, but he chalked it up to normal bureaucratic infighting. And, after all, he quickly moved to another assignment, with Murphy's help. "To give Dave his due, he got me a good job as chief, foreign intelligence, Western European division." In 1965, after Garbler had worked in his new post for several months, a major reorganization took place inside the DDP. The Central and Western European divisions were merged into a new European division (EUR), headed by Rolfe Kingsley, a senior officer who had been chief of station in Copenhagen and Ottawa.

Early in 1966, Kingsley selected Garbler to be chief of operations in the new division. He sent the nomination up to Desmond FitzGerald, the deputy director for plans. Two weeks later, Garbler said, Kingsley called him into his office, all smiles. He showed him the memorandum he had sent to the DDP. It had come back with a notation penciled on the margin by FitzGerald: "Excellent choice, I agree."

For Garbler, it was a prestigious new job at the center of the agency's operations in Europe. He put the unfortunate experience in the Soviet division behind him and settled into his new post. Three weeks later, on a Friday evening, a shaken Kingsley summoned Garbler to his office. "He told me Tom K. wanted to see me right away." Thomas H. Karamessines was FitzGerald's deputy.

It was late, and Garbler remembered his steps echoing in the almost deserted building as he made his way to Karamessines's office. What could Tom K. possibly want?

Karamessines, a short, stocky man with black horn-rimmed glasses, was ill at ease. But he came quickly to the point. He and FitzGerald had been talking about it most of the afternoon, and they had reached a decision. The agency had a new responsibility for Garbler, Karamessines said. "We're sending you down to the Farm."

The Farm! Garbler was staggered; Karamessines might as well have said Siberia.

It made no sense; Garbler pointed out that the DDP had just agreed to his appointment as chief of operations for all of Europe.

"We need someone with your operational experience to motivate the trainees," Karamessines replied smoothly. "We're lucky to have you."

Garbler managed to ask how soon he was needed at the Farm.

"Within a week," Karamessines said.

Garbler, years later, still remembered the anger that rose within him. "I asked myself, what the hell was going on? What about my family? We'd bought a house believing we would be in the Washington area for at least three years. My wife was deep in plans for decorating it. My daughter had just been placed in school. What was I to tell them?"

Garbler argued with Karamessines for an hour. His demand to see either FitzGerald or the director of the CIA was turned down. He could refuse the assignment, Karamessines finally told him, only if he resigned.

After fifteen years in the CIA, Garbler had too much of a career investment to quit. Dutifully, but puzzled, he went off to Williamsburg, where he spent the next two years as deputy director of the Farm, working with young trainees. All the while, he kept expecting word from headquarters that a terrible mistake had been made.

The other CIA officers on the staff at Camp Peary were quick to realize that something odd was going on with Garbler, and they shunned him, lest something rub off on them. "It was as if I had contracted leprosy," Garbler remembered.

Two years to the day, Garbler was back in the office of Karamessines, who was by now the DDP. The chief of clandestine operations was upbeat; he had discussed Garbler's next assignment with Richard Helms, the new CIA director. Garbler was really going to like his new job.

"Great," said Garbler. With his background as chief of station in Moscow, perhaps he had been selected for COS in one of the major Eastern-bloc countries. Or maybe a senior post had opened up back in the Soviet division.

"We're sending you to Port-of-Spain, Trinidad," Karamessines said.

Garbler was stunned.

Karamessines, like a travel agent selling passage on the *Titanic,* cheerily extolled the advantages of Garbler's new post. The situation in the Caribbean was "very bad." Dick Helms was greatly concerned. The agency needed a reliable, experienced man as station chief in Trinidad.

Garbler was incredulous. "I couldn't believe this was happening," he said. He had visited the island once, years before, on an aircraft carrier, and knew that the major preoccupation of the residents was the annual carnival. "I had worked for years to learn my trade in Soviet operations. What was I going to do in Trinidad?"

Outraged, Garbler protested the decision, marshaling all his arguments, demanding to know the real reason for his exile. In return, Karamessines provided only soothing replies. Garbler was being assigned to one of the agency's most important nerve centers in the Caribbean. Helms wanted him there. Once again, Karamessines reminded Garbler that he could always resign if he did not want the assignment.

By now, Garbler was sure there was a conspiracy against him in the agency, although he did not suspect the reason. When he left Karamessines, he went directly to the office of Howard J. Osborn, the chief of the Office of Security. An old friend of Garbler's, Osborn said yes, he knew of the appointment. The security chief admitted, Garbler said, that sending him to Trinidad was a bit like "assigning Dick Helms to run the incinerator." He laughed and bantered with Garbler. But he shed no light on what was really going on.

At age fifty, Paul Garbler, former dive-bomber pilot, Berlin operative at the height of the Cold War, and the first CIA chief of station in Moscow, swallowed his pride and went off to Trinidad for four years.

Midway through his tour, Garbler finally learned the truth. A DDP officer who was an old and close friend arrived in Trinidad on agency business and stayed with Garbler at his home. After dinner, Garbler invited his colleague into the study, which had been swept for electronic bugs only a few days earlier by CIA technicians. Garbler turned up the stereo anyway.

After several cognacs, the visiting CIA man put security aside and confided in his old friend.

Headquarters wanted Garbler out of the way, he said, because he was suspected of being a spy for the Soviet Union. He was believed to be a Soviet mole inside the CIA. He had been sent to Trinidad so he would be cut off from access to secret operations and classified documents involving the Soviets.

There was a moment during World War II that Garbler often remembered. He was flying his Navy Helldiver in terrible weather on a mission to Japanese-held Chichi Island, in the far Pacific, and Grafton B. "Soupy" Campbell, the squadron leader, was having trouble finding a way through the thick cloud cover. The planes were running low on fuel, and if they did not attack soon, they would not make it back to the carrier. Suddenly there was an opening in the clouds below, and Garbler and all the other pilots got on the radio at the same instant. In unison, they yelled, "Dammit, Soupy, dive!"

Now, almost thirty years later, with the carnival music of Trinidad blaring on his hi-fi, the clouds had parted once again for Garbler. Finally, he understood.

At the time, Garbler was unaware that an intense hunt for penetrations was underway within the CIA. Nor did he yet know how or why the agency had come to focus on him as a major suspect.

The key, of course, was Igor Orlov, whom Garbler had called "the little man" when he had run him in Berlin almost two decades earlier. But how did the mole hunters get from Orlov to Garbler?

Garbler, after all, did not have a name that began with the letter K. Ed Petty, a former member of the Special Investigations Group, explained what had happened.

Within the SIG, he said, there was general agreement that Orlov was Golitsin's "Sasha." Bruce Solie had reached that conclusion after studying the Berlin operational files. "But there was a problem. They went to Golitsin. 'You said it was a staff penetration,' they said. 'This guy [Orlov] was never a staff officer.' Golitsin came up with this theory. 'The Russians are running Orlov, and doubling the agents run by Orlov, and their real target is your staff officers. You can be sure among officers who ran Orlov you will find one or more serious penetrations. The Russians will have gone to them, the CIA staff officers, and said, "We control your network, you had better cooperate with us or your careers go down the drain." ' I could never understand how Angleton or anybody bought the logic.[1]

---

[1]Some former CIA officers thought that Golitsin had not warned of moles in the CIA when he defected, but only about two years later. Donald Jameson, for example, who

"Upwards of a dozen case officers had handled Orlov and they all came under suspicion. They were all gone over with a fine-tooth comb."

Scotty Miler, Angleton's former deputy and a key member of the SIG, defended the decision to broaden the investigation. "You have to make a presumption that if Igor Orlov was a spy, he in turn would recruit some of the people he was associated with," Miler said. "From a CI point of view you have to assume one spy may recruit another."

Not only were all of the case officers who ran Orlov investigated, he continued, "but also other agency people he might have known or socialized with."

But Miler insisted that the mole hunt was not solely the responsibility of the SIG. Others played a part as well. "The Counterintelligence Staff," he said, "did not do the investigations. We did the research. OS [the Office of Security] did the investigation if it became a good case. OS, the DCI [the Director of Central Intelligence], chief of CI, and the DDP would know about it. In almost every instance of a referral to the FBI the DCI gave the approval."

It was through Orlov, therefore, whose previous operational names had begun with the letter K, that the mole hunters made the quantum leap to the first chief of the Moscow station. Like an electric current that arcs between electrodes, the mole hunters had moved from Orlov, whom they were convinced was Sasha, to every case officer, secretary, or other CIA employee who had ever had any contact with him.

Once the SIG had focused on Garbler, the counterintelligence men dug into his file and found additional information to feed their grow-

---

had been an officer in the Soviet division, remembered taking Golitsin to dinner in August 1962 at the home of former CIA director Allen Dulles in Georgetown. "Dulles said, 'The thing that interests me most is, do you know of any penetrations in the CIA?' Golitsin said no. Dulles knocked on wood, on the table, and Golitsin did, too." But Golitsin was telling his CIA debriefers a different story. The evidence is clear that Golitsin spoke of moles from the start. Even before he arrived in Washington, he told Frank Friberg that he had seen information that had leaked from "high inside the CIA." At the outset, he warned of a penetration named Sasha. And he disclosed that the KGB knew about the CIA's effort to copy the Soviet bug in the Great Seal. By January 15, 1962, within four weeks of Golitsin's defection, and as a result of his leads, wiretaps were in place on Peter Karlow, and a full-fledged FBI and CIA investigation of Karlow was under way. The mole hunt reached an even greater level of intensity in 1963 and afterward as it spread from Orlov, and beyond Karlow to other staff officers.

ing suspicion. In Korea, for example, where Garbler had served as assistant naval attaché and as President Rhee's pilot, he had played tennis, the mole hunters triumphantly discovered, with George Blake. Blake, who was captured and imprisoned under harsh conditions when the North Koreans overran Seoul, was later unmasked as a Soviet agent inside MI6.

As the "evidence" mounted against Garbler—including the discovery that his father had emigrated from Russia and his mother from Poland—the CI Staff became persuaded that the former chief of the Moscow station was a Soviet spy. The CIA referred the Garbler case to the FBI.

In Trinidad, after Garbler had learned he was a suspected Soviet mole, there was little he could do except serve out the rest of his tour. Stuck in Port-of-Spain, more than two thousand miles from headquarters, he could not even begin the process of trying to clear his good name.

There was time to brood and think, time to despair. Although he now knew why he had been sent to the Caribbean, he tried to make the best of it. Trinidad was, after all, an island paradise. Rum and sunshine were abundant. Garbler liked the people; he found them hedonistic and unpredictable, but also generous and kind. Among them he made many lasting friends, both black and white.

But for the better part of nine years, he now realized, he had been shunted into blind alleys, cut off from the mainstream in the CIA, and finally isolated under the coconut palms, a suspected traitor to the country he loved and had served all of his adult life.

Garbler reviewed the last half-dozen years, reevaluating events in the light of what he now knew. What might have seemed bureaucratic errors or innocent events took on new meaning. It was like seeing a movie over again, this time knowing the plot.

He thought back to Moscow. Was it possible that the agency's suspicions, of which he had still not officially been informed, had begun there? In Moscow, Garbler had been told almost nothing by headquarters about developments in his most important case, that of Oleg Penkovsky. If he was already under suspicion, headquarters would have told him as little as possible.

He remembered when he was recovering from his ski accident in the hospital in Wiesbaden and Hugh Montgomery, his deputy chief of station in Moscow, had paid him a visit. At the time, he had thought that Montgomery had been sent by David Murphy, the division chief, "to report to Murphy whether I had enough marbles left to return to Moscow and run the station." But in retrospect, Garbler wondered whether Montgomery's true purpose was "to see if I was carrying KGB money in my pajamas."

Garbler had been determined to return to his post in Moscow. "The bunglers at headquarters may have thought my insistence on return-ing was linked to my need to see my KGB handler one more time, if for no other reason, to get instructions for future contact in the U.S. Murphy would infer from my position that I had to go back and satisfy the people who were controlling me from the other side."

In 1972, when his tour in Trinidad ended, Garbler returned to headquarters and immediately made an appointment with William V. Broe, the CIA inspector general. A complaint to the inspector general, Garbler knew, would earn him the displeasure of Karamessines, the deputy director for plans, but at this point, Garbler had nothing to lose.

Garbler told his story to Broe, whom he was certain already knew it. He had achieved senior status in the DDP at age forty-five, Garbler said, and could normally have looked forward to another fifteen years of increased responsibility. Instead, he had been sidetracked, the vic-tim of invisible charges that he had never been told about officially. Garbler demanded to know why, if he was a suspect, he had not been informed.

Broe did not respond, but promised to talk to Karamessines, who then wrote a memorandum praising Garbler's sterling performance in Trinidad, but making no mention of the mole charge. But Garbler's protests had some effect; after nine years as an unperson in the CIA, he was partially rehabilitated and in 1973 sent to Stockholm for three years as chief of station.

The knowledge that he had been suspected by his own service of committing espionage for the Soviet Union had placed a terrible strain on both Garbler and his wife, Florence, and their daughter. In the midst of Garbler's fight to clear his reputation he was awakened one night from a deep sleep by his wife.

"Paul," she said, "I've never asked you this, and I know it's not true. But now I want to hear it from you. Did you ever spy for the Russians?"

"Christ, hell no, you know I didn't," Garbler said.

Garbler had still not been told officially that he was a suspected mole. He had never been given a chance to confront his faceless accusers. Sweden was a pleasant assignment, but Garbler was not ready to give up. In December 1976, after he returned from Stockholm, he wrote to the inspector general again.

This time, he demanded an inquiry.

Chapter 15

Murphy's Law

By the mid-1960s, the CIA's Soviet division was in turmoil. The division, staffed as it was by so many Russian-speakers and persons of Russian origin, had become the primary target of the mole hunt triggered by Golitsin.

Literally dozens of its officers were under suspicion, and many were being actively investigated by the SIG, the Office of Security, and in some cases the FBI. Down on the Farm, Yuri Nosenko was being held incommunicado, a ticking time bomb for the agency. Paul Garbler, the first chief of the Moscow station, had been exiled to Trinidad, an unwitting suspect. All of the other case officers who had run Igor Orlov were also under investigation.

Because Golitsin had predicted that any defector who followed him would be a plant, virtually all of the cases being run by the division were viewed as bad by the CI Staff. The Soviet division was supposed to be recruiting Soviet intelligence officers around the world, but what was the point if the powerful counterintelligence officials at headquarters regarded every new recruit or walk-in as an agent sent by the KGB?

The result was that the CIA's Soviet operations had ground to a halt. At the time, during the height of the Cold War, the CIA existed primarily to gather intelligence on the Soviet Union; other targets were secondary. Now the mole hunt had paralyzed the Soviet division and thereby the CIA itself.

While some agency officials dispute this, it was precisely the conclusion reached by William E. Colby, the director of the CIA from 1973 to 1976. "From the mid-1960s on," Colby said, "Soviet operations came to a dead halt. Helms and Karamessines had launched a program we called hard targets. 'Let's recruit hard targets. Soviet. Chinese. That's what we're in business for.' It wasn't happening.

"As I understood it, it was because of the high degree of suspicion that was exhibited about any operational opportunities. The insistence of CI that defectors be looked at as probable fakes. There was an awful impasse between the CI staff and the Soviet division."

A former high-ranking official of the agency said the problem went far beyond the Soviet division. "The Soviet division had people in stations all over the world," he said, "but they were not the only ones who could recruit Soviets. Other officers in the stations could recruit Soviets as well.[1] The divisions went ahead and tried to recruit people, but they were constantly getting into disputes with Angleton because he claimed that anyone we recruited was being sent to manipulate us. Angleton believed everyone was bad. We kept on working, we kept on recruiting, but it was totally undermined by the CI Staff."

According to one former senior CIA officer, Angleton tried to persuade the British to reject Yuri Krotkov, the first Soviet defector to vouch for Nosenko. A Moscow filmmaker, Krotkov had defected in London in the fall of 1963. "Krotkov was a KGB co-optee," the CIA man said. "He gave us a lot of information about Soviet dissidents. He was a tremendous source of interesting information. All scoffed at by Angleton. All throwaway, Angleton said—who cares about a bunch of dissidents?"

Nosenko had defected early in 1964. "Krotkov was immediately asked if he knew Nosenko, and yes he knew him, and verified that Nosenko was an officer in the Second Chief Directorate. That sealed his doom. Jim said, send him up to Scotland and put him in a castle and let him rot there for a couple of years. The Brits wouldn't do it. Then he said, send him back. Dick White [the chief of MI6] said, 'Send him back, are you mad? We'll never get another Soviet defector.' White was horrified. The Brits intervened and Krotkov was allowed to stay. He lives in California now."[2]

[1]There was one major exception. In the Soviet Union only officers of the CIA's Soviet division could recruit a Russian. Any recruitment of a Soviet, regardless of the country where it was taking place, required approval of Langley headquarters.

[2]Krotkov revealed to Western intelligence that one of his successful missions for the

•   •   •

Murphy's Law states that if anything can possibly go wrong, it will. And as it happened, during this tumultuous and difficult period in the 1960s, when so much in the CIA went wrong, the Soviet division was presided over by David E. Murphy.

Tall and bespectacled, with a high forehead and a shock of gray hair that contrasted with his blue eyes, Murphy was square of jaw and rather distinguished-looking, with a faint resemblance to the actor William Holden. At CIA headquarters Murphy looked like a man who was always in a hurry, a slightly stooped figure striding rapidly down the corridors. He gave the impression of a high-powered executive who thought fast and acted fast.

To most of his colleagues, Murphy was an Irishman from Syracuse, in upstate New York. "Of course he was Irish," said one ex-CIA officer. "I was in his house, there were shillelaghs on the wall." But considerable mystery surrounded his roots. Wild rumors persisted in the agency that Murphy was an orphan, that he was adopted, that he wasn't really Irish, that his true name was Moscowitz, and that he might even have had a Russian background. Some of this chatter may have stemmed from the fact that Murphy's first wife, Marian Escovy, was a White Russian. Or perhaps from the fact that Murphy was fluent in Russian, as well as in German and French.[3]

Second Chief Directorate had compromised the French ambassador to Moscow, Maurice Dejean. Krotkov had introduced him to a beautiful young actress, a KGB "swallow" with whom Dejean had an affair. The story is related in John Barron, *KGB: The Secret World of Soviet Secret Agents* (New York: Bantam Books, 1974), pp. 170–92. Krotkov later wrote a book about his life, *I Am from Moscow* (New York: Dutton, 1967).

[3]Murphy, retired for more than a decade, was living in McLean, Virginia, in the shadow of the CIA, in 1991. He declined to be interviewed, although we spoke by telephone and he agreed at first to answer written questions subject to review—and deletions—by the agency. After reading the questions, he declined to answer any. Much of the information circulating about his background, he said, was "garbled or in some cases untrue. . . . The 'Murphy is a White Russian syndrome' is a good example. There is no way I could respond to such garbage about my background in a manner which would satisfy those who have spread those falsehoods. In a way I'm reminded of the Polish rabbit joke. It was on the Polish-Soviet frontier during the great purges of the thirties. A Polish rabbit's solitude was shattered when a Soviet rabbit came tearing across the border in obvious panic. 'What's your hurry?' asked the Polish rabbit. 'They're killing camels back there,' gasped the Soviet rabbit. 'But

What little is in the public record about Murphy reveals that he was born on June 23, 1921, in New York State, was graduated from State Teachers College in Cortland, New York, south of Syracuse, in 1942, and served in the Army during World War II. After that, the official biography lists him as a "consultant" to the "Department of Defense." In fact, Murphy served with Army intelligence in Korea and Japan, then joined the CIA. By 1949, or soon after, he was chief of the agency's Munich operations base.

In 1953, Murphy came to Berlin to be deputy chief of base under Bill Harvey. In Berlin, his backyard adjoined that of Paul Garbler, who was there running "Franz Koischwitz," later to be known as Igor Orlov. By 1959, Murphy had briefly succeeded Harvey as chief of base, and in 1963 he was promoted to chief of the Soviet division at headquarters. As such, he was at the center of the period of the mole hunt, the intense conflicts over Golitsin and Nosenko, and the freeze in Soviet operations.

Murphy was a senior player in the agency, and his career advanced rapidly, but along the way he got into some highly publicized scrapes. In Vienna, CIA legend has it, Murphy wound up in a barroom brawl with a KGB man and had to escape, ignominiously, out the men's-room window. Scotty Miler recalled that something like that happened. "Apparently he went to a beer hall or bar after receiving an indication that this KGB guy could be recruited. Dave made his pitch and then the guy blew up, threw beer in his face, and started yelling 'American spy!' "

In 1966, while serving as chief of the Soviet division, Murphy starred in another Keystone Cops episode, this time in Japan. It made headlines around the world, although Murphy was described in the news stories as a "tourist."

The trouble began when Murphy flew into Tokyo to try to recruit the KGB resident, Georgy P. Pokrovsky, who was there under cover as first secretary of the Soviet embassy in Tokyo. It was unusual for a division chief personally to participate in a high-risk field operation, but Murphy was not one to shy away from danger or intrigue.

George Kisevalter remembered the episode. "As chief of SR [Soviet

---

you're not a camel,' answered the Polish rabbit. 'Try proving that to them!' sadly replied the Soviet rabbit." Letter, David E. Murphy to author, January 7, 1991.

Russia] division," he said, "Murphy went to Japan using his true name. To show the boys how to do it. He took with him a case officer who got hit in the head with an umbrella. It was a scandal and got into the press."

Indeed it did, and the news stories centered on some odd goings-on at the Clean Breeze apartments in Tokyo on the night of St. Patrick's Day. Pokrovsky, according to the published accounts, returned to his residence at the Clean Breeze to find a Colombian neighbor, one José Miguel Moneva Calderón, seemingly ill in the lobby. The Colombian asked Pokrovsky to help him to his apartment to get some medicine. The Russian obliged. Who was waiting in a nearby stairwell but the two American "tourists," Murphy, whose residence was given as McLean, Virginia, and Thomas A. Ryan, of Vienna, Virginia. A scuffle ensued. Pokrovsky got away, but returned with Soviet reinforcements. The KGB goon squad encountered the two Americans outside the apartment, and a free-for-all took place. Pokrovsky hit Ryan with the umbrella and one of the CIA men had his glasses broken.

Pokrovsky charged that the Americans had tried to kidnap him. The Japanese police smoothed over the affair, calling it merely "a quarrel with two Americans and a Colombian." In Washington, Robert J. McCloskey, the State Department spokesman, was asked whether there were "any American government representatives involved in this."

"No, sir," he replied sturdily.

And it was under Murphy that the Soviet division ran, and then began to suspect, the KGB illegal Yuri Loginov, code name AEGUSTO. Loginov, it will be recalled, had been recruited in Helsinki in 1961 by Richard Kovich, who later became one of the CI Staff's prime mole suspects as a result of Golitsin's analysis of his career. Kovich not only had a name that began with the letter K, a Slavic background, and service in Germany, he had handled Ingeborg Lygren, the Norwegian CIA agent, Mikhail Federov, the GRU illegal, and Loginov.

Although Loginov was run in the field by a succession of CIA officers after Kovich, the case was supervised at headquarters from the start by Joseph C. Evans, a counterintelligence officer who worked for Murphy and Bagley in the Soviet division. A short, stocky, compact man who chain-smoked filter cigarettes, Evans was a former newspaper reporter who had edited a weekly in Lewisburg, Pennsylvania. He joined the agency and was sent to London in the 1950s to analyze traffic from the Berlin tunnel that the CIA had dug to wiretap the Soviets. Back at headquarters in 1959, he concentrated on a narrow specialty, Soviet illegals. A thoughtful man with an analytical turn of mind, he had faith in Loginov, at first.

Evans took part in the debriefing of Golitsin. "I debriefed him thoroughly on Loginov," he said. It was in May 1961, while Kovich was in Helsinki, that Golitsin and another KGB officer had met there with Loginov. "Golitsin said the other officer from Moscow was from the illegals directorate and was shepherding Loginov and 'staging' him—the term they use is *stazhirovka,* a familiarization test before a final mission." At the time, Evans said, "I was quite apprehensive about Loginov returning to Soviet hands," since he was now ostensibly a double agent for the CIA.

Loginov flew to Paris in the fall of 1962. In the spring of 1964, he arrived in Brussels on his third trip to the West. He traveled to Germany, then left for Beirut in June, went on to Cairo, posing as a Canadian, and later returned to Moscow. In January 1967, the KGB dispatched Loginov to Antwerp on his fourth trip to the West. He was instructed to go to several countries and finally to the United States, his main target.

Although Richard Kovich continued to believe in Loginov, there were growing suspicions about the KGB illegal in the Soviet division and the CI Staff. To Bagley and Evans, the counterintelligence officers for the Soviet division, the *stazhirovka* process appeared endless. "He never seemed to handle anybody," Bagley said. "Here we had an illegal who spent all his time documenting himself. Most illegals handle cases, like Lonsdale."

"There were several other reasons," Bagley added. "Specific reasons. Not just that he was unproductive. There were concrete points. He made a mistake about a radio transmission. He knew something he hadn't yet received from Moscow. His legend didn't check out. He was always being promised he would handle important assignments, but it never happened." By about 1965, the decision had been reached: Loginov was a plant.

Joseph Evans said that "the decision was made because of two reasons. One was, we despaired of getting to the bottom of the story. We questioned him about contradictions and gaps in his story. Here was someone who could infer from the types of questions that clearly we doubted his story and never a reaction of anger and surprise. And, two, we had a loose cannon. If we break off and let run free a man who has a passport, we don't know where he's going to go."

If Loginov came to the United States, his ultimate target, he would be under FBI surveillance. But the CIA's concern, Evans said, was that "this man was capable of changing identities and disappearing. We'd lose him."

"Loginov gave us nothing of CI value," Evans insisted. "He gave us no illegals or agents. His false documentation never led to any illegal support apparatus, no accommodation addresses of [Soviet] agents, which illegals have, nothing."

Loginov's failure to identify illegal support agents was significant, Evans insisted, because "if they support one, they could support others. He identified none who could lead to other illegals." Loginov's real mission, Evans believed, was "to find out how much we knew about illegals and how they operated."

To be sure, Evans said, Loginov had turned over his codes to the CIA. " 'This is my cipher system,' he said. So yes, we were able to read his traffic. But were there other systems? Were there two? He had one-way communication from the [Moscow] Center by radio, unread-able unless you had the cipher system. We were able to listen—he told us frequencies, times—and confirm his messages." But, Evans re-peated, Loginov might have been getting radio messages the CIA didn't know about.

Another reason for the CI Staff's conclusion, Evans said, was that Loginov never explained his motive for volunteering his services to the CIA. "I never sensed a hatred of KGB or of his assignments. Nor was he doing it for the excitement of being a double agent. He said he liked to work for the Americans, but he never displayed the counter feeling of animosity to the Soviet system. 'I just want to work for the Ameri-cans,' Loginov said."[4]

---

[4]In a series of interviews, Evans said he could not reply to some questions because they involved classified information. I put these queries in writing, and Evans submitted a four-page reply to the CIA, which deleted almost two pages—his entire answer to the question asking him to list in detail the reasons why he doubted Loginov. In their initial response in December 1990, the CIA's censors left only one answer of any substance. I had asked Evans whether the CIA had officially taken the position that Loginov was a plant. The agency let stand his reply: "The official CIA position was

Brussels, said: "Loginov was arrested with the approval of the division and Angleton. It was Dave Murphy's decision and Jim's. He was exposed to the South Africans. We gave him to the South Africans."

The South African intelligence service was told that the CIA had been running Loginov as an agent, but that the CIA had been unable to establish Loginov's bona fides and suspected he was a KGB plant.

Joseph Evans said the decision to expose Loginov was a "collective recommendation; what should we do? We discussed the alternatives. Dave Murphy signed off on that, and Angleton, maybe. I assume it was cleared with the DDP and discussed with Angleton, but I don't know that."[6]

Another senior former CIA officer, a retired station chief, had no doubt that Angleton was at the heart of the decision. "He was the master figure behind the scenes who moved the puppets around, whether the puppet was young Bagley, who thought he was smarter than everyone else, or some old buddy like Kingsley, who was unsure of himself, or Tom K. The point is that Jim never made overt power moves. But as chief of CI, Angleton got every piece of eyes-only traffic. He saw it all. Any exposure of Loginov would not have taken place without his permission. It couldn't."

On September 9, the South African security police announced that Yuri Loginov had confessed to espionage in that country and twenty-three other nations. Major General H. J. van den Bergh, the chief of the security police, released a long list of Soviet diplomats in other countries whom he said Loginov had identified as KGB agents.

Evans, posing as a South African security official, met and questioned Loginov after his arrest. "He admitted to me in South Africa that he had not told us everything about his relationship with the KGB," Evans said. But Loginov would not say more. Evans reported to the CIA that Loginov had teetered on the edge of admitting he was a dispatched agent, but never did. Convinced, nevertheless, that Loginov was a fake, the CIA allowed him to languish in a South African prison, which was, of course, where it had put him.

•   •   •

[6]Desmond FitzGerald was the deputy director for plans (DDP) from mid-1965 until July 23, 1967, when he collapsed on a tennis court at his country home in The Plains, Virginia, and died. The South Africans arrested Loginov that same month.

As Evans recalled it, "I reached the decision he was bad and I was supported in this decision by Dave Murphy and Pete Bagley. They felt as I felt on the same grounds—that something was wrong."

One thing that was wrong, of course, was that Loginov had backed up the bona fides of Yuri Nosenko. At the time, Nosenko was imprisoned by the CIA, and the agency, in David Murphy's blunt language, was attempting to "break" him. The CIA case officers in contact with Loginov were ordered to question him about Nosenko. Loginov's answer, that Nosenko was a genuine defector, would, by itself, have been enough to cast doubt on Loginov. "Loginov supported the bona fides of Nosenko and that was what got him in trouble," said one former agency officer.

Meanwhile, Loginov was maintaining contact with the CIA. He had arrived in South Africa late in January 1967. In May, he flew to Kenya, where he was met by a CIA case officer, and the following month he was back in Johannesburg, traveling on a Canadian passport as Edmund Trinka.[5] He moved into an apartment on Smit Street.

Now, at CIA headquarters, an extraordinary decision was made. Convinced that Loginov was a plant, the agency decided to "burn" its own agent. It tipped off the South African intelligence service to the fact that Yuri Loginov, a Soviet illegal, was in Johannesburg, living as Edmund Trinka.

In July 1967, agents of the South African security service raided Loginov's apartment and arrested him. He was jailed and a long series of interrogations began.

If the CIA was right, it was turning the tables on the KGB and putting a Soviet spy out of action. If the agency was wrong, it was causing the arrest and imprisonment of one of its own agents. It might even be placing his life in jeopardy. As might be imagined, it was not a decision that most CIA officials want to talk about, even today.

Pete Bagley, careful to note that by 1967 he had left his job as deputy chief of the Soviet division to become chief of station in

_____

that Loginov had not established his bona fides." Evans appealed, and in June 1991 the CIA permitted him to reply in writing, but only in generalities, to the core question of why Loginov was suspect.

[5]For this purpose, the KGB, as it usually does in such cases, used the identity of a real Canadian who had returned to Lithuania and died. The real Edmund Trinka was born on January 16, 1931 in Fort Whyte, Manitoba.

The mole hunt was not going well. Karlow had been forced out, Garbler shunted aside, the career of Richard Kovich stalled, and countless other officers investigated, and in some cases, transferred to less sensitive work. But no moles had been found, unless one counted Igor Orlov, who admitted nothing. In any case, Orlov had never been a CIA officer, only a contract employee in Germany.

But in the late 1960s, the Special Investigations Group began focusing on a new and astonishing target. This time it was no low-level agent running hookers out of bars in Karlshorst. This time it was the head of the Soviet division himself, David Murphy.

To begin with, Murphy was accused as a possible Soviet agent by Peter Kapusta, one of his own officers (who had handled Yuri Loginov). William R. Johnson, a former senior member of Angleton's staff, recalled the episode. Johnson, a trim, pipe-smoking man with the manner and mustache of a British regimental colonel, went to Yale with Angleton, who recruited him into the agency and sent him to Vienna. Later, Johnson served all over the Far East for the agency, ending as chief of base in Saigon.

According to Johnson, Kapusta went to Sam Papich, the FBI's veteran liaison man with the CIA, and voiced his allegations about Murphy. It was an unusual and rare move for a CIA officer to go outside his own agency to the FBI.

Papich had good reason to remember the accusation against Murphy. "Kapusta called in the middle of the night," he said. "It was one or two o'clock in the morning." But, Papich added, "The FBI did not investigate. From the beginning, the bureau looked at the Murphy matter strictly as an internal CIA problem. We received certain information, including Kapusta's input. By our standards, based on what was available, FBI investigation was not warranted."

William Johnson said, "I never could figure out why he [Kapusta] accused Murphy. I could not follow his reasoning. It involved the fact that Murphy and Blake were in Berlin together. I wrote a report and fired it off to Helms. I was in shock. I saw Sam [Papich] a couple of days later. He couldn't make head or tail of it, either."

Since Papich and the FBI had declined to take up the case, that might have been the end of it, but for the fact that the SIG was investigating Murphy. That meant that Angleton, too, had become suspicious of David Murphy, one of his closest colleagues and the senior CIA official in charge of operations against the Soviet Union. The mole hunt had now taken a mind-boggling twist: the chief of counterintelligence suspected the chief of the Soviet division.[7]

Scotty Miler confirmed that the SIG had conducted a full-dress investigation of Murphy while he headed the Soviet division. The Murphy investigation, he said, was "not directly in connection with Sasha. Just a series of failures, things that blew up in his face. Odd things that happened. The scrapes in Japan and Vienna. They [the KGB] may have been setting up Murphy just to embarrass CIA. But you have to consider these incidents may have been staged to give him bona fides."

Miler lit a cigarette and slowly exhaled. "Maybe Murphy was like Joe Btfsplk. He may have just been unlucky."[8] Then, too, Miler said, Murphy had been in Berlin at the same time as Orlov. "Orlov and Murphy overlapped in several places."

And Murphy's family could not be ignored, Miler added. "Murphy's wife was a White Russian from China who emigrated to San Francisco. It was a factor, just as in the investigation of anyone of that White Russian background. There were a lot of salted émigrés, particularly coming out of China. So, yes, that had to be looked at."

But, Miler finally conceded, the beer hall and umbrella-bashing scrapes, Murphy's overlaps in Berlin with Igor Orlov and George Blake, his wife's background, were not really the root cause. What really led the Counterintelligence Staff to suspect Murphy, who headed all CIA operations against the Soviet Union at a critical time, was his link to a White Russian whom the mole hunters believed was a KGB agent. The background and activities of the man who cast a shadow over Murphy's career is one of the most intriguing, and previously untold, stories of the Cold War.

"Murphy was instrumental in getting him into the agency," Miler said. "It was like Ivory Soap that he was a spy.

"The man was not a staff employee, he was contract. And he was let go. And some things went very badly wrong when he worked for

[7]Asked to comment on the investigation of him by the SIG as a suspected Soviet mole, Murphy chuckled and replied: "I know who I am." He made it clear he did not wish to be interviewed about his own turn as a mole suspect, or about any other aspect of his long and somewhat stormy career.
[8]Joe Btfsplk, as every fan of Al Capp's comic strip L'il Abner knows, had the misfortune to go through life with a black raincloud hovering over his head.

us. We lost some agents. It was during the Korean War. This chap was managing agents working behind the lines in North Korea who were lost. The suspicion was this wasn't just incompetence, but he betrayed these agents."

The man whom Miler was talking about was a character who might have stepped from the pages of a le Carré novel, or more likely one by John Buchan. His name was Arseny "Andy" Yankovsky.

He was born in 1914 in Vladivostok, Russia, into a landed family of the czarist aristocracy. The Yankovskys had a coat of arms, a huge estate, cattle and horses. They were, in fact, famous for breeding horses. When the revolution came in 1917, Andy's father, George, joined the White Russian forces and fought against the Red Army. Three years later, the Yankovskys were driven from their estate. George, his two brothers, Andy, and about two dozen other family members, along with the best of their cattle, fled Russia, crossed the border into North Korea, and settled in Chongjin. They later bought land in the mountains near Chuŭl and built their homes there.[9]

George Yankovsky had been a famed hunter in Russia, and in North Korea, he and his three sons hunted wild boar, leopards, and Korean tigers, which are bigger, and said to be fiercer, than the tigers of India. He sold furs, and trapped tigers for zoos. The Yankovskys also sold powdered reindeer antlers, much prized as an aphrodisiac throughout Asia. An accomplished lepidopterist, George had twenty species of butterflies named for him.[10]

In this exotic if rugged environment, Andy Yankovsky grew up speaking Russian, Korean, and Japanese. Other White Russians joined the colony in North Korea, and in 1934, young Andy took a bride, Olga Sokolovskaya, the divorced mother of two young children. They had met during her summer vacation trips to the colony. Like many White Russians, Olga had made her way to Harbin, Manchuria, where her daughter, Anastasia (Nata) Sokolovskaya was born in 1925. The same year the family moved to Shanghai, where a son, Rostislav, known as Slava, was born about 1930. But when Olga

[9]At the time, all of Korea was occupied by Japan, which annexed the country in 1910 and called it Chosun. In Potsdam in 1945, the United States and the Soviet Union divided Korea at the 38th parallel. Russian troops entered North Korea in August 1945, and U.S. troops moved into the south the following month.
[10]Including *Saturnia jankowskii, Marumba jankowskii,* and *Actias jankowskii,* as well as a swan, *Cygnus jankowskii,* and a beetle, *Captolabrus jankowskii.*

married Andy Yankovsky, her children were separated; Slava remained in Shanghai with his father and Nata lived with her mother and her new stepfather in North Korea.

By 1947, the good life the Yankovskys had lived in Chuŭl was over. The Soviets, who had occupied North Korea, rounded up most of the White Russian colony, including Andy, his two brothers, and his father. "The Soviets marched in and arrested everybody," said Andy Yankovsky's stepdaughter, Nata. "The army troops were everywhere. They arrested men only. Andy was arrested. He escaped, and got out on foot. They walked across the 38th parallel, Andy and Olga."

At the time, Nata, twenty-two, was in Chongjin. "I got out on a fishing tug in 1947, in the hold with smelly fish," she said. She joined her mother and stepfather in Seoul. But Andy's father and two brothers were sent to a labor camp in Siberia, she said, where his father soon died. In the meantime, she said, her brother Slava in Shanghai, lured by Soviet promises, boarded a ship and returned to the Soviet Union, where he was promptly imprisoned in the gulag for ten years.

In Seoul, American intelligence was looking for recruits among the White Russian refugees. "David Murphy is the first one who interviewed us," Nata said. "He interviewed Andy and then me. He [Murphy] was stationed in Seoul. We were interrogated endlessly."

For a year, Nata worked in Seoul as a typist for the Army. Then the Yankovskys were transferred to Tokyo. Andy Yankovsky went to work for the CIA. By 1949, Nata had also been hired by the agency as a translator and interpreter in Yokosuka.

That's where she met Ed Snow.

Edgar Snow (no relation to the well-known writer) was a Russian-speaking case officer for the CIA, a six-foot-tall, blue-eyed, personable man whom women found attractive. Andy Yankovsky, as a contract agent, worked for Snow, as did Nata.

Snow's background was almost as colorful as Andy Yankovsky's. He was born in Seattle in 1922, the son of Nikolai Snegerieff, a Russian from Novosibirsk who had fought in the White Army. After the defeat at Irkutsk, Snow's father remained in that city and met and married Snow's mother, then sixteen. He and his wife, then pregnant with Ed, escaped from Russia and made their way to Canada and then to Seattle, where the family name was changed to the more manageable Snow.

The senior Snow was offered a job with Continental Can in Japan, and young Ed went to the American School there and learned Japanese. The family returned to the United States when Ed was ten, living first in Los Angeles and then in Phoenix, where he worked as a disk jockey while still in high school. He joined the Navy, got into intelligence work, and was an observer at the atomic tests on Bikini Atoll. After the war he finished college at UCLA, approached the CIA with some ideas about Soviet operations, and was hired. In 1948, the agency sent him to Japan under military cover.

There he ran Andy Yankovsky, who was building a network of agents in North Korea. And when the agency took on Yankovsky's stepdaughter as a translator, Snow was attracted to her. At twenty-seven, Nata was petite and vivacious, with long sandy hair in curls. They were married in 1954.

According to Scotty Miler, the agency had hired Yankovsky after David Murphy had recommended him. The Korean War broke out in June 1950, and in time almost all of Yankovsky's agents in the north were caught, Miler continued.

"Yankovsky was running agents from South Korea and training them to go into North Korea, infiltrate across the border, some by boat, some in air drops. To gather military intelligence. A lot of his agents were rolled up. The vast majority. Somewhere between two dozen and fifty.

"Snow was in Soviet operations in Japan. He was running his father-in-law, in essence. His wife was a White Russian. Snow had permission to marry her, since normally you can't marry a foreign national. And then it turned out later she had relatives behind the Curtain."

Nata Sokolovskaya insisted that she had fully disclosed her background to the CIA from the start. "Not only my brother, but also my other relatives in the gulag. They knew about him as they knew about every single relative. If they were so upset about my brother, why did they recruit us in the first place? Why did they grant permission to marry Ed? Of course, when I got the job I told them about Slava. With lie detectors. I don't remember whether I put it on written forms or not, but I told them."

Edgar Snow and Nata returned to CIA headquarters from Tokyo in 1954, soon after they were married. By that time, pregnant with a daughter born later that year, Nata had left the CIA.

Snow rose within the Soviet division to the key post of chief of operations. In 1959, he was slated to go to Berlin to work with George Kisevalter on the Popov case.

By this time, however, the CI Staff and the Office of Security had been turned loose on the Snow-Yankovsky case, the problem of the lost agents in Korea, and Nata's relatives behind the Iron Curtain. A major mole hunt now took place inside the agency, two years *before* Golitsin defected and triggered the larger search for penetrations. In a very real sense, the great mole hunt had begun in 1959 with the investigation of Ed Snow, his wife, and his father-in-law.

"There were horrible interrogations," Nata said. "For years I had nightmares. They called me in. There was a big room, a lot of officers, a huge table, everybody glaring at you. But the questions are all the same. Helms was there, I think, and Dulles, too. All during the summer of '59. They mainly asked me about the two years we spent under Soviet occupation in North Korea, from 1945 to 1947."

Snow and his wife were interrogated separately. Also drawn into the case was Vivian L. Parker, a British-born CIA case officer who immigrated to America and became a naturalized citizen in 1942 at the age of thirty-four. The CIA sent Parker to India in the mid-1950s, to Madras and Calcutta, and he had the misfortune to have met and married Andy Yankovsky's cousin, Marianne. Now the mole hunters had *two* case officers linked by marriage to Yankovsky.

According to George Kisevalter, CIA director Allen Dulles summoned Snow to his office at the end of the investigation and fired him. Kisevalter said Dulles told Snow, "We have a tragedy here, your security is shot. We have to let you go." At the age of thirty-seven, having achieved a senior position in the division, Snow was through.

"Dulles personally got him a job," Kisevalter continued, "and then he became vice president of Litton Industries, thanks to Dulles. Dulles acted very kindly, because he felt Snow had been mousetrapped and the agency had done him an injustice. But it ruined his whole life."[11] Vivian Parker and Yankovsky were fired as well, along with Ed Snow.

Andy Yankovsky, his stepdaughter insisted, "was the most loyal person to this country. We thought we had found our haven." She was

[11]The strains told on Snow's marriage; three years later he and Nata were separated, and in 1968 they were divorced. After Andy Yankovsky left the CIA, he was hired by TRW, the aerospace firm, and worked as the company's public relations man for the Far East. He had homes in Tokyo and in San Francisco, where he died on February 13, 1978. Ed Snow died in Los Angeles on April 1, 1990, at the age of sixty-seven.

still bitter, even thirty years later, about what the CIA had done. Her husband, her stepfather, and Parker, all three men, had been fired on the same grounds, she said, "relatives behind the Iron Curtain. Relatives dying of starvation and freezing to death in the gulag.

"Both Andy's and my family have fought Communism for three generations, and lived in exile as stateless White Russian immigrants. In the eyes of the Soviet government, we were their worst enemies. We were all on the list for deportation to Siberian labor camps. If we had known, all of us would have tried to make it across the 38th parallel. We had no great plans or ambitions, we 'just wanted to live,' as Dr. Zhivago said in Pasternak's book. If we had outlived our usefulness to the CIA, we should have been dismissed in a more humane manner. We were totally defenseless and devoted to this country. We have served this country well."

Mole hunters have long memories. The books were never closed with the dismissals in 1959, and less than a decade later, the Snow-Yankovsky-Parker case rose up to haunt David Murphy, the chief of the Soviet division. It was, as Miler confirmed, one of the major threads of the SIG's investigation of Murphy himself. As farfetched as it might seem in retrospect, the mole hunters were trying to find out whether Murphy, by helping to recruit Yankovsky, was somehow responsible for the loss of CIA agents in the Korean War.

Ed Petty was one of the members of the SIG who had investigated Murphy. Angleton not only considered Murphy a prime suspect, but, according to Petty, "even stated outright on certain occasions that Murphy was a KGB agent." After studying the files, Petty wrote a long paper concluding that Murphy was not a mole, after all. But with the suspicions of treason swirling around Murphy, his days as chief of the Soviet division were numbered.

In 1968, a major upheaval took place within the division. Murphy was forced out—replaced as head of the Soviet division and sent to Paris as chief of station. At first, William Colby was in line to succeed him. But President Johnson reached down into the agency's ranks and plucked Colby out to go to Vietnam. As a result, Rolfe Kingsley succeeded Murphy.

According to Miler, not only the suspicions of Murphy played a part in his departure, "but also the decision to incarcerate Nosenko. And the whole Nosenko case." It was Murphy who had played a primary role in subjecting Nosenko to his terrible ordeal. Helms had by now demanded that the issue of Nosenko's bona fides be resolved; the case had gone on too long. The Soviet division was an obvious target. "It was decided a change was needed, new management, new style," Miler said.

Just how far Angleton had turned against the former division chief soon became clear in startling fashion. On a trip to Washington, Count Alexandre de Marenches, the three-hundred-pound director of the SDECE, the French intelligence service, was buttonholed by Angleton. The counterintelligence chief warned de Marenches that David Murphy, the new chief of station in Paris, was a Soviet mole.

William Colby said that he learned of Angleton's astonishing warning about Murphy several years later. It happened, Colby said, when he visited Paris a few months after he had been appointed director of the CIA. "De Marenches drew me aside and said, 'Did you know that Angleton told me that Murphy was a Soviet agent?' "

Colby said de Marenches had good reason to be upset. "He meant, 'You've got to get your agency under control. You shouldn't be speaking with two voices.' " As soon as Colby returned to Langley, he said, "I read the files on Murphy. There were allegations, the thing had been looked at." In his memoir, without naming Murphy or de Marenches, Colby said that the files revealed that the officer, "a brilliant and effective one at that, was given a totally clean bill of health. But our counterintelligence had never accepted the conclusion."[12]

After reviewing the file, Colby recalled, "I wrote a memo saying there should be no suspicion of this man." Moreover, Colby gave Murphy an important assignment coordinating the agency's technical operations with human intelligence. "I called him after I reviewed the file. I said, 'I want you to know this is over.' I was taking a chance, putting him into a highly sensitive activity. I did it deliberately."

The story of Angleton's warning about Murphy to the French has circulated for years in the murky world of counterintelligence. But members of Angleton's inner circle refused to believe it. "Colby is the only source for that," Scotty Miler said.

However, Alexandre de Marenches himself confirmed that Angleton had warned him that Murphy was a Soviet spy. An urbane aristo-

[12]William Colby and Peter Forbath, *Honorable Men: My Life in the CIA* (New York: Simon & Schuster, 1978), p. 365.

crat who speaks colloquial English without a trace of an accent, de Marenches said he remembered the conversation very well. "Around '71 I was in Washington," he said. "To be told that the liaison officer with me [Murphy] was a Russian agent was a bit of a surprise, to put it mildly." And Angleton had told him that? "Yes, Angleton told me this. It was flabbergasting."[13]

Even before Colby learned of Angleton's suspicions about Murphy, de Marenches had alerted a senior CIA official to Angleton's warning about the Paris station chief. According to a former agency officer, "De Marenches said to the official, 'My dear friend, why does the CIA send me a Soviet spy as chief of station?' This was a conversation in Paris. The CIA man said, 'I don't believe it.' De Marenches said, 'It comes from your Monsieur Angleton.' "

When the incredulous CIA man got back to Langley, "he asked Jim for an explanation and got a three-page memo giving all the reasons that Dave Murphy was a spy. When you read the three pages you realize Angleton was really off the wall. Angleton wanted Helms to send a letter incorporating the material in the three pages. Helms ducked it. Instead, the senior official wrote back a nice letter to the French saying there's nothing to support it."

Richard Helms insisted he could not recall the incident and had been unaware of the suspicions about Murphy. But then Helms found it difficult to remember almost any controversial matters that occurred on his watch. He could not remember who had made the decision to imprison Nosenko; he had never approved the Shadrin operation. Interviewed in his office on K Street in Washington, where the former CIA director was an international business consultant, Helms at seventy-seven was a symphony in gray—gray hair, gray suit, and shades of gray as he talked about his years as head of the CIA and the need for a delicate balance between intelligence and counterintelligence. He was tall, slim, elegant, and relaxed; in contrast to years past, he agreed to be quoted.

[13]De Marenches said he had no memory of having told Colby of Angleton's warning. "It was not Colby," he said, "it was Helms." He said he had informed the CIA director of Angleton's warning about Murphy during the same visit to Washington. "I saw Helms in his office," he said. But, de Marenches added, "During my eleven years [as head of the SDECE] I saw six directors of CIA." Richard Helms said he did not remember "de Marenches coming to my office in Langley and telling me my station chief in Paris is any Soviet agent."

"I don't recall Jim coming to me and saying anything about a problem with David Murphy," he said. "I heard about this later, after I left the agency. My best recollection is that at the time I sent David Murphy to Paris I wasn't aware of Angleton's suspicions. I never believed it. I had no reason to doubt Dave Murphy's loyalty."

But Angleton did. And what makes Angleton's warning to the French even more bizarre is that Howard J. Osborn, head of the CIA's Office of Security, had cleared Murphy of the mole charges before he ever went to Paris, according to a former senior agency officer. "When Murphy was about to go to Paris he was under suspicion," he said. "Helms would not send a COS to Paris under a cloud. He insisted it be resolved. Osborn gave Murphy the toughest interrogation he ever ran, and a long polygraph. It was nasty. And Dave Murphy came up absolutely clean. It was negative all the way."

Angleton, the former CIA officer said, "not only warned de Marenches personally but also Marcel Chalet, then head of the DST [the French counterespionage service]. I'm convinced he gave Chalet a message similar to one he gave to de Marenches. Poor Murphy. It's a wonder he was able to go to the bathroom while he was in Paris. It was the most egregious, outrageous conduct I've ever heard of."

But there is an unknown sequel to the story. According to a former high-ranking CIA counterintelligence officer, Angleton also voiced the same warning about Murphy's successor as COS in Paris, Eugen F. Burgstaller. "It happened around 1974," the CIA man said. "Angleton said Burgstaller was a Soviet agent, too. It didn't convince the French. By that time, Angleton had less and less credibility. He warned Chalet, and I think he went over and saw Chalet."[14]

Marcel Chalet declined to comment on whether Angleton had warned him that two successive CIA station chiefs in Paris were Soviet agents, although he did not deny it, either.[15]

[14]Burgstaller, who served as chief of station in Paris for five years, beginning in 1974, was startled to be told of his colleague's assertion. "I must say I never have heard that," he said. "And I never got any indication from any of the senior people [in French intelligence] that they had received such a warning."

[15]"You won't be surprised that I prefer not to answer questions relating to David Murphy, Eugen Burgstaller, and James Angleton dealing with the internal problems of the American services," he said. "Somehow, to be precise I must tell you that the first two men cited were and are my friends and that James Angleton has served his country well. This said, you know as well as I do that the job that was theirs exposed them to controversy." Letter, Chalet to author, July 19, 1990.

Rolfe Kingsley, the new head of the Soviet division, had been chief of the European division and before changing jobs had approved Murphy's assignment to Paris. Kingsley was not aware until after he took over the Soviet division that Murphy had been a mole suspect.

Murphy, as matters turned out, was only the first to go. According to a senior former officer in the Soviet division, when Kingsley came in, "the division was cleaned out. Literally hundreds of people, all of the Russian-speaking officers, were transferred without being asked to other divisions. The Soviet division had hundreds of people and most were Russian-speakers. Most were children of Russians, some were born in Russia. Virtually the whole division was transferred. It was all designed to cleanse the division of a possible mole."

If the Counterintelligence Staff couldn't find the mole, he said, then the transfers meant that at least the suspected penetration would in all probability no longer be in the Soviet division. It was a new approach; instead of pinpointing the penetration, which it could not do, the SIG had cast its net wide in an attempt to scoop up the mole along with everyone else.

The former officer said most of those transferred never knew what hit them. "The excuse given was we were not successful in recruiting Soviets. Each person developed an individual rationale for being transferred. No one realized it was because we were *all* suspect. Angleton decided to freeze everyone of Russian origin."

To staff the depleted Soviet division, he said, the agency turned to officers from the old Eastern European division, which had been absorbed into the Soviet division two years earlier. "EE would take over, they knew how. Hundreds of people were affected by the search for the mole," he concluded, "because hundreds were transferred out of the division."

Another former officer of the Soviet division said, "I think Kingsley permanently injured the clandestine capability." He added, "I don't know if he was under orders or setting policy."

Donald F. B. Jameson, who served in the Soviet division at the time, confirmed that "there were a substantial number of changes" as officers were shifted out of the division. "It was related to their affiliation with Murphy. And, as it now appears, there was the presumption that they were all spies."

Kingsley strongly disputed these accounts of a wholesale purge. Asked whether hundreds of Russian-speaking officers had been transferred, he said: "That's a lot of baloney." Kingsley declined, however, to say how many officers he *had* removed.

Richard Helms, the CIA director at the time, could not remember mass transfers. "That's nonsense," Helms said. "It never happened as far as I'm concerned. It's simply untrue." Was Helms aware of any transfers from the division for security reasons? "No, I was not," he responded. But Scotty Miler thought that perhaps "fifty, plus or minus," had been transferred. "Out of maybe three hundred people in the division."

Whatever the totals, among the officers who remained, those under suspicion were secretly identified to Kingsley by Thomas Karamessines, the DDP. In addition, Kingsley sat on a hush-hush committee of three, consisting of himself, Angleton, and a representative of the Office of Security. The secret committee kept Kingsley abreast of the latest suspicions of the SIG.

Kingsley was not, he later claimed, much impressed with the evidence that was presented to him in the arcane committee of three. He realized he had stepped into a can of worms; morale in the Soviet division was at a low ebb, operations had ceased, everyone was looking under the chair for moles. The division, Kingsley felt, had lost sight of its purpose, to penetrate the Soviet Union.

But with Murphy gone, Kingsley was soon caught up in the endgame of the Loginov case. The decision to betray Loginov to the South Africans, after both Angleton and the Soviet division decided he was a fake, had taken place before Kingsley headed the division. But Kingsley shared the prevailing view that Loginov was not genuine; he had never produced what the agency wanted.

To this day, many former CIA officers consider what happened next one of the worst blots on the agency's record. With the approval of the CIA, South Africa traded Loginov back to the Soviet Union in a three-cornered swap for some half-dozen West German agents imprisoned by East Germany.

According to George Kisevalter, Angleton was the key figure in arranging the trade of Loginov. "Angleton decided he was a plant and engineered the swap with the East Germans to release the West Germans in return for Loginov, who was then given back to the Soviets."

"Angleton," said one former CI officer, "would have to have been consulted every inch of the way." Even though Loginov was suspected by the CIA to be a plant, no one was *sure,* and to trade him back to the KGB might be signing his death warrant if the agency was wrong.

After Loginov's arrest in Johannesburg in 1967, the South Africans had announced the Soviet spy had revealed the names of KGB officers all over the world. Asked how Loginov could have been a plant, given the large numbers of KGB officers he exposed, Pete Bagley replied: "He named his Soviet handlers in Africa, Kenya, and Belgium. But those were giveaways. Loginov gave away the names to deceive us on the rest."

In fact, the KGB officers' names had been provided to the South African security service by the CIA, and had been culled from the agency's files. They did not come from Loginov at all. The release of the names, according to one CIA officer, was designed to put Loginov in the worst possible light with the KGB. But Loginov's "confession," although bogus, might nevertheless have endangered his life if he was sent back to the Soviet Union.[16]

When South Africa, before agreeing to the swap, asked the CIA whether it was sure it did not want Loginov, Rolfe Kingsley said he did not. Angleton agreed; the CIA had no further use for Yuri Loginov.[17]

A CIA officer familiar with the Loginov case explained what then occurred. "Loginov was taken from South Africa to West Germany, and the arrangements were made for him to be pushed back by Jim. When Loginov arrived in Germany and realized fully the horror of his situation, he was scared to death and resisted very strongly being sent back. The story at the frontier is pretty sad. He literally had to be pushed across. Into the hands of the KGB, who took him away."

This account, related as well by several other CIA sources, was disputed by Bagley, who claimed that Loginov was "happy" to go back. "At the reunion with the Soviets, they fell into each other's arms. It is unthinkable we would have thrown anyone over the line against his will." The fact that Loginov provided information to the

---

[16]Joseph Evans, the headquarters officer in charge of the case, denied that the provision of the names to the South Africans by the CIA would have jeopardized Loginov. The KGB, he argued, knew that as an illegal, Loginov did not have access to the names.

[17]On a decision of this importance, with its potential for opening the agency to criticism, logically the director of the CIA, Richard Helms, would have to have approved. But Helms said, "I have no recollection of the case whatever." Could he explain why Loginov was traded back? Helms put up his thumb and forefinger, forming a zero. "That's what I recall," he said. "I have no memory of it."

South Africans proved he was not a true illegal, Bagley argued. "Illegals like Abel keep their mouths shut. Illegals don't talk."

Evans, too, clung to the hope that he and the other CIA officers who swung against Loginov had not made a terrible, fatal mistake. He was not persuaded that Loginov had been sent to his death. But the CIA, according to several knowledgeable sources, obtained information from later defectors that Loginov had been executed. Richard Kovich, the man who recruited Loginov, learned of his agent's fate when he was called back to the CIA as a consultant some years after he had retired; by that time the agency had a Soviet defector who said he had attended Loginov's funeral.

George Kisevalter had heard much the same. "A later defector came with the story that Loginov had been shot," Kisevalter said.

"He was sent back to goodbye."

Chapter 16

Downfall

■

John Denley Walker, the station chief in Israel, knew that a visit from a senior official at headquarters always meant a certain amount of extra preparation and effort. The VIP would have to be entertained and looked after.

But he was not prepared for what happened when James Angleton arrived on one of his periodic trips to Israel. The visit had come soon after Walker had taken up his duties as station chief in 1967.

At the time, Angleton was drinking heavily. The counterintelligence chief asked Walker to arrange to have a case of whiskey delivered to his hotel room.

After it arrived, Angleton told Walker he suspected the bourbon had been poisoned by the KGB. Walker tried to explain that he had bought the whiskey at the embassy commissary and had delivered it himself, but to no avail. Angleton would not be dissuaded.

To Walker, Angleton looked exhausted. The CIA station chief feared that the chief of counterintelligence was on the edge of a nervous breakdown.

"I'm sending you home," he said.

Angleton was enraged. "You can't do that," he replied.

When Walker insisted, Angleton warned angrily of retribution; he would see to it that Walker never got another decent job in the CIA. But the conversation had its effect; Angleton took some time off to rest. He went, not back to Washington, but to Elat, on the Gulf of Aqaba.

By this time, Angleton's power was beginning to unravel. His warning to the French that David Murphy was a Soviet agent had not been taken seriously by the SDECE, and eventually boomeranged to undermine the counterintelligence chief. In addition, Angleton had lost Pete Bagley, one of his closest allies and strongest supporters in the Soviet division.

CIA director Richard Helms had decided it was time for a change in the leadership of the Soviet division. Early in 1967, Bagley, then the deputy chief of the division, was offered the post of chief of station in Brussels. By September, he was in place. Bagley's exit was soon followed by David Murphy's departure for Paris.

But no one was safe from the suspicion pervading the CIA. Now, Bagley himself became a target of Angleton's mole hunters. Ed Petty, a member of the SIG, began digging into his background.

Petty fastened on an episode that had taken place years earlier, when Bagley had been stationed in Bern, handling Soviet operations in the Swiss capital. At the time, Bagley was attempting to recruit an officer of the UB, the Polish intelligence service, in Switzerland. Petty concluded that a phrase in a letter from Michal Goleniewski, the Polish intelligence officer who called himself Sniper and who later defected to the CIA, suggested that "two weeks after approval of the operation by headquarters," the KGB had advance knowledge of the Swiss recruitment attempt—advance knowledge that could only have come from a mole in the CIA.

Bagley said it proved nothing of the sort. "I was running the correspondence phase of Sniper in Switzerland," he said. "We wrote a letter to a Polish security officer when I was in Bern station." The letter, an attempt to recruit the Pole to work for the CIA, "mentioned the man's boss. Some time later, Goleniewski wrote again, mentioning the name of the UB chief in Bern, 'whose name you already know,' which meant that Goleniewski knew of our letter. But that doesn't mean there was a mole in CIA. It means the target turned the letter in to his service and our guy [Sniper] was high up enough to know it."

Bagley said that Petty had interpreted the episode to mean that "the UB knew of the recruitment attempt in advance, which is quite different." Petty, nevertheless, wrote an analysis of the Swiss recruitment episode, and of Bagley's file, and concluded that "Bagley was a candidate to whom we should pay serious attention." The study gave Bagley the cryptonym GIRAFFE. Petty said he submitted his paper "with some trepidation" because "I was well aware that Bagley had long been a protégé of Jim Angleton."

Petty turned in his report to James Ramsay Hunt, Angleton's deputy. "Hunt said, 'This is the best thing I've seen yet.'" But, Petty added, he heard nothing from Angleton.

"The Bagley report stewed in Angleton's in box for a considerable time," Petty said. "Then one day he called me in to discuss the Nosenko case. He brought up some of the points in Bagley's nine-hundred-plus-page study. And I said, 'If there is a penetration, then Nosenko could not have been genuine.'" A mole in the CIA, Petty argued, would have told the KGB of Nosenko's initial contact with the agency in 1962, and, Nosenko, had he been a true asset, would never have come back in 1964. "I said to him, 'You don't need all these points in Bagley's nine-hundred-pager—it's much simpler than that.'"

"Angleton sat there and mulled this point over for some time. Then he said to me, 'Pete is not a Soviet spy.'"

At that moment, Petty saw the light, like Saint Paul on the road to Damascus. It suddenly hit him; not Bagley but Angleton himself was the mole. "I was flabbergasted," Petty said. "Because the subject of my paper about Pete had not arisen. It was at that point that I decided I'd been looking at it all wrong by assuming Golitsin was good as gold. I began rethinking everything. If you turned the flip side it all made sense. Golitsin was sent to exploit Angleton. Then the next step, maybe not just an exploitation, and I had to extend it to Angleton. Golitsin might have been dispatched as the perfect man to manipulate Angleton or provide Angleton with material on the basis of which he [Angleton] could penetrate and control other services."

Angleton himself must be the traitor, Petty decided. "Angleton made available to Golitsin extensive sensitive information which could have gone back to the KGB. Angleton was a mole, but he needed Golitsin to have a basis on which to act."

Petty was now sure he had unlocked the key to everything that had been going on inside the agency for the past decade. "Golitsin and Angleton. You have two guys absolutely made for each other. Golitsin was a support for things Angleton had wanted to do for years in terms of getting into foreign intelligence services. Golitsin's leads lent themselves to that. I concluded that logically Golitsin was the prime dispatched agent."

The more Ed Petty thought about it, the more convinced he became that Angleton had been the mole all along. Angleton had extraordinary access, after all. "The only place in the CIA besides the cable room where there was total access was on James Angleton's desk. From the indications we had, the penetration had to be at a high and sensitive level, and long-term. You could say the director's desk fit that description, but there were several directors. All the operational cables went through Angleton."

By now, the mole hunt had run out of control. Like a Frankenstein monster, it had finally attacked its own creator.

In 1971, Petty said, "I started working on it. Putting stuff on index cards, formulating my theory." He did not dare to discuss what he was doing with Jean Evans, then his boss. Instead he went to a close friend, a senior officer, and told him what he was thinking. "I said, 'I can't do this without some backstop.' He said he would take it to the director and a few days later he came back and told me go ahead. He said he had talked to Helms."

Helms denied that while CIA director he knew that his counterintelligence chief had himself become a mole suspect. "I never heard about it when I was in the agency," he said. "I knew Ed Petty—he'd worked for me years before." But no one "ever told me that Petty's study was under way." Petty's conclusion that Angleton was the mole, Helms added, "didn't make any sense to me."

The senior officer to whom Petty had confided was James H. Critchfield, who had been Petty's boss in Munich years earlier and rose to head the Eastern European and Near East divisions. Critchfield said he was indeed aware of Petty's investigation, and Petty had discussed it with him. But, Critchfield added, he never told Helms about it until after he and the CIA director had both left the agency.[1]

Petty's belief that his mentor had seen the director was not far off the mark, however. For in 1974, Critchfield, as it turned out, had

---

[1] Petty kept Critchfield informed. "He used to stop by my office from time to time," Critchfield said, "and tell me about fragments of information that led him to believe there was a penetration. Angleton was one of the common denominators that ran through the cases. I listened because it seemed important and because of my respect for Ed Petty, who had been one of my two chief analysts."

informed William Colby, then the CIA director, about Petty's investigation of Angleton. Critchfield was about to retire. "I conveyed that Ed Petty had told me of possible security problems in the CI Staff. Of course I mentioned Angleton. I did not want to walk out the door without bringing it to the attention of the director."[2]

Petty worked in absolute secrecy, never revealing to anyone except Critchfield that he was gathering information to accuse his own boss, James Angleton, as a Soviet spy. By the spring of 1973, after toiling for some two years, Petty felt he could not develop his theory any further. He decided to retire.

"I told my intermediary, 'I'm going to retire.' He said, 'You've got to have a talk with somebody.' By now Colby was director, but he was not available. I finally saw the assistant DDO, David Blee. I told my story and he said, 'We would like you to stay.' The clear implication was 'Keep doing what you're doing.' So I stayed and kept at it. I stayed another year."

In 1974, Petty said, he reached a firm decision to retire. Blee, he said, urged him to prepare a report on Angleton.[3] "I said, 'It's only on cards.' So they sat me down with a senior officer, James Burke, and I talked to him on tape for twenty-six hours. Plus I turned over two safe drawers full of collateral material. On the tapes, I said quite clearly, to my best hypothesis, Angleton had to be the person. The penetration. We didn't say moles. I didn't say he's the only possibility. But he's the only one who has been here all that time and has seen it all. I said they should get rid of Angleton. Fire him."

Even before William Colby became director of the CIA, he had begun zeroing in on Angleton's counterintelligence turf. After Colby returned from Vietnam in 1971, Helms had named him executive director of the agency.

[2]Colby said he did not specifically remember Critchfield's visit, but had been told of the Petty study by William E. Nelson, the DDO, after it was finished. "I said, 'Aw, c'mon. It was nonsense." The Petty study, Colby said, was a "nonstarter" and did not affect his later decision to dismiss Angleton.
[3]Blee, who was later to head the Counterintelligence Staff, regarded Petty's study of Angleton as a serious effort that would have to be carefully considered, not simply filed and forgotten. Without taking a position on whether Petty's conclusion about Angleton was valid, he moved to make sure that the study was preserved.

When President Nixon, in the midst of the Watergate scandal, appointed Helms ambassador to Iran, Colby, in February 1973, became the DDO under James R. Schlesinger, the new CIA director.

"I'd had minimum contact with the CI Staff," Colby said. "I knew they were highly secretive and a separate power. I'd had one contact with Angleton in Rome, in the mid-fifties. The CI Staff was running an agent, and eventually I took over the agent. I had my doubts that was the way to run a railroad." The clash in Rome was not very important, but it planted the seed in William Colby's mind that counterintelligence had become too much a law unto itself.

Colby and Angleton did not often cross paths again until 1967, when Colby was asked to take over the Soviet division, a job that David Murphy got instead when Colby was unexpectedly sent to Vietnam. During the period when Colby was preparing for what he thought would be the post of Soviet division chief, Angleton asked to see him. "Jim invited me down for 'the Briefing.' I went through several hours of his briefing. The KGB was everywhere, it was penetrating Americans, foreign political leaders. The presumption was that the agency was the main target. Being a lawyer, I wanted to hear evidence. There wasn't any."

When Colby became the DDO under Schlesinger, he was now in charge of counterintelligence—and had suddenly become Angleton's boss. "I began to look at it and found the CI Staff had several hundred people. I was under pressure to reduce. That seemed an awful lot of personnel slots."

Colby was DDO for only a couple of months, but in that period, he also found out that Angleton had a hammerlock on anything to do with Israel. "I discovered the Israel account was being run through the CI Staff, and to my amazement I learned that the chief of station Cairo could not communicate with the COS Israel. Everything had to go through the CI Staff."

Colby also discovered that the agency had for twenty years been opening first-class mail in violation of the law. During most of that period, Angleton and the CI Staff intercepted letters between the United States and the Soviet Union and other Communist countries. "I got into the mail-opening thing and wrote a memo saying it should be terminated," Colby said. "The Post Office guy running it was getting scared. I couldn't find it had produced anything. Angleton objected. Schlesinger cut the baby in half and said, 'Let's suspend it but not terminate it.' "[4]

In May, Colby was promoted to director of the CIA. "I began to talk to Jim about these things shortly after I took over," he said. "I raised taking away the Israel account several times and he had resisted it. I did not want to push it through. I can tell you the reason now, since he is no longer living. He was so intense I was really worried that if I got rid of him he would have done harm to himself."

Colby feared that Angleton would commit suicide?

"Yeah. So I was trying to ease him out." As part of his campaign to get rid of Angleton, Colby gradually began dismantling pieces of the CI Staff. Up to then, the Counterintelligence Staff had exclusively handled liaison with the FBI. That meant that often Sam Papich, Hoover's man, dealt directly with Angleton, with whom he had developed a close personal friendship.

"I put liaison with the FBI under the DDO," Colby said. "Nobody could tell what the CI Staff was doing. Yet the FBI relationship was important. So I designated a guy on the DDO's personal staff who became liaison with FBI."

Methodically, Colby took other steps to chip away at Angleton's power. Until then, no proposed clandestine operation anywhere in the world could take place without approval of the CI Staff. Colby decided that division chiefs should make those decisions; the CI Staff "should give advice, not have a veto or approval of the operation." The Counterintelligence Staff was reduced to running name checks on people proposed to be used in operations. "They could give a clearance that there was nothing bad on someone," Colby said, "but they didn't approve the overall operation."

With operational approval removed from Angleton's domain, Colby next took away Angleton's power to review operations already in progress. According to Colby, the CI Staff and several other CIA units engaged in these periodic reviews. To an extent, he said, "these

---

[4]The Post Office, however, refused further complicity in the illegal program, and on February 15, 1973, the mail-opening program in New York, the largest of four such programs run by the CIA over the years, was shut down. During the twenty years from 1953 to 1973 that the CIA opened first-class mail, under the code name HTLINGUAL, 28 million letters were screened, 2.7 million envelopes were photographed, and 215,000 were opened in New York City alone.

staffs had developed an operational function and were running their own operations. I thought that was a mistake. A division should run operations." Now the CI Staff was out of the business of project review.

In addition, Colby removed the small international Communism unit from Angleton's fiefdom. As each of these offices were plucked out, the size of Angleton's staff dwindled from hundreds to some forty people.

"Taking away FBI liaison and the other units was designed to lead him to see the handwriting on the wall," Colby said. "He just wouldn't take the bait."

Angleton, of course, realized what was happening, as did Scotty Miler. Colby did not explain his changes, Miler said, "but it was clear why. He felt CI approval for each operation was inhibiting ops. It got rid of people looking over the operators' shoulders. There was nobody second-guessing them. To use extreme language, it got rid of the Gestapo.

"There was a direct connection between Colby's dislike of the mole hunt and his decision to break up CI in 1973," Miler continued. "Colby didn't understand CI. And he said every case officer will be his own CI officer. Jim's reaction? 'There goes counterintelligence.'

"We knew the handwriting was on the wall," Miler went on. "Jim and I talked about it. This was the first step toward firing Jim. I saw little future for CI. At age forty-eight I presumably had some places to go. But we certainly realized that CI as Jim conceived of it, and as I did, could not function under the reorganization."

When Colby had finished, Angleton and his staff had little to occupy themselves. "We were left with penetrations and double agents, a few of which CI ran," Miler said, "and we were left with approval of double-agent operations, and day-to-day oversight. Maybe a couple of dozen such operations. We were turning more to research and analysis, and we reexamined the penetration cases to see if we had missed anything."

Recalling the curtailment of Angleton's power, Colby was frank about what he had done and why. "As DDO and then as director, I sliced into his empire. He'd developed a direct relationship with Dulles, Helms, and McCone. He tried it with Schlesinger." It had not worked under Schlesinger, and Angleton knew there was no hope of maintaining the same kind of clout under Colby.

"I determined a long time ago I had to get rid of him and the question was how," Colby said. "I thought it essential to run a clear-cut organization where different parts worked together. His idea was to be totally secretive and cross lines all over the place. Second, I found several hundred people in there. I honestly couldn't figure out what the devil they were doing. What benefits was this giving us? I couldn't find any.

"I finally decided if I was to be responsible for CI, I had to have control over it. And I didn't have confidence I had control with him there. Counterintelligence needed a sweeping with a good new broom."

In Colby's view, the mole hunt had hobbled CIA operations and all but destroyed its main mission at the time, spying on the Soviet Union. "I couldn't find we'd identified any penetrations. And I concluded his work had hampered our recruitment of real agents. I'd be happy to get two false agents if I could get three real ones. We weren't recruiting any because of the negative effect of the super-suspicion. I said that has to stop. We've got to get agents. We've got to recruit Soviets. That's what the agency's in business for."

Angleton, Colby concluded, had stopped the agency dead in its tracks. "The big factor was what he was doing was counterproductive. If you find a reason to reject everyone you want to recruit, you don't have ops. Jim thought the fact you can get at a potential Soviet agent means he's being manipulated from the other side. The most important thing was the lack of agent recruitment, and from a discipline point of view the way he worked in total secrecy. I thought his fixation on the wily KGB was exaggerated and out of the real world. We shouldn't have anything as important as this in the hands of anybody so intense. And then, there was the question of fairness to my officers. I couldn't accept that they be placed under suspicion for inadequate reasons."

Finally, there was the embarrassment of the David Murphy episode. When Alexandre de Marenches took him aside and said Angleton had warned that David Murphy was a Soviet spy, Colby said, "I was infuriated. How can a service operate if a man is sent as COS Paris and another man goes over and tells the French he is a Soviet agent?"

For Colby, it was the last straw. "I had already come to a decision we had to make a change, and this was one other factor, a big one. It was another indication that Jim seemed totally out of control. By then it was a question of how to do it."

While Colby was pondering how to get the reluctant Angleton to walk the plank, the problem solved itself in the person of Seymour M. Hersh. A brilliant and tireless former police reporter from Chicago in the tradition immortalized in *The Front Page,* Hersh had come to national prominence in 1969 when he broke the story of the My Lai massacre in Vietnam for an obscure news service, for which he won the Pulitzer Prize. He then joined the *New York Times,* where his reporting on Watergate in the early 1970s helped that newspaper to keep up with, and occasionally even surpass, the stories broken day after day by Bob Woodward and Carl Bernstein in the *Washington Post.*

While covering Watergate in 1973, Hersh said, "somebody I was dealing with told me there was a big problem inside the agency. Muskie had hearings on reorganizing the intelligence community in the fall of '74. There was a witness there and I was talking to him afterwards. I said to him, 'What the hell is the problem inside the agency?' I started meeting this person."

That was when Hersh learned about the Family Jewels.

In May of that year, Schlesinger—shocked by the wigs, spy gadgets, and other support that the CIA had given to Nixon's White House plumbers—issued a decree forbidding illegal activities by CIA employees, and requiring that they report any knowledge of past or present violations of the agency's charter. Thus was born the "Family Jewels," an agency euphemism for a 693-page compilation of the worst skeletons in the CIA's closet. The list included assassination plots against foreign leaders, drug tests on unsuspecting Americans, mail intercepts, and Operation CHAOS, a program of domestic spying on Americans opposed to the war in Vietnam.

Hersh soon heard of this extraordinary list and managed to learn part of its contents. "I eventually got in contact with someone who had access to the Family Jewels," he said. "I got hard numbers on how many mail openings, wiretaps, unauthorized break-ins there were, and, of course, the domestic spying. I remember talking to Angleton, and he initially said he had nothing to do with it."

Angleton also cast a lure in front of Hersh, with no effect. "Angleton said, 'Look, forget what you're working on, I have a better story for you.' And he told me about two [espionage] nets, in North Korea and a net in Moscow. 'Trap lines' he had laid in Moscow. I called Colby and told him what Angleton had said, and I thought I heard him gasp, suck in his breath. That Angleton would say that on an open phone line.

"By the time I got ready to see Colby I had hard numbers. I called up Colby and he agreed to see me on a Friday morning at the agency, and I laid out what I knew. I just came off a very hot year, all of Watergate, and Colby had sat down with me on the *Glomar Explorer,* and we held it, which by the way was not my decision.[5]

"He simply reviewed my domestic spying story with me. I said there were so many mail openings, so many break-ins, and he went over the numbers, in general reducing them. The big number was the ten thousand files—I said they were dossiers—on American citizens. He said, 'Sy, they were more like files.' If I said there were sixty-two break-ins he said, 'No, there were nineteen.' From his point of view it was damage limitation. But he was also confirming everything."

As soon as he got out of the building, Hersh telephoned Abe Rosenthal, his editor at the *New York Times.* "I said, 'Abe, I got it. I don't have him on the record but he confirmed it.' I remember being amazed I got that detail out of him. I went into the office on a Friday and wrote it and they ran it on Sunday."

Colby described how, in his meeting with Seymour Hersh, he had tried his best to downplay the CIA's role. "He came to me with what he said was a story bigger than My Lai. That we were engaged in a massive domestic intelligence operation. I said, 'Sy, you've got it all wrong.' He asked me about wiretaps. I said we weren't wiretapping a

---

[5]The *Glomar Explorer* was a CIA ship operating under cover as a Howard Hughes mining vessel supposedly searching for minerals in the deep ocean floor. Its true purpose was to recover a Soviet submarine that had sunk in the Pacific. The CIA had named the supersecret operation Project Jennifer. In February 1974, Colby learned that Hersh was investigating Project Jennifer. He went to the *New York Times* Washington bureau and met with Hersh and Robert H. Phelps, the *Times* Washington editor, pleading with them to wait. Colby was given no commitment ("We didn't offer any promise whatsoever," Phelps said), but Hersh, busy covering Watergate, did not yet have enough information to write about the submarine project anyway. A year later, after the story briefly peeped out in the *Los Angeles Times,* Colby, on grounds of national security, asked the *New York Times* (as well as several other newspapers and television stations) to hold off on further coverage. The *Times* agreed, but Hersh, who by now had prepared his story about Project Jennifer, protested vigorously. All the news media went along with the CIA request until columnist Jack Anderson broke the story on his national radio program on March 18, 1975.

lot of people, a few cases of CIA employees or ex-employees who were suspect. He said we were opening the mail. I said it was very, very limited. Just a small amount of mail to and from Moscow.''

Colby realized that he had not succeeded in throwing Hersh off the scent—an impossible task, in any event. "I had a sense he was going to run with something," Colby said laconically. With one of the CIA's most onerous cats about to poke its whiskers out of the bag, Colby determined he could delay his dismissal of Angleton no longer.

"Some time before," Colby said, "I had pointed out to Angleton that if he left before a certain day, he would get a better pension arrangement. He said no the first time I raised it. It came up again in December of 1974, before I saw Sy. I had a session with him a few days or maybe a week before. I pointed out it was time to go on, and if he didn't want to retire I had this other job of writing a history of his contribution to the agency. It was a way to keep him gainfully employed. He turned me down on that, too. I said, 'Well, think about it, Jim.' I said I wanted him to leave by the end of December.''

With the Hersh story about to explode, Colby telephoned Angleton and told him that the *Times* was on to Operation CHAOS, the domestic surveillance program, and other potentially embarrassing secrets. "I called Jim up. I said, 'I'm sorry this has happened. It really doesn't relate to our discussions. You and I know we've had these discussions over a long period of time. But I insist you go now.' I wasn't going to go into the uproar that was coming with Jim there and have to defend him and work with him. Because some of the Jewels were things he did, like the mail opening. I said, 'There's not a person in the world going to believe us, Jim, that it wasn't caused by Sy.' "

But, in retrospect, Colby agreed that the "precise timing" of his dismissal of Angleton was indeed a result of Hersh's story in the *Times*. He had, after all, fired Angleton in anticipation of its appearance.[6]

[6]Hersh suspected that Angleton's indiscretion in telling him about CIA networks in North Korea and Moscow was the real reason that Colby finally dismissed the counterintelligence chief. Remembering Colby's gasp when he related this conversation to the CIA director, Hersh said: "I think *that's* why he fired Angleton." *Time* magazine reported that Angleton himself claimed that "his resignation was solely because of an indiscretion in the course of an interview with the *Times* that could have jeopardized a U.S. agent in Moscow." However, Colby said he had no memory of

Hersh's story led the paper on Sunday, December 22, 1974, under a four-column headline: "HUGE CIA OPERATION REPORTED IN U.S. AGAINST ANTIWAR FORCES, OTHER DISSIDENTS IN NIXON YEARS." The *Times* story reported that the CIA, in violation of its charter, had conducted "a massive illegal domestic intelligence operation" against the antiwar movement, and had engaged in break-ins, wiretaps, and "the surreptitious inspection of mail."[7]

Hersh's story set off a political chain reaction. President Gerald R. Ford, skiing in Vail, Colorado, announced he would tolerate no illegal spying and ordered Colby to prepare a report on the CIA operation. Colby ordered the DDO, William E. Nelson, to draft it. "By eight A.M. Monday," Miler said, "I had been advised I was to stand by to review some material being prepared by Nelson's office for the White House about the Hersh article. We had to review the Family Jewels report about mail opening and other things for the report that Colby flew out to Vail. Then I was told to be in Nelson's office at seven o'clock that night.

"During the day Jim called in me and Ray Rocca, and explained he was retiring." Rocca was the deputy chief of the CI Staff. Also present at the meeting in Nelson's office that night, Miler said, were Angleton; Nelson, slim, blond, well-tailored and smooth of manner; and Nelson's deputy, David Blee.

"Nelson explained Jim was retiring, they were making big changes in CI, Rock [Raymond Rocca] and I were no longer to be in CI. Then he turned to me and said, 'What are you going to do?' 'I guess I'll retire.' 'Good.' He turned to Rock and he said, 'I guess I'll retire.' That was it."

Two days later, Hersh reported the resignation of James Angleton, and soon after, of Rocca, Miler, and William J. Hood, another Angleton deputy and a thirty-year veteran of the OSS and the CIA. Hood, a latecomer to Angleton's inner circle—he had joined the staff as

---

Hersh telling him about Angleton's lapse. "Maybe he did," Colby said. "But it wasn't a factor in firing Angleton. I determined a long time ago I had to get rid of him and the question was how."

[7]Colby's adversaries in the intelligence community later launched a whispering campaign that the CIA director had leaked the mail-opening program to Hersh to torpedo Angleton. Both Hersh and Colby firmly denied it.

executive officer only in 1973—had planned to retire anyway, Miler said, but was caught up in the mass departures.

On the day that Angleton's dismissal became known, Daniel Schorr of CBS News received a telephone call from his office at 6:00 A.M. A camera crew was on the way to Angleton's home in Arlington, and Schorr was instructed to meet it there. Schorr vividly recalled what turned into an off-camera interview that lasted four hours. "I arrived, he opened the door, sleepy-looking, wearing a robe over pajamas. He invited me in. He sat down and we talked for a long time. 'I've been up all night,' Angleton said. 'My family is away, but I can offer you apple juice or Sanka.'

"He was emaciated-looking, and his glasses came down over his nose, and he sometimes tended to look over them. He was soft-spoken. He talked at enormous length about Yasir Arafat. How Arafat went to Moscow and laid a wreath on Lenin's tomb. He showed me a photograph of a beaming Arafat at the tomb. 'The man standing next to Arafat at Lenin's tomb is his KGB case officer,' Angleton said. 'Petrovakov. He was head of KGB headquarters in Karlshorst when Blake was in Berlin.' "

No pictures, Angleton told Schorr; the camera crew would have to remain outside. "He said, 'You've blown my cover. I sent my family to several states, they're scattered all over, because of the story. It's caused me a lot of trouble. If my picture is taken, my wife will be killed. My wife of thirty-two years is gone, and here I am.' He went on, bewailing his troubles. Then back to Arafat again."

Angleton rambled on circuitously, the conversation disjointed. He had been to Israel thirty times. He had never met Howard Hunt, the Watergate burglar. Then a long dissertation on how Georgi Malenkov had taken over in Moscow, and other Kremlin maneuvers, all controlled by the KGB. Dzerzhinsky ran four thousand agents, Stalin changed the OGPU to a terror organization.

"He talked about Watergate," Schorr said. "He said, 'When Watergate occurred, Helms was deeply victimized. Helms was set up as the scapegoat for President Nixon.' " Angleton was disturbed by détente. " 'Public opinion favors détente, everything swirls around détente, which is just another word for peaceful coexistence, used by Stalin. The Nixon-Kissinger détente bothers me deeply.'

" 'For twenty-two years I handled the Israeli account. Israel was the only sanity in the Middle East. They wanted to transfer this account—that was unacceptable.' Colby was planning a trip to Israel, and Kissinger forbade him to go to East Jerusalem, because it would recognize Israeli control, and Colby canceled it. Angleton was furious at this.

"Angleton said the Yugoslav break with the Soviet Union was false, as was the Sino-Soviet split—neither happened, it was all part of KGB disinformation designed to mislead us. They remained under central control. That's when I decided he was really crazy. I said, 'Mr. Angleton, do you really *believe* that?' He didn't answer, and went on speaking almost as though I wasn't there. He was talking as though he was looking into his own mind.

"Then Angleton said he was leaving. I said, 'Mr. Angleton, you realize there are sixteen cameras out there. You've just told me if your picture is taken your family will be killed.' He went out anyway and seemed mesmerized by the cameras. He spoke for some time. Then he got into his blue Mercedes and drove away."

Colby's broom had now made a clean sweep of the leadership of the Counterintelligence Staff. But the fallout from Hersh's story was just beginning. President Ford named an eight-member commission headed by Vice President Nelson A. Rockefeller to investigate the charges. By early in 1975, a full-dress inquiry had begun in the Senate under Frank Church, the Idaho Democrat. In the House, a similar investigation was conducted by Representative Otis G. Pike, a Democrat from Long Island.[8]

James Angleton reluctantly emerged from the shadows for a memorable appearance before Senator Church's Senate Select Committee on Intelligence. It was the first time he had ever testified in public. As

---

[8]The Rockefeller Commission and the two congressional committees reported widespread abuses by the CIA and other intelligence agencies, including assassination plots by the CIA against foreign heads of state. As a result of these investigations, Congress belatedly established permanent intelligence committees in the Senate and House to watch over the CIA and the other intelligence agencies. And the President was required to inform Congress of covert operations. Efforts to pass broader "charter" legislation, defining the tasks of the spy agencies and setting strictly defined limits on their activities, failed to pass, however. Despite this, the myth arose that the Church committee and other investigations had somehow hobbled the intelligence agencies.

the cameras clicked and whirred, the tall stooped figure was sworn in at the witness table under the bright lights of the chandeliered Senate caucus room.

After some initial sparring between Angleton and Church, Senator Richard Schweiker, a Pennsylvania Republican, began questioning the former counterintelligence chief. At an earlier, executive session, the senator pointed out, Angleton had been asked why the CIA had failed to comply with a presidential order to destroy the deadly shellfish toxin that it used to coat the microscopic missiles fired by its dart guns.

Angleton had replied: "It is inconceivable that a secret intelligence arm of the government has to comply with all the overt orders of the government." Had Angleton really said that? Schweiker asked. "Well, if it is accurate, it shouldn't have been said," Angleton replied.

That wasn't enough for Schweiker. Did Angleton believe the CIA had to obey the President or didn't he? The remark was "imprudent," Angleton said; he wished to withdraw it.

Senator Church joined the questioning. "Did you not mean it when you said it the first time?" he asked.

"I do not know how to respond to that question," Angleton replied. "I said that I withdrew the statement."

"But you're unwilling to say whether or not you meant it when you said it?"

"I would say the entire speculation should not have been indulged in."

Senator Robert Morgan of North Carolina was troubled by Angleton's answers. He wanted to know how "the actions of that Central Intelligence Agency can be monitored in such a way as to protect the fundamental rights of the American citizens of this country? . . . How can we act if . . . the intelligence agencies refuse to obey the guidelines? . . . what assurances do we have that an intelligence agency would follow any mandate of the Congress or the President?"

"I have nothing to contribute to that, sir," said James J. Angleton.

In the days immediately before the fall, Miler said, "Jim was very discouraged. What was going to happen to CI? What was going to happen to efforts to keep the government from being penetrated? There were many nights we would go to the Shanghai for dinner, out on Lee Highway. Or Jim would go to La Niçoise, a restaurant in

Georgetown.''[9] Over lunch there the two men would talk about the dim future of counterintelligence.

"He was very concerned we hadn't found the mole," Miler said. "He asked me, 'Where should we be looking? What should we be doing? Did we miss something? What were we doing wrong?' "

[9]La Niçoise, where Angleton lunched regularly, was notable for the odd fact that in the evening the waiters wore roller skates.

Chapter 17

Aftermath

The Norwegian counterintelligence man was puzzled. He had spotted a KGB officer in Oslo and followed the Soviet to a resort. What puzzled him was the woman the Russian had met there. She was older than might have been expected, in her mid-sixties perhaps, not the sort of young lovely a KGB man might choose for a weekend tryst.

A former FBI counterintelligence agent told what happened next. "Norwegian security identified her, and then, 'Oh my God, she had worked in Moscow.' She fit Golitsin's case."

It was the late seventies, more than ten years after Ingeborg Lygren had been arrested and grilled—and eventually released for lack of evidence—as a result of Anatoly Golitsin's identification of her as a Soviet spy. Angleton had warned the Norwegians about Lygren and had continued to insist on her guilt, even after her release.

The woman at the resort was Gunvor Galtung Haavik, sixty-five, who had been a secretary at Norway's embassy in Moscow for nine years before Lygren had served there.[1]

[1]The Soviet defector Oleg Gordievsky, a KGB officer who began working for British intelligence in Copenhagen in 1974, has said that in the mid-1970s he warned MI6 about a Soviet agent in the Norwegian foreign ministry. But he did not indicate whether he was able to identify Haavik by name, nor is it known whether the British passed along the information to Norway. Christopher Andrew and Oleg Gordievsky, *KGB: The Inside Story* (New York: HarperCollins, 1990), p. 567. A former high-

By 1977, Gunvor Haavik was assigned to trade and political matters in the Norwegian ministry of foreign affairs in Oslo. Checking their records, Norwegian security found that she had worked in the Moscow embassy from 1947 to 1956.

"The original Golitsin story," the FBI counterintelligence man went on, "was that the KGB had targeted the Norwegian embassy in Moscow, decided that the woman who turned out to be Haavik was lonely, and sent a handsome officer to sit next to her at the opera. It worked."

James E. Nolan, Jr., an FBI counterintelligence official in the Soviet section at headquarters when Haavik was spotted, explained how the case had gone awry. "Golitsin talked about a Norwegian woman recruited in a Moscow honey trap who was an important KGB source in the Norwegian foreign service. That was absolutely, totally accurate. The agency with the help of the Norwegians came up with five or six candidates and showed him the files. 'This is the woman,' Golitsin said. They arrested her. Big stink. Trouble is, it was the wrong woman."

Once they had picked up Haavik's trail, Norwegian security police followed her for months. On January 27, 1977, she was under surveillance as she rode a streetcar to a rendezvous with Aleksandr K. Printsipalov, a KGB man listed as a third secretary in the Soviet embassy. She got off the streetcar, met the Soviet intelligence officer, and handed over documents. At that point, a group of police dressed as joggers closed in, arrested her, and held Printsipalov until he could prove his diplomatic status, at which point he had to be let go.

During interrogations and in court hearings, Haavik admitted she had handed over stacks of secret documents to the KGB, first in the Moscow embassy and then for nineteen years as an employee of the ministry in Oslo. The KGB had equipped Haavik with a special Russian-made bag with secret pockets, the better to take documents from the ministry. She delivered the documents to her KGB controllers at outdoor meetings in the Oslo area, at which she was paid.

---

ranking CIA counterintelligence official doubted that a tip from Gordievsky had resulted in Haavik's detection. "To protect Gordievsky, the Brits would absolutely not pass it on to Norway," he said. "Gordievsky was too valuable to the Brits to risk passing on this little tidbit."

Haavik was run by Gennady F. Titov, a KGB officer stationed in Oslo who was later promoted to general.[2] One day after Haavik's arrest, Norway expelled five Soviets for espionage, including Printsipalov and an embassy driver, S. Z. Gromov, both of whom were accused of receiving classified material from Haavik. Titov was in Moscow on leave at the time, but the Norwegian government made it clear he would not be allowed to return.

According to correspondent Per Hegge, of Oslo's *Aftenposten,* there was more to the story. The Soviets had a personal hook into Haavik. The KGB agent whom Golitsin said had been placed next to her at the opera in Moscow was a man she already knew. "In 1945," Hegge said, "Haavik had served as an interpreter for a Norwegian physician, who was trying to improve health conditions in the camps of Soviet war prisoners whom the Germans had sent to Norway, and who were being repatriated. She struck up a friendship, a romance perhaps, with a Soviet soldier. He, unlike the others, was not sent to Siberia when he returned to the Soviet Union. He wrote to her. They used him to control her; if she didn't cooperate, something dreadful would happen to her Soviet soldier friend. I'm told he was let out of prison to see her. And if she didn't cooperate, he would go back."

The full details of the case were never made public in court. On August 5, 1977, six months after her arrest and before she could be brought to trial, Gunvor Galtung Haavik died in jail of congestive heart failure.

Just after Christmas in 1974, Colby called George T. Kalaris home from Brasilia, where he was chief of station, and appointed him chief of counterintelligence to replace James Angleton.

Kalaris, the son of Greek immigrants who owned restaurants in Billings, Montana, had joined the agency in 1952. He had served for the most part in the Far East, where he had been deputy COS in Laos

---

[2]Titov, who was known in the KGB as "the Crocodile," also ran Arne Treholt, a high-level Soviet spy in the Norwegian diplomatic corps. In 1984, Norwegian police arrested Treholt at Oslo's airport as he was about to leave for Vienna to meet General Titov. He carried a briefcase containing sixty-six classified documents. Treholt was convicted and sentenced to twenty years. Early in 1991, Titov was named chief of counterintelligence of the KGB. He was dismissed in the aftermath of the failed coup in August against Soviet President Mikhail S. Gorbachev. All of the KGB's top leaders were fired in the wake of the coup, which had been led by KGB chairman Vladimir A. Kryuchkov.

and chief of station in the Philippines. There he had gotten to know Colby, who headed the Far East division. Kalaris was part of the "FE Mafia," the Asian hands whom Colby had brought in to staff a number of high-level positions in the agency.

As one of his first acts when he took over the CI Staff, Kalaris assigned William E. Camp III, a CIA officer who had served in Oslo at the time of Lygren's arrest and whom Kalaris had recruited for the CI Staff, to do a study of the case. Camp concluded, even before Haavik's arrest, that the CIA—relying on Golitsin's information—had bungled, alerting Norway to arrest the wrong woman.

Mortified, Kalaris felt the agency should express its regret to Norway for the false imprisonment of Lygren. In 1976, Camp was dispatched to Oslo with a letter from the CIA, signed by Kalaris, apologizing to the government of Norway for the monstrous error in the Lygren affair. Camp, accompanied by Quentin C. Johnson, the CIA's Oslo station chief, called on the Norwegian authorities and delivered the letter and a verbal apology as well. The CIA also offered Lygren money, in addition to the small compensation she had received from her own government, an offer that the Norwegians turned down.

Kalaris also took steps to ensure that Lygren herself was made aware of the agency's contrition. But the official CIA apology to the government of Norway was never made public. By that time, Ingeborg Lygren had retired into obscurity near her native Stavanger, in southwest Norway, her telephone unlisted, her only wish to live out her days quietly and unnoticed.

On January 22, 1991, it was disclosed through an item inserted in the Oslo paper by her family that Ingeborg Lygren had died in Sandnes, a suburb of Stavanger, at the age of seventy-six.

George Kalaris, the new chief of counterintelligence, was a tall, thin man with a quick mind and no social pretensions. In an agency run largely by Ivy Leaguers, Kalaris was an anomaly. Whereas many of his colleagues were Easterners who communicated in the languid accents of Groton and Andover, Kalaris grew up in Billings, Montana; in appearance and style, he was faintly reminiscent of Jimmy Durante. His prep school was the streets of Nazi-occupied Athens.

When Kalaris was eleven, his mother took him and his two brothers to Greece to be educated there. His father would come to visit every year. World War II broke out, and Kalaris and his mother and brothers were caught in Athens during the Nazi occupation. The family acquired false identity cards in their true names and posed as Greeks. Kalaris's ID card said that he had been born in Athens. During the war, Kalaris attended law school at the University of Athens. In 1944, Greece was liberated and the American embassy reopened. When an eager Kalaris contacted the embassy, an official told him cheerfully: "We're holding something here for you." It was his draft notice. Kalaris returned to the United States in April 1945 and was inducted in August, just after the war's end. He served two years in the Army, finished law school at the University of Montana, and earned a master's degree in labor law at New York University. He worked as a lawyer for the National Labor Relations Board, then joined the CIA in 1952.

The CI Staff, having been whittled down by Colby, was already small when Kalaris was summoned back from Brazil to run it. Kalaris decided to keep it that way. As his deputy he brought in Leonard V. McCoy, who had been a reports officer in the Soviet division. Reports officers do not run agents, but they write up and evaluate the information flowing in from case officers in the field. McCoy had written the reports, among other major cases, on Penkovsky and Nosenko. A big, balding, slow-spoken man, McCoy was appalled as he read the files of the Angleton era, to which he now had access. Strongly pro-Nosenko, and a bitter foe of Angleton, he became even more outraged when he realized the full extent of what had been going on behind the closed doors of the CI Staff and the SIG.[3]

A former colleague of McCoy's sketched in the background. "As a relatively junior officer in the reports section, McCoy wrote a memo to Helms at the height of the Nosenko controversy and said Nosenko was bona fide, and the whole treatment of Nosenko was wrong. Helms sent the memo to Angleton for comment. McCoy became a marked man. He damn near lost his job. Bagley and Angleton came down on

[3]For example, a 1987 article by McCoy in the CIA retirees' newsletter was a stinging indictment of the Angleton era and its devastating effect on CIA operations. Leonard V. McCoy, "Yuriy Nosenko, CIA," *CIRA Newsletter*, Vol. XII, No. 3 (Fall 1987), published by Central Intelligence Retirees' Association, p. 20. The unpublished portions of McCoy's manuscript are if anything even stronger in their criticism of Angleton. In the longer version, McCoy defended Paul Garbler and Richard Kovich, as well as Peter Karlow, who is not mentioned by name, and said all three were completely innocent of charges that were "dredged from Golitsyn's imagination" and given "monstrous life" by Angleton.

him like a ton of bricks. You could hear the spatter for a block. Boy, he [McCoy] was put in the back room and given a dressing down by Bagley.

"The memo so angered Angleton that I think he put McCoy on the suspect list. That was what he frequently did. If someone was difficult to deal with, Angleton concluded he was under Soviet instructions to frustrate the mole investigation." The colleague shook his head. "But when he became deputy for counterintelligence McCoy had the misfortune to get involved in the Shadrin business, and that didn't do his career any good." Shadrin was the Soviet destroyer captain who defected in 1959 and disappeared in Vienna in 1975 after American intelligence played him back against the KGB.

As his other deputy, Kalaris appointed Lawrence M. Sternfield, a tough, heavyset CIA veteran who had worked for the agency in Chile, Brazil, and Bolivia and then handled Cuban operations in Miami. Under Kalaris, the CI Staff had but two components, Research and Analysis, headed by McCoy, and Operations, headed by Sternfield.

Sternfield was astonished to learn that Golitsin had agency files in his possession, files that had been shown to the defector by Angleton during the height of the mole hunt. By now the CIA had stashed Golitsin on a farm in upstate New York. Quietly, Sternfield began recovering the CIA's files. Every weekend for weeks, he sent a station wagon to the farm; it would come back to Langley loaded with documents. Ernest J. Tsikerdanos, a CIA officer on the Counterintelligence Staff, was at the wheel.

The Special Investigations Group was still going strong, looking for penetrations. Kalaris placed the SIG under McCoy. But after fourteen years, the SIG had not uncovered any moles inside the agency, and Kalaris ordered that it spend no more time chasing Golitsin's leads.

The new CI team was later criticized by Angleton's former aides as lacking counterintelligence experience. Perhaps so, but Kalaris had the wit to try to find out what Angleton had been doing for the past twenty years. To that end, he commissioned a series of classified studies. Some dealt with major Soviet cases, such as Nosenko, Orlov, Loginov, and Shadrin. But the most important study of all was a massive, detailed history of the CI Staff itself under Angleton.

To undertake this gargantuan task, Kalaris turned to Cleveland C. Cram. A rotund, friendly man with a scholarly manner, Cram had impressive qualifications for the job—he was a Ph.D. Harvard historian, of which the Clandestine Services did not have large numbers, and a former station chief. Moreover, as a liaison man in London between the CIA and British intelligence, he had lived through the British mole hunt and was already familiar with Golitsin's charges.

A farmer's son from Waterville, Minnesota, Cram was educated at St. John's University, a Benedictine school in Minnesota. He earned a master's degree in European history at Harvard, served four years in the Navy in the South Pacific during World War II, and returned to Harvard for his Ph.D. Cram had looked forward to teaching in some lovely small college and spending the rest of his life in an ivory tower. But the CIA offered him a job. Cram accepted it, and never looked back. In 1953 he went off to London, where he stayed five years and met Kim Philby. He ran the British desk at headquarters after that, returned to London for a second tour, then served as chief of station in Holland and in Ottawa.

In 1975, after twenty-six years in the agency, Cram had retired. In the fall of 1976, he was attending a cocktail party in Washington given by Harry Brandes, the representative of the Royal Canadian Mounted Police, the Canadian security service. Theodore G. Shackley, the assistant DDO, called over Kalaris, and the two CIA men cornered Cram.

"Would you like to come back to work?" he was asked. The agency, Cram was told, wanted a study done of Angleton's reign, from 1954 to 1974. "Find out what in hell happened," Cram was told. "What were these guys *doing?*"

Cram took the assignment. For the duration, he moved into a huge vault down the hall from what had been Angleton's office. It was a librarylike room with a door that had to be opened by a combination lock. There many of the materials he needed were at hand—the vault, for example, contained thirty-nine volumes on Philby alone, all the Golitsin "serials," as Angleton had called the leads provided by his prize defector, and all of the Nosenko files.

But even this secure vault had not been Angleton's sanctum sanctorum. Inside the vault was another smaller vault, secured by push-button locks, which contained the *really* secret stuff, on George Blake, Penkovsky, and other spy cases deemed too secret for the outer vault.

Kalaris thought Cram's study would be a one-year assignment.

When Cram finally finished it in 1981, six years later, he had produced twelve legal-sized volumes, each three hundred to four hundred pages. Cram's approximately four-thousand-page study has never been declassified. It remains locked in the CIA's vaults.[4]

But some of its subject matter can be described. Cram obviously spent a substantial amount of time reviewing the history of the mole hunt that pervaded the era he studied. In doing so, he had considerable difficulty. The names of the mole suspects were considered so secret that their files were kept in locked safes in yet another vault directly across from Angleton's (then Kalaris's) office.

Even though Cram had carte blanche to conduct his study, he had trouble at first gaining access to this most sensitive material. In part, he was hampered as well by the chaotic and often mysterious nature of Angleton's files.

Eventually, Cram got access to the vaulted files on individuals kept in the locked safes. But among Kalaris and his staff, Cram detected an edginess that Angleton, in Elba, might somehow return and wreak vengeance on those who had dared to violate his files by reading them.

Even with access, it was hard for Cram to tell which of the penetration cases were most important and which were less important. The files were shrouded in ambiguity.

One former agency officer familiar with the secret study described the nature of what Cram must have grappled with as he toiled for years, like the Benedictines who had taught him, in the CIA's secret vaults.

"Angleton might be discussing a division chief's plan to send a man as station chief overseas," the ex-CIA man said. "Angleton would say, as an aside, 'I wouldn't assign that man.' 'Why not?' the division chief would ask. Jim would pull out a pack of Marlboros or whatever, light one, and say 'Sorry, I can't discuss that with you.' Well, that was enough."

The numbers were hard to pin down. But after analyzing all the files, Cram concluded that there had been roughly fifty suspects.[5] Of

---

[4]Cleveland C. Cram, "History of the Counterintelligence Staff 1954–1974," classified unpublished study (Langley, Va.: Central Intelligence Agency, 1981).
[5]The SIG initially screened more than 120 suspects, a much higher figure. The total of fifty arrived at by Cram probably represents those officers who were subject to further and more intensive investigation.

those, about sixteen or eighteen fell into the category of serious, major suspects who were subject to massive and detailed investigations, first by the Counterintelligence Staff, which had the task of pinpointing possible Soviet moles, and then by the Office of Security, which was responsible for further investigation.

As his study progressed, one thing became clear to Cram: an officer could easily be hurt once he was placed on the list of fifty, even if he wasn't on what Angleton's mole hunters had called the "hard core" list. Careers had been damaged simply because a man had been placed on the longer list.

A former officer who was aware of Cram's study said it must have been a challenge. "People just didn't know what the hell Jim and company were doing," he said. "Angleton was a little like the Wizard of Oz. There wasn't anything there. But he made a lot of trouble."

The former CIA man paused as though wondering if he should go on. Then he took the plunge. "The place was a morass of irrationality. You can use the word 'crazy.' These people were a little bit crazy. Not a little bit. Quite crazy. Jim was a tortured, twisted personality. Oh, he could be charming, and pleasant, but at bottom, he was a son of a bitch. He was a bad man."

Other studies commissioned by Kalaris were in progress. Cram would often ride to work with Jack J. Fieldhouse, a Yale man by way of Ohio, who had worked for the agency in Vienna. Fieldhouse, who was working on a study of the Loginov case, was appalled by what he found in the agency's files on the KGB illegal. The Fieldhouse report remains classified in the agency's vaults, but it concluded that Loginov was genuine and had been traded back to the KGB against his will.[6]

Later, in the spring of 1981, after William J. Casey had become CIA director, Fieldhouse wrote a study of the Nosenko case. Again, it concluded that Nosenko was a bona fide defector.

Kalaris commissioned yet another study in an effort to clear the mists that had enveloped the CI Staff. Early in the spring of 1975, he called in Bronson Tweedy, a retired, British-born CIA veteran who had twice served as London station chief. Kalaris had Golitsin on his

---

[6]As already noted, in other studies conducted for Kalaris, Vasia C. Gmirkin concluded that both Shadrin and KITTY HAWK were genuine CIA assets, William E. Camp III determined that the CI Staff had made a terrible mistake in the Lygren case, and John L. Hart concluded that Nosenko was bona fide and had been horribly mistreated by the agency.

mind. He turned to Tweedy because he wanted a dependable person outside the agency.[7]

Kalaris told Tweedy to study the entire Golitsin case; he wanted to know how much reliance he could put on anything Golitsin had said. Tweedy worked for months and produced the first study on Golitsin, a ninety-page report that he handed in to Kalaris later that year. It concluded that Golitsin was indeed a bona fide defector but that his value to the agency had been far less than his supporters claimed. With prompting from the Counterintelligence Staff, the idea had gained currency that somehow Golitsin had exposed vast numbers of spies and penetrations in allied intelligence services. In fact, the report found, Golitsin had furnished information that led to the arrest of Georges Pâques, the Soviet spy in France; he gave the first lead on William Vassall, the spy in the British Admiralty; and he had supplied some leads in Finland. That, Tweedy concluded, was about all. Despite Tweedy's findings, in 1987 the CIA awarded Golitsin a medal for outstanding service.

Kalaris also pressed Tweedy into service to conduct yet another, lesser-known study. The new CI chief had been left an irksome problem in the form of the Petty report, the reels of tape, index cards, and bulging file cabinets in which the former SIG member had accused Angleton himself of being the Soviet mole in the CIA. Kalaris could hardly overlook the possibility, however farfetched, that his predecessor had been a traitor. Again, Tweedy produced a written study that dismissed the charges against Angleton as illusory.[8]

---

[7]Tweedy was certainly dependable. As chief of the Africa division, he had been asked to explore the feasibility of assassinating Patrice Lumumba, the first Prime Minister of the Congo, who was inconveniently opposing the CIA's handpicked leaders in that country. Dr. Sidney Gottlieb, the CIA biochemist respected for his expertise in such matters, suggested that a lethal biological agent—a disease indigenous to Africa—be placed on Lumumba's toothbrush. Lumumba eluded Langley's dentifrice but was captured and killed in January 1961 by the troops of Joseph Mobutu. Although Tweedy's role in the Lumumba assassination plot became embarrassingly public during the Church committee's investigation, he was well regarded inside the agency as an objective and honest officer. The son of a prominent American banker in London, he was educated in England and then at Princeton, class of '37. In an agency of Ivy Leaguers with a strong streak of Anglophilia, Tweedy, for his time, was almost the perfect specimen of an upper-echelon officer.

[8]According to a former CIA official, "There was a joke going around the agency at one point that Angleton thought *he* might have been the mole. That he had a dual personality and suspected himself. Of course, it was only a joke."

Although Angleton was now cleared of the charge that he, the prime mole hunter, was himself the head mole, from exile he fought back. The chosen instrument of his battle was the author and journalist Edward Jay Epstein. With Angleton playing the role of Deep Throat, Epstein in 1978 published his book *Legend,* which for the first time revealed the war of the defectors, the backstage clashes between Golitsin and Nosenko, Angleton's conviction that Nosenko had lied about Lee Harvey Oswald, and J. Edgar Hoover's faith in FEDORA.[9] Angleton emerged in the book as Epstein's hero, a master counterspy with "prematurely silver hair and a finely sculptured face," a "superbly patient" fisherman who "played defectors much like trout."[10]

At the time the book appeared, it was widely assumed in Washington that Angleton was Epstein's source, an assumption that Epstein himself confirmed in a later book.[11] He had, Epstein disclosed, conducted a series of interviews with Angleton for a decade, beginning in 1977. In the second book, Angleton is quoted directly and admiringly.

Angleton had extensive connections in the press, and he managed, through Epstein and others, to air his grievances and his unique worldview. After the fall, he became a celebrity of sorts, a subject of endless fascination for journalists, writers of nonfiction books, novelists, and filmmakers.

But exile proved frustrating for the old CI chief. Stung by John Hart's testimony to the House Assassination Committee about the handling of Nosenko—Hart had called it "an abomination"—Angleton in 1978 sued Stansfield Turner, the director of the CIA, to try to gain access to his own former files, in order to prepare a rebuttal. Claiming he needed to review the files of the Nosenko case to complete his own testimony to the committee, Angleton got only two; but in a settlement that must have been bittersweet, he was eventually allowed to go back into the CIA headquarters, where he had once wielded so much power, and read more of the secret documents. He had to wear a visitor's badge.[12]

[9]Edward Jay Epstein, *Legend: The Secret World of Lee Harvey Oswald* (New York: Reader's Digest/Press McGraw-Hill, 1978).
[10]*Ibid.,* pp. 26, 31.
[11]Edward Jay Epstein, *Deception: The Invisible War Between the KGB and the CIA* (New York: Simon & Schuster, 1989).
[12]On Angleton's visit to CIA headquarters, which took place on March 29, 1979, the

With no agents to run and no Counterintelligence Staff at his beck and call, Angleton nevertheless fought back in other ways, applying the operational skills he had honed over more than three decades. It began to be whispered around Washington that Colby was the mole. But somehow the rumors could never be tied to Angleton directly. The former counterintelligence chief took a "Who, me?" attitude if questioned about the whispering campaign against the man who had fired him.

Colby himself, when asked if Angleton had accused him of being a mole, replied: "I've never heard him quoted as saying that. I've heard that some of his aides said it.[13] I'd heard rumors that members of Angleton's staff were saying I was a mole. Or it may have been in the vein of 'Colby couldn't have done more harm to the agency if he were a mole.'

"Several years later I got a call from Jim. 'How are you?' I asked. 'I'm not feeling very good.' 'What do you mean?' '*The New Republic* says this week that I said you were a Soviet mole.' I said, 'Jim, as I understand it, you have not said that, but some of your [former] assistants have made that statement.' He said, 'That's right.' I said, 'What do you want me to do?' He wasn't very responsive. I said, 'I'll write a letter to *The New Republic* saying it's my understanding you've never said that.' So I did, and they ran it.[14] I often wondered what his problem was, and I suspect he may have been afraid of a libel suit."

And what was Colby's response to the rumors about him that floated around the capital? "I've said I am not a mole," he replied. "There's nothing to it. I don't fudge around on that one. I hit it right on the head."

---

former counterintelligence chief was accompanied by his lawyer, Philip L. Chabot, Jr. It was Angleton's last hurrah, and Chabot remembered the scene vividly. "I sat nearby and he reviewed documents from the file. He was in there for more than four hours." Soon afterward, Angleton completed his classified testimony to the committee, Chabot said.

[13]In an interview in *New York* magazine in 1978, author Epstein was asked if Angleton knew the identity of the mole in the CIA. His published reply: "Angleton refuses to say, but one of his ex-staff members told me with a wry smile, 'You might find out who Colby was seeing in Rome in the early 1950s.' " "The War of the Moles: An Interview with Edward Jay Epstein by Susana Duncan," *New York,* February 27, 1978, p. 28.

[14]*New Republic,* February 21, 1981, p. 7.

•   •   •

When Paul Garbler returned from Sweden in 1976, he had demanded an official inquiry into the shadowy accusations against him. No one had ever confronted the former Moscow station chief. But he now knew informally that for close to a decade he had lived under a secret stigma as a suspected Soviet penetration of the CIA, a suspicion that explained his exile to Trinidad for four years when his career in Soviet operations should have blossomed.

In a letter to the agency's inspector general, Garbler wrote: "I found myself the victim of a charge against which I was never given the opportunity to defend myself. . . . I felt a strong sense of personal outrage at what had been done to my family and myself." Without an inquiry, Garbler wrote, the security charge might never be resolved. "I would like finally to defend myself and clear my name."[15]

Eight months later, in August 1977, Garbler received a letter from John F. Blake, the CIA's acting deputy director, reporting that the "security issue has been fully resolved in your favor." It was the first time that the CIA had informed Garbler that there had been a security charge against him. Blake went on to acknowledge that the spy charge had indeed had an "adverse effect" on Garbler's career. "Your feelings of frustration and bitterness are understandable," Blake added, "and I am only sorry that there is no way to turn back the clock."[16]

Was the agency's apology enough? After thinking about the question for several months and talking it over with his family, Garbler decided it wasn't. He wrote to Stansfield Turner, the director, asking for compensation "for my family and myself for nine lean and unhappy years." The charges, Garbler wrote, had called into question "my loyalty to the Agency, the government, and the country." His friends and colleagues had shunned him, he wrote. "I became a person one dealt with warily, a kind of pariah."[17]

Garbler had chosen his words with precision. For years, he had read distrust in the eyes of his associates at the CIA. "People I worked with turned over the papers on their desks when I entered the room," he recalled. "If I was walking down the hall and a group of my colleagues were chattering away, they would see me approach and quickly dis-

[15]Letter, Garbler to Inspector General John H. Waller, December 8, 1976.
[16]Letter, Blake to Garbler, August 3, 1977.
[17]Letter, Garbler to Turner, November 29, 1977.

perse. Friends turned their backs to me at cocktail parties. Even people who knew me well would sometimes stop in midsentence, to make sure they didn't say too much."

Late in December, three days before Garbler was due to retire, he received a reply from Turner, who said he found the "spurious security charge against you abhorrent." At the same time, Turner said there was nothing he could do about it. There was no way Garbler could be compensated, Turner wrote, unless Congress passed a private bill for that purpose. An "injustice" had been done, Turner added, yet the agency appreciated his many years of fine service.[18] It amounted to a hearty handshake, but no cash.

More than two decades later, Garbler was living in Tucson, to where he had retired with his wife, Florence. He spoke without rancor.

"I retired on December 31, 1977," Garbler said, "and got the usual retirement party on the seventh floor. Turner did not appear. Helms did not appear. Angleton did not appear."

Ten days after he retired, Garbler received a routine letter from Stansfield Turner expressing the director's sincere appreciation for "the important work you have done and my warmest hopes that you will find full enjoyment in the years ahead."

What did Garbler think that wintry day when the farewell party was over, he had cleaned out his desk, and he walked out of the building for the last time? "I looked back a lot that day," Garbler said, "but I thought the Lord had been good to me. I had an unfortunate time in my life. Nine years out of my life, but that all in all, it had been worth it. I would always be proud of the fact that I had served with the CIA.

"I did feel I would like very much to be able to refute what people thought about me and what this small group of people had tried to do to me." Then he remembered something. "At the farewell ceremony, they gave me a little CIA seal in plastic."

Garbler, standing now, turned and stared out the picture window of his study for a long moment. "No medals," he said. "No apologies."

---

[18]Letter, Turner to Garbler, December 26, 1977.

Chapter 18

The Mole Relief Act

In 1964, even though Richard Kovich realized his CIA career had mysteriously stalled, he dutifully continued to work as an agency "headhunter," a Russian-speaking officer who could fly anywhere on a moment's notice to make a recruitment pitch to a KGB man.

In the fall of 1966, Kovich was assigned to the Farm to teach agency trainees the skills he had acquired. After three years, he returned to headquarters, did some lecturing and training, but seemed to be marking time. By the beginning of 1974, at age forty-seven, it was clear he was going nowhere. In February, "Dushan" Kovich decided to pack it in.

By now he was aware that Ingeborg Lygren (SATINWOOD 37), Mikhail Federov (UNACUTE), and Yuri Loginov (AEGUSTO), three of his important agents, were suspect. But he did not know that he himself had come under intense investigation as a presumed Soviet mole.

At Kovich's retirement ceremony, William Colby presented him with a CIA medal and two other awards he had earned in his twenty-four years of distinguished service with the agency.[1] With his wife, Sara, Kovich disappeared into a life of retirement. Or so he thought.

Soon afterward, Kovich got a telephone call from a CIA colleague.

---

[1]Normally, CIA officers receive medals during the course of their careers for particular operations. Checking the files, someone in the bureaucracy noticed that Kovich had received none. Colby remedied the oversight.

Could he get on a plane and go and meet someone? Kovich protested that he was retired. But, like an old firehorse, he responded to the call and by 1975 was back globe-trotting for the agency on contract, making his recruitment pitches as of old.

Early in March 1976, Kovich was finally told that he had been suspected of working for the Soviets. Three aides on the staff of John H. Waller, the CIA's inspector general, met with Kovich and broke the news. Kovich was also informed that he was no longer under suspicion. By now, Colby had fired Angleton and himself been dismissed by President Ford in the wake of the various investigations into the intelligence agencies touched off by Seymour Hersh's story about CIA domestic spying in the *New York Times*.[2] But before Colby left, he ordered that Kovich be allowed to see his files.

As he read the files, Kovich's hair stood on end. He had not realized the enormity of the charges against him. He had not known it was a cause for suspicion to have a name that began with the letter K. It was like watching his life through the wrong end of the telescope. The mole hunters in SIG, the gumshoes in OS, had really thought he was a traitor. To Kovich, it was unbelievable.

He discovered that in December 1965, after Ingeborg Lygren's false arrest, the CIA was so worried that Kovich might bolt that it asked the FBI to prevent him from entering any Soviet installation in the United States. Kovich had laughed bitterly when he saw that in the files; he had never had any intention of fleeing to the Soviets, of course, he was a loyal CIA officer, but he knew that the FBI had no blanket authority to stop anyone from entering a Soviet building. The FBI knew it, too, and had rejected the CIA request.

[2]Colby was dismissed by Ford in November 1975 but agreed to remain on until George Bush could be sworn in to succeed him as CIA director on January 30, 1976. Colby thought he knew the immediate cause of his dismissal; he was convinced that he was done in by the CIA poison dart gun he had produced at the demand of the Church committee. Chairman Frank Church had waved the gun at a Senate hearing, and the resulting photograph made front pages around the world. It was too much for the White House, which already felt that Colby had been excessively candid with the investigating panels. At one point, Vice President Rockefeller, whose commission was supposed to be uncovering the abuses of the intelligence agencies, drew Colby aside and asked: "Bill, do you really have to present all this material to us?" In the White House situation room, during a meeting to map strategy to deal with the investigations, Secretary of State Henry Kissinger, aware that Colby was a practicing Roman Catholic, turned to him and said: "The trouble with you, Bill, is that whenever you go up on the Hill, you think you're going to confession."

After reading the files, Kovich realized he could no longer work for the CIA, and he so informed George Bush, the new director. In a letter to Bush in July, Kovich summarized the false accusations that had destroyed his career. Soon afterward, Bush wrote back, expressing regret for what had happened. He hoped, Bush added, that Kovich might take some comfort from the fact that he had been cleared.[3] In the fall, after winding up the project he was working on, Kovich retired from the agency again, this time for good.

Kovich was determined to remove any doubts about his loyalty, however, and if possible to receive compensation. He contacted Stanley H. Gaines, a former CIA colleague who had also retired from the agency and was practicing law. It wasn't the money primarily, Kovich told Gaines. He had given his best for his country, and now he wanted his good name restored and a terrible injustice rectified.

Gaines and Kovich opened discussions with the CIA's inspector general and with its Office of General Counsel. Around the same time, Robert B. Barnett, an attorney for Paul Garbler, had also contacted the agency for the same reason. By now, President Carter had been elected and had appointed Stansfield Turner as CIA director.

Just as Paul Garbler had been told by Admiral Turner he would need an act of Congress to be compensated, Kovich was informed that a law would have to be passed. "We couldn't find any specific authority we could fit this kind of relief into," a representative of the CIA's Office of General Counsel recalled. "What this required was legislation on the Hill to grant relief by the agency to people whose careers had been damaged by unfounded mole allegations. The inspector general explored this with us—he said, 'We think this is a case where some injustice was done. What can we do for these people?' That's when we decided we needed legislation, which we supported."

Although the CIA attorney, who had reviewed the files at my request, thought the agency had given its backing to remedial legislation, initially, at least, that was not the case.

In a letter to Paul Garbler's attorney in 1978, Anthony A. Lapham, then the CIA's general counsel, wrote: "I continue to feel that any tangible damages suffered by Mr. Garbler are speculative at best."

[3]Because Bush's letter mentioned some of the sensitive cases Kovich had handled, Kovich could not hang it on the wall or show it to anyone. He had to read the original in a special room at headquarters; later he was given a copy to keep.

While Garbler's career had without question been "sidetracked," Lapham argued, there was no guarantee that he would have been promoted anyway. It would not be "appropriate for the Agency to initiate or formally support" legislation to redress Garbler's misfortunes, Lapham wrote, but "neither would we oppose such a measure."[4]

Stansfield Turner's general counsel was saying that the agency would not back a private bill to help Garbler, although it would not stand in his way. A private bill applies only to one individual, a public law to whole classes of people. Now with Kovich pushing for action, the agency was saying it could not compensate anyone without a public law that would apply to all those who had been wronged by the search for moles. Within the CIA, however, there were strong pockets of resistance to the idea.

The reason for the agency's ambivalence was easy to see. A law giving the director of the CIA power to pay victims of the agency's own mole hunt might slip through unnoticed by the press, but there was always a chance that an alert reporter would spot the provision, that the law would attract unfavorable publicity, leading to all sorts of questions. It was, after all, a breathtaking concept: a secret agency that had wronged its own officers was being asked to turn around, admit its mistakes, and compensate those injured. No bureaucracy, let alone a powerful secret agency, likes to admit error.

Moreover, the CIA feared that a law providing compensation for victims of the mole hunt might be opening up a Pandora's box. The agency had visions of dozens, even hundreds, of ex-officers filing claims running into millions of dollars.

But Kovich, acting as the point man, kept plugging away. In 1977 he wrote to Senator Daniel K. Inouye, Democrat of Hawaii, the chairman of the Senate Intelligence Committee, and in August 1978 he testified to the senators for several days in closed session.

William Green Miller, the powerful staff director of the permanent Senate Intelligence Committee, was impressed by Kovich's arguments. Senator Birch Bayh, who had succeeded Inouye as chairman of the intelligence panel, and Senator Charles McC. Mathias, Jr., the Maryland Republican, supported the idea of legislation. Kovich met with Daniel B. Silver, who had replaced Lapham as general counsel of

---

[4]Letter, Anthony A. Lapham to Robert B. Barnett, December 6, 1978.

the CIA in 1979, and with Ernest Mayerfeld, another CIA lawyer and a former clandestine officer for the agency. The House Intelligence Committee joined with its Senate counterpart in supporting the bill.

"The issue," Miller said, "was how do you compensate for a mistake that jeopardized, harmed an individual personally or inflicted mental distress? The reason for the legislation was to make clear in law the right to rectify. There was an earnest desire by the CIA to resolve the issue in a fair way."

The CIA's desire was perhaps more earnest because by now Miller, Birch Bayh, and the Senate and House intelligence committees were breathing down its neck. On September 30, 1980, Congress passed the Intelligence Authorization Act for fiscal 1981. Tucked away in its pages was an obscure clause, Section 405 (a). In its entirety, it read:

"Whenever the Director of Central Intelligence finds during fiscal year 1981 that an employee or former employee of the Central Intelligence Agency has unfairly had his career with the Agency adversely affected as a result of allegations concerning the loyalty to the United States of such employee or former employee, the Director may grant such employee or former employee such monetary or other relief (including reinstatement and promotion) as the Director considers appropriate in the interest of fairness."

On October 14, 1980, the bill was signed by President Carter and became Public Law 96-450. Within the CIA, the law became known as "the Mole Relief Act."[5]

The following month, Ronald Reagan was elected President and named his campaign manager, William J. Casey, as the new CIA director. Both Kovich and Paul Garbler had been told they would receive compensation under the Mole Relief Act. On February 3, 1981, Garbler received a check from the United States Treasury, under the new law. In the spring, Kovich received a letter of apology from the CIA, and by July, he, too, had received his settlement. Although neither former CIA officer wished to discuss the amount

---

[5]See, for example, "Serge Peter Karlow—Request for Relief Under Section 405 of Public Law 96-450 ('Mole Relief Act')," memorandum, Stanley Sporkin, CIA general counsel, to Director of Central Intelligence William J. Casey, August 21, 1981, declassified and approved for release February 5, 1987. Although many CIA officers disdain the word "mole" as an invention of John le Carré, life imitates art, and the term, as noted earlier, has crept into the vocabulary of real spies.

he received, intelligence sources said one payment was more than $100,000, the other somewhat lower.

Four other former CIA officers, including Peter Karlow, applied for compensation under the 1980 act. They were all turned down. But Karlow resolved to continue his fight.

There was a catch to the Mole Relief Act, however. The provision was good for just one year. It opened up a window for the victims of the mole hunt, but only if they knew about it and could persuade the agency of the merits of their case before the law expired.[6]

From the CIA's viewpoint, everything was being managed well, that is, quietly. The agency was pleased that the number of mole victims who actually came forward was low. It was pleased as well that the press, except for one article in *Newsweek,* had missed the extraordinary story.[7] A secret government agency had falsely accused its own officers and was now paying them large sums of money under an act of Congress of which the public was, for the most part, unaware.

The CIA today refuses officially to confirm the names of the officers compensated under the Mole Relief Act, or the amounts paid out, or even the total amount of the payments it made to victims of the mole hunt. "Under the terms of the settlement I'm not at liberty to disclose the amounts," the attorney in the CIA's Office of General Counsel said. "They didn't all get the same amount." But it was, nevertheless,

[6]For some reason, most of those who brought about the passage of the Mole Relief Act were reluctant to discuss it. Almost all of the CIA and congressional officials whom I was able to interview appeared to have suffered severe memory lapses about the legislation they helped to create. For example, Daniel B. Silver, Admiral Turner's general counsel when the bill was enacted and a participant in the discussions that led to the passage of the measure, professed to have almost no memory of it and said he could find no one else who knew anything about it. Silver said he had checked with some former members of his staff but could not shed any light on the legislation. The conversation then went this way:

Q: Is there anyone who served on Turner's staff who would know about this?
A: I can't recall anyone.
Q: Well, it wasn't every day that the CIA handed out millions or at least hundreds of thousands of dollars to its former officers. I can't believe that it was done casually or that no one on Turner's staff would be aware of it.
A: [Grunts] I can't help.

[7]The article, by Tom Morganthau with David C. Martin, of the magazine's Washington bureau, appeared on August 11, 1980.

an astonishing story, even if the CIA had been able largely to keep the lid on it.

The fact that many former CIA officers, including those whose careers were affected, were not aware that the law existed in part explains the low numbers of those who came forward during the one-year window. An example was Stephen Roll, who spent twenty-six years as a CIA officer but strongly suspected Angleton had blocked his promotions because of suspicions of his Slavic background. "In 1980, I didn't know about the law," he said. "I heard about it much later through the grapevine." By then it was too late.

Roll was born in central Pennsylvania, and both his parents were Ukrainians. His father worked as a track repairman for the Pennsylvania Railroad. Roll went to college, learned Russian, did graduate work at Yale, and joined the CIA in 1949. He worked in Munich as chief of counterintelligence, parachuting émigrés into the Ukraine in the CIA's ill-fated Red Sox operation, then moved to the Soviet division as a counterintelligence officer. After serving as a chief of base in Libya, he applied for an opening on Angleton's staff. Given his strong counterintelligence background, he expected to get the job, but was rejected without explanation.

Roll remembered what he had been told by Peer de Silva, a fellow officer in the Soviet division. De Silva had sat on a promotion board that considered the name of Richard Kovich. There were comments around the table. When it was Angleton's turn to speak, de Silva said, he turned thumbs down on Kovich, saying: "We can't trust these Slavs."

Roll had realized that something was wrong. "I asked myself, why didn't I get better jobs? Why wasn't I given a promotion? Why was I rejected for the job on Angleton's staff? I can only assume it was because of Angleton, given his attitude toward Russian-speakers. They needed us, but didn't want us to get too high."

Other case officers despaired of proving that their careers had been affected by the search for penetrations. They may have suspected what went on, but producing the evidence was like chasing a will-o'-the-wisp.

Angleton loyalists made the opposite argument—that it was easy for mediocre officers whose careers had fizzled to blame it on the mole hunt. "Everybody denied a promotion said the mole hunt was the reason," Scotty Miler, Angleton's former deputy, contended.

But the fact remained that it was difficult to prove harm, and years later to pinpoint decisions made by unidentified bureaucrats whose reasons for shunting aside some officers may never have been committed to paper.

There was another even more basic problem that prevented many agents from taking advantage of the Mole Relief Act: most CIA officers placed on the SIG's list of "hard core" suspects were unaware of that fact. They did not realize that their careers were affected, because they were never told. Still others chose not to reopen old wounds; they had retired and did not care to fight the agency, or to go to the expense of hiring a lawyer to present their cases.

In the months of maneuvering that led to his financial settlement, Paul Garbler was also determined to find out more about how and why he had come under suspicion as a traitor. He understood that the main reason for his years of exile was the fact that he had been Sasha Orlov's case officer in Berlin—and that the mole hunters suspected that Orlov had recruited him.

But he could hardly believe the file of CIA documents, several inches thick, that he ultimately received from the agency under the Freedom of Information Act. Garbler was astonished to discover from the documents that he had also become a suspect because he had played tennis with George Blake.

"When I lived in Korea," Garbler said, "there was a British legation active until June of 1950. The minister was Sir Vivian Holt, one of few living holders of the Victoria Cross. Florence and I became friendly with Holt, who was an eccentric bachelor. He had two officers working for him, Sidney Faithful and George Blake. Up pops the devil. My next-door neighbor was an army major, and he and I played doubles with Faithful and Blake. When the North Koreans came south, Holt said, 'I'm not leaving; this is my legation and British soil. If I have to, I'll fight them with my sword.' He kept a sword over the mantel and brandished it frequently. So he and Faithful and Blake were taken and imprisoned. At least theoretically, that's when Blake was turned."[8]

To the counterintelligence mind, the fact that Garbler had been a tennis partner of George Blake took on ominous significance. The CI men, after all, were paid to perceive sinister patterns. Their occupa-

---

[8]"When Holt was released," Garbler said, "he came through Berlin, and Florence and I went out to Tempelhof to meet him. He was just passing through. He cried when he saw us. We cried a little bit. He told us Faithful and Blake were alive and well. Or as well as he was. He'd lost about fifty pounds; he looked haggard and wan."

tional weakness was that they might see those patterns even, as in Garbler's case, where they did not exist.[9]

To his dismay, Garbler also discovered from the documents that the CIA had asked the FBI to investigate him, his sex life, his bank accounts, even his parents. "The FBI never called me in," Garbler said. He no longer has his file. "After I got the documents from the CIA, I burned them in disgust around 1979 or 1980. I was made quite nauseous."

As he thought back on his case, Garbler was disturbed by the role of Richard Helms. Admittedly, Garbler had little use for Helms. He would see him in the basement gym where both went to run. Helms nodded but never spoke.

But why, Garbler wondered, had Helms never tried to help? "He must have known I was a loyal and capable officer. He should have known that I was a case officer who just wanted to serve the company and his country." But Helms had never intervened, Garbler said. "He left me swinging in the wind."

Late in 1977, Helms had been convicted in federal court of misleading Congress about the CIA's role in Chile. But to the agency's old boys, Helms was a hero for stonewalling. Like many former CIA officers, Garbler was a member of the Association of Former Intelligence Officers, based in McLean, Virginia. At an association lunch at nearby Fort Myer some months after Helms's court appearance and around the time Garbler got his CIA file, "when Helms walked in everyone rose and applauded. Some had tears in their eyes. The entire room was on their feet applauding for Helms." But not Paul Garbler.

"Why should I?" he asked. "He left me out there to rot."

---

[9]As it happened, George Blake had almost derailed Garbler's career for another, unrelated reason. In 1961, as Garbler was getting ready to go to Moscow, the CIA learned that Blake, who had been arrested in April, told British authorities that he had rifled the files of the MI6 officers who had talked with Garbler and other CIA representatives some months earlier about a CIA program to debrief tourists who traveled behind the Iron Curtain. The worldwide CIA operation was known as the "legal travel program." Blake, the CIA was told, transmitted all the information to the Soviets. Garbler recalled a confrontation with Sheffield Edwards, the director of the Office of Security at the time. "Sheff Edwards said, 'Y-y-you can't go to Moscow, you are known to the Soviets.' Sheff stuttered. Jack [Maury] and I argued with him. I said I'd waited all my life to go to Moscow. Also that the Blake operation would be so highly compartmented it would not circulate within the KGB. He finally gave in."

Chapter 19

Son of Sasha

In mid-April 1987, James Angleton had only a month to live when he granted an interview to David Binder of the *New York Times.* The former counterintelligence chief had been diagnosed as having lung cancer five months earlier, but he smoked filter cigarettes throughout the interview.[1]

Although Angleton had told the newspaper he would not discuss intelligence matters, he could not stay away from the subject of moles. It was clear that with time running out, Angleton consoled himself with the belief that he had at least identified one mole.

Although he did not reveal the man's name, it was equally clear that he was talking about Igor Orlov, who Angleton was convinced was Golitsin's "Sasha." There was a case, Angleton told Binder, where the Soviets had infiltrated a man into the CIA.

The article, paraphrasing Angleton's words, said, "In an elaborate ruse in WWII, he was parachuted behind German lines. . . . The Germans picked him up and made him into a double agent. But his true loyalty had remained with the Russians. After the war, he was employed by the C.I.A., working under cover in Soviet émigré organizations based in Berlin and was eventually taken on"—and here the

[1]David Binder, "A Counterspymaster's View: Assessing Intelligence Breaches," *New York Times,* April 10, 1987, p. A18.

article quoted Angleton directly—" 'as a full-fledged intelligence officer.' "[2]

Referring to Golitsin without naming him, Angleton said that a high-level KGB man had defected and alerted American counterintelligence, which became convinced that the CIA operative in question was a Soviet agent. Again paraphrasing Angleton, the interview continued: "Ultimately, through a number of clumsy bureaucratic actions, the suspect was able to avoid prosecution and, as far as Mr. Angleton knew, lived quietly in the Washington area. 'The man was a genius,' Mr. Angleton recalled with genuine professional respect."

The reference to "clumsy bureaucratic actions" may have been Angleton's way of saying that the FBI had been unable to build a case against, or arrest, Igor Orlov. Angleton's conviction of Orlov's guilt was undoubtedly reinforced by information provided to American intelligence in 1985 by the controversial defector Vitaly Yurchenko.

Yurchenko, a high-ranking KGB man in charge of operations in the United States and Canada, defected in August 1985. Before he redefected in November he provided a great deal of information to the CIA and the FBI, some of which proved accurate. Yurchenko identified Orlov as a Soviet agent. Moreover, in a statement that threw both agencies into a tailspin, he announced that Orlov had recruited one or more of his sons as a Soviet spy.

On Saturday, January 9, 1988, a whole new generation of FBI agents, none of whom remembered the investigation twenty-three years earlier, descended on the Gallery Orlov in Alexandria. Simultaneously, other FBI agents in Chicago and Boston fanned out and called on Orlov's two sons, George and Robert, in their suburban homes.

George Orlov, the younger of the two Orlov sons, remembered the agents coming to his home in Hinsdale, Illinois, that afternoon. A physicist and a nuclear engineer who once held a "Q" clearance, Orlov was working as a private consultant on nuclear power plants when the FBI came calling.

"They knocked on the door—the bell doesn't work—in the early afternoon," he said. "There were two agents, Vincente M. Rosado, he is Cuban, an ex-state trooper out West, and Steven Vass. They flash their ID, and announce, 'FBI. We'd like to talk to you.' "

[2]Orlov was never a CIA officer. He was always a contract employee of the agency.

"I've been expecting you," Orlov replied.[3]

"I invited them in and they said, 'We'd like to ask a few questions, but we'd rather not do it here. We have a place we'd like to take you.' We hop into their little blue Celica, drive to the Hyatt Regency in Oak Brook, and go to this nice suite. They had rented several suites.

"At the hotel they say they think I'm a Soviet agent. I said, 'Why am I working as a management consultant instead of in the technical field, missiles, something the Russians would be interested in?' " Both George and his brother, Robert, a computer expert, had graduated from the Massachusetts Institute of Technology, but in 1988 neither was engaged in defense work.

The FBI continued to question George Orlov. "They offer me lunch, I ordered up a Cobb salad. They say, 'There's something we have to show you.' So they showed me a transcript and said it was Yurchenko. They said it was a transcript of Yurchenko saying that my father had recruited my brother and myself.

"It was about five pages long. It said there's a Russian agent working for us, his name is Igor Orlov, he has a frame shop, he has two sons, both of whom went to schools in the Northeast, the sons are technically oriented, he recruited them, they're working for us. He gave vague descriptions of what Robert did and I did. He said that I travel a lot.[4]

"Then they played the tape. He [Yurchenko] spoke in broken English, very halting English, that's why they gave me the transcript, so I could hear it and follow along at same time. I don't know if it was Yurchenko, but they said it was.

"I don't know if my jaw dropped, but mentally my jaw dropped. I

[3]Orlov said he had been expecting the FBI because "they left a trail." The FBI ran a credit check, he said, and he discovered that when he applied for a mortgage; and "one day my mail came along with a Xerox copy of two pieces of mail addressed to me. So it was obvious somebody was copying my mail. Then two days later the actual pieces of mail came in. The third clue was my brother had noticed he was being followed. He ran a check on the license plates and found they were FBI vehicles. This was just a few weeks before."

[4]Igor Orlov had died six years earlier, and Yurchenko should have known this. Had he really spoken of Orlov as a current agent? "He said they have an agent in the U.S. with an art gallery," George Orlov replied, "but I don't remember whether he used the past or present tense. There was no doubt he was talking about us. I remember he did not say my father was no longer alive, he made no reference to that. He definitely did not say he is no longer working for us, or he has died. His grammar was not the best in the world, so it could be that explains it."

looked at them in disbelief. I said this guy is confused, this is a mistake. I'll do anything I can to clear it up."

The FBI agents then asked George why Yurchenko had made these statements. There were "maybe a couple of reasons," George told the FBI men. "To keep the FBI busy investigating a family that wasn't agents. Maybe to divert from real spies. I'd read a little bit about Angleton in the sixties, and I knew how a couple of words could tie us up in knots.

"They had questions. 'Why did I go to Canada in 1978?' 'To plan an experiment on a research reactor.' 'Why did I go running at the Institute for Advanced Studies at Princeton?' I was visiting my in-laws—they live in Princeton—in the mid-eighties. Apparently they followed me and found red and blue nylon strings tied to a fence post along the trail."

The FBI suspected that the nylon strings were signals that George Orlov had left for a Soviet agent. "They asked, 'You didn't put them there?' 'No.' 'You didn't know there was a Soviet scholar named so-and-so in one of the compounds?' 'No.' They said when I went for a run near Hinsdale, I crossed a bridge over a little creek, and they found some white chalk marks on the bridge. They had it chemically analyzed and figured it was surveyor's chalk, and since I was working on a construction site at the time at a nuclear power plant, they figured it was me. Of course, our surveyors use paint."

That was about the point in the interview when the FBI accused George of having received "the sign of life" from a KGB agent. It had happened when George came East and visited his mother. "I went running in Washington, and afterward I went up to the third floor of the gallery. They saw I came to the window wearing the same red jogging suit. They said they had traced some Russian spy out of the embassy who was walking up and down across the street and making the 'sign of life.' I said, 'What does that mean?' They explained that a sign of life was letting me know, 'We're around, we're still here.' They showed me the Russian's picture—had I ever seen him before? No. They thought my driving habits were suspicious. They thought that I kept losing them, a technique used by people who are professionally trained to lose tails. At the time I had a 911 Porsche Carrera and I was driving it fast. I was not aware that I was being followed.

"They asked me if my father was a spy. I said I didn't know. They showed me a lot of pictures of people they believed had come into the gallery—did I know these people? I said no."

More than two decades after the FBI had first searched the gallery, "they were still trying to uncover people who had visited the gallery. They asked, 'Who were his friends, who were his acquaintances?' Basically, they said they are still looking today for people who might have been associated with my father or who my father might have converted, turned. They firmly believed I was a Russian agent. My father had converted me."

The FBI also questioned George Orlov about a trip he had made to San Diego, the headquarters of Science Applications, Inc., where he had worked seven years earlier. "They do management of defense contracts. They were prime contractors for SDI, the Star Wars program, in the early 1980s."

The FBI had little choice, of course, but to take Yurchenko's information seriously. An important defector, the KGB official in charge of North America, had said that Igor Orlov, the man at the very heart of the CIA mole hunt two decades earlier, was a Soviet agent and had recruited one or more of his sons. Once Yurchenko had made that statement, the FBI was obliged to follow up by interviewing Orlov's sons.

Nor was the FBI's concern about George Orlov's previous work surprising, since after graduating from MIT in 1977 he worked for a time for a defense contractor who was developing instruments to measure the accuracy of ballistic missiles.[5]

After playing the Yurchenko tape and questioning George Orlov, the FBI agents asked if he would be willing to take a lie-detector test. Orlov agreed. "We went into another room, where they bring out two experts from Washington. They hooked me up and started asking questions. Did I speak Russian? I said, '*Da, nyet,* maybe *do svidaniya.*' I don't speak Russian at all. They asked eight questions over and over again in various order. 'Is your name George Orlov? Are you working for the Soviet government? Did you ever give secrets to the Russians?'

---

[5]"We were looking for ways to measure the ablation of nose cones as they reentry," he said. "The burning off of the nose cone material. You want to know the shape of the nose cone because it will tell you the course of the reentry vehicle. You will know your CEP [Circular Error Probable, a measure of ballistic-missile accuracy]. The better you know the shape, the more accurate the reentry vehicle."

'No.' One question I took issue with: 'Did your father recruit you?' They asked me that over and over again. I said, 'No.' It took an hour and a half. They told me I passed on seven of the eight questions. They got an anomalous response on 'did my father recruit me.' I told them the question was insulting to me. My father wouldn't do that, if he loved me, he obviously wouldn't do that. He had always told me, 'Don't get involved with the government, with the CIA. The American CIA are a bunch of no-good, unprofessional people.' He said they are a bunch of kids right out of prep school, 'cowboys without honor.' When he found I had applied to the Defense Intelligence Agency after college, he said, 'You don't want to work for them, or any of the intelligence services.'

"Recruiting me—you can't be a loving father if you recruit your own children and put them in harm's way. It pissed me off. [FBI agent] Rosado had told me his father escaped Castro's Cuba. I said to him, 'How would you like it if I told you your father was a Commie and said your father recruited you to work for Castro.' He said, 'I'd be pretty pissed off.' They said they would take the results back to Washington and they would be in contact.

"We went to dinner that night. They were playing good guy, bad guy. Rosado was the good guy, he seemed honestly friendly. After all the things they thought I was doing, I think they realized I wasn't a big bad Soviet agent. At first, they were ready to lock me up and throw away the key."

His father, George Orlov said, "voted for Nixon. He was a conservative as far as conversation around the dinner table went. He worked twelve to sixteen hours a day. He believed people should work for what they get, no handouts. How Republican can you get? My wife is a Harvard-educated liberal and I'm a conservative. I'm to the right of Attila the Hun."

Igor Orlov, George said, had never spoken to him of the Soviet Union. "He never talked about his life there, or about the war. To this day I don't know who my grandparents were on my father's side. I haven't seen it, but my mother told me I have a false birth certificate, doctored by the CIA. That I was born under a false name.

"I'm not going to tell you my father is or isn't a spy, but I don't know. In 1963 I was six years old and had no reason to believe he was a spy. I had no reason to believe he was a spy anytime after that. He seldom left the shop, he never met with anyone. I know he had very few friends—he was almost a recluse. I didn't see him recruiting people, I didn't see him trying to cultivate people."

Robert Orlov, who lived with his wife in Sudbury, Massachusetts, declined to comment on the FBI interview, but Richard Laurent, a close friend who grew up in Alexandria with him, said he had visited Robert around the time of the FBI inquiry. He described Robert as "pretty mad" because the investigation was taking up a lot of time and energy.

He remembered that Robert Orlov had been suspicious of a nearby vacant house, apparently believing he was being watched from it. Laurent said Robert turned up the stereo so they could talk. "He thought they might have a directional mike."

Robert Orlov told him some of the questions the FBI had asked, Laurent said. " 'Isn't it true you're a photographer?' 'Yes.' 'Isn't it true you're a pilot?' 'Yes.' 'Then what's to stop you from taking pictures over Portsmouth Naval Base in New Hampshire?'

"They kept asking him the same questions over and over again. At one point, he told them, 'It's no wonder the Walkers and the Pollards did so well, because you wasted this time going after me instead of the real spies.' "

For Eleonore Orlov, the FBI visit in 1988 was, in the immortal words of Yogi Berra, *déjà vu* all over again. By now, she was an experienced hand at FBI investigations. "They came on Saturday, January 9, 1988, about five P.M.," she said. "There were two FBI agents, they gave me their cards, Stephanie P. Gleason and Charles K. Sciarini. The woman was twenty-five and the man was maybe twenty-nine. There were very young, friendly. They showed up and said what Yurchenko said, and I couldn't believe it. They had no warrant. They asked to search the house." The agents, she recalled, said they were looking for "a lot of money, and some equipment. A shortwave radio transmitter. I said the only radio we had was a Grundig and it was burned in the fire. We had a fire in January of 1987.

"They tried to dig up the backyard. They asked, 'Did your husband ever dig in the backyard? What did he dig for?' I said by a tree, for burying our cat. 'Where?' I said, 'Look, it's just a dead cat.' It was already eleven o'clock at night. They searched for five hours, opened all the drawers, found his wallet, credit cards, and took everything with them. They took a binder with my husband's English lessons. A grammar book. They left at midnight."

Her son George had called from Chicago the next morning to report his FBI visit. "Georgie said, 'Tell them everything you know about Papa. You know what they can do with me. They can put me in prison and throw away the key for twelve years and no one would ever hear from me.'

"When the FBI came to see Robert," Mrs. Orlov continued, "he said, 'Do you guys have a warrant? No? Make an appointment.' 'We can come in now,' they said, 'it's a matter of national security.' They stopped him outside his house. 'Let's call my congressman,' he said. No answer. He had just come back from sledding with his daughter."

On Sunday morning, Eleonore Orlov called her old friend Fred Tansey, the former FBI agent. "I called Mr. Tansey and said, 'I don't think these people are for real—can you find out if they are real FBI agents?' He was here in five minutes. He said, 'Come in my car.' We drove for two hours in his car. He said, 'The best thing is to call the two agents and talk more. You have to convince them the children are not agents. Forget your husband, whatever he did he paid ten thousand times.' He called the FBI on his car phone. It was Sunday and he asked for Gleason and Sciarini. Both were in church, but they were beeped and called him back, and he said, 'I'm a friend of Eleonore Orlov and I'm sitting here in the parking lot of the courthouse in Alexandria in a black car. Please meet me there. And show me your ID.'

"In half an hour, Sciarini came in a big station wagon with the baby seat still there. He got out and said, 'I'm Sciarini and I'm working for the FBI.' Tansey said, 'If you ever go in their house, she will sue you. You ruined their business. You did this twenty-five years ago. If you would like to talk to Mrs. Orlov, go to a hotel or anyplace, but not her house.'

"They made a reservation for the Holiday Inn. I went to the hotel. Gleason and Sciarini met us there and they started asking me about Berlin, who I met, and they started showing me pictures. They showed me a lot of pictures of people, did you meet this guy or that guy. They showed me pictures of both Kozlov and Mrs. Kozlov. After all those years I didn't recognize them. I had worked with her in the censorship office, but that was thirty years ago. They wanted to know a lot about Kozlov. I only knew my husband hated him, that's all I could say.

"They came back on Tuesday to the basement and went through the children's things. They came back in blue jeans—I warned them the basement was full of soot and oil, from the fire. They went through games, toys. They packed everything in big cartons. I'm a citizen since '76. Sasha became a citizen in 1971, approximately. They said, 'We don't need a search warrant. This is a matter of national security.'

"It was eerie. It was like a bad dream. They asked if my husband did carpentry during the restoring of the house. He could have put in some secret compartments. I asked, 'Could he? For what?' 'For the money he got from the Russians.' They said they were looking for a place where Sasha could hide hundreds of thousands of dollars. I said, 'Let's search for it. May I help you? For whom did he hide it? He would have told me, he knew he was dying.'

"They came to the gallery twice a week for three months. The FBI found no money, no secret compartments, no clues. Finally, I agreed to a polygraph. They got me—they said, 'If you do a lie-detector test for us we will leave your boys alone for twenty years.' 'And if I don't?' They just smiled. But I got the message.

"Thirty years ago, when I took the polygraph in Germany, before I started the letter-translating business they gave me one. It was the first time I worked for the CIA. The CIA asked sex questions which bothered me. So I made one condition, no sex questions."

The polygraph took place in the Morrison House, an Alexandria hotel. "There was a polygraph operator from New York and Gleason and Sciarini. The polygraph took place in the bedroom, five hours, from six to eleven P.M. Gleason and Sciarini were in the living room. They asked twenty-seven questions. 'Was your husband a spy for Soviets? Did he have connections with KGB?' And so on. 'Why did Robert take flying lessons?' I said, 'He liked it.' "

And then, as suddenly as it had begun, it was over. The FBI faded away, and the Orlov sons resumed their normal lives. Eleonore went back to running the gallery. It kept her busy, but sometimes at dusk, when the last customer had gone, and there were only the cats to keep her company, she had time to wonder whether she would ever know the truth about the man she had met on streetcar No. 8 in Schwabing a lifetime ago.

James Angleton never lived to see the second unsuccessful investigation of Sasha, his nemesis. On the morning of May 11, 1987, he died of lung cancer at Sibley Memorial Hospital in Washington at the age of sixty-nine.

He was mourned by his friends, if not by his enemies. But even those who admired him the most, and there were many, seemed to realize that his obsession with moles and his fascination with Anatoly Golitsin had become a fatal flaw.

Rolfe Kingsley, who had taken over the Soviet division at the height of the mole hunt, had valued his close relationship with Angleton and admired him personally as a Renaissance man. But even Kingsley saw Angleton's limits. "Jim was one of the most brilliant officers I've ever worked with until Golitsin appeared," he said. "I won't say any more."

Mrs. Angleton shared Kingsley's view. She told a former CIA station chief, who had known her husband well, that in part she blamed Richard Helms: "The worst thing that happened to Jim was Golitsin. Why didn't Dick take him away from him?"

They held the memorial service on Friday, May 15, at the Rock Spring Congregational Church in Arlington. There were hymns and scripture readings, and the poet Reed Whittemore, Angleton's old friend and Yale roommate, gave a reading from T. S. Eliot. The closing hymn was "My Country, 'Tis of Thee."

Daniel Schorr, who had interviewed Angleton for four hours thirteen years earlier and had had some contact with the former counterintelligence chief since then, decided to attend the service. He was struck by the fact that no one had spoken about Angleton's life and work.

Walking up the aisle afterward, Schorr remarked, to no one in particular, "Gee, there was no eulogy."

Someone in front of Schorr turned around and snapped: "It's classified."

Chapter 20

Triumph

Peter Karlow never gave up hope.

Although forced out of the CIA at the age of forty-two, his intelligence career destroyed by the mole hunt, he continued to try to clear his name. It was a slow and frustrating process, and he received no encouragement from Langley.

In the 1970s, Karlow had several conversations with James Angleton after the counterintelligence chief had been fired. Karlow believed that James Angleton held the key; if he could somehow get Angleton to open up, some of the mists might clear away. Twice he had been able to speak with Angleton when they were both still in the agency. It was in Angleton's office that the counterintelligence chief had warned Karlow not to discuss his case with anyone. In a later encounter in the hall, Karlow tried again.

"I said, 'I've been asking more and more questions about this and there is nothing that ties what this defector said to me.' Angleton reacted strongly and said, 'Don't talk to anybody about this—it's too secret.' I said, 'I'm keeping my own bigot list of who I have talked to, and you're welcome to see it.' He said okay. But he never asked for it."

Soon after Angleton was dismissed in 1974, Karlow encountered him at a Georgetown cocktail party. The two men chatted about the past. "At the party, he said I was the prime suspect." Karlow saw

Angleton again at a reception at the embassy of South Africa. Karlow suggested lunch, and somewhat to his surprise, Angleton agreed.

They met at L'Escargot, a small, out-of the-way French restaurant on upper Connecticut Avenue that was one of Angleton's favorites. "He said to me again, 'You were the prime suspect.' I said, 'How is it possible for a Soviet defector to knock out a staff officer of the CIA? Why don't we do something like that to the KGB? With a simple rumor.' I assumed Golitsin was running down and came up with me. Something to keep interest alive in him."

To Karlow, Angleton appeared to have a guilty conscience, but he admitted nothing. "Angleton never expressed any regret. He took the position it wasn't his doing. He said he never recommended my being fired. It was not something he had control over. He explained it was better from a CI viewpoint not to fire a suspect, but to keep him in place. He said the problem was I had become a security case."

This was pure double-talk, since the counterintelligence chief and the Office of Security worked hand in glove. OS had seized upon trivial security violations to make a case against Karlow because Angleton suspected he was a Soviet agent. If the CIA could not prove Karlow a spy, they would push him out the door on lesser grounds. He would be hung for a sheep.[1]

Karlow's meetings with Angleton were extraordinary, mole hunter and quarry, both fired by the CIA, sparring over the *pâté maison*. But this was no Stockholm syndrome at work; Karlow had known Angleton for years, and had tried to help him develop ways of detecting Soviet bugging devices. One night in the late 1950s, Angleton had come to Karlow's house for dinner to discuss espionage equipment. Karlow's wife, Libby, gave up at midnight and retired, but Karlow and Angleton kept at it until four in the morning, when the counterintelligence chief finally went home.

By questioning Angleton, Karlow was trying to gather evidence to help his case; perhaps somehow he could still clear his name. At a

[1] A former CIA officer familiar with the case speculated that Karlow had been dismissed on "security" grounds because the agency had feared embarrassment if it became known publicly that Karlow had been wiretapped without cause. "They had a tap on Karlow," he said, "and it was alleged he and his mother talked about classified matters. But this was stuff they didn't want to bring into a court of law. The legal department stonewalled and didn't want any of this aired. They never had anything against Peter except these minor indiscretions, the telephone chatter."

second lunch at a restaurant in Alexandria, Virginia, "we went further into the same thing. We were talking like two ships that cross in the night. I was interested in getting a handle on this thing for my purposes and Jim was providing me with nothing that I felt I could use.

"Angleton confirmed the business about letter K. He told me it was logical that I was the person—I was in Germany, my name began with K, I'd been in East Berlin, I had access to just about everything."

But there was one key fact that Angleton neglected to disclose. Karlow did not know that he had also come under suspicion of leaking to the Soviets the CIA's efforts to copy the bug found in the seal in the American embassy in Moscow. Nor did he know that Angleton had been informed by Peter Wright, of MI5, that the source of that leak was George Blake. The information from MI5 would have exonerated Karlow of this allegation, but Angleton never disclosed it, at the lunch or any other time.[2]

Karlow pressed the former CI chief. How could it all have happened? How could so many officers have fallen under false suspicion? "He said, 'There was literally panic when Golitsin said there was a mole. We were under so much pressure after Burgess and Maclean.' "[3]

At the time of these encounters with Angleton, Karlow was back in Washington as international affairs director for Monsanto. At first, after he was fired by the CIA, it had not been easy for Karlow, who had a wife and two children to support. Often it is difficult for officers in the Clandestine Services to make the transition to the private sector. Since their work has been secret, there is the delicate problem of what to put down on their résumé.

---

[2]After Blake confessed, Sir Dick White, the head of MI6, came to Washington with a damage report on the Blake case that omitted the fact that Blake had told the Soviets about the work on the bug by the CIA and the British. But later Peter Wright tipped off Angleton that Blake had confessed to this. The CIA believed that the KGB requirements circular that Golitsin brought with him when he defected, and which revealed Soviet knowledge of the CIA research, was based on the information Blake gave to the KGB. A former CIA man who knew the story said, "Jim had knowledge it was Blake, not Karlow. He acquired this information from Peter Wright *after* Karlow had been fired and sat on the information and never revealed it. The horrific thing was, Jim knew that Karlow had been wrongly treated and suppressed that information and didn't do anything about it."

[3]Interestingly, Angleton, in explaining the pressure, never mentioned Philby, who was far more important than Burgess or Maclean. It may have been too painful, since Philby had been Angleton's regular luncheon partner in Washington but was never detected as a Soviet agent by the CIA counterintelligence chief.

"After scratching around for a year, I got a job with Monsanto," Karlow said. "The job paid better than the government, there were stock options, promotion after six months." Karlow worked for Monsanto in St. Louis for several years, and in 1970 the company sent him to Washington. As an executive of a Fortune 500 company, Karlow prospered.

But the improvement in his bank account hardly erased the painful memory of his departure from the CIA. His wife, Libby, had died in 1976, not knowing how the story would end.

Karlow retired from Monsanto but stayed on in Washington as an international business consultant. Determined to clear his name, he began talking to lawyers, including an old friend from the OSS, Edwin J. "Ned" Putzell, Jr. "I had to get at the root of what happened," Karlow said. "Who had it in for me, what had really gone on."

In September 1980, Karlow applied for his entire CIA file under both the Privacy Act and the Freedom of Information Act. When the Mole Relief Act passed in October, Karlow got wind of it. Two months later, on December 18, Putzell wrote to Admiral Turner formally filing a claim under the new law. And Karlow and his attorney met with CIA officials to press his case.

But, as it happened, the one-year window that opened in October 1980 for claimants under the Mole Relief Act spanned two administrations. In January 1981, with the inauguration of President Reagan, a new team took over the CIA. Karlow's case ended up on the desk of William J. Casey.

The new CIA director asked his general counsel, Stanley Sporkin, to check into the matter. Secretly, a special three-man panel was convened, including Sporkin, to review the case. In a memorandum to Casey, Sporkin concluded that the facts placed Karlow's case "on a different footing" from those of Kovich and Garbler, who had been granted compensation.[4]

The Sporkin memo went on to review what supposedly had occurred. In December 1961, the memo said, a KGB defector—Golitsin—had reported that the Soviets had penetrated the CIA. "The

---

[4]"Serge Peter Karlow—Request for Relief Under Section 405 of Public Law 96-450 ('Mole Relief Act')," memorandum, Stanley Sporkin, CIA general counsel, to Director of Central Intelligence William J. Casey, August 21, 1981.

defector was not able to provide a positive identification of this 'mole,' but the descriptive data provided by the defector fit Mr. Karlow to such an extent that he came under serious suspicion and an extensive investigation of Mr. Karlow followed. The investigation did not result in the conclusion that Mr. Karlow was the mole. . . ."

Then came the bombshell in the secret memo. Since Karlow had not been proved to be the mole, Sporkin wrote, it might appear he was entitled to compensation. "However, information developed during the course of the investigation of Mr. Karlow led to the decision that he must be dismissed on security grounds quite apart from the fact that he had been accused . . . of being the mole."[5] The panel, Sporkin added, had concluded that Karlow's claim should be denied.

The agency had trotted out the same old shopworn goods—Karlow had been unclear about his father's birthplace, he had been vague about where he had traveled on certain dates, he had left his safe open, and so on.

But official records often fail to give a complete picture. For Sporkin and the other CIA officers reviewing the files almost two decades later, it may have been difficult to grasp the truth—that once Karlow was tarred as a mole suspect, the agency had been determined to get rid of him come what may. If it could not prove he was a traitor, then other grounds would do. A senior CIA officer who knew what had happened in 1963 declared, "They used the security material to frame Karlow with this chickenshit stuff."

Karlow as yet knew nothing of the Sporkin memo. In October 1981, after the one-year window had slammed shut, Casey wrote to Karlow explaining why his claim had been turned down. Karlow remarried that year—his new wife, Carolyn, was a respected college administrator—and he engaged Stanley Gaines, who had successfully represented Richard Kovich, to carry on the fight.

Gaines tried to convince the Senate Intelligence Committee that justice had miscarried in Karlow's case, but he was too late; the agency had persuaded the committee's staff that there were sound, albeit murky and elusive, reasons for rejecting his client's claim.

Karlow, normally a temperate man, now let his frustration boil over. "There is a deliberate concealment or frame-up here," he told

[5]*Ibid.*

Gaines. The agency, Karlow added, was "making me a scapegoat for something."[6]

In October 1986, Karlow got his first break. By now, he and Carolyn had moved to northern California, where he continued to work as an international business consultant. Back in Washington to attend an OSS symposium, Karlow gave a speech to his wartime colleagues. So did Casey, who had served in the OSS in London.

Afterward, the two men had a chance to chat. "Casey came up to me and we talked," Karlow remembered, "and he said, 'What the hell is going on with your case?' "

Volatile, quick-tempered, and mercurial, Casey was nevertheless an approachable man, and for all of his flaws, he did not have a closed mind. Within days of his conversation with Karlow, Casey personally ordered the case reopened. He telephoned Karlow in California and asked him to work with the agency's new general counsel, David Doherty, to prepare new recommendations to compensate Karlow. At the same time, the floodgates opened; more than 150 documents dealing with his case were suddenly declassified and released to Karlow.

But there was one crucial fact that the CIA had never disclosed to Karlow, and it dared not reveal it now. In 1963, Peter Karlow had been cleared by the FBI.

The former FBI agent in charge of the investigation confirmed this. "The agents who questioned Karlow," said Courtland J. Jones, "felt he was not the person described by Golitsin. Both FBI men who questioned him were top-notch." Maurice "Gook" Taylor and Aubrey "Pete" Brent had been tough and unrelenting in their five-day interrogation. But they came away convinced of Karlow's innocence. Jones was sure of it because he remembered Taylor's reaction. "I recalled Gook saying how good he felt that he had cleared a man who had been painted guilty." Jones added: "Our inquiry cleared Karlow."[7]

According to Jones, a report would normally have been sent by the

[6]Letter, Peter Karlow to Stanley H. Gaines, September 23, 1982.
[7]Not only was Karlow cleared by the FBI, he passed the polygraph test that the bureau had administered during his five days of interrogation. Alexander W. Neale, Jr., the case agent who handled the Karlow inquiry, said, "The results of the polygraph did not reveal any facts that would indicate the man's guilt." So the lie-detector test showed that Karlow was innocent? "You can take it a step farther," Neale replied, "and say he was innocent."

Washington Field Office of the FBI, which conducted the interview, to headquarters, and from there to the CIA. And was that done in the Karlow case? "Of course," Jones replied. No such document was ever released to Karlow by either agency.

Under the Freedom of Information Act, Karlow did finally obtain Sporkin's memo, which shocked him when he was finally able to read it. It was the first he had learned of the CIA's spurious claim that he had been forced out for any reason other than the mole charges. The 1963 memo written by Lawrence R. Houston, the CIA's lawyer, when Karlow was pushed out, said just the opposite—that although Karlow had not been shown to be the mole, his usefulness was over because of that accusation. To Karlow's dismay, the CIA initially could not even find Houston's memo. It was lost in a sea of paper.

At the request of the general counsel, Karlow wrote a detailed rebuttal of the Sporkin memo and the old charges. As the CIA lawyers went over the case once more, they quickly perceived that the minor "security" matters that had been developed during the course of the mole investigation were not, in fact, the real reason that Karlow had been asked to resign. The agency had made a mistake, it now realized, in rejecting Karlow's claim under the Mole Relief Act.

But there was a problem: the one year law had expired five years earlier. The CIA had no legal authority to compensate Karlow.

Moreover, Karlow's case was soon swept aside by the tidal wave of Iran-Contra. In the very month that Casey had ordered the Karlow case reopened, the arms-for-hostages scandal was coming down around his ears. By November, the incredible facts had emerged: Ronald Reagan, staunch opponent of Iran and the Ayatollah Khomeini, had secretly provided arms to that country in the hope of gaining the release of American hostages, and millions in profits from the arms sales had been illegally diverted to support the Contras in Nicaragua. White House aide Oliver North, the Marine lieutenant colonel at the center of the scandal, became a household name. For the Reagan administration, Casey, and the CIA, it was a disaster.

Casey was in his office on December 15 preparing for another appearance on Iran-Contra before the Senate Intelligence Committee when he suffered a seizure. He was operated on for a malignant brain tumor and never returned to work. He died on May 6, 1987, five days before the death of James Angleton.

Robert M. Gates, the deputy director of the CIA, had become

acting CIA director when Casey underwent surgery, and on February 2, Reagan nominated him to be director. But Gates, who had also played a role in the arms-for-hostages scandal—and had helped to keep Congress in the dark about it—faced a bruising confirmation fight in the Senate. In March, Gates withdrew and Reagan nominated FBI director William H. Webster as the new CIA chief.[8]

For Karlow, the chain of events touched off soon after his promising encounter with Casey at the OSS meeting in October must have had a why-do-these-things-happen-to-me? impact. The timing of Iran-Contra was a cruel joke. "They were going to make a settlement with me," Karlow said. "After Casey died, Gates didn't want to pick it up. Webster stalled."

But after Webster, a former federal judge, had settled into the CIA, he took another look. "Webster brought a group of aides from the FBI," Karlow said. "They went over my case and Webster agreed I'd been screwed."

The agency's lawyers worked out an amount of damages that they felt Karlow was owed for having his career unjustly destroyed twenty-five years earlier. And they solved the problem of how to pay the money. They would quietly ask Congress to pass the Mole Relief Act all over again, just for Peter Karlow.

On September 15, 1988, the House and Senate passed the Intelligence Authorization Act for fiscal 1989. Buried in its provisions was Section 501 (a), which contained language identical to that of the 1980 Mole Relief Act. Two weeks later, President Reagan signed the bill.[9] The Mole Relief Act of 1988 was now law.

The press failed to notice the obscure provision or to uncover for whom the law had been passed. Since the CIA did not provide any public notice of the new law, or attempt to contact ex-employees who might have been affected, no other victim of the mole hunt came forward.

William Webster approved the settlement. Early in 1989, Peter Karlow flew to Washington. At CIA headquarters, in the general counsel's office, he was handed a check for close to $500,000.

Karlow declined to discuss numbers; all he would say was: "It was

[8]President Bush nominated Gates on May 14, 1991, to succeed Webster. The Senate, after lengthy hearings and renewed controversy over Gates, confirmed him on November 5.
[9]Public Law 100-453, signed by the President on September 29, 1988.

under a million." Karlow drove back to downtown Washington to try to find a bank where he could deposit the check. Ironically, perhaps, he found himself on K Street, the city's main business thoroughfare.

"It was a funny feeling to stand on K Street at three P.M. with a check that size in your hand and what do you do with it?" Karlow found a bank. "Fortunately," he said, "it was open until four P.M." The bank was happy to take the money.

The payment was nice, but, Karlow said, "There is no way to compensate for being called a traitor, and kept in that position for twenty years." He wanted something "to hang on the wall," some visible symbol of his vindication. Webster agreed. Karlow was invited to come back to Langley in the spring.

The CIA wanted to give him a medal.

Chapter 21

The Legacy

■

As he looked back on the era of the mole hunt, Richard Helms had no regrets. It was warm in his office in downtown Washington, but he preferred to keep on the jacket of his exquisitely tailored suit as he talked.

Angleton may have been the point man, but it was Helms who had presided over the period of the mole hunt, first as the deputy director for plans from 1962 and then as the Director of Central Intelligence from 1966 to 1973. Little of importance could have occurred during that period without his personal approval. Helms knew.

In retrospect, what did he think of the handling of the mole investigation? It had to be done, Helms said. "One of the real nightmares the DCI lives with is that someone is going to walk into his office and say, 'We found a penetration.' Any director worthy of his stripes is bound to pay attention to allegations and to try to run them down. We had to check these things out. I felt it then, and now.

"When I was director, I refused to sign off on getting rid of anybody until it was clearly demonstrated that they were indeed a penetration." But, he conceded, some officers had been "put on a siding while the allegations were being checked out.

"What are you going to do with these people in the meantime? You can't hang them from the ceiling. When these cases came forward it was Angleton who raised the possibilities, but investigations had to be conducted by OS, not by Angleton."

How many CIA officers had been investigated? "I don't know the numbers," Richard Helms said.

And no one was found?

"Not that I'm aware of."

Any large organization rests on trust, or it could not function. Among its members, there is a presumption of loyalty to the organization, to their common goals, and to each other. As Robert T. Crowley, the veteran Clandestine Services officer, put it graphically, "In operations you have to ask, 'Would I want this guy on my air hose at two hundred feet?' "

The CIA, too, rests on trust, but assumes betrayal. That is its continuing dilemma.

The era of the mole hunt brought into sharp relief the potential threat posed to any organization that has built into its basic structure a powerful unit in charge of suspecting everyone. A Department of Paranoia, as it were.

James Angleton, who directed the agency's counterintelligence for two decades, devoted the last thirteen years of his career to finding "the mole" or moles in the agency. Angleton was the CIA's Captain Ahab, endlessly pursuing the great white whale. He never even got close enough to throw a harpoon.

It is tempting but too easy to say that Angleton was paranoid. By the dictionary definition, a paranoid is "characterized by oversuspiciousness, grandiose delusions, or delusions of persecution."[1]

Yet it is hard, and perhaps unfair, to make the case that Angleton was paranoid. His suspicions had a rational basis. There *were* moles and traitors in other intelligence agencies, notably MI6. Even in the CIA, moles and traitors would surface (although none of the CIA cases took place, or at least were discovered, until after Angleton left the agency). Some cases may remain unpublicized, because the CIA preferred it that way, but the known list is long enough:

Edwin Gibbons Moore II, a former CIA officer who had hundreds of classified documents in his home, and offered them to the Soviets for $200,000. Convicted and sentenced to fifteen years imprisonment in 1977.

[1] *Webster's New World Dictionary of the American Language,* Second College Edition (Cleveland: William Collins Publishers, 1980), p. 1030.

William P. Kampiles, a former CIA watch officer, who received $3,000 from the Soviets for a copy of the manual for the KH-11 spy satellite. Convicted and sentenced in 1978 to forty years.

David Barnett, a former CIA case officer in Indonesia, who sold agency secrets to the Soviets for $92,600. Pleaded guilty to espionage in 1980 and sentenced to eighteen years.

Karl F. Koecher, a CIA contract employee who worked as a translator from 1973 to 1975 while an agent of Czech intelligence. Arrested in 1984, pleaded guilty to espionage, and traded in an East-West exchange of prisoners in 1986.

Sharon M. Scranage, a CIA clerk in Ghana, who passed agency secrets to her lover, an agent of the Ghanaian intelligence service. Arrested in 1985, pleaded guilty to revealing classified information, and sentenced to five years.

Larry Wu-Tai Chin, a former CIA broadcasting analyst who passed secrets to Chinese intelligence for thirty-three years, for which he received about $140,000. Arrested in 1985, convicted the following year, and committed suicide in February 1986 while in jail and awaiting sentence.

Edward Lee Howard, a CIA case officer about to be sent to Moscow when he failed a polygraph test and was fired. Howard then sold the secrets of the CIA's operations in Moscow to the KGB and put the money he received in a secret Swiss bank account containing upwards of $150,000; he buried an additional $10,000 in the New Mexico desert. Escaped from the FBI in 1985 and was granted asylum in the Soviet Union.

The list is sufficient evidence that moles and traitors exist, and logically must be pursued and, if at all possible, detected. "Today," Sam Papich insisted, "we have moles in every agency, including the FBI. We'd be stupid if we don't think so."

But like so much in a democratic system, rooting out spies requires a delicate balance between security and liberty. The CIA is not exempt from due process. It is part of the American government. The agency is free to practice its full range of black arts against other nations, subject to certain minimal presidential and congressional restrictions, but logically it cannot—at least when dealing with its own officers—operate outside the democratic norms of the system it professes to defend. It cannot, without great cost, trample on the values it was created to protect.

If Angleton was brilliant, as his admirers claim, he was also warped, as his detractors maintain, a tortured and twisted man who saw conspiracy and deception as the natural order of things. His mind, and his universe, was a hopeless bramble of false trails and switchbacks, an intricate maze to nowhere. He was, in the end, truly lost in a "wilderness of mirrors."

A former case officer, a white-bearded, wise old owl who left the agency years ago to settle in the foothills of the Colorado Rockies, perhaps put it best:

"The wilderness? More people found their way into it than out of it. There is something inhuman about the CI mind, and the manipulation of human beings. It's always tempting for a counterintelligence officer to take a case and double it back. That leads you into the wilderness."

The old case officer added: "Much of the trouble we get into is due to stupidity rather than to evil design, sabotage, or treason. Normally it's stupidity.

"If you have good control over CI, and it works, that's fine. If it doesn't, it ought to be stopped. I'm not even saying that it should be stopped if it damages careers. Those are casualties of war."

He gazed out the window, toward the nearby mountains. A breeze was rippling the trees. "There must be control over Angletons," he said. "We can't afford to run the risk of getting the whole outfit screwed up. Angleton went over the line."

A former chief of the Soviet division, although he had admired Angleton personally, agreed. Guarding against penetration was "absolutely basic," he said, but it was a question of the methods used. "It's a matter of dealing with facts, not theories. If you're going to move, you have to have hard evidence."

But the basic conflict between trust and betrayal that gave rise to the mole hunt inside the CIA was larger than any one individual. The problem was, and is, endemic.

Angleton, after all, exercised great power under five directors—Walter Bedell Smith, Allen Dulles, John McCone, William Raborn, and Richard Helms. Angleton could not have amassed and wielded that power unless the CIA as an institution wanted him to do so. Angleton operated in a supportive environment, not in a vacuum.

The mole hunt in the CIA destroyed the careers of loyal officers, shattered lives and families, and paralyzed the agency, bringing to a halt its operations against the Soviet Union at a time—during the height of the Cold War—when those operations were the CIA's *raison d'être.*

Leonard V. McCoy, the reports officer in the Soviet division who later became deputy chief of the reorganized CI Staff, said as much in an article circulated privately among former CIA employees. He wrote: "The negative effect of the Golitsyn era on our Soviet operational management was in fact devastating—the inevitable culmination of a long-standing belief that CIA could not have a *bona fide* Soviet operation. Potential cases were turned down, ongoing operations were judged to be deception operations (including Penkovskiy), and defectors who gave information supporting Nosenko . . . were judged to have been dispatched by the KGB."[2]

Another veteran CIA officer, F. Mark Wyatt, in a review of a BBC film about the Nosenko case, put it even more succinctly: "Because of this case and its many ramifications, careers had been ruined, operations against the Soviet Union paralyzed, and relations with several friendly intelligence services crippled."[3]

The mole hunt spread to several other Western allies, touching off a particularly destructive and inconclusive search for traitors at the top levels of British intelligence. It claimed innocent victims in other countries, such as Norway's Ingeborg Lygren. And it created a climate of fear in the CIA.

It was not an unfamiliar atmosphere. Senator Joseph R. McCarthy's hunt for Communists in the American government flourished in the early 1950s. What happened inside the CIA in the 1960s paralleled the McCarthyism that had taken poisonous root in America a decade earlier. That in itself was ironic, since the CIA had been one of the Wisconsin senator's targets in his destructive witch-hunt. It was almost as though the CIA, insulated by its walls of secrecy, was caught in a time warp, experiencing its own witch-hunt several years after that in the larger society.[4]

[2]Leonard V. McCoy, "Yuriy Nosenko, CIA," *CIRA Newsletter,* Vol. XII, No. 3 (Fall 1987), published by Central Intelligence Retirees' Association, p. 20.
[3]Mark Wyatt, "Yuri Nosenko, KGB," *CIRA Newsletter,* Vol. XI, No. 4 (Winter 1986/1987), p. 11.
[4]It is perhaps of passing historical interest to note that Senator McCarthy was condemned by the Senate, 67–22, on December 2, 1954, eighteen days before James J. Angleton became chief of counterintelligence.

Like a speeding locomotive with no brakes, the mole hunt had gathered a momentum of its own until, inevitably, it went completely off the rails.

The "war of the defectors," the conflict over Golitsin and Nosenko, a central event of the mole hunt, split the agency into two camps, creating scars that had yet to heal decades later.

The harm done was so great that the agency even agreed to an act of Congress to compensate the victims of the mole hunt, although it did not take the initiative in seeking to redress the wrongs it had committed. But the payments to Karlow, Garbler, and Kovich, substantial though they were, did not make up for the harm done to them, and to dozens of other loyal officers, some of whom to this day do not even realize that they were victims.

Like a snake eating its tail, the mole hunters eventually devoured each other. The mole hunt turned on itself, and led to the spectacle of the chief of the Soviet division, the chief of counterintelligence, even the director of the CIA being accused. David Murphy, James Angleton, and William Colby—all were touched by the corrosive finger of suspicion. The Soviet division's operations virtually ground to a halt.

In the greatest irony of all, as a direct consequence of the mole hunt, counterintelligence within the CIA was also diminished, its size, influence, and effectiveness greatly reduced. When William Colby took over as CIA director in 1973, he was rightly convinced that Angleton had become a destructive force within the CIA. The belief of the Counterintelligence Staff that all Soviet defectors or volunteers were plants and that the agency itself was deeply penetrated had frozen the CIA's operations against the Soviet Union around the world. Determined to change this and to maneuver Angleton out of the agency, Colby dismantled his empire. The pieces were never put back together.[5] "CI," said Sam Papich, "has never been reconstructed."

With his excess of zeal, Angleton had succeeded in destroying all that he had worked for. The world of counterintelligence is rather like a cave, so deep, so dark, that no one can fully see into all of its crevices. But the basic task of CIA counterintelligence is to prevent penetrations within the agency and to help detect foreign spies.

[5]There was one exception, however. The power of the Counterintelligence Staff to approve clandestine operations—such as the recruitment of an agent—in advance was restored by Angleton's immediate successor, George T. Kalaris. Operational approval was one of the functions that had been removed by Colby.

While the work of counterintelligence—precisely because it is carried on in secret—is difficult to measure, one reasonable yardstick is the number of espionage cases that surface in a given period. And the proliferation of spy cases in the mid-1980s, from Edward Lee Howard in the CIA, to Ronald Pelton in the NSA, to John A. Walker, Jr., and his confederates in the Navy, to Richard W. Miller in the FBI, and to the Army's Clyde Lee Conrad, all suggest that something had gone very wrong with U.S. counterintelligence.

Indeed, more than one official study reached the same conclusion. In 1988, a subcommittee of the House Intelligence Committee investigated the nation's counterintelligence agencies. The panel directed its heaviest criticism at the way the CIA had handled the case of Edward Lee Howard, the agency's first defector to the Soviet Union. In its report, the House committee called the case "one of the most serious losses in the history of U.S. intelligence."[6] It published excerpts from secret testimony by Gardner R. "Gus" Hathaway, then the CIA's counterintelligence chief, who admitted for the first time that "what Howard did to us was devastating," and that Howard had revealed to the Russians "some of the most important operations we have ever run in the Soviet Union." Hathaway also conceded that in the Howard case "the agency did not do its job properly."[7] Reviewing the counterintelligence problems facing the United States, the House committee concluded that "something is fundamentally wrong."[8]

That same year, a Senate-House conference report found "basic flaws" in the nation's security apparatus. It called the intelligence community "poorly organized, staffed, trained and equipped to deal with continuing counterintelligence challenges."[9]

So many espionage cases broke in 1985 that it became known as "the Year of the Spy." In the wake of these cases, and the defection and redefection of the KGB's Vitaly Yurchenko, CIA director William Webster quietly reorganized the agency's Counterintelligence Staff, replacing it with a new Counterintelligence Center and upgrad-

[6]"U.S. Counterintelligence and Security Concerns: A Status Report," Report of the Permanent Select Committee on Intelligence, House of Representatives, Subcommittee on Oversight and Evaluation (Washington: U.S. Government Printing Office, October, 1988), p. 15.

[7]*Ibid.,* pp. v, 15.

[8]*Ibid.,* p. 19.

[9]*Congressional Quarterly Weekly Report,* August 20, 1988, p. 2345.

ing its director to the level of associate deputy director for operations for counterintelligence. Whether the changes would prove to be more than a bureaucratic shuffle remained to be seen.

Scotty Miler, Angleton's former deputy, lamented what he saw as the demise of counterintelligence in the wake of Angleton's dismissal and his own departure. But Miler, who spent years in the SIG looking for moles, and never found any—except, perhaps, Igor Orlov—was aware that counterintelligence was an inexact science. He liked to quote a remark by the CIA's former deputy director for plans: "Desmond FitzGerald once said CI is nothing but a couple of guys in the back room examining the entrails of chickens."

In the end, Angleton had self-destructed. He had mesmerized a succession of CIA directors, but the Wizard of Oz analogy was apt. With the agency tied up in knots, he could no longer maintain the mystique.

As John Denley Walker, the former station chief who had clashed with Angleton in Israel, put it: "Angleton became like the spider king and he never knew what was in the web. Colby was pretty nearly right."

David H. Blee, one of Angleton's successors as chief of counterintelligence, grasped the problem very well. Blee headed the CI Staff for seven years. "In counterintelligence," he said, "we're all paranoid. If we weren't, we couldn't do our jobs."

Another former CIA counterintelligence chief did not want to be identified, but he was astonishingly frank about the hazards. "You go berserk in this job," he said. "You lose your orientation completely. You become demented. You're looking for spies everywhere." It might be a good idea, he added, if the CIA's counterintelligence chief were limited to a term of one year.

Angleton's deep-seated belief that Soviet walk-ins or defectors after Anatoly Golitsin were all plants died hard, even after Angleton himself had gone. Some former CIA officers insist that the agency had recovered rapidly from this mind-set.

But in 1976, two years after Angleton's departure, Adolf G. Tolkachev, a Soviet defense researcher working on Stealth technology for aircraft, began leaving notes in the cars of U.S. diplomats near the American embassy in Moscow. Tolkachev, fearing KGB surveillance, did not dare to approach the embassy itself. The CIA's Moscow station relayed these approaches to Langley.

Three times, it can be revealed, Tolkachev was turned away by the CIA, which feared he might be a plant. Finally, the agency decided to take a chance and began accepting material from the Soviet defense researcher. For almost a decade, Tolkachev proved to be the CIA's most valuable asset inside the Soviet Union, his existence a closely guarded secret. Because of the agency's initial suspicion, it had come close to losing his rich haul of Soviet secrets. Tolkachev was finally caught, betrayed, almost certainly, by Edward Lee Howard.[10]

In the end, it all came back to betrayal. The need for trust, the reality of betrayal, transcend the dilemma faced by the CIA and the mole hunters of the 1960s. They are at the core of every human relationship.

On one level, James Angleton's obsessive quest for the mole was a search for the evil within. The parallel to the human condition is obvious. In a sense, Angleton and his band of mole hunters were exorcists. Ultimately, they had about as much success as others who have attempted to ply that difficult trade.

John Denley Walker, who saw it all from the inside but managed to keep a sense of balance, summed up: "The mole hunt," he said, "probably did more to protect the Soviet agent, if there was one, than to unmask him. While everyone was being investigated and accused, the real mole was sitting back laughing."

[10]On June 14, 1985, Tolkachev was arrested in Moscow during a meeting with his CIA case officer, Paul M. Stombaugh, Jr., who was expelled for espionage. On October 22, 1986, TASS, the Soviet news agency, announced that Tolkachev had been tried, convicted, and executed. When I interviewed Edward Lee Howard in Budapest in June 1987, he admitted that Tolkachev "could very well have been one of the assets I would have handled." Asked if he had betrayed Tolkachev, Howard said: "I don't believe I did that." David Wise, *The Spy Who Got Away* (New York: Random House, 1988), pp. 261–62.

Epilogue

On May 26, 1989, Peter Karlow, accompanied by his wife, Carolyn, drove to CIA headquarters in Langley, Virginia, for the ceremony.

It took place in a briefing room on the seventh floor, near the office of William H. Webster, the Director of Central Intelligence. Webster looked on as Richard F. Stolz, Jr., the DDO, presented the agency's Intelligence Commendation Medal to Karlow.

Stolz, the chief of all clandestine operations for the CIA, was an ordinary-looking man with heavy horn-rimmed glasses. In his dark blue suit and red tie, he might have been an insurance executive presenting an employee with a gold watch at a retirement party.[1]

In addition to the small bronze medal, Karlow also received a large blue leatherette binder with the gold seal of the CIA on the front. Inside was a two-page citation that went with the medal. "THE UNITED STATES OF AMERICA," it began, above the CIA seal with eagle and shield, "To all who shall see these presents, greeting: This is to certify that the Director of Central Intelligence has awarded the Intelligence Commendation Medal to Serge Peter Karlow for especially commendable service." The text said the medal was awarded to Karlow

---

[1] Stolz himself retired in December 1990. He was replaced, on January 1, 1991, by Thomas A. Twetten, former head of the CIA's Near East division and one of the officials involved in the events that led to the Iran-Contra scandal.

"in recognition of his more than twenty-two years of devoted service to the Central Intelligence Agency. He distinguished himself in a series of increasingly responsible assignments both at Headquarters and overseas. Mr. Karlow demonstrated inspired leadership, operational wisdom, and good judgment throughout his career, reflecting credit upon himself, the Central Intelligence Agency, and the Federal service."

The citation was signed by William Webster.

Karlow remembered Stolz: "He was a junior officer when I was in Germany." And although Stolz was never photographed in public, a CIA photographer was on hand this day to record the presentation. Later, Stolz inscribed a copy of the color print: "For Peter Karlow, in small recognition for an outstanding professional career of a great gentleman, Dick Stolz, May 26, 1989." Karlow hung it on the wall.

Except for Stolz, there was a new cast of characters at the CIA. None of the officials who had driven Karlow from the agency twenty-six years before attended the ceremony. They were all long gone.

But one of Angleton's successors as chief of counterintelligence, Gardner R. "Gus" Hathaway, came to the presentation. "I guess he wanted to get a look at me," Karlow said. "I had a brief chat with Gus. I had mixed feelings about having him there."[2]

There was a party afterward, at the International Club of Washington, on K Street, and many of Karlow's old friends and retired colleagues came. Trapper Drum was there, from the Technical Services Division, Reid Denis from Berlin base, Peter Heimann from Bonn. And Richard Helms.

"Everyone there was relieved," Karlow said. Many of his former colleagues had refused to believe he was anything but a loyal American, but until the director of the CIA ordered that Karlow be given a medal, the doubts had lingered.

Smiling, one of the CIA men raised a glass and said to Karlow: "You've won, you beat 'em."

---

[2]Hathaway retired in March 1990 after five years as chief of counterintelligence. He was replaced by his deputy, Hugh E. "Ted" Price, fifty-two, a short, sandy-haired man who favored tweeds and fiddled constantly with a pipe. Price, a Far East hand who spoke Mandarin Chinese, switched over to the job of assistant deputy director for operations early in 1991. His successor as CIA chief of counterintelligence was James Olson, a six-foot, slender, blond Iowan who several years earlier had served in the Moscow station.

But Karlow didn't really feel that way. He was not bitter, or angry, but he had waited twenty-six years for this day. When he left the CIA in 1963, he was forty-two. When he returned in 1989, he was a sixty-eight-year-old man. Certainly, he had done well in the private sector, and there was the compensation from the agency.

But the mole hunt had robbed him of a lifetime. It had destroyed his career. It had accused him of treason. It had taken him away from doing the work he loved, for his country. He had already given his left leg, but it wasn't enough. Peter Karlow also had to give his reputation, and his best years.

There is an emptiness to the New Mexico landscape. The rolling high desert north of Albuquerque has a special beauty, but it is the beauty of desolation, the barren hills relieved only by the occasional juniper or prickly pear cactus.

Scotty Miler, living there, far from Langley, had plenty of time to look back. He lit a cigarette and inhaled deeply. "I wish there was some way the government could lay all this to rest, because it's unfair," he said. "If you go into intelligence you have to expect you will be investigated, that there may be allegations about you."

It had not been so easy for the mole hunters, either, he said. "Even while I was investigating these people I was obliged to deal with them on a day-to-day basis." That had created "a certain uneasiness."

And what was his view, in retrospect, about the lives and careers that were damaged, that had been in his hands?

"Regrettable. You're concerned—have you been fair? It's regrettable that it has to happen. But you have to have a system if there is sufficient cause for suspicion. . . . You're trying to protect something larger than an individual. If there is one thing that you learn, it's that there are no certainties about who's going to be a spy."

Miler stubbed out his cigarette and looked up. "As far as we know, none of these people we investigated turned out to be spies."

Did that mean there was no mole?

"No, I didn't say that," Miler replied. "It means we didn't find one."

Scotty Miler's rear porch faced west, toward Arizona. To the north, the Sangre de Cristo mountains darkened the distant horizon. With his wife, Miler had come to New Mexico from Washington in 1976, "to get away from the long arm of the investigating committees."

The Milers had set out hummingbird feeders on the porch, filled with sugar water. They loved to watch the aerial acrobatics of the tiny creatures, swooping and buzzing around the porch. But Miler's wife had died in 1988, and he was alone in the house with his memories, and the hummingbirds.

There were fewer hummingbirds now, but they still came to feed. "On a good day," he said, "you can see twenty-five."

Author's Note

Almost ten years ago I had lunch in Washington, at an appropriately inconspicuous restaurant, with a former officer of the CIA's Clandestine Services whom I had come to know and like. I respected this man for many reasons, not the least of which was that he had never told me anything that proved to be untrue.

But that day I thought his record of verity might be strained to the limit. In the course of our lunch he told me that a Soviet defector had said there was a penetration in the CIA whose name began with the letter K, and that this had cast a shadow on many officers, including one who was forced out.

A CIA man dismissed because his name began with the letter K?

My friend nodded. Clearly he was serious. And just as clearly, I knew it was a story I had to write. In a low voice, he confided the man's name: Peter Karlow.

Other projects intervened, but I was determined to return one day to the subject of the mole hunt that had taken place inside the CIA and to find the man whom I had begun to think of as Mr. K. It was almost five years later that I found him. He had been working for most of that time in Washington, ironically in an office on K Street. He had moved to California but agreed to meet with me on his next trip back East.

A few weeks later, on a sunny spring day, I was sitting opposite Peter Karlow at an outdoor restaurant in the capital. The story I had heard about him was true, he said. He might be willing to tell it to me.

But Karlow, it became clear, was a modest man, and he did not want a book written only about him. He pointed out that what had happened was part of a much larger pattern.

And I knew he was right. I had by now read David C. Martin's ground-breaking book *Wilderness of Mirrors,* and from that and other sources, I was well aware that the mole hunt that had paralyzed the CIA was intertwined with the "war of the defectors"—the clash over Anatoly Golitsin and Yuri Nosenko—and with dozens of secret operations that the United States and the Soviet Union had mounted against each other during the height of the Cold War.

I had stepped into a maze, and friends in the intelligence world warned me that I might become lost in the wilderness. In truth, the paths and byways seemed to lead in a hundred directions. The story *was* complex, but not, as it turned out, beyond reach.

Around the same time that I had met Peter Karlow, I had also begun conversations with Paul Garbler. At first, I was puzzled. He, too, had been a major suspect, but his name did not begin with a K.

I was interviewing Garbler in his study in Tucson when a moment of revelation came. I knew that Igor Orlov, whose wife still ran the picture-framing gallery in Alexandria, was a key to the mystery, but where did he fit? When Garbler revealed that the agent he had run in Berlin was Orlov, I realized with mounting excitement that I was getting close. Then he walked over to the bookcase, reached up, and took down the book that Orlov had inscribed and presented to him in Berlin as a farewell gift thirty-three years earlier. It was signed "Franz Koischwitz."

Orlov's operational name had begun with the letter K! That was the nexus, the missing link that explained how the mole hunt had spread far beyond Karlow. The pieces began to fall into place.

To research this book, I conducted 650 interviews with more than two hundred persons. Although my interest in the mole hunt extended over a decade, most of my effort was concentrated in the last two years. While much of the research was based on the interviews, there are additional references to books, congressional hearings, and other documentation, including CIA and FBI files, and these sources are cited in the footnotes included in the text.

A book about secret operations and agencies presents special problems of attribution. Wherever possible, sources are identified by name and quoted directly. But the book also contains some information attributed to former intelligence officers who, given the nature of their work and having been anonymous all their lives, preferred to remain so. I have respected their wishes.

Every writer wrestles with this problem. On balance, it seemed more important to me to use the material from former CIA and FBI officers, and to let them speak in their own voices, than to sacrifice the information because they declined to be identified. Many of these former officers believed the facts should come out, but did not want to open themselves to criticism by their colleagues for breaking the code of silence. All of these men and women have my thanks and deep appreciation. They know who they are.

Many former and some present intelligence officers and officials, as well as other sources, were willing to be interviewed on the record. While the list is too long to permit me to mention everyone, I am especially grateful to a number of former CIA officers, including S. Peter Karlow, Paul Garbler, George Kisevalter, Newton S. Miler, Robert T. Crowley, Tennent H. Bagley, William E. Colby, Richard M. Helms, John Denley Walker, George Goldberg, Donald F. B. Jameson, Frank F. Friberg, Clare Edward Petty, Joseph C. Evans, William R. Johnson, F. Mark Wyatt, Thomas W. Braden, Stephen Roll, Peter M. F. Sichel, Eugen F. Burgstaller, George L. Cary, David H. Blee, James H. Critchfield, Rolfe Kingsley, Anthony A. Lapham, Bela Herczeg, and Stanley H. Gaines; and to Joseph R. DeTrani, director, and E. Peter Earnest, deputy director, of the CIA's Office of Public Affairs.

Among many former FBI officials, I am particularly indebted to James E. Nolan, Jr., Donald E. Moore, Sam J. Papich, Eugene C. Peterson, Courtland J. Jones, Phillip A. Parker, James H. Geer, Edward J. O'Malley, and Alexander W. Neale, Jr. In France, I am also grateful to Count Alexandre de Marenches, the former head of the Service de Documentation Extérieure et de Contre-espionnage, and Marcel Chalet, the former chief of the Direction de la Surveillance du Territoire, for their assistance.

Others deserve my thanks. John V. Abidian generously explained his role in inspecting Oleg Penkovsky's dead drop in Moscow. Eleonore Orlov was unsparing of her time, and always patient with my endless questions, as was her son, George Orlov. William G. Miller helped me to reconstruct the legislative history of the Mole Relief Act. Vera Connolly kindly shared her memories of her brother, Edgar Snow, and I could not have reconstructed the remarkable story of the Yankovskys without the help of Anastasia Sokolovskaya. I am grateful as well to Joseph A. Mehan, Earl D. Eisenhower, Spencer Davis, Irene Thompson, Philip L. Chabot, Jr., G. Robert Blakey, George S. Pinter, Nicholas R. Doman, Victor Gundarev, and Dr. John W. Walsh.

Many writers and colleagues in the press were generous as well, especially Seymour M. Hersh; Andrew J. Glass, chief of the Washington bureau of the Cox newspapers; Per E. Hegge, the Washington correspondent for Oslo's *Aftenposten;* Daniel Schorr, senior news analyst of National Public Radio; David C. Martin, of CBS News; Thomas J. Moore; Francis Lara; Bill Wallace, of the *San Francisco Chronicle;* Elizabeth Bancroft, editor of the *Surveillant;* Michael Evans, defense correspondent of the *Times* of London; Robert J. Donovan; Tom Lambert; Don Cook; Marianne Szegedy-Maszak; Arnaud de Borchgrave, of the *Washington Times;* William R. Corson; Aslak Bonde, of the Norwegian Broadcasting Corporation; John Costello; Henry Hurt; Aaron Latham; Robert H. Phelps; Jukka Rislakki, of the *Helsingin Sanomat;* Dean Beeby, news editor of the Halifax bureau of the Canadian Press; Michael Littlejohns, former chief of the United Nations bureau of Reuters; John Scali, of ABC News; Kathy Foley, deputy director of the *Washington Post* news research center; David Binder, of the *New York Times* Washington bureau, and Barclay Walsh, the bureau's research supervisor; and Camille Sweeney, former researcher for the *New York Times Magazine.*

A special word of appreciation must go to Carol Monaco, who conducted the research for this book with great patience and with resourcefulness that enabled her to overcome many of the obstacles we encountered along the way. I am grateful as well to William A. Wise, who provided additional research assistance, and to whom this book is dedicated. My thanks also go to Kate Sawyer, who cheerfully helped me to keep my newspaper files current.

None of the former and present CIA and FBI officials or other individuals thanked here are in any way responsible for the conclusions reached in this book, which are, of course, entirely my own.

Those who must live with writers are indeed noble, and my family is no exception. Without their love and support, I would hesitate to try to navigate the deep and murky waters I encountered in bringing forth *Molehunt.* I am, as always, indebted the most to Joan, Christopher, and Jonathan.

David Wise
Washington, D.C.
June 19, 1991

Index

ABOUT THE AUTHOR

DAVID WISE is America's leading writer on intelligence and espionage. He is coauthor of *The Invisible Government*, a number one best-seller that has been widely credited with bringing about a reappraisal of the role of the CIA in a democratic society. He is the author of *The Spy Who Got Away, The American Police State,* and *The Politics of Lying,* and coauthor with Thomas B. Ross of *The Espionage Establishment, The Invisible Goverment,* and *The U-2 Affair.* Mr. Wise has also written three espionage novels, *The Samarkand Dimension, The Children's Game,* and *Spectrum.* A native New Yorker and graduate of Columbia College, he is the former chief of the Washington bureau of the *New York Herald Tribune* and has contributed articles on government and politics to many national magazines. He is married and has two sons.